Aerosmith: Tapes From The Cellar 1970 to 1986

A few of the tapes from the cellar...

Aerosmith: Tapes From The Cellar 1970 to 1986
Introduction

Aerosmith is a band that made its name by relentless, grind-it-out, city-by-city touring. Since its inception in 1970 and for the following decade, nary a year went by without the band being on tour. It was not until 1981 that they were not on the road. In fact, it was not until the early 1990s that the band was off the road for an extended period.

Yet, for a band that built its reputation through incessant touring, the fans have been left with just a few bones of that live experience so critical in establishing Aerosmith.

Aerosmith grew from a burgeoning band into a colossus in the 1970s, but there is precious little official documentation of the band on stage from that period.

"Live! Bootleg" is the lone piece of work entirely dedicated to that era, focusing primarily on 1977 and 1978. Few studio overdubs (although there are some) and the band riding the edge of musical anarchy made that album loved or loathed. For the true rock fan, it was brilliant in its honesty and reaffirmed why Aerosmith had become such a giant.

Part of that package included two tunes from the band's early career set at Paul's Mall in Boston from 1973, illustrating how the band developed its live sound.

But what about the rest of 1973? Or 1974, 1975 or 1976 for that matter? Certainly, two songs from a lone gig from among hundreds of shows were not enough to tell the tale of Aerosmith during its formative years, the band hungry for success.

Future live releases "Classics Live I and II" did little to shed additional light on the band's life on the road. While there were diamonds, the collections had a hodgepodge feel, studio alterations and drew primarily from shows in the 1980s.

Then there were video-only releases of parts of the massive Pontiac gig in 1976 and the Texxas Jam two years later that helped shape a perspective of Aerosmith on stage, but certainly not definitive. The "Pandora's Box" set provided bits and pieces of live material, but nothing comprehensive.

What has been left is a seeming gaping hole in the band's story, hundreds of shows and a live legacy lost in the mists if time.

But all was not lost.

On its rise to prominence, and even when the band had arrived as legend, they decided to broadcast shows over the radio. Those were recorded by fans, and those in the know could locate and listen to them.

Between 1973 and 1986, all or parts of 16 shows went out over the airwaves. Some of those gigs ended up on the 1970s-era bootleg vinyl: "Rattlesnake Shake," "Look Homeward Angel," and "Rock This Way," the latter two iterations of the same show from New York City's Central Park in 1975.

These broadcasts illustrate the band growing musically on stage over the years, continuing to deliver live. But even with the broadcasts, there are holes: nothing substantial went out over the air in the touring years of 1976, 1977, 1979, 1982 or 1985.

The radio broadcasts are the gems in a sea of live recordings that have been buoyed by a group of live music enthusiasts who brought their own recording gear to shows.

Some were "bootleggers" looking to make a profit by pressing their recordings onto vinyl, but a vast majority were rock fans and members of the band's Blue Army wanting a document of the show to hear again. Those tapes were then traded between fans and collections were built.

Those audience recordings fill voids in the band's tour history quite nicely. Sometimes the sound quality is brilliant, at other times it borders on dire or worse, but each recording plays a role in unveiling the band's live legacy. Most importantly, they are honest documents. As Jimi Hendrix once said, "Music doesn't lie."

No editing, no overdubs, just pure, raw and live, a window to a night at a concert hall that otherwise would be largely forgotten. While news clippings grow tattered and memories distort over time, recordings are as fresh as the night they were made. You are in the crowd and in front of the band.

Taken alone, the recordings are a point of interest, but when looked at in the whole, they weave a more complete narrative of the band's early touring history. The shows fit together like a jigsaw puzzle, and piece by piece create a picture and bring context.

A few mixing board tapes have also slipped out from under lock and key over the years, further helping tell the band's live story.

4

These documents are not subject to revisionist history, or foggy memories, and allow for a detailed look at the band live on stage, the pulpit from which Aerosmith carved its legend.

"Aerosmith is a *live* band, something that can't be captured any way but live," Steven Tyler is quoted in Stephen Davis' book *Walk This Way*. "The beauty of a concert is the energy of a show, the event, *that* night."

Joe Perry told *Hit Parader* in 1985: "We've always been a live band more than anything else."

And Brad Whitford said being on stage is what made the band.

"When we initially started out, a lot of critics and music people were cool toward us," Whitford told the *Ottawa Journal* in 1977. "So, we decided to get on the road and play for anyone who would listen to us. It's grown from that."

What is documented in the coming pages are more than 200 shows during the band's classic period from 1970 through 1986.

Grades are provided for the sound quality of each show as a guide. Those given an A grade are very, very good. These are always FM or soundboard recordings. Some of the audience recordings are quite good too, giving a feel for what it's like to be among the fans listening to the band. The best sounding of those have been assigned a B grade.

From there, things get a little dicey in terms of sonic quality and C and D grades are issued, and we even have a partial F. But as beauty is in the eye of the beholder, music appreciation is in the ear of the listener. There are no doubt excellent performances to be found in the din – you just have to listen more closely.

And what about the performance quality of the shows? That, again, is left to the listener. Aerosmith certainly could be messy at times on stage, but that's rock and roll! If a listener wants a precise rendering on stage of what is heard on record, that's not what early Aerosmith is about. Early Aerosmith is dangerous and chaotic on stage, an amalgamation of rock, garage band and even punk music.

It also makes listening to these shows and adventure, one never knows what's around the corner! It's all a high wire act: there is success, but once in a while there is a spectacular fall. Most importantly, songs are never played the same way twice. Each concert is unique.

With a little gumption, fans can dig and find these recordings.

Songs listed are ones that were recorded, not all the tunes played at a gig. Many shows are complete, but several are not. Tape deck problems, running out of recording tape or getting to a show late are some of the reasons for incomplete audience recordings. And some of the radio concerts were edited before going out over the airwaves.

Days of the week on which the show was played are also provided, which can play a role in the energy of a concert. A Friday or Saturday night gig might have a more exciting feel than, say, a Tuesday night show. But there are no rules there.

Vintage print ads and notices have been included to enhance the flavor of the hype around the concerts. There are a few reviews of albums, shows and other articles, but they are limited and presented to highlight aspects of the band's early career.

Aerosmith's early live period is important, playing a key role in the development of American rock and roll music in the 1970s. It has been somewhat obfuscated by the band's later, greater commercial success. But the band's early period should be respected, celebrated and documented for history.

With that…*Good evening, people, welcome to the show...*

The band's first live show came at a gymnasium at Nipmuc Regional High School in Mendon, Massachusetts on November 6, 1970. Interestingly, a setlist from that first show has appeared:

Route 66, Rattlesnake Shake, Happenings Ten Years Time Ago, Movin' Out, Somebody, Think About It, Walkin' The Dog, Live With Me, Great Balls of Fire, Good Times Bad Times, Train Kept A-Rollin'.

A recording has yet to emerge from the inaugural gig from a nascent Aerosmith, and it's hard to know if the setlist is in any way accurate. One thing we know is that memories are fuzzy, and the tale of the tape is really all that can be trusted! But it's fun to imagine the young band tearing through this setlist, covering The Yardbirds, Zeppelin, The Stones and even Jerry Lee Louis!

For the next several months, the band plays more high schools, colleges and small clubs in Massachusetts, Vermont and New Hampshire, building a name for themselves.

Rogers High School, Lowell Massachusetts. Saturday, May 15, 1971. Soundboard. Sound quality: A

Jam, Somebody, Reefer Headed Woman, Walkin' The Dog, Major Barbara, Dream On/You See Me Crying, Mama Kin.

A fascinating document, the earliest known recording of the band to have surfaced. Ray Tabano is still in the band at this juncture.

A loose, brief Rolling Stones-type jam kicks off the recording, and then voices can be heard in the background as "Somebody" gets off to a rollicking start. It's very similar to the version that would appear on the band's first album.

"Reefer Headed Woman" gets the heavy blues treatment, with Tyler blowing on his harmonica to set the mood.

A somewhat slowed version of "Walkin' The Dog" follows, this one with a flute interlude that flows into a Doors-like "Riders Of The Storm"-type jam.

The tune that could never quite make it onto vinyl in the early days, "Major Barbara," gets a fun work through, finishing with a short version of

7

"Here We Go Around The Mulberry Bush" that increases in speed to finish out the song.

"Dream On" is played, and aside from some small lyric changes ("sing with me, this mournful death") it sounds very similar to the recorded version. The big difference is the movement at the end, which would become "You See Me Crying" on "Toys In The Attic."

Tyler uses an affected voice on "Mama Kin," which finishes out the interesting recording. This very well could be an audition tape or rehearsal, rather than a gig at the high school as an audience can't be heard.

On January 5, 1973 the eponymous "Aerosmith" is out in record stores. While failing to chart initially, the band's future success will put it at as high as No. 21 on the Billboard charts on April 2, 1976 when it is re-released on the strength of "Dream On" and the band's rising success.

Of note: When the album was re-released in 1976, "Dream On" and "Write Me" featured re-mixed versions.

8

AEROSMITH:
FACT SHEET

Like most good things, Aerosmith wasn't planned, it just happened.

It began to happen in late summer of 1970. Guitarist Joe Perry and bassist Tom Hamilton had been playing in a band in New Hampshire which had just broken up. They were familiar with the talents of a drummer, Steve Tyler, whose band had likewise recently dissolved. The initial connection among the three flickered a bit, and another drummer, Joey Kramer, was asked by Hamilton and Perry to play with them. Soon afterward, Tyler joined up again, this time as the lead singer, and the band moved to Boston. There, a fifth member, guitarist Brad Whitford, was finally added.

That much wasn't planned. But the rest . . .

"When we all got together," says Tom, "our intention was to be a concert and recording band." During the first months together, Aerosmith played gigs at colleges, high schools, sometimes at fraternities, as well as writing and collecting material for an album. Their refined style of rock and roll attracted more than just highly partisan reactions from the audiences: They were brought to the attention of Columbia Records, and signed in August, 1972. Their first Columbia recording is, appropriately, **Aerosmith.**

The band has been most effective in urban college audiences, although when they did sneak into a club or two, the reactions were usually quite favorable. When they made their New York club debut at Max's Kansas City,

Cash Box wrote:

"Are you looking for that extra spurt of energy that is often missing from the new wave of 'mellow' musicians? Fear not, the search is over. Aerosmith is bursting with rhythm and raunch, carrying on with the tradition of the Stones, but with the innuendos of the '70's. The sound radiates total energy, but is still dynamic enough so that this quintet managed to play tastefully in a room as contained as the upstairs at Max's."

To describe their music one of the band members said, "Our music is R&B with a lot of arrangement and refinement; it is rough and raunchy, but melodic at the same time."

The members of Aerosmith are:

Brad Whitford, 20, guitar, born in Winchester, Massachusetts, and raised in Reading, Massachusetts. He's played the guitar five years, after studying both the trumpet and piano.

Joey Kramer, 22, drums, born in Manhattan, raised in Yonkers; moved to Boston about five years ago, where he joined Aerosmith.

Steve Tyler, 24, lead singer, born in New York City, also the lyricist of the group.

Tom Hamilton, 20, bass, born in Colorado Springs, began playing when he was 14.

Joe Perry, lead guitar and backup vocals, born and raised just outside Boston.

Aerosmith's first LP is simply entitled **Aerosmith,** and it is for the most part hot 'n' heavy rock 'n' roll.

Side One:

Make It Starts things out with an explosion of sound. Rhythm and lead guitars dominate the beginning of the song, and a very heavy bass picks up later.

Somebody Again, another explosion of heavy mettle. Joe Perry on lead is a powerhouse. Steve Tyler's voice quivers in and out throughout the song.

Dream On A beautiful ballad with excellent vocals by Steve and great drumming by Joey Kramer. Adrian Barber's clean production techniques really pay off here.

One Way Street A high powered rocker that has a heavy message about the other side of the tracks. Guitar solos by Joe Perry and Brad Whitford highlight this tune.

Side Two:

Mama Kin Written by Steve Tyler, the tune has a real high energy feel to it. There are some great back-up vocals with unusual guitar playing.

Write Me A song with an early Stones feel to it. Steve overdubs the vocals to make it a very effective rocker.

Movin' Out By now they're dripping wet with the energy that they create. Just when you think things are going to let up, they smack you with another Tyler cut. Slicing guitar and tremendous drumming by Joey do the number here.

Walkin' the Dog They teach an old dog new tricks here and the result is the best rendition of this old hit ever to hit the wax.

Insert from the first album. "Aerosmith" received very good reviews (following page) from the Los Angeles Times (top left), Hartford Courant (top right) and a syndicated piece that ran in several newspapers. All the reviews were published February 17, 1973.

9

Aerosmith. Columbia KC 32005. This young group from Yonkers achieves all that punk rock bands strive for but most miss. Cliched but properly raw lyrics are growled and rasped by a fine, manic voice. The guitarist packs a Rory Gallagher wallop, especially sounding like the funky Irishman on the great "Movin' Out." Irresistible riffs u n d e r l i e "Made It" and most of the other songs. Side two is a thorough delight, ending with a "Walking the Dog" that cooks as well as the Rufus Thomas and Stones versions. The band's longest song, "One - Way Street," could have been more diversified, or simply shortened, to good effect, but it's still a good song. "Aerosmith" is a hearty, sensual, hip-shaking serving of hot rock. Play it loud.

Aerosmith (Columbia KC 32005) is a Boston-based band that's best feature is its snappiness and tightly-knit sound. Joe Perry's lead guitar is good and strong, and the whole group sounds well-practiced (that's often the case with first albums, because a group finally commits to vinyl the songs it's been doing live for a year).

"Mama Kin," which leads off Side Two, is an excellent steamer, and even the slower material, such as "Dream On," has a quiet perseverance that makes it well worth the listening.

Aerosmith really moves into its own at album's end, however, as a midnight mover called "Movin' Out" segues into what is absolutely the best version of "Walkin' The Dog" that's been done in the last 10 years. Everything is perfect, and the rhythm is just changed enough to keep the song from being so much recycled soul food.

The group has a tendency to rip off certain Stones and Who riffs, but that's a l m o s t unavoidable when doing this type of hard rock. Aerosmith are new, and they are good.

REVIEWS

★ ★ ★ ★ ★ **EXCELLENT**
★ ★ ★ ★ **VERY GOOD**
★ ★ ★ **GOOD**
★ ★ **FAIR**
★ **POOR**

Aerosmith (Columbia KC 32005)

Aerosmith, a new hardrock band from New England, is good enough to become America's answer to the Rolling Stones.

Those who doubt that prediction are invited to listen to their debut album, one of the best albums of hard rock by an American band in years. The music is tough, gutsy, blues-tinged rock at its best.

The album is not perfect, but it consistently demostrates such great strengths that the future of the band appears exceedingly promising.

The music is almost all original, written primarily by lead vocalist Steve Tyler, who is good enough to hold his own with anyone. The group consists of Joe Perry and Brad Whitford on guitars, Tom Hamilton on bass, and Joey Kramer on drums.

Guitar and vocals are very powerful, and supporting roles of bass and drums are also excellent. The group's playing is extremely together, even though the group still has rough edges.

There are several tunes in the album which could and should emerge, with "Make It" and "Somebody" and "Dream On" the best. Any one could pop, particularly "Dream On," a beautiful rock ballad.

If Aerosmith can hang together, it can make it big.

Five stars.

For the rest of 1971 and into 1972 the band continues to play in the Northeastern United States, dropping into Connecticut for shows and most famously playing Max's Kansas City in New York City in the summer of 1972 where Clive Davis saw them.

By this time Tabano has been replaced by Brad Whitford. Late in 1972 the band continues its shows at Max's Kansas City and has a string of gigs at K-K-K-Katy's in Boston.

As 1973 progresses, the band plays shows at the Academy of Music in New York City, the Orpheum in Boston and the Palace Theater in Providence, among other locales.

Ad for the now famous Paul's Mall gig.

NIGHT CLUBS

Hoyt Axton, Mimi Farina — Paul's Mall, 733 Boylston st., now through March 18. Coming March 19: Aerosmith; March 20-25: Tracy Nelson, Mother Earth; April 2-8: Billy Paul.

Paul's Mall, Boston, Massachusetts. Tuesday, March 20, 1973. WBCN radio broadcast. Sound quality: A

Make It, One Way Street, Somebody, Write Me, I Ain't Got You, Mother Popcorn, Movin' Out, Walkin' The Dog, Train Kept A-Rollin', Mama Kin.

This FM broadcast is the first definitive evidence (to date) of Aerosmith playing in front of an audience. The band had been together for more than two years at this point and it shows. With its first album now out, the band is in a groove, even if largely unknown beyond the Northeast.

On the recording, WBCN DJ Maxanne Sartori, a supporter who gave them early radio airplay, introduces the band members. After some tuning, there is a second introduction from the house: "Ladies and gentlemen, welcome to Paul's Mall. Now if you will, a warm hand for Columbia recording artists, Aerosmith."

Tyler lets out a yell and then "Make It" gallops like a thoroughbred as the set opener here, a fitting start to the show as it is on the band's album. It clears the way for a trio of tunes from "Aerosmith" before the now famous renditions of "I Ain't Got You" and "Mother Popcorn," culled for the band's "Live Bootleg!" release some five years later. Joined at the hip, the pairing provides an insight to their influences, The Yardbirds and James Brown. It's a blissful workout of the two. David Woodford steps up to "blow some sax" for good measure.

Someone in the Aerosmith camp must have remembered the moment as "Live Bootleg!" was prepared. The raw tape reveals a more complete "Mother Popcorn" as there is an edit on the live album.

The first Tyler/Perry composition, "Movin' Out," is next and is dedicated to the band's landlord. A now sped up version of Rufus Thomas' "Walkin' The Dog," a tune that would dip in and out of the band's setlist for years to come, continues the show.

"Train Kept A-Rollin," done in The Yardbirds staccato fashion, ends in chaotic fashion, segueing nicely into the opening notes of "Mama Kin," which finishes the 50-minute set.

All in all, a wonderful gig in sublime quality, one that can be listened to over and over. The first flash of Aerosmith on stage!

On "Live Bootleg!" April 23, 1973 is given as the date of this show. While the band may have played Paul's Mall on that date, March 20, 1973 is the real date here. Tyler poetically says after "Make It": "To the breath of spring, to energy..." Spring typically begins on March 20 or 21. A fan who recorded the show from the radio also noted the March date.

ROCK — With the release of its first album, (Columbia 32005), Aerosmith takes its place in the growing number of good new groups putting Boston back on the musical map. The sound is a straight-on, hard driving rock featuring the vocals of Steve Tyler and the guitar of Boston-born Joe Perry.

Michael Nicholson

★

ROCK — With its first album (Columbia), Aerosmith takes its place with the growing number of good new groups putting Boston back on the musical map. The sound is a straight on, hard driving rock featuring the vocals of Steve Tyler and the guitar of Boston-born Joe Perry. They are two-year veterans of the local club and college circuits. Seven of the album's eight cuts were written by the group, with the exception of an interesting hard rock treatment of the R&B "Walkin' the Dog." For a debut album, it is surprisingly devoid of weak material. "Dream On," the only slow tempoed number, impressed me the most with its fascinating musical themes, but the group's great appeal is in its hard, rolling-stonish rock. You'll be hearing more from this group. — **Michael Nicholson**

★

The Boston Globe took two bites of the apple in reviewing Aerosmith's debut album. A blurb ran February 2, 1973, followed by a slightly longer write-up March 16, 1973.

Interesting ad in that it shows the band ventured as far west as Cincinnati early in 1973.

Frolics, Salisbury Beach, Massachusetts. Thursday, August 16, 1973. Audience recording. Sound quality: C+

Write Me, Whit's Tip (Downtown Baby), Woman Of The World, Somebody, Pandora's Box, Make It, S.O.S. (Too Bad), Dream On, One Way Street, Walkin' The Dog, Train Kept A-Rollin', Mama Kin.

There is a fervor in the crowd to see the band play, as it claps and cheers in anticipation during a delay before Aerosmith hits the stage. Interesting, in that it is so early in the band's career.

"Thanks for waiting and here's what you have been waiting for: Aerosmith!" The MC says as Kramer starts "Write Me."

The rarity "Whit's Tip" or "Downtown Baby" is a blues rocker, and while a good workout, it never really fully catches fire, a sign that these types of numbers from the band's early touring days need more work or are better left behind.

"We are going to do a song off our next album, dedicated to Mr. David Krebs," Tyler says as the band plays the first known "Woman Of The World" live, part of it sped up compared to what would end up being pressed on vinyl on the next Lp. It's a very muscular version that breaks out into a jam.

"Pandora's Box" also gets an early outing, with Tyler noting not many in the crowd had probably heard the tune that Tyler wrote pre-Aerosmith. It features some alternate lyrics, with Kramer executing some precise rat-a-tat drums to bring the song to a close. Tyler also introduces "Make It" as a song that's rarely heard.

"You know, last night we got ripped off in our dressing room and it's funny because the culprit took some little pills that belonged to Joey Kramer, who happens to have a Great Dane with a laxative problem," Tyler relates before "S.O.S. (Too Bad)." The tune has some early lyrics with Tyler seemingly faking his way through parts of the song.

The band plays the first known stage outing of "Dream On." Tyler says the band has just re-learned the song again to play live, but he is off the mark, missing his cues twice. It's almost as if he is singing an edited version while the band is playing the complete take. In fact, Columbia released an edited version of the tune June 27 to jump start it for radio play. It may have been Tyler re-learned this version, while the band re-learned the album version! A rather ignominious first-known live take, but that's rock and roll, and it's not altogether awful. The "You See Me Crying" movement is no longer present as it was in 1971.

Tyler gets the crowd clapping along to "One Way Street." Some feedback begins "Train Kept A- Rollin'" with "Mama Kin" closing out the show with Tyler saying, "this ain't no sunshine song." The song cuts off after a couple of minutes as the tape runs out.

The Box Club, Boston University. Friday, September 14, 1973. Audience recording. Sound quality: C
S.O.S. (Too Bad), Somebody, Dream On, Pandora's Box, One Way Street, Walkin' The Dog, Train Kept A- Rollin', Mama Kin, Make It, Milk Cow Blues.

This is one of those recordings in which one must wear "bootleg ears" to listen because of the quality: it's rough, but not altogether unenjoyable if the challenging sonics are put aside.

After an energetic "S.O.S. (Too Bad)" joined in progress to start things off, Tyler says "rags to riches" after the tune, perhaps noting the band's uptick in popularity after the initial sluggish sales of its debut that almost got them booted from Columbia Records.

We have another "Dream On," which Tyler mentions has been getting some radio airplay. Unlike the Salisbury Beach show, this version is polished, quite spectacular and interesting to hear in a small room before it would be played to thousands in large venues in the coming years. Perry and Whitford's guitar interplay on the song is spot on, providing an emotionally pondering backdrop for Tyler's vocals.

"Pandora's Box" is played as a wide-ranging, eight-minute jam that brings the best out of the band. That's followed by an elongated eight-minute "One Way Street." Despite the length of these two pieces, they flow nicely, and the music is never dull as the band changes the pace and timing from the versions heard on the studio albums.

The crowd is in a tizzy after the "Train Kept A Rollin'"/ "Mama Kin" ending and calls the band back for a resounding "Make It."

A first known live "Milk Cow Blues" was the last song recorded and likely was the last of the evening. It features a lead vocal by Perry, which comes off quite well, fitting the grit of the song. Half of the tune is comprised of a solo by Kramer, although the drummer himself has said it was years later before he did one. A nice thing about these recordings: the tapes provide better documentation than memories do.

Counterpart Creative Studios, Cheviot, Ohio. Wednesday, September 26, 1973. WKRQ radio broadcast. Sound quality: A
Make It, Somebody, Write Me, Dream On, One Way Street, Walkin' The Dog, Pandora's Box, Rattlesnake Shake, Train Kept A-Rollin', Mama Kin.

A bit of good fortune for Aerosmith fans as the band enters a recording studio, playing a show in front of a handful of people which is captured in excellent quality. Counterpart Creative Studios, the brainchild of Cincinnati music producer Shad O'Shea, opened operations in 1971. Two years later it was hosting bands for live radio shows and Aerosmith was booked, likely with the help of Columbia.

The great quality here brings out all the good and bad; there are a few flubbed notes along the way, but nothing that detracts from the energy the band brings.

But there does seem to be a sterile vibe during the first part of the show. The band is used to playing live in smoky clubs, small theaters and school gymnasiums, not recording studios.

Maybe sensing the low-key vibe, Tyler gets the small crowd assembled to begin rhythmically clapping before "One Way Street." "Not too fast" he advises as the clapping helps launch the tune, improving the flow of the rest of the show.

Before "Pandora's Box," Tyler announces the name of the new album will be "Night In The Ruts."

Tyler's seeming obsession with "self abuse" has found an outlet in the form of Fleetwood Mac's "Rattlesnake Shake." The blues jam really takes off with an improvised middle section that later found its way onto "Woman of The World" and "Rats In the Cellar."

The recording ended up on the 1970s vinyl bootleg "Rattlesnake Shake," which mistakes the location as New York. A pre-FM in studio recording of the show has off air comments from the DJ included.

The songs "Walkin' The Dog" and "Rattlesnake Shake" end up on the "Pandora's Box" compilation, but an incorrect date of 1971 is provided on that collection.

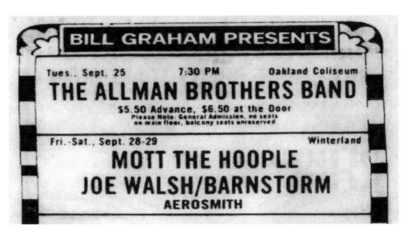

Aerosmith playing their first dates in San Francisco. Or did they? Given they were in Maine the following day, it's possible the band didn't play these gigs.

University of Maine, Gorham Campus Gym, Gorham, Maine. Sunday, September 30, 1973. Audience recording. Sound quality: B-

Write Me, Downtown Baby, Somebody, S.O.S. (Too Bad), Dream On, One Way Street, Walkin' The Dog, Pandora's Box, Train Kept A-Rollin', Mama Kin, Make It, Rattlesnake Shake.

"Are we going to raise the roof!" Tyler shouts before the show begins as Kramer starts the proceedings by banging out the intro to "Write Me" over the intro by tour manager Robert "Kelly" Kelleher. It's an exciting start to the show captured by the well-balanced audience recording. Kelly's intros marked many of the band's 1970s shows. "Somebody" emerges in a smooth segue from the previous tune and picks the energy right back up.

Tyler introduces "S.O.S. (Too Bad)" and again says the new album will be titled "Night in the Ruts" and will be out by December, both of course, will end up not being true. Kramer is really the standout on "S.O.S. (Too Bad),"

17

his rollicking drumming driving the song. The "Son of Shit" (S.O.S.) lyric reference is here, but jettisoned for the album, likely out of fear of losing radio play.

"This song is all over the radio, so we decided to learn it," Tyler quips before "Dream On." Given Perry's known dislike of the tune, it's possible the band had not played it live for much of 1973 until it gained radio prominence after it was released as a 45. It is warmly received this night and gets a strong response by its end, building energy into "One Way Street," which segues into "Walkin' The Dog."

"Pandora's Box" features some alternative lyrics from what appeared on the album version. "Make It" is effective as a first encore. The lively tune would not be heard on stage much after 1974. "Rattlesnake Shake" makes another appearance to bring the show to a close.

Palace Theater, Providence, Rhode Island. Wednesday, October 24, 1973. Audience recording. Sound quality: C

Make It, Write Me, Somebody, S.O.S. (Too Bad), Dream On, One Way Street, Walkin' The Dog, Pandora's Box, Train Kept A-Rollin', Mama Kin, Rattlesnake Shake.

"Good evening people, welcome to the show," Kelly says has he warms up the crowd before the band comes on stage. Tyler repeats that same opening verse moments later as Aerosmith hits the stage. The music on the recording is somewhat distant, but it captures the crowd's reaction to the show well. "Dream On" is met with wild applause; the song is taking off from radio play in the region.

Hard to imagine how the Columbia bosses didn't initially hear the potential of the tune as a single that would have more easily helped break the band, with execs taking six months to make the move.

"Pandora's Box" gets a loud crunchy intro by Perry that meets with approval from someone in the crowd who yells "Yeah!"

No doubt photos of Tyler through the years holding a finger to his ear to be able to hear his own voice during shows can be traced to Perry's propensity for playing at a pleasingly loud volume as is evidenced here.

18

"Aerosmith" (Columbia) — Boogie at its very, very best is the only way to describe Aerosmith.

On its debut album for Columbia, this Boston fivesome has assembled a foot stomping package for those who love to turn up the volume and move to a driving beat.

Unlike other boogie bands, Aerosmith is not three chords, a beat and "hello Sue, you know I'll be true," lyrics.

The group is an evolved band which encompasses a wide range of driving scores that, when added together, comes out pure boogie.

Album highlights include "Mama Kin," "Make It" and a great version of "Walkin the Dog."

An astounding tribute to the band is that one of its guitarists, Brad Whitford, is only 20-years-old and so is bassist Tom Hamilton.

Aerosmith is one of the few honestly good boogie groups to come out in awhile and its worth hearing them. —J.B.

Hard Rock Returning

Good hard rock is coming back, and among the best new pounders is Aerosmith, whose new album of the same name is real roll-back-the-rug-and-cut-loose-music.

The best cuts are "One Way Street," Guitarist Joe Perry's chance to star, and "Mama Kin," a real piledriver, although several other of their songs would make swell singles.

These five new Englanders will open Mott the Hoople's show T h u r s d a y at Syria Mosque. They have what it takes to go a lot further.

More reviews for "Aerosmith." (Left) appeared in the San Pedro News Pilot (California.) The second in the Pittsburgh News. Both published October 14, 1973. Also, a concert ad for the Pittsburgh gig.

Orpheum Theater, Boston. Saturday, October 27, 1973.

Audience recording. Sound quality: C+

Make It, Write Me, Somebody, S.O.S. (Too Bad), Dream On, One Way Street, Walkin' The Dog, Train Kept A-Rollin', Mama Kin, Pandora's Box.

The beginning of the show sounds like a scene from a Hollywood movie as the hometown heroes are welcomed to the stage by the MC (who mentions something about a large pair of Aerosmith underwear) and a cheering crowd as the first notes to "Make It" ring out into the theater. There is a palpable excitement about Aerosmith that can be heard on this night, the band has really "arrived," at least locally.

Tyler tells the crowd a new album will be out in December or January and refers to "S.O.S. (Too Bad) as "Son of Shit."

"Dream On" is again the highlight of the show, getting a delirious response from the assembled.

"One Way Street" follows, with Whitford playing a flawless, spot on solo. Tyler calls out for "Mr. Perry" right before his solo, though on this night he delivers a discordant effort. In fact, if there was a sour note to be played during these early shows, it usually came from Perry, likely from his devil may care swagger on stage that is part of his persona. Paradoxically, Perry squeezes notes out during the show closer "Pandora's Box" that sound as though he is playing a horn as heard on the studio version. Quite amazing.

This night in Boston is a non-stop party, an hour of blistering blues rock. No doubt the headliner Mott the Hoople had a tough time following this one! *The Real Paper* of Boston reported: "The reaction of The Orpheum crowd was tumultuous. (It was) like the Ed Sullivan show in 1964. They're really rocking in Boston."

11:00 A.M.
❹ TREASURE
❺ AMERICAN BANDSTAND
Billy Preston and Aerosmith guest.
(1 hr.)
⑬ FOOTBALL
Detroit Lions vs. Miami Dolphins. (3 hrs.)

American Bandstand. Saturday, December 15, 1973.

Dream On.

A recording of this has not surfaced. Likely a lip-sync affair shot earlier in the month when the band was in town to play two gigs in Los Angeles at the Whiskey A-Go-Go.

SPOKANE'S TOP TEN

Following is a list of the top recordings in Spokane compiled from the top ten listings of sales and radio favorites:

1. Angie ....Rolling Stones
2. Midnight Train to Georgia
   ....Gladys Knight and the Pips
3. Top of the World ....Carpenters
4. Half-Breed ....Cher
5. Heart Beat It's a Lovebeat ...De Franco Family
6. I Got a Name ....Jim Croce
7. China Grove ....Doobie Brothers
8. Dream On ....Aerosmith
9. Ramblin Man ....Allman Brothers Band
10. Sail Around the World ....David Gates

"Dream On" helped the band gain traction outside of the Northeast.
Spokane Spokesman-Review, Nov. 4, 1973.

KC 32005
The group that puts the raunch in rock and roll will devastate you on this, their first record. Contains the smash hit single, "Dream On."

"Get Your Wings." Aerosmith is taking off.

They burst out of Boston heralded by the screams of thousands of their fans, won over by their first explosive album. Now after a cross-country tour, highlighted by devastating Steven Tyler performances, Aerosmith has combined their talents to make "Get Your Wings" bulge with all the compressed energy and drive one record can hold.

"Get Your Wings" is the album that's going to take Aerosmith and everyone else even higher.

"Get Your Wings."
New rock and roll from Aerosmith.
On Columbia Records and Tapes

March 1, 1974 marks the release of the band's second album, "Get Your Wings." It's a solid sophomore effort and gives the band a foothold as they begin playing more shows outside the Northeast, headlining some shows, while opening others for the likes of Mott the Hoople, The Kinks and most notoriously, The Mahavishnu Orchestra. The band also shared the stage with REO Speedwagon, Santana, Lynyrd Skynyrd, Quicksilver Messenger Service, Queen, Rush, Mahogany Rush, Country Joe and the Fish, Bob Seger, Blue Oyster Cult, Three Dog Night and Mountain.

The touring takes them across the country, the band building a loyal following along the way. Detroit, in particular, takes a keen liking to the band. The album peaks at No. 74 on the Billboard charts on October 17, 1975, buoyed by the release of "Toys In The Attic."

The touring commences before the album is released.

Of note: A quadrophonic version of this album is prepared and released. It features unique mixes, most prominently on "Woman Of The World," which has a female backup singer and a different arrangement. Also, a single of "Train Kept A Rollin'" is shorter, punchier and eschews the "live" treatment found on the Lp.

Michigan Palace, Detroit, Michigan. Friday, February 1, 1974. Stage recording. Sound quality: B+

Make It, Lord Of The Thighs, Somebody, Write Me, Same Old Song And Dance, Dream On, One Way Street, S.O.S. (Too Bad), Train Kept A-Rollin', Mama Kin, Walkin' The Dog, Milk Cow Blues.

A fine recording here, even if its making is a bit of a mystery. The MC mentions something about "the radio" during the clipped introduction, but nary a mention is made during the show of a broadcast by Tyler, typically something he would do. The sound is solid, and it could be an FM broadcast. More likely, the gig was recorded from the stage by unknown persons, possibly by the band themselves for future study.

"My man, my man," Tyler says in acknowledgment of the MC as the band launches "Make It," the tune bursting with energy and setting the tone for a hot night in one of the band's early supportive cities. The band would play Detroit close to 20 times between 1973 and 1986.

The new album is now to be out in mid-February (1974) Tyler tells the crowd as "Lord Of The Thighs" gets one of its first live plays. More truncated at four minutes than versions to come, it's played in a straightforward manner only hinting at the Whitford/Perry legendary interplay that would occur within the song's framework in the coming years.

Tyler tells the crowd not so happily that the "higher ups" have declared "Same Old Song And Dance" is the single off the forthcoming album. A trimmed "Seasons of Wither" may have been the better option! Nonetheless, we hear the first known live take of the funky "Same Old Song And Dance," which would be a stage staple for years to come.

"Dream On" does not quite get the strong response heard in the Northeast, hinting that it had not yet been picked up by radio in the Midwest. The tight, efficient early version mirrors what is on the album.

Perry again takes the mic for vocals on "Milk Cow Blues" and does a more than admirable job, his rough-hewn voice a fit for the dirty blues tune penned by Kokomo Arnold in 1934 that got the Aerosmith treatment on this night.

The date January 7 is often associated with this show, but the band was in the studio early in the month working on "Get Your Wings."

Michigan Palace, Detroit, Michigan. Sunday, April 7, 1974. WABX radio broadcast. Sound quality: A-

Write Me, Mama Kin, Lord Of The Thighs, Woman of the World, Dream On, Pandora's Box, Same Old Song And Dance, One Way Street, Somebody, Train Kept A- Rollin', Walkin' The Dog, Milk Cow Blues.

This show is part of a benefit for the clean-up of Belle Isle, a park in the Detroit River. What better way to celebrate a "Kite In and Balloon Fly" held earlier in the day at the park than to have

Aerosmith close out this night of rock, though rain spoiled the daytime activities.

Detroit's WABX is on hand to broadcast the 80-minute show, the band's longest concert caught on tape to date. The loose, flowing gig is a great listen.

Kramer starts off the proceedings with the drum shuffle of "Write Me," maybe a more plodding opener than "Make It," but effective in its own way. "Get Your Wings" is now out and the band wants to bring it to the public.

"Woman Of The World" again takes on a jam feel within its structure, with Perry and Whitford trading licks throughout and Tyler doing some impromptu vocals and harmonica work. Parts of the jam that formed inside of "Rattlesnake Shake" in 1973 is now heard in the tune. "Pandora's Box" has a new ending on this night, the same one heard on the studio version.

The guitarists have a tough time getting in tune before "Same Old Song And Dance." "You gotta be in tune, you know!" Perry says. Out of the on-stage tuning session, the opening notes of the song emerge. More tuning issues follow upon the song's conclusion.

"Instead of wrecking your ears with bad notes, we're gonna kill you with volume," Perry says, then, "As you know every band from Boston has to have a harp player, so here's our harp player right now," as Tyler blows away, making vocal gesticulations behind it before the band crashes into "One Way Street." It sees a new arrangement on this night, with Perry bringing out a talk box to great effect. It adds to the groove and swagger of the song, a rollicking blues jam.

Hamilton's bass drives "Train Kept A- Rollin'," which features a Kramer solo as well. The fantastic show concludes with "Milk Cow Blues" and Perry again singing from the gut, joined by Tyler on some verses. A night to remember.

Felt Forum, New York City. Friday, May 31, 1974. Audience recording. Sound quality: C
Write Me, S.O.S. (Too Bad), Lord Of The Thighs, Dream On, Same Old Song And Dance, Woman Of The World, Train Kept A-Rollin', Milk Cow Blues.

A real onslaught here at what attendees later called deafening volume. The band is opening for Slade and burns through a 50-minute set at a non-stop pace. One song leads to another, with Tyler rapping intros along the way.

The rapid-fire approach leaves the audience trying to keep pace. Only "Dream On" provides a breather. It's a take no prisoners kind of show that helped build legions of fans.

Rolling Stone famously documented the show, claiming Slade was even louder, and that Aerosmith "paled in comparison" to Britain's glam rockers. While Slade may have been a bigger band at the time, there is no doubt those in attendance took notice of the burgeoning Aerosmith.

The recording is well documented, with the taper announcing the date and venue after he hits "record." The sound is rough here, but these uneven documents have a way of focusing the listener's attention to what's going on.

My Father's Place, Roslyn, Long Island, New York. Tuesday, July 2, 1974, WLIR radio broadcast. Sound quality: A-
Write Me, S.O.S. (Too Bad), Lord Of The Thighs, Dream On, Same Old Song And Dance, Woman Of The World, Train Kept A-Rollin', Walkin' The Dog.

Another radio broadcast, one of a series at this venue delivered over WLIR-FM in New York beginning in 1971.

The intro of "S.O.S. (Too Bad)" coming out of "Write Me" gets a complete makeover since the last time we have heard it. There is more than a minute of instrumental jamming before the song starts proper, quite a cool start to this gig.

After the song, Tyler complains the band was rushed on stage and didn't have time to get high. "It's hard to come up here and do this straight," he mutters, maybe waiting for his stimulants to kick in.

Kramer pounds out a slightly extended intro into "Lord Of The Thighs," as Perry and Whitford get into a fantastic rhythm/lead interchange as they make their way through the song. The chemistry is palpable between the two players.

Tyler introduces "Dream On" as the song "that made us all rich and famous, it gave us something to believe in." The wistful "Woman Of The World" has a whole new mid-section, with Tyler playing some blues licks on harmonica as the band jams behind him. Perry plays a chaotic solo toward the end of the song before bringing it to a close.

"Train Kept A- Rollin'" sounds particularly muscular on this night, delivered in full glory via the great recording. Kramer gets in an extended solo as well as he has done during recent shows on the tune, playing the intro of Hendrix's "Little Miss Lover" at one point. Perry hints at "Mama Kin" as an encore, but the gig ends with "Walkin' The Dog."

Aerosmith must have been a late ad to the Ozark Music Festival as they were not included in this ad.

Today's concert began about 10 a.m. and will run about 12 hours. The lineup consisted mostly of hard rock groups such as Aerosmith, Tower of Power, and the Amboy Dukes. Tomorrow, the show will focus on bluegrass and country music. Performers will include the Earl Scruggs Revue, Jim Stafford and Leo Kottke.

Ozark Music Festival, Missouri State Fairgrounds Grandstand, Sedalia, Missouri. Saturday, July 20, 1974. Radio broadcast of a soundboard recording. Sound quality: B

Write Me, S.O.S. (Too Bad), Dream On.

"Here we go folks, Beantown boogie from Boston, Aerosmith!" the MC

27

announces to the crowd as the band starts with "Write Me." The guitars are buried in the rough soundboard mix.

The rapid fire "S.O.S. (Too Bad)" lyrics can be heard clearly here, a fun listen. Tyler announces, "Dream On" as "the only laid-back tune we do." It would be nice if more of this show turned up.

There are some fabulous photos online of this gig. Temperatures for the festival were well over 100 degrees and 150,000 came over the weekend, according to reports. Only 50,000 were expected and the event caused much consternation among locals.

❹ Midnight Special
Host: Little Richard. Guests: Golden Earring, Kool & the Gang, Aerosmith, Eddie Kendricks, David Clayton Thomas.
⑩ ⑬ Midnight Special

The Midnight Special television show. Friday, August 16, 1974. Soundboard. Sound quality: A
Train Kept A-Rollin', Dream On.

Little Richard hosts the venerable music program that was a staple for rock fans across the United States in the 1970s. The performance no doubt helped millions see the band in one fell swoop.

"Train Kept A- Rollin'" is performed in a truncated (Kramer's solo is excised for TV) but powerful way.

"Dream On" is replete with dry ice billowing across the stage in true 1970s rock fashion. While musically strong, the visual impact is almost as stunning.

The band's look is classic rock and roll – they have the image down pat. Tyler's outfit is something to behold, fashionable attire that has a timeless quality.

Thank you, Columbia, for believing.

This week our first album, "Aerosmith", (released Jan.'73) is 181 Bullet.

Our second album, "Get Your Wings," (on the charts 42 weeks already) is hot again at 167 Bullet. It includes our new single, "S.O.S." ₃₋₁₀₁₀₈

Aerosmith. On Columbia Records® and Tapes

Management: Leber-Krebs, Inc.
Agency: I.C.M.

29

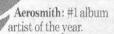

Aerosmith: #1 album
artist of the year.

NUMBER ONE, TIMES TWO.

Aerosmith: #1 album
group of the year.

A fitting tribute from *Billboard* to America's premiere rock and roll band.
Aerosmith. There's nothing like them anywhere in the whole wide world.
On Columbia Records and Tapes.

Shaefer Music Festival, Wollman Skating Rink Theater, Central Park, New York City. Saturday, September 7, 1974. Audience Recording. Sound quality: C

Lord Of The Thighs, Woman Of The World/Movin' Out/Woman Of The World, Dream On, One Way Street, Same Old Song And Dance, Train' Kept A-Rollin'.

The legendary – or maybe infamous – show that coupled Aerosmith and Irish blues rocker Rory Gallagher. Aerosmith was set to open for Gallagher, but organizers decide to flip the order right before the show given Aero's rising popularity. That move alone angers Gallagher fans, who will now see a shorter set from their hero. Too make matters worse for his following, the guitarist turns in an absolutely blistering set and only left the stage because of his time restriction as the opener. Feeling they had been robbed, fans pelt the stage with debris as roadies set up for Aerosmith.

The first two songs or so are missing from this recording – reports have Aerosmith being booed as they walked on stage. The tape begins with the crowd chanting "We want Rory!" then picks up the middle of a strong "Lord Of The Thighs," which is greeted with applause upon its conclusion, but there is a sense of uneasiness in the air. The earthy "Woman Of The World" is next and is not to the liking of everyone, especially the Gallagher fans.

One report has more than three-fourths of the crowd walking out at this point. Perry seeing this starts in on "Moving Out" in the middle of "Woman Of The World" and the band picks up on the song and plays it in its entirety, a commentary on what they were seeing from the stage. "I see the signs of moving out," Tyler says.

Whitford plays a sublime solo in the middle and eventually Kramer smartly picks right back up into "Woman Of The World" seamlessly, and the band finishes the tune. After some hesitancy, the band gets into "Dream On." Tyler appears ready to end the night after the song, calling for the show closer "Train Kept A- Rollin'."

But Perry has other ideas and starts playing "One Way Street" with a hard edge and the band joins him. Perry is not done yet, without taking a breath he jumps into a loud and nasty "Same Old Song And Dance."

It's obvious this has become Perry's show; he does not want to be shown up by Gallagher. "Train Kept A- Rollin" is played with equal frenzy to close out the show, but is marred when someone throws a bottle at the stage and it shatters, cutting Kramer. "There is blood all over my tubs!" the drummer yells. Projectiles from audiences will be something that dogs the band for years, as we will see.

In this case, the incident didn't stop the drummer, who finishes off his solo and leads the band back into the song to end the wild show. Some reports have the band wilting during the show after Gallagher's onslaught and leaving the stage after three songs, tails between their legs. Not so. As the tape shows, they gave a spirited performance, and in many ways equaled Gallagher.

Over the years some have made the night about Gallagher versus Aerosmith. Nothing could be further from the truth. Tyler has said he knew his band was in trouble after watching Gallagher's set, and went on to say the guitar seemed to be an extension of the Irishman's body. And in his autobiography, Perry acknowledged Gallagher blew Aerosmith off the stage "fair and square." But Perry might want to revisit the tapes, it reveals that Aerosmith more than held its own in large part because of his efforts.

Variety wrote about the gig and termed Aerosmith's performance "relentless." How apt.

Palace Theater, Providence, Rhode Island. Friday, October 4, 1974. Audience recording. Sound quality: D-/F

Somebody, Pandora's Box, Lord Of The Thighs, Woman Of The World, Seasons Of Wither, Think About It, Same Old Song And Dance, Train Kept A-Rollin'/Kramer solo.

The worst sounding recording of the band reveals a historically significant show. Overall, the playing is excellent, and the excitement of Aerosmith live is on full display.

We also get our first known live renditions of "Seasons Of Wither" and The Yardbirds' "Think About It," songs that would not see the light of day again on stage until the late 1970s.

"Are you ready? C'mon, let's hear it, the Bad Boys from Boston, Aerosmith!" says the MC. There is a short gap, then the recording picks up with an energetic "Somebody." Perry strums some 1960s-sounding notes until starting "Woman Of The World," which turns into a mini-epic clocking in at more than 11 minutes. Tyler asks what the crowd wants to hear, and shouts of "Dream On" go up. The singer says that will come later.

The opening notes of "Seasons Of Wither" get a great response from the crowd, which recognizes the song instantly. Kramer starts his parts early in the song during this fabulous version. The drummer's beats standout through the song. We are left to wonder why the band didn't play this more on stage in the coming years.

"Think About It" was rumored to have been played early on by the band and now we have evidence. It's a great lively version, which has an intricate, long ending that builds to a crescendo before a snappy finish, a segment not heard on later versions. Another gem in the sea of cacophony.

Before the tune, Tyler tells the audience they must be tired "of hearing the same old shit over and over" and says "Think About It" will be on the band's new album. Whether that was the plan, or an off-hand remark is unclear.

The end of "Same Old Song And Dance" has sustained, low feedback until the first notes of "Train Kept A Rollin'," which Tyler mentioned is being released as a single. It features a powerful Kramer solo set up by a short music interlude. The solo itself threatens to destroy the fragile magnetic tape! While in full flight, Kramer's drumming goes silent as the tape runs out.

A great early show. The downside? The recording suffers from awful distortion. Our taper was simply too close to the stage and his recorder couldn't handle the volume. But "hearing" the early versions of "Seasons Of Wither" and "Think About It" make what would be an excruciating listening experience rather satisfying.

Morris Civic Auditorium, South Bend, Indiana. Sunday, October 20, 1974. Audience recording. Sound quality: C
Woman Of The World, Dream On, Milk Cow Blues, Somebody, Same Old Song And Dance, Walkin' The Dog, Train Kept A-Rollin', Mama Kin.

The feel is that of a mellow show, maybe because the excitement of the beginning of the gig is missing here. The tape picks up before "Woman Of The World." The crowd is excited to see the band, but some can't see: "Sit your ass down!" one fan yells to another.

Some in the crowd call out for "Walkin' The Dog." "You like the stuff from the first album, huh?" Tyler says. Perry has some trouble finding the beginning notes to "Milk Cow Blues," but he finally captures them and then plays a rollicking version.

"Same Old Song And Dance" continues nonstop into "Walkin' The Dog," giving the crowd what it wanted to hear.

Kramer plays his longest recorded solo to date in the middle of "Train' Kept A Rollin'" and Perry sneaks in a snatch of the "Peter Gunn" theme that would be heard at future shows.

The crowd begs the band for an encore and is treated to a taut "Mama Kin." The fans hope for another song, but it's not to be. The lights go up and there is a collective groan.

McKeesport Okays Rock Fest

A free rock concert, sponsored by a local radio station, has found a home and will go on as schedule tomorrow in McKeesport's Renziehausen Park, a station spokesman said.

Renziehausen Park Bandshell, McKeesport, Pennsylvania. Sunday, October 27, 1974. Audience recording. Sound quality: C+

S.O.S. (Too Bad), Somebody, Lord Of The Thighs, Woman Of The World, Pandora's Box, Dream On, Same Old Song And Dance, Walkin' The Dog, Train Kept A-Rollin'.

A free outdoor show where the band is not the headliner, Brownsville Station is. But the band still makes a dramatic entry via helicopter to the site, landing at a nearby field. It's not exactly Woodstock, but more than 20,000 crowd into the park to watch the show. The ambiance is well captured on tape, with Tyler checking his mic before the gig starts by counting.

"Must behave, so they say...we'll behave," Tyler mutters, maybe told to watch his words before the gig. There had been opposition to the show from some locals.

"S.O.S. (Too Bad)" and "Somebody" get the show off to a rocking start as a wave of energy surges through the crowd. Perry plays a little of "Jailhouse Rock" before Tyler introduces the next tune that is about "ladies who drive Corvettes and some of the men that put them there." He then voices an impromptu rap over Kramer's intro into "Lord Of The Thighs," something he would do often.

The crowd is happy and digging the band. Perry joins Tyler on vocals for the first verses of "Pandora's Box" to great effect as the brunettes share a single mic.

A 15-minute "Train Kept A- Rollin'" with a Kramer solo finishes off the hour-long set that still remains legendary in the Pittsburgh area to this day. Did Aerosmith really play the Renz? Indeed, they did!

35

Academy of Music, New York City. Saturday, November 2, 1974. Audience recording.

Sound quality: C

S.O.S. (Too Bad), Somebody, Lord Of The Thighs, Woman Of The World, Dream On, Same Old Song And Dance, Walkin' The Dog, Train Kept A-Rollin'.

A warm reception from an audience that is in tune with the band. Tyler "raps" during the intro to "Lord of the Thighs" again, long before the genre would become popular.

Perry noodles on "Think About It" before "Woman Of The World." Tyler's harmonica soulfully fills "Woman Of The World" at every opportunity.

Aerosmith is the headliner this night, playing with Mahogany Rush and the James Montgomery Band. But Aero's gig is only 45 minutes. Hawkwind has been booked for a midnight show and the venue needs to be cleared!

Convention Center, Niagara Falls, New York. Friday, November 29, 1974. Audience recording. Sound quality: C+

Same Old Song And Dance (fragment), Train Kept A-Rollin'.

Opening for Johnny Winter on this night, the taper must have had only a passing interest in Aerosmith. Just a bit of "Same Old Song And Dance" was recorded and most of "Train Kept A-Rollin'," although the very end is missing.

What we hear most of is Kramer's expanding solo, with the drummer yelling out after going at his kit for several minutes.

ROCK AND ROLL'S
NEWEST GOLDEN BOYS.

TOYS
MADE TO
LAST.

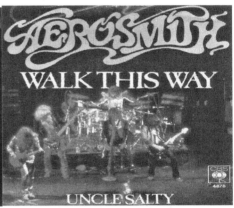

The band's breakthrough album. "Toys In The Attic" is released April 8, 1975. The album hits No. 11 on the Billboard charts on September 12, 1975. Despite the band playing more than 70 shows across the country on the "Toys In The Attic" tour, only nine have surfaced to date. A real shame.

Of note: A quadrophonic version of the album is also prepared and released. As with other Aerosmith quad albums, it features different mixes. The ones here are more subtle than on other releases.

Aerosmith, Foghat — Boston Garden. April 18, 8 p.m. Open seating, all tickets $7. High energy and glittery hard rock.

NIGHT LIFE

Aerosmith, Foghat· and Barnaby Bye — It's a veritable Garden party for dancers and listeners, so sing and sway. Tonight (sold out) and Saturday, Boston Garden.

DON LAW presents
· **AEROSMITH**
OPEN CONCERT
Friday, April 18, 1975, 8:00 P. M.
ALL SEATS UNRESERVED $7.00
PATRON - RETAIN THIS STUB
SEE REVERSE SIDE
OCCUPANCY OF ALL AREAS IS POSITIVELY RESTRICTED TO LEGAL LIMIT

Boston Garden, Boston, Massachusetts. Saturday, April 19, 1975. Audience recording. Sound quality: D
Toys In The Attic, S.O.S. (Too Bad), Somebody, Adam's Apple, Lord Of The Thighs, Sweet Emotion, Dream On, Walk This Way, No More No More, Write Me, Same Old Song And Dance, Train Kept A-Rollin', Make It, Big Ten Inch Record, Mama Kin, Walkin' The Dog.

After dates in the Midwest and Northeast, the band lands back home in Boston.

Major gigs for the band, playing the biggest venue in their hometown for two nights with a new album fresh in the record store bins. It must have been surreal for the band to play the Garden, a venue where they saw their heroes – Hendrix, The Stones and Zeppelin – play.

This second gig starts with an ominous drone on tape that plays before the band appears: "All right Boston, Massachusetts, are you ready to rock tonight! What can I say? Let's all get together and give a warm welcome home to those boys from Boston, Aerosmith!"

The crowd erupts as Kramer starts "Toys In The Attic" and the band is off and flying. This is the first known live recording of "Toys In The Attic," but the cacophonous recording makes it hard to hear what's happening with all the band's members, though Tyler and the guitars are clear enough.

It's then a return to two tunes from the first album before Perry starts in on the opening riff to "Adam's Apple." Oddly, Tyler – who had to be coaxed by Perry to address the crowd during the band's early gigs – stops the guitar player. "Hold on, will you, hold on a second!" Apparently, Tyler wants to explain the song to the thousands. "This is something that brings us way, way, way back to the beginning. It ain't a revival trip, but it is. It ain't about Noah's Ark, but it is. It's about Adam and Eve and what we believe, and she bit into whatever it was that somebody said don't bite into," Perry then starts the song again, the first known live recording of the tune. The volume washes over the blissful crowd, absorbing the new song with cheers and excitement.

"Sweet Emotion" also gets caught live for the first time along with "Walk This Way." Tyler sings the verse "Walk This Way" like the album version, without the swagger that would come later.

"No More No More" gets its debut too, with Tyler telling the crowd it's about "life on the road," something the band knew all too well. "Write Me" gets a short piano solo from Scott Cushnie, who played on the "Toys In The Attic" album and joins the band for parts of the tour. He also adds vocal harmonies.

Hamilton's bass is dialed up in the mix toward the end of "Same Old Song And Dance" to great effect. "Make It" makes a return to the setlist as an encore on this night. "Big Ten Inch Record" also is caught on tape for the first time, with Tyler saying AM radio had no interest in playing the song. "Walkin' The Dog" closes out the show, a real red-letter gig for the band. Aerosmith was on its way to big, big things.

War Memorial, Rochester, New York. Monday, April 28, 1975. Audience recording. Sound quality: D+

Toys In The Attic, S.O.S. (Too Bad), Somebody, Adam's Apple, Lord Of The Thighs, Sweet Emotion, Dream On, Walk This Way, No More No More, Write Me, Same Old Song And Dance, Train Kept A-Rollin', Big Ten Inch Record, Mama Kin.

"Toys In The Attic" jumps out of the gate on this night, followed non-stop by "S.O.S. (Too Bad)" and "Somebody."

"Adam's Apple" and "Lord Of The Thighs" are also joined at the hip, the latter featuring intense guitar work from Perry, who seems to be able to shift the air in the auditorium with his snaking solo. He is joined by Whitford for some unique interplay as Tyler picks up the vocals again.

Hamilton plays his exotic intro to "Sweet Emotion," one of the most recognizable bass intros in the history of rock. The song builds to an intense crescendo as Kramer begins the outro with his relentless rat-a-tat on the drums. Tyler would often stick his vocal mic in front of the drum kit for some added volume.

"Train Kept A-Rollin'" approaches the 15-minute mark with Kramer's solo added in. The "Peter Gunn" theme is again played briefly within the song. The overdriven, distorted recording highlights Hamilton's bass work here. It was seeing his older brother play "Peter Gunn" that made Hamilton want to be a musician and here he was onstage in Rochester doing just that.

"Big Ten Inch Record" features a Scott Cushnie piano break that fits seamlessly into the song, which then segues into "Mama Kin" which ends the night to thunderous applause.

Hara Arena, Dayton, Ohio. Saturday, May 24, 1975. Audience recording. Sound quality: C

Toys In The Attic, S.O.S. (Too Bad), Somebody, Sweet Emotion, Lord Of The

Thighs, Dream On, Walk This Way, No More No More, Write Me, Same Old Song And Dance, Train Kept A-Rollin'.

It was during a trip to Ohio a month earlier, in Toledo, where the term "Blue Army" was coined by band members who saw fans lined up dressed in blue jeans in the Rust Belt state.

On this night in Ohio, a group of Blue Army pals brought a tape recorder along. The goal was to make a document of the night, but not a pristine recording, but it is interesting, nonetheless.

"Toys In The Attic" is joined in progress and the recording mic seems to be jostled about. The tape does reveal the interplay in the song between Tyler and Perry alternately singing "Toys!" not easily heard on earlier versions on the tour.

By the time "Sweet Emotion" comes around, the taping crew seems to be meandering about the Hara, buying food, using the restroom and debating the worthiness of Aerosmith in a jocular manner.

The band can be heard throughout the journey, a testament to the volume at which they played. Things settle down somewhat for "Lord Of The Thighs," which stretches out in good fashion to almost eight minutes as Perry and Whitford trade licks.

"Dream On" is given a hero's welcome here, the crowd cheering wildly during the first part of the song, as though dubbed in, as we here on some studio-produced "live" albums. But this is the real thing. The song concludes with a flash pod going off and an immense roar inside the Hara.

Scott Cushnie becomes the star of "No More No More," his jangly piano out front in the mix during parts of the song, which features a crunchy guitar intro from Perry. Cushnie is also very prominent in "Write Me" giving the song a honky-tonk feel.

Tyler signals the beginning of "Train Kept A-Rollin'," but Perry has another idea. He begins playing "Moving Out" then stops. Then it's a few notes of "Pandora's Box." Then the beginning of "Train Kept A-Rollin'." "You want, Number 1, Number 2, or Number 3?" Tyler aks. The cheer goes up for 3 and "Train Kept A-Rollin'" gets going. We get another Kramer solo and then it's back into the main movement, then suddenly: it's over. The tape runs out.

Albums that go gold,
a single ("Sweet Emotion") that's bulleting up the charts,
a sold-out tour*
and reviews like these:

"Aerosmith is the best hard rock group in the United States." — *L.A. Times*

"'Toys in the Attic' will no doubt take a deserved place in the Rock Hall of Fame." — *Creem*

"'Toys in the Attic' is a remarkably clean, raw and delicious rock album." — *Raves*

"One of the finest rock records of the year." — *Pop Top*

*July 19,
Long Beach, California;
July 20,
San Jose, California,
July 24,
Houston, Texas;
July 25;
San Antonio, Texas;
July 26,
New Orleans, Louisiana;
July 27,
Tulsa, Oklahoma,
July 31,
Dallas, Texas;
August 23,
Providence, Rhode Island;
August 28,
Largo, Maryland;
August 29,
Central Park, New York

Aerosmith, on Columbia Records and Tapes.

Aerosmith to Headline Bill

The rock group Aerosmith will headline a concert at 8 p.m. Sunday at the Long Beach Arena. The opening group will be Mahogany Rush, which will also appear Monday and Tuesday at the Starwood.

Arena, Long Beach, California. Sunday, July 20, 1975. Audience recording. Sound quality: B-

Walkin' The Dog, S.O.S. (Too Bad), Somebody, Sweet Emotion, Lord Of The Thighs, Dream On, Walk This Way, No More No More, Same Old Song And Dance, Train Kept A-Rollin', Big Ten Inch Record, Toys In The Attic.

The first time the band is heard at a proper concert west of the Rockies. Scott Cushnie gets an introduction before "Sweet Emotion." Perry then slips in the intro into "Lord Of The Thighs" as he and Whitford create a wall of guitar sound within the tune.

"Walk This Way" features a funky intro by Kramer, and Perry uses a talk box throughout the tune, singing some verses with Tyler through the device. Cushnie again moves to the front of "No More No More" during sections of the song.

"Same Old Song And Dance" gets a strong workout, very powerful on this night. Kramer's solo during "Train Kept A-Rollin'" is one of his best to date, precise and energetic playing that excites the crowd. Perry plays a blues riff, then the "Batman" theme and "Peter Gunn" theme back to back during Kramer's solo.

Tyler improvises some lyrics on "Big Ten Inch Record." "Toys In The Attic" moves from the opener at recent shows to the final encore here; the fast-paced song leaves the crowd in a frenzy by the end, and they yell for more.

The recording is not bad for the time, seemingly made from very close to the stage (Kramer's off mic yells are audible at points) but is still rough in spots and overdriven at times. But that sound adds to the intensity of the gig.

Tad Gormley Stadium, City Park Stadium, New Orleans, Louisiana. Saturday, July 26, 1975. Audience recording. Sound quality: B-

Walkin' The Dog, S.O.S. (Too Bad), Sweet Emotion, Walk This Way, No More No More, Same Old Song And Dance, Train Kept A-Rollin', Toys In The Attic.

"Their first visit to New Orleans, ladies and gentlemen, Aerosmith!" shouts the MC as the band plays this outdoor venue in support of ZZ Top.

Fleetwood Mac and Jeff Beck are also on the bill, but it's Aerosmith that makes a strong impression on this rainy day.

The audience recording is clear and atmospheric and details the excitement the crowd has for the band. Hoots and hollers and the taper's signature whistle are heard throughout. Hamilton's bass is captured well and his rhythmic patterns that lock in songs are well evident throughout.

Kramer pounds out an intro for "Walk This Way," but Tyler seems a little confused, rapping "she was a floozie, all she wanted to do was walk in the mire and the muck," as he often did during the "Lord Of The Thighs" intro. Perry's guitar mostly drops out toward the end of the song, so we end up hearing Whitford leading the rhythm section to the end of "Walk This Way," locking in the groove of the song, and it sounds great! The band seems to get a little lost toward the end of "No More No More" and Perry ends it by launching "Same Old Song And Dance."

"Train Kept A-Rollin'" gets another Kramer solo, even though as an opener, the band is onstage for only 45 minutes. Yet his solo further propels the audience frenzy.

As "Train Kept A-Rollin'" ends, the crowd screams for more and they get it. "Toys In The Attic" ends the show, but the crowd lingers, hoping for more. Quite a show in NOLA.

Municipal Stadium, Cleveland, Ohio. Saturday, August 23, 1975. Audience recording. Sound quality: B-

Walkin' The Dog, S.O.S. (Too Bad), Somebody, Big Ten Inch Record, Sweet Emotion, Dream On, Write Me, Walk This Way, Same Old Song And Dance, Mama Kin, Train Kept A-Rollin', Toys In The Attic.

The largest crowd Aerosmith sees to date. More than 80,000 come out to see them, along with Mahogany Rush, Blue Oyster Cult, Uriah Heep and Rod Stewart and The Faces in the city's "World Series of Rock" shows. Aerosmith played in the middle of the bill. The recording is very good given the massive venue.

After a trio of songs from the band's first album, Tyler apologizes for their tardiness. "Sorry for taking so long to get on stage, one of our roadies locked himself in our dressing room getting his rocks off." More likely the band was getting high, and it shows in the performance.

"Big Ten Inch Record" gets moved up in the setlist and Scott Cushnie gets an introduction as the tune lifts off with Kramer's falsetto counting the band in. At its end, Tyler gives full credit to the song's author: Bull "Moose" Jackson, a Cleveland native.

The band has trouble launching "Sweet Emotion" and in buying time, Tyler claims "this is something we never have done before." Of course, we know that's a fib. More likely they were vexed by technical trouble, finding drugs or both.

Then Cushnie is again given an introduction by Tyler as the band appears to be heading into "No More No More." After a delay, and with Perry seemingly having trouble finding the notes to the song, he suddenly starts "Same Old Song And Dance" with the rest of the band taking his cue, then "Mama Kin" follows without a break.

"Train Kept A-Rollin'" features another "Batman" theme from Perry, but no "Peter Gunn" theme. Before the "Toys In The Attic" encore, Tyler says to the crowd: "I want it quiet, I want to hear my voice echo. Shhh. Shhh. Shhh. Shhh. I might be shitfaced, but I ain't more shitfaced than you. Shhh."

Not sure what his bandmate will say next, Kramer beats his drums to start "Toys In The Attic." A fan in the crowd keeps asking for "Uncle Salty," but it's not to be and the gig is over. A good show, but some of the band's drug excesses are starting to creep onto the stage.

Shaefer Music Festival, Wollman Skating Rink Theater, Central Park, New York City. Friday, August 29, 1975. Soundboard recording. Sound quality: A

Walkin' The Dog, S.O.S. (Too Bad), Somebody, Big Ten Inch Record, Sweet Emotion, Dream On, Write Me, Walk This Way, No More No More, Same Old Song And Dance, Train Kept A-Rollin', Toys In The Attic.

The famous show broadcast over the King Biscuit Flower Hour live music program. The accessibility spawned several well-known vinyl bootlegs: "Rock This Way" (Which Tyler has mistakenly referred to as "Monkey Grip"), "Look Homeward Angel," and "Live in New York, Nineteen Seventy Eight." Perry has heard "Look Homeward Angel" calling it in a radio interview "the one (made in) Guatemala City," as noted on its back cover. None of those records or subsequent re-airings of the concert provide the complete show. The entire show is available at Wolfgang's Vault as of this writing.

"Awhooo! Good evening Central Park," Tyler yells out before we get some tuning (in stereo!) and a more proper intro from Kelly: "Good evening New York City, are you ready to rock?!" and the familiar, "Let's all get together and give a warm welcome to the Boys from Boston, ladies and gentlemen Aerosmith!"

"No, I never seen nothing like this before, no I never, no I nev..." Tyler says as the band strikes up "Walkin' The Dog" with great zest. Perry's solo starts off discordant before he reins it in. The recording is a delight to listen to, especially with headphones as the dynamics can be heard quite clearly. The first three songs meld into one another to start the onslaught.

Cushnie (who is quite near-sighted) is dubbed by Tyler as "Blind Boy" during the "Big Ten Inch Record" intro. Perry gets too amped and comes in early, blowing the intro and throwing the band off for a second, but they quickly recover.

Tyler renames "Sweet Emotion," "Sweet Implosion" as he thanks New York City rock station WNEW for playing it. Hamilton's intro is spot on and taut, launching the thrill-a-second, driving rhythm that propels the song. Cushnie's backing of the main verse keeps Tyler in tune as the band powers through a fantastic version. "Thank you kindly, Yonkers," says Tyler as the band tries to get the tortured instruments back in tune. "Every rose, every rose has a thorn," the singer says at the song's conclusion.

"This is for you, Jack," Tyler says before "Walk This Way" to producer Jack Douglas who is at the gig. Tyler has found the groove to the song, rapping the lyrics in a relaxed fashion lacking during earlier live takes. The drugs no doubt helped loosen him up on this night as he seems to improvise lyrics as the song progresses.

"Anybody have a cold beer down there," Tyler says as the band plays on into the warm summer night, winning over the Big Apple with each song. "No More No More" again sees Tyler venture into alternative lyrics that are not entirely decipherable. "Train Kept A-Rollin'" stretches to 15 minutes with Kramer's solo thrown in. Perry's "Batman" theme during the track features cool, understated rhythm guitar from Whitford.

Recalling the 1974 Central Park debacle from the year prior, Perry says, "I think this is the first gig we have done in New York where we haven't walked away cursing," before the band crashes into "Toys In The Attic." Perry is not quite in tune during the song – the pristine recording makes that all too clear – but it does little to diminish the spectacular show that helped win them legions of fans in the venue and across the nation via radio and bootleg vinyl. A couple of minutes of 8mm footage has turned up on the internet with matching sound.

The King Biscuit Flower Hour
on Sunday, September 28, 1975 presents:

★AEROSMITH★
and
Gentle Giant

On September 28 The King Biscuit Flower Hour will present a taped live radio show featuring Aerosmith* and Gentle Giant.

The show hosted by Bill Minkin (on FM only) is in Quadraphonic Sound. So you can hear it the way you'd be seeing it.

In the future, shows will be every Sunday. The first Sunday features "The Best of the Biscuit", (repeats of our most requested shows). The second Sunday, a brand new Biscuit Show. The third Sunday "The British Biscuit", concerts recorded live in England. The forth Sunday a completely new

Biscuit show. Check the listing below for time and station in your area.

For further information, contact Bob Meyrowitz, Peter Kauff or Alan Steinberg at D.I.R. Broadcasting Corp., 445 Park Ave., New York, N.Y. 10022. Or call (212) 371 - 6850.

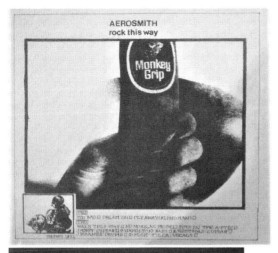

Various vinyl bootlegs of the Central Park gig.

Ambassador Theater, St. Louis, Missouri. Thursday, September 18, 1975. Soundboard recording. Sound quality: A-

Walkin' The Dog, S.O.S. (Too Bad), Somebody, Big Ten Inch Record, Sweet Emotion, Dream On, Write Me, Walk This Way, No More No More, Same Old Song And Dance, Train Kept A-Rollin'.

An interesting "dry" soundboard recording that has Tyler high up in the mix for much of the show. It's almost like you are on stage with the band. He ad-libs new lyrics throughout the gig, which can be heard clearly. With the audience but a distant piece in this unbalanced recording, the band's harmonies during "Sweet Emotion" are up front and raw, providing a unique perspective.

Keyboardist Scott Cushnie – so prominent on this tour – is not on stage this night, but it doesn't detract from the band's sound in the least. Tyler's soulful harmonica work comes through loud and clear on "Write Me."

Tyler dedicates "No More No More" to the capture of Patty Hearst, the newspaper heiress, kidnap victim and fugitive nabbed by police earlier in the day. Then Perry dedicates the tune to his dog "Stash."

Later, Tyler holds the mic into the crowd's first rows to have them sing "all night long" in anticipation of "Train Kept A-Rollin'" and suddenly the fans are clear, almost as if the whole affair is in a club, rather than a large auditorium.

Kramer plays what would become the drum intro to "Lick And A Promise" during his solo in the middle of "Train Kept A-Rollin'." During the song's final solo, Perry plays a little of the theme music from the TV show "Perry Mason," then it's "Think About It," "Movin' Out," "Pandora's Box," and finally the "Peter Gunn" theme with the band joining in before closing out the tune.

Tampa Tribune

Civic Center, Lakeland, Florida. Thursday, October 16, 1975.
Audience recording. Sound quality: D

Walkin' The Dog, S.O.S. (Too Bad), Somebody, Big Ten Inch Record, Walk This Way, Dream On, Lord Of The Thighs, Sweet Emotion, Adam's Apple, Same Old Song And Dance, Train Kept A-Rollin', Toys In The Attic.

The last known recording from the "Toys In The Attic" tour is a rough one. Tyler and Kramer can be heard well enough, but much of the rest of the band is obfuscated by the poor recording. There are still some interesting moments.

"Dream On" is the star on this night, getting a strong reaction at its conclusion. Otherwise, the crowd seems to be in a fog and rather listless until the end of the gig.

"Adam's Apple" takes the place of "No More No More" and segues into "Same Old Song And Dance." Perry sounds out the theme song for the Burger King restaurant chain during "Train Kept A-Rollin'."

The band plays a short blues intro into "Toys In The Attic" before closing the show out to wild applause. Rod Stewart and the Faces canceled, leaving Tyler's crew and Jeff Beck to carry on.

The same bill was set to play in Miami outdoors at the Gulfstream Race Track the following Saturday, but poor organization and rain bumped Aerosmith from the show. The band did return to Miami November 29, playing at the Jai-Alai Fronton with Ted Nugent.

Stewart was scheduled to perform Wednesday, Oct. 15, and Thursday, Oct. 16. However, late Wednesday, he canceled the show and the entire performance was rescheduled for Friday. Then Thursday night, Stewart announced he would not perform either Thursday or Friday, but the support talent of Jeff Beck, Aerosmith and Brian Bowers would perform for the fans who wanted to see them.

However, late Friday afternoon, Stewart decided to perform that night. But, according to Mrs. Littlejohn, the turnout was a "small house" since many fans did not think he would be performing.

Tampa Tribune

Aerosmith. Pure Gold.

Congratulations, boys, on a year well done. "Toys in the Attic," released this year, went over the half-million mark and pulled down a Gold Award. "Get Your Wings," album #2 for the group, raised its total to the magic number and earned Gold recognition.

And the album that started it all, "Aerosmith," this year also joined the select circle of Gold Records.

Congratulations, Tom Hamilton, Joey Kramer, Joe Perry, Steve Tyler and Brad Whitford, from all your friends and admirers at Columbia Records.

And Aerosmith says "Why stop at Gold?" Their tour continues:

Nov. 11 Milwaukee, Wis.
Nov. 12 Davenport, Iowa
Nov. 14 Minneapolis, Minn.
Nov. 15 Des Moines, Iowa
Nov. 16 Madison, Wis.
Nov. 19 Charlestown, Ill.
Dec. 2 New Haven, Conn.
Dec. 3 New York City, N.Y. (Madison Square Garden)
Dec. 5 Los Angeles, Calif. (Forum)
Dec. 6 San Francisco, Calif.
Dec. 7 Sacramento, Calif.
Dec. 9 Spokane, Wash.
Dec. 11 Seattle, Wash.
Dec. 12 Portland, Ore.
Dec. 17 San Diego, Calif.

Produced by Jack Douglas for Waterfront Productions Limited and Contemporary Communications Corp.

54

Aerosmith- the heights of rock and roll.

3⁹⁹ LP
OUR REG 4.96

SALE ENDS DEC 31

4⁹⁹ TAPE
OUR REG 5.97

Aerosmith played to a SRO crowd at the Forum.

A thundering, captivating rock and roll show that epitomizes music in the 1970's was a thrill shared by thousands of ecstatic fans. Even more have been pleasantly shocked into the recognition that Aerosmith is one of America's biggest phenomenons.

Witness three straight gold albums, "Get Your Wings," "Aerosmith" and their latest, "Toys in the Attic."

Thank you, L.A.

Aerosmith. On Columbia Records and Tapes.

55

Rocks Sessions, The Wherehouse, Waltham, Massachusetts and the Record Plant, New York February 1976 and March 1976. Soundboard recording. B

Nobody's Fault, Rats In The Cellar, Home Tonight, Last Child, Back In The Saddle, Combination, Get The Lead Out, Lick And A Promise.

The music for the album is just about complete here, but there are zero vocals. Tyler was known for delivering his lyrics as the last element of albums after the music was near done.

What we have here appears to be exactly that: almost finished music that Tyler then put lyrics to, which then allowed the guitar players to add leads.

Without the leads, the songs' rhythms are emphasized and really stand out, such as on "Nobody's Fault," which features more of a proper ending here, instead of a fade as heard on "Rocks."

"Rats In The Cellar" features a vocal count-in to launch it. The beginning of the track is just the rhythm guitar, so we don't hear the "answer" that the later lead would supply.

A guitar solo does appear on "Home Tonight," but not the one that would be on the final version. Tyler can be heard scatting in the distance as that track comes to a close.

"Last Child" is fairly well-formed, but is missing guitar parts, including Whitford's lead.

"Back In The Saddle" does not have its ending yet; it fades out here and is missing all its signature aural accoutrements: vocals, spurs and whip sounds. "Combination" has a couple of yelps not heard on the final version, likely from Tyler.

The session is an interesting document without the vocals, which, when added later, would make these iconic Aerosmith songs.

....A HISTORY

AEROSMITH was just beginning to break the ice. To build up a broader reputation for the group, their management promoted AEROSMITH shows throughout New England, where for several months the group played clubs and colleges four or five nights a week. The New England dates were supplemented by touring dates for AEROSMITH throughout the country with groups like the Mahavishnu Orchestra and the Kinks. And in the fall of 1973 an extensive tour with Mott the Hoople brought the sound and performance of AEROSMITH all across America.

In early 1974, the group's second Columbia album, "Get Your Wings" produced by Jack Douglas, was released. Steady touring and constant musical improvement by the group resulted in sales much better than the first album. By late summer 1974 AEROSMITH had earned their place in rock 'n roll. By the time AEROSMITH'S third LP, "Toys in the Attic" (also produced by Jack Douglas) was released in April 1975, "Get Your Wings" was gold. In August, just four months after release, "Toys in the Attic" joined "Get Your Wings" as a gold album; the first LP "Aerosmith" followed closely by. Summer of 1975 saw AEROSMITH become one of the major concert attractions in the country, selling out halls in cities they'd played before, as well as places they were playing for the first time. In December 1975, all three AEROSMITH albums were back on the charts! Understandably, the group took some time off the road in early 1976. But that didn't slow their popularity down. In January, Columbia released "Dream On" which not only hit the Top 10 on the national charts, but also brought AEROSMITH AM airplay for the first time. By May 1976 the first three AEROSMITH albums all went platinum. Their fourth Columbia album, "Rocks" was released in May 1976 and shipped Gold. It is their "most impressive and sophisticated effort to date. The band retained Jack Douglas as producer; and while the mostly hard rock songs are in the same vein as those on their previous albums, the songwriting on "Rocks" is more of a group project than before. The invaluable experience of three previous studio albums and two years of almost constant touring are evident in AEROSMITH's latest work. With this new national tour even more fans will find out —AEROSMITH: they've come a long way since Sunapee, New Hampshire—Listen—they'll be around for a long time to come.

57

A girl's best friend.
"Rocks" from Aerosmith. On Columbia Records and Tapes.

ROCKS TOUR

"Rocks" is released May 14, 1976, with the band going out on tour before it was out. The album peaks at No. 3 on the Billboard charts on June 25, 1976. The new album brings the band more success, boosting sales for their previous Lps. It also gets them dates outside North America for the first time.

The reaction to the band on stage in the States is tremendous, while the European dates bring mixed results. Japan, meanwhile, greets the band with delirium.

Of note: A quadrophonic version of this album is also prepared and released. It features different mixes. This is the last quad mix of an Aerosmith album as the technology never finds a mass audience.

Aerosmith tickets available

McElroy Auditorium, Waterloo, Iowa. Friday, April 30, 1976. Audience recording. Sound quality: B

Walkin' The Dog, Walk This Way, Adam's Apple, Lick And A Promise, Same Old Song And Dance, Train Kept A-Rollin', Toys In The Attic.

As the band takes the stage at this out of the way, sold-out venue, "Rocks" has yet to be released, but the band is playing the new songs anyway. The recording is fabulous, almost as if it was done on stage – maybe it was. Unfortunately, the recording captures only part of the concert, with the first section missing.

The crew adds some reverb to Tyler's voice, but that backfires during "Walkin' The Dog" as the effect overpowers the main vocals at one point. The tape yields a great clean version of "Adam's Apple" with Tyler calling out "story time!" during the opening licks. He uses a maraca to great effect during the tune.

We get the first known live version of "Lick And A Promise." The reverb unit

60

works well on the tune, but it again goes awry during "Same Old Song And Dance" as Tyler gets the crowd clapping by yelling "ha!" But the echo builds on itself, causing Tyler to say "Bob!" likely referring to sound expert Bob "Nitebob" Czaykowski to cut the device. Towards the end of the song, Tyler shouts "Sing it Elyssa!" to Perry's wife hanging out in the wings.

Nitebob (who began working with the band in September 1975) deserves high praise for helping deliver the band's sounds in a crystalline manner on a nightly basis throughout the early touring years.

A 15-minute version of "Train Kept A-Rollin'" follows with a Kramer solo, then with "Toys In The Attic" closing out the gig, the latter in slightly lesser quality than the rest of the show – Perry's solo is in the distance. The taper likely moved during the encore break.

An enjoyable document from the middle of the country. While a reported 10,000 people turned out, the audience is quite well behaved, probably due to their salt of the earth upbringing in Iowa. Nonetheless, locals didn't like the size of the crowd and called for limited attendance at future concerts.

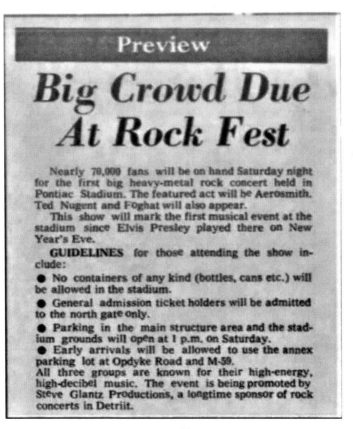

Preview

Big Crowd Due At Rock Fest

Nearly 70,000 fans will be on hand Saturday night for the first big heavy-metal rock concert held in Pontiac Stadium. The featured act will be Aerosmith. Ted Nugent and Foghat will also appear.

This show will mark the first musical event at the stadium since Elvis Presley played there on New Year's Eve.

GUIDELINES for those attending the show include:

● No containers of any kind (bottles, cans etc.) will be allowed in the stadium.

● General admission ticket holders will be admitted to the north gate only.

● Parking in the main structure area and the stadium grounds will open at 1 p.m. on Saturday.

● Early arrivals will be allowed to use the annex parking lot at Opdyke Road and M-59.

All three groups are known for their high-energy, high-decibel music. The event is being promoted by Steve Glantz Productions, a longtime sponsor of rock concerts in Detriit.

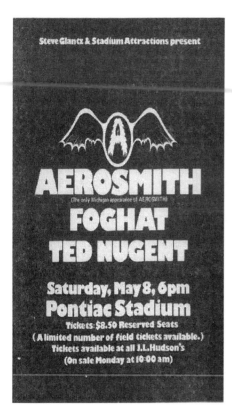

Steve Glantz & Stadium Attractions present

AEROSMITH
(The only Michigan appearance of AEROSMITH)

FOGHAT

TED NUGENT

Saturday, May 8, 6pm
Pontiac Stadium
Tickets: $8.50 Reserved Seats
(A limited number of field tickets available.)
Tickets available at all J.L.Hudson's
(On sale Monday at 10:00 am)

Silverdome, Pontiac, Michigan. Saturday, May 8, 1976. Soundboard from video. Sound quality: A.

Toys In The Attic, *S.O.S. (Too Bad), Adam's Apple, Sweet Emotion, Walk This Way, Same Old Song And Dance, Train Kept A-Rollin'.*

From the cornfields of Iowa to the gritty world of Detroit, the band in front of its biggest crowd to date as a headliner.

Tyler muddles the words during "Sweet Emotion" with Perry playing some wild notes in the middle. Some cool, locked-in twin guitar work during "Adam's Apple" highlights the tune. Perry plays the "Peter Gunn" theme as well as the "Batman" theme during "Train Kept A-Rollin'."

It sounds as though the drugs were flowing freely on this night; the band's focus is just not there.

Tyler was quoted as saying the gig was just too big and had a surrealistic feel, which may have added to the strange feel of the show.

This is an officially-released video recording from the "Scrapbook" VHS tape. But the audio was never officially released in a separate manner.

even in the Big City. Meanwhile, Aerosmith is the headline attraction tonight in the jai-alai fronton. So, there still is a chance to see a young band very much on the way up, already white hot in the Northeast.

Miami Herald

62

Jai-Alai Fronton, Miami, Florida. Monday, May 17, 1976. Audience recording. Sound quality: C

Somebody, Sick As A Dog, Big Ten Inch Record, Lord Of The Thighs, Sweet Emotion, Dream On, Walkin' The Dog, Walk This Way, Adam's Apple, Lick And A Promise, Same Old Song And Dance, Train Kept A-Rollin', Toys In The Attic.

The "Joe Perry Experience" is in full force on this night. The guitarist is playing out of his mind at the Miami venue, finding new and inventive ways to put his mark on each song.

During "Somebody" he solos throughout the song as if possessed. The tape reveals the first known live airing of "Sick As A Dog" with the twin guitars driving the song along.

Tyler works some harmonica into the beginning of "Big Ten Inch Record," adding more funk and groove to the already swinging tune. His harmonica intro would grow more elaborate in future versions, his work always a treat to hear live. There is more harmonica later in the song, before turning it over to Whitford.

"Lord Of The Thighs" is another Perry vehicle, his tortured tones filling the arena, and he adds a bit of trilling coming out of one of the mid-tune solos. The song stretches to seven minutes, Whitford and Perry taking the assembled for a wild ride.

Perry stretches out the intro to "Train Kept A-Rollin'" bending the strings, and when it comes time for Kramer's solo, Perry gives him a guitar intro. During his final solo, Perry uses feedback leading to the "Batman" theme and then gets into the "Peter Gunn" theme with a tremolo bar swoop, the type Eddie Van Halen would often use two years later on his band's first album. Then it's more feedback before the song finishes off. The segment is breathtaking, Perry displaying how far he had come as a player.

"Toys In The Attic" is the encore and features a longer than usual blues intro. When the song begins properly, chaos ensues as the start falls apart until Tyler sings the first lines. While it's a rough version, it's a fitting way to end the wild night that features many gems throughout.

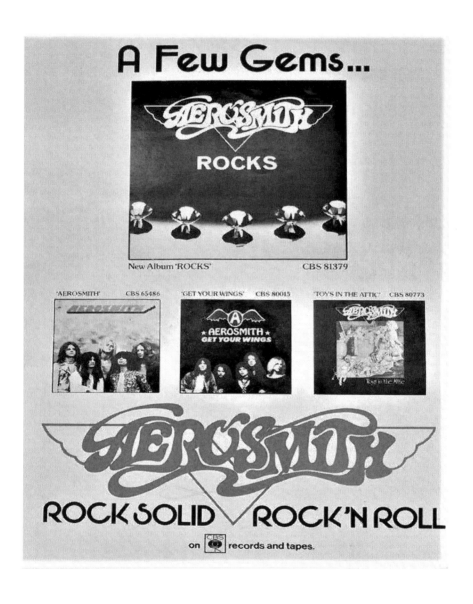

The Mecca, Milwaukee, Wisconsin. Thursday, July 8, 1976. Audience recording. Sound quality: D

Mama Kin, Write Me, S.O.S. (Too Bad), Lick And A Promise, Big Ten Inch Record, Sweet Emotion, Dream On, Lord Of The Thighs, Last Child, Walk This Way, Train Kept A-Rollin', Toys In The Attic.

Finally, a complete recording of a "Rocks" show, but the quality is challenged. We do learn how the band opens its shows: music from the movie "Jaws," followed by Sebastian Bach's "Tocatta and Fugie in D minor BWV 565," certainly a nice way to get the crowd revved up before Kelly's introduction.

Interestingly, despite the more sophisticated new material, the band kicks off their shows with older songs for the tour. This gig starts out with the familiar pattern of three back to back tunes, no breaks. "Write Me" returns to the lineup, with Kramer's funky, rhythmic intro.

Firecrackers pop at various times during the show, no doubt fans had some leftover pyrotechnics from the Fourth of July a few days earlier. The intro to "Sweet Emotion" gets the crowd into a frenzy and many stand at the Mecca as cries of "sit down!" follow.

"Dream On" gets a strong response. Seeing the band on the rise, Columbia smartly re-released the song as a single in the spring, entering the charts on March 20 and peaking on April 10 at No. 6, spending four weeks in the Top 10.

The tape also reveals the first known live version of "Last Child," although Whitford's intro can barely be heard. The band plays a straight-ahead rendition of what would be a concert standard for years to come. The band is off the stage within 75 minutes, much to the dismay of the crowd who wants to hear more after the "Toys In The Attic" encore.

65

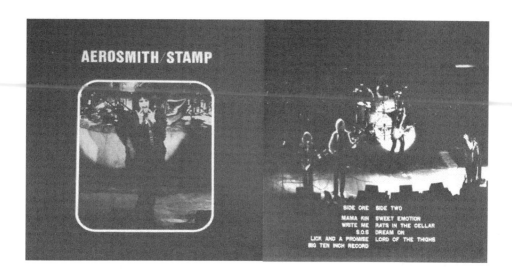

AEROSMITH/STAMP

SIDE ONE   SIDE TWO
MAMA KIN   SWEET EMOTION
WRITE ME   RATS IN THE CELLAR
S.O.S   DREAM ON
LICK AND A PROMISE   LORD OF THE THIGHS
BIG TEN INCH RECORD

Civic Center, Peoria, Illinois. Thursday, July 15, 1976. Audience recording. Sound quality: C

Mama Kin, Write Me, S.O.S. (Too Bad), Lick And A Promise, Big Ten Inch Record, Sweet Emotion, Rats In The Cellar, Dream On, Lord Of The Thighs.

Perry and Whitford use the rolling of the intro tape as a time to tune their guitars, maybe there was not enough time for a soundcheck on this night. Kelly gives an odd intro: "Say, what are you fellows doing here, and a queer, no shit. Ladies and gentlemen, from Boston, Aerosmith."

The reverb device we heard in Waterloo is back and more controlled here, used during "S.O.S. (Too Bad), "Lick And A Promise," "Sweet Emotion," "Rats In The Cellar" and "Dream On." During "Sweet Emotion," Perry plays notes sounding like an English-style ambulance siren.

The recording gives us the first known live version of "Rats In The Cellar," which seemingly starts from a standstill, though maybe the count-in is not heard on the tape. Oddly, right before the guitar solo, someone gets a hold of a mic and yells, "sweet emotion." The breakneck reading of the tune has an extended ending not heard on the "Rocks" version. That ending was played as part of the band's earlier version of "Rattlesnake Shake."

The reverb does get the best of Tyler during "Dream On" as "fools" from "fools and from sages," echoes wildly and he seems to listen to it, then has to catch up to the rest of the verse. He also sings "sing for your daddy and sing for your Pap smear" a reference that would continue off and on for years within the song. The end of the tune has Perry holding a long note that continues into the beginning of "Lord Of The Thighs," a cool effect. No more tape exists of this show apparently.

The bootleg vinyl "Stamp" is the source for this show. Named for its basic stamped artwork, only 25 copies of the album were pressed, according to lore.

CNE Grandstand, Toronto, Ontario, Canada. Saturday July 24, 1976. Audience recording. Sound quality: B-

Mama Kin, Write Me, Sweet Emotion, Dream On, Same Old Song And Dance, Train Kept A- Rollin'.

The first known tape from foreign soil. It's a well-done recording by a fan, unfortunately many of the songs are edited out, leaving about 30 minutes. Why? Who knows.

What we do have provides an enjoyable listen, the subtle guitar work on "Dream On" – often hard to hear in more cacophonous recordings – is displayed nicely here and is quite haunting, helping lay the emotional backdrop for the song.

Tyler interestingly changes the tone of his voice during parts of "Same Old Song And Dance," while Perry fires off some frantic notes during the song. Afterward, someone from the crowd seems to be passing money to Tyler, as he makes a reference to it. Odd!

During "Train Kept A- Rollin'," Perry hints at "Back In The Saddle." Oddly the tune – a crowd favorite that would see many live airings – seems to have not been played during the first "Rocks" shows. All in all, a cool stereo recording on this night, just too bad more of it has not surfaced.

Akron Beacon Journal

Richfield Coliseum, Richfield, Ohio. Wednesday, July 28, 1976. Audience recording. Sound quality: D

Mama Kin, Write Me, S.O.S. (Too Bad), Lick And A Promise, Big Ten Inch Record, Sweet Emotion, Dream On, Lord Of The Thighs, Last Child, Walk This Way, Sick As A Dog, Same Old Song And Dance, Train Kept A-Rollin'/Get The Lead Out/Helter Skelter, Toys In The Attic.

This was a make up gig as Cleveland Stadium officials wouldn't allow "World Series of Rock" fans to sit on the grass out of worry fans would ruin the baseball field. That gig was set for July 11.

68

This is one of the longer Aerosmith shows committed to tape up to this point as the band is on stage for close to 90 minutes.

Whitford's solo during "Last Child" cuts through the din like a laser in the dark. The highlight of the night is an epic, 19-minute version of "Train Kept A-Rollin" featuring a fantastic Kramer solo and significant parts of "Get The Lead Out" and The Beatles "Helter Skelter" before the band returns to the main theme.

The crowd doesn't want to go after the "Toys In The Attic" encore as we can hear calls for the band as the house music comes on along with the lights, and there is a palpable buzz in the air.

Cow Palace, San Francisco, California. Friday, August 27, 1976. Audience recording. Sound quality: B-

Rats In The Cellar, Dream On, Lord Of The Thighs, Last Child, Walk This Way, Sick As A Dog, Same Old Song And Dance, Train Kept A-Rollin'/Get The Lead Out/Jailhouse Rock, Toys In The Attic.

Strong recording of the band on this night, capturing the power of Kramer's drumming and the crunchy dual guitars very well.

The crowd calls for "Back In The Saddle" throughout, but it was not to be. After some dead air Tyler says, "Take your time Mr. Kramer" who then pounds the intro to "Sick As A Dog."

During "Same Old Song And Dance," Tyler is hit by a flying object to which he retorts: "Don't throw any shit at me!"

The solid recording brings out more details of the "Batman" theme during "Train Kept A-Rollin'." "Jailhouse Rock," which Perry hinted at during a show in McKeesport, Pennsylvania two years prior, comes into more full form here as the band joins in.

A slow, delicate blues is savagely broken by Kramer pounding out the "Toys In The Attic" intro. One of the few West Coast gigs found on tape during the band's early success.

Anaheim Stadium, Anaheim, California. Sunday, September 12, 1976. Audience recording. Sound quality: C

Train Kept A-Rollin', I Ain't Got You.

A massive show at Anaheim Stadium, known as the "Big A." Also, on the bill: Jeff Beck, who joins Aerosmith on stage. The event was a thrill for Perry, a huge Beck fan, and the pair take turns taking leads on "Train Kept A-Rollin'," the song Beck's Yardbirds help revive. The song is cut on the recording, and then suddenly Beck and the Boston Boys are into "I Ain't Got You," with a brand-new set of lyrics courtesy of Tyler.

A magical rock and roll moment.

As the song comes to a close, Tyler says, "That ain't all!" But that is all as the taper shuts down his gear after a couple of notes of the "Batman" theme and an audible pyrotechnic pod flash. It's likely the taper did not care for Aerosmith and was there to record Beck.

We are left with a tantalizing eight minutes of tape. It would be nice to put Tonight" being played. Another report has Perry listening to a recording of the show afterward.

AEROSMITH
Lynrd Skynrd, Jeff Beck
Anaheim Stadium — Sept. 12

'Live' Aerosmith

KNAC—FM, 105.5 on the dial, will provide live remote coverage of the Aerosmith concert at Anaheim Stadium Sunday.

The event includes performances by Jeff Beck, Lynyrd Skynyrd, Rick Derringer and Starz.

Joe Perry phoned from Los Angeles to say that Jeff Beck jammed with him onstage at Aerosmith's Anaheim Stadium concert on the songs "Train Kept A Rollin' " and "Ain't Got You." While Joe sounded almost as blase as usual, wife Elissa was slightly more extroverted in her enthusiasm about the event.

"It was history in the making," she laughed, "and it was the first time I can remember Joe smiling onstage during a show.

"Also," Elissa added, "Jeff's never jammed with an American band before, it was in front of a sold out crowd of 50,000, and it was the day after Joe's birthday."

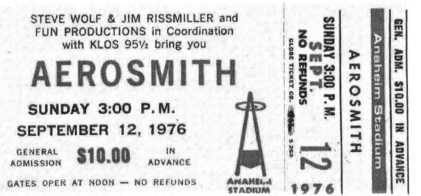

STEVE WOLF & JIM RISSMILLER and FUN PRODUCTIONS in Coordination with KLOS 95½ bring you

AEROSMITH

SUNDAY 3:00 P.M.

SEPTEMBER 12, 1976

GENERAL ADMISSION **$10.00** IN ADVANCE

GATES OPEN AT NOON — NO REFUNDS   ANAHEIM STADIUM

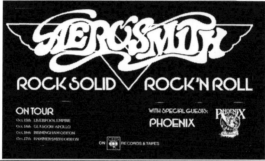

BRAD WHITFORD/STEVEN TYLER/JOEY KRAMER
JOE PERRY/TOM HAMILTON

AEROSMITH

EUROPEAN TOUR 1976

U.K. DATES

Presented by Harvey Goldsmith
in association with Neil Warnock for
Bron Agency Ltd.

October

13
Liverpool Empire
14
Glasgow Apollo
16
Birmingham Odeon
17
Hammersmith Odeon

EUROPEAN DATES

20
Cologne Sartory Saele
21
Erlangen Stadthalle
23
Stockholm Concert Hall
25
Amsterdam New Rai
26
Offenbach Stadthalle
28
Ludwigshafen Friderich Ebert Halle
30
Zurich Volkshaus
November
1
Paris Pavilion Theatre

FAN CLUB

c/o
15 Great Western Road
London W.9. England

MAIL ORDER
If you require further copies
of this programme
please forward 60p
(special mail order price inc. post)
to: Souvenir Book Publishers,
Dept. A.
13 Oxford Circus Ave. London W.1.

Programme designed,
produced and published,
for your pleasure, by
THEATREGRAPHICS
Publishing Enquiries
DAVID FELLERMAN
01-437 3926

Tour co-ordination
HUW PRICE/MEL BAISTER/DOUG SMITH
P.A. and sound engineer
M.E.H. LTD/BOB CZAKOWSKI
Lighting and lighting engineer
SEE FACTOR/NIGEL GIBBONS/JOHN BRODERICK
Equipment manager
NICK SPIEGEL
Trucking
EDWIN SHIRLEY LTD
Tour managers
MEL BAISTER/BOB 'KELLY' KELLAHER
Promotion/Press
RICHARD OGDEN/STEVE GILMORE
American/European Direction
DAVID KREBS/STEVE LEBER/DOUG SMITH

73

Given its success in the United States, Aerosmith looks to break the European market. Several dates are set across the continent. Unfortunately, none of the British dates have surfaced on tape. They would be a fun listen, no doubt.

RAI, Amsterdam, Holland. Monday, October 25, 1976. Audience recording. Sound quality: C

Mama Kin, S.O.S. (Too Bad), Lick And A Promise, Big Ten Inch Record, Sweet Emotion, Rats In The Cellar, Dream On, Lord Of The Thighs, Last Child, Walk This Way, Same Old Song And Dance, Train Kept A-Rollin/Get The Lead Out, Milk Cow Blues.

The first evidence of the band in Europe. Maybe because the show was on a Monday, maybe because the band was not well known in Holland at this time, or maybe because the crowd is high on famed Amsterdam hash, the energy on this night is next to non-existent.

That's not to say the band played poorly, but the tepid response to songs and Tyler's exhorting of the audience to get involved make it all a lackluster affair.

"Come on!" Tyler implores the audience after "Lick And A Promise" and the band does get a better reception after the next song, "Big Ten Inch Record."

The crowd does acknowledge the first verse of "Dream On," which jumped into the U.S. charts in 1976 and no doubt filtered over to Holland. But Tyler sums it all up before "Train Kept A-Rollin:" "I want to hear you sing. You have been so fucking quiet, sitting on your asses all night." Ouch.

Kramer's solo is excised from "Train Kept A-Rollin" as it is from all the European gigs, at least those that have been captured on tape on this tour.

"Milk Cow Blues" is revived for the gig, with Perry taking over the lead vocal for the first verses, an interesting ending to a sleepy, sleepy gig.

Stadthalle, Offenbach, West Germany. Tuesday, October 26, 1976. Soundboard recording. Sound quality: B

Mama Kin, Write Me, S.O.S. (Too Bad), Lick And A Promise, Big Ten Inch Record, Sweet Emotion, Rats In The Cellar, Dream On, Lord Of The Thighs, Last Child, Walk This Way, Sick As A Dog, Same Old Song And Dance, Train Kept A-Rollin'/Get The Lead Out, Toys In The Attic.

What a difference a day and a new country make! Dragging along with the audience the night before, the band comes out on fire this night as does the audience. German beer trumps Dutch hash? Kelly starts his introduction with: "Good evening everybody, are you ready to rock tonight!?" A resounding roar comes back. "All right, all right, that sounds good!"

The whole band sounds on hyperdrive as the show lifts off, energy bounding as though they can hardly contain themselves within the structure of the songs.

Perry and Whitford play interesting staccato riffs during the first and second verses of "Sweet Emotion," which is dedicated to road manager Kelly, as Tyler again calls the tune "Sweet Implosion" during the intro.

"We ain't home," Tyler says before "Rats In The Cellar," reminding his bandmates they have to win over the crowd. It's not easy like it is back in the States for the band.

Perry plays the intro to "Dream On," but then the band launches into "Rats In The Cellar," flying down the rails with an intense version, an all-out aural assault. Tyler's initial verses get lost in echo, but this time the effect is good. Perry's solo is inventive and leaves the band far behind. But he lands on his feet and rejoins his mates soon enough.

These European gigs show off Perry's skills, and his solos are never played the same way twice. Even during "Dream On" he pushes and prods the song's structure, part of what makes Aerosmith's sound so exciting live.

"Lord Of The Thighs" gets off to an odd start. Tyler usually raps over Kramer's intro, but not tonight, and it leads to a tepid intro for the guitar players who may be waiting for Tyler. But Whitford and Perry weave their magic during the solos, just pure listening pleasure as they trade licks.

"I'm bleeding tonight..." Tyler sings during the "Last Child" intro verse, again switching up lyrics on the spot. Perry again ventures way out on "Train Kept A-Rollin'" his playing satisfyingly erratic as it is inventive. A pair of good sounding recordings preserves the night, one likely taken from the soundboard.

Volkshaus, Zurich, Switzerland. Saturday, October 30, 1976.
Audience recording. Sound quality: B
Mama Kin, Write Me, S.O.S. (Too Bad), Lick And A Promise, Big Ten Inch Record, Sweet Emotion, Rats In The Cellar, Dream On, Lord Of The Thighs, Last Child, Walk This Way, Sick As A Dog, Same Old Song And Dance, Train Kept A-Rollin/Get The Lead Out, Toys In The Attic.

The recording starts out with a talk from the MC in German, then suddenly "Tocatta and Fugie in D minor BWV 565" strikes up. "Let's all get high!" someone in the audience yells after Kelly's proper introduction and the band launches into its back-to-back-to-back series of tunes to open the show.

Tyler is absent on the first verse of S.O.S. (Too Bad) before jumping back into the song. Kramer's drum intro into "Lick And A Promise" has a groove, but is machine-like in its power. Hamilton plays along with Kramer and Tyler's harmonica on "Big Ten Inch Record," adding to the looseness of the gig.

In 1976, Aerosmith is definitely not a "paint by the numbers" band. Like in Offenbach, the audience is tuned into the band in Zurich, and starts an unprompted "Aerosmith" chant before Kramer pounds his bass drum along with the mantra. Tyler then playfully gets the crowd to quiet: "Shhh, shhh, shhh, we are going to slow the whole business down..."

Not really, as Perry blasts into "Rats In The Cellar." The song is a highlight as the guitars wreak havoc, jamming out as Kramer keeps the steady beat behind the duo.

Kramer pounds out a strong intro into "Walk This Way" as Perry joins in with the talk box before starting the song proper. The band gets into a whole minute of a "I'm A Man"-type jam before the dam breaks way into "Toys In The Attic" to end a fantastic show. The lively, atmospheric recording makes it that much more enjoyable.

concert
Pavillon de Paris 21h
1ᵉʳ Novembre
Nouvel album

CBS

Nouvel album

CBS 81379

en 1ᵉ partie: PHOENIX

Paris Pavillon porte de Pantin, Paris France. Monday, November 1, 1976. Audience recording. Sound quality: B-

Mama Kin, Write Me, S.O.S. (Too Bad), Lick And A Promise, Big Ten Inch Record, Sweet Emotion, Rats In The Cellar, Dream On, Lord Of The Thighs, Last Child, Walk This Way, Sick As A Dog, Same Old Song And Dance, Train Kept A-Rollin/Get The Lead Out, Toys In The Attic.

Aerosmith lands in Paris for its last European gig of the tour. Like the Dutch, the Parisians need a little push from Tyler.

"I can't hear you!" says the singer, who then uses some alternative lyrics for the first verse of "Lick And A Promise." But the band is more confident by the end of the European run and they are going to take the crowd on a wild ride, willing or not, as the notes come fast and furious.

Perry steps on Tyler's first word on "Dream On," and we imagine the guitarist smiles. Tyler changes the lyrics to "dream on, cream on, scream on" during its climactic moments.

Tyler's "Lord Of The Thighs" rap over Kramer's drum intro often referred to France, and it's no different once in the country: "She was a honey, south side of France, all she wanted to do was get down my pants."

The recording on this night captures one of the best versions of the song, as fluid playing throughout gets the crowd clapping along to the beat. A perfect live version of the tune.

Perry's "Batman" theme during "Train Kept A-Rollin'" also gets the crowd going; if they were sluggish at the outset by the end they are fully tuned in to what's happening on stage.

Perry again is the dynamo on this night, making his guitar swoop and swoon, perfect notes mix with feedback during the penultimate tune. He even tosses in a bit of "Movin' Out."

The cool Parisians are in a frenzy and spend two minutes yelling for the band to come back to the stage. The band obliges them (as we knew they would) and plays a bone-crushing "Toys In The Attic" to finish off the affair.

A rock show at 7:30 p.m. Wednesday at the Civic Arena is to feature Aerosmith and Rick Derringer.

Civic Arena, Pittsburgh, Pennsylvania. Wednesday, November 10, 1976. Audience recording. Sound quality: D+

Mama Kin, Write Me, S.O.S. (Too Bad), Lick And A Promise, Big Ten Inch Record, Sweet Emotion, Rats In The Cellar, Dream On, Lord Of The Thighs, Last Child, Walk This Way, Sick As A Dog, Same Old Song And Dance, Train Kept A-Rollin/Get The Lead Out, Toys In The Attic.

Aerosmith's tour of Europe had been an uneven journey. Now they are back on their home turf and the difference is palpable. The audience claps along to every song and the old Pittsburgh arena is rocked to its foundation.

Pittsburgh was one of the hard scrabble towns that was a Mecca for the band. "I'll tell ya, it's great to be back in the States," Tyler observes as the band teases to "Dream On," but instead breaks into a whip-cracking "Rats In The Cellar."

"Dream On" does come next and the intro gets a "Stairway To Heaven" - type response as the crowd recognizes the tune. Tyler switches up the lyrics to "all these lines of the lives getting clearer."

Tyler breaks out a maraca during "Lord Of The Thighs" to add a little rhythm, a new wrinkle to the song which stretches out to just over eight minutes on this night.

A ponderous Whitford intro to "Last Child" is featured next. Tyler introduces "Walk This Way" as a new single. At one point, Tyler seems to refer to the gig as in Buffalo, but likely was an error.

"It's your turn, I'm getting tired" says Tyler as he cajoles the crowd into singing "Train Kept A-Rollin'."

Aerosmith (who take off this week for their first-ever European tour), will play Detroit's Cobo Hall on Dec. 1 and 2 to correct what they feel was a "bad show" at Pontiac Stadium last spring. "We'll never play those huge, enclosed places again," they vow. They also plan two shows in November at Madison Square Garden — a satisfying prospect for a band that at one time felt they couldn't sell out a New York venue.

Cobo Arena, Detroit, Michigan. Wednesday, December 1, 1976. Audience recording. Sound quality: C

Mama Kin, Write Me, S.O.S. (Too Bad), Lick And A Promise, Big Ten Inch Record, Sweet Emotion, Rats In The Cellar, Last Child, Lord Of The Thighs, Walk This Way, Sick As A Dog, Same Old Song And Dance, Train Kept A-Rollin'/Get The Lead Out, Toys In The Attic, Train Kept A-Rollin'/Get the Lead Out, Toys In The Attic.

Weird night in Detroit. The crowd is distant on the recording and quiet, and Tyler chastises the audience all evening.

"You're awfully quiet tonight," he says during the intro into "Big Ten Inch Record." Mr. Reliable, Whitford, delivers a sterling solo on the song, but Perry stumbles into his solo. After some fits and starts, he gets it off the ground and then it goes longer than usual.

Tyler again comments on the crowd's lethargy: "What did they do frisk you before you came in here tonight?" before "Sweet Emotion." During the song Whitford and Perry get into some pleasant harmonics before Kramer breaks in with his rat-a-tat amplified by Tyler's mic. Perry's soloing on the outro is quite the journey as he weaves adventurous sonic waves that rebound off the arena's walls – the guitar outlaw at his best.

Tyler goes at the crowd again during the "Lord Of The Thighs" intro, "Detroit, you need to shake your ass." That seems to throw the band off as Whitford and Perry are slow to start the song.

Then during the "Walk This Way" intro: "You people, get up and shake your ass." The whole second half of the concert sounds like all are on quaaludes as the music seems to slow. Perry's second solo during "Same Old Song And Dance" is discordant, and he pauses for a moment in one place to find the groove of the song. The song finishes with extended bass lines from Hamilton that reverberate around the arena.

Tyler gets one final jab at the crowd: "What a bunch of zombies you are. I can't believe you are still on your ass. Will you sing at least?" As Tyler leads them through "Train Kept A-Rollin'," Kramer is slow to start the second part of the song. Perry sounds out "Have Yourself A Merry Little Christmas" briefly during his solo. After all the carrying on and criticism of the audience by Tyler, the crowd calls the band back for the "Toys In The Attic" encore.

Overall, a strange gig. Aerosmith played Detroit often in the mid-1970s and had the massive Silverdome show only seven months earlier. Maybe they had oversaturated the market, hence a response Tyler was not pleased with. Or maybe it was too reminiscent for him of the recent European gigs.

Madison Square Garden, New York City. Thursday, December 16, 1976. Audience recording. Sound quality: D

Mama Kin, Write Me, S.O.S. (Too Bad), Lick And A Promise, Big Ten Inch Record, Sweet Emotion, Rats In The Cellar, Dream On, Lord Of The Thighs, Last Child, Walk This Way, Sick As A Dog, Same Old Song And Dance, Train Kept A-Rollin'/Get the Lead Out, Toys In The Attic.

The first of two sold out gigs at Madison Square Garden. After touring like demons and putting out four albums in four years, the band's hard work had paid off.

How far the band had come in a few short years. The band is met with a din created by the throng of 20,000 as they walk on stage.

The band does its usual "Dream On" tease, playing the first notes that drives the crowd into a frenzy, but then they break into "Rats In The Cellar." But people are equally amped to hear that song as yells of approval can be heard.

Then when "Dream On" gets its proper reading, the Garden erupts. How satisfying that must have been for Tyler. Kramer's intro to "Lord Of The Thighs" almost sounds like the "Walk This Way" intro. As the song progresses, Perry eschews his slide guitar work for cool, clipped, rhythmic, staccato notes.

Tyler is strangely quiet for most of the show, maybe using his energy to focus on the high-profile gig.

Whitford delivers a sublime solo during "Last Child" on the big stage of Madison Square Garden. Perry again plays part of "Have Yourself A Merry Little Christmas" during his "Train Kept A-Rollin'" solo.

After the tune, the band leaves the stage and the crowd yells for more than two minutes to get them back for the "Toys In The Attic" encore.

This was one of the last of the "Rocks" tour shows in the U.S. The band was a hot commodity and a new land beckoned.

WHO is WHO

Management Direction:
DAVID KREBS, STEVE LEBER
for LEBER/KREBS inc.

ROAD PERSONNEL

BOB KELLEHER "KELLY"
Tour Director

JOE BAPTISTA
Stage Manager

NICK SPIGEL
Crew Chief

DICK HANSEN "the RABBIT"
Stage Crew

B.J. REISCH
Stage Crew

HENRY SMITH
Asst. Tour Director

BOB CZAYKOWSKI "NITE BOB"
Sound Engineer

NIGEL BERESFORD "JINX"
Monitor Engineer

GILL MACNEIL
Transportation Director

Merchandising– RAY TABANO   **Sound**– TASCO

Publicity– LAURA KAUFMAN   **Lighting**– SEE FACTOR

Travel– STARFLITE   **Security**– SUNRISE SECURITY

Special thanks to special folks...
    Jack Douglas, Jay Messina– RECORD PLANT– Sam Ginsberg, Dave Hewitt, Van the Man– RECORD PLANT MOBILE Unit
– Billy Murry, Ed Cooper, Dave Radibush and all of E.V. WURLIZTER'S people, Zildjian Cymbals, Terry Hanley, Walter Link,
Gail Smith, Sue Tabano, Francine Lamess (Steven's seamstress), Michel & Anovchka (Joe P. wardrobe), Danny Gatton–
CHARVEL GUITARS, George Abdon and Compant, Michael B. & Anne P., Captain Harold & Zunk, Jack Baldwin, Mickey
Kramer, Michael Cohen & Jim Stepp, Karen Shields, Helen Morgan, Bruce Polley, Mel, Kevin, Fran, Dan, John and the rest
of the DEDICATED STAFF at NEW YORK HEADQUARTERS (LEBER/KREBS)– There's more– Peg Griffen, Norman Jacobs, Cosmo
Taglino, Leo I. along with everyone else who believed, Ronnie Cohan & Shelly Schultz, Hal Lazareff (ICM)

Thanks,
It feels good

P.S. Arma Andon, Bruce Lunvali & Bill Freston (CBS)

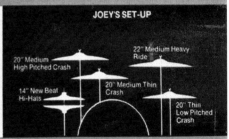

DOUBLE PLATINUM
ON THE ROCKS.

AEROSMITH "ROCKS" ON COLUMBIA RECORDS AND TAPES.

The band lands in Japan for an absolute stellar series of shows. It was a wildly successful tour with many highlights.

"If only management had the foresight to tape those shows..." Tyler wrote in his autobiography. The fans had the foresight to do just that. There is even a vinyl document.

Japanese radio also produced a documentary complete with Tyler trying his hand at a stringed koto and shamisen.

Sports Center, Maebashi, Gunma, Japan. Saturday, January 29, 1977. Audience recording. Sound quality: B-

Mama Kin, Write Me, S.O.S. (Too Bad), Lick And A Promise, Big Ten Inch Record, Sweet Emotion, Rats In The Cellar, Dream On, Lord Of The Thighs, Last Child, Walk This Way, Sick As A Dog, Same Old Song And Dance, Train Kept A-Rollin', Toys In The Attic.

The band has described parts of the Japanese tour as Beatle-esque, with fans screaming at every turn. This is evident during this first show as the band hits the stage as thousands of young women squeal in the auditorium.

"Write Me" has sped up significantly since its more metered readings back in 1973. In fact, the whole show feels sped up, the band playing on adrenaline on the opening night in a new land for them.

Tyler gives a premature toot of his harmonica on "Big Ten Inch Record," a song greeted with great applause at its conclusion. One wonders if the crowd understood all the lyrics!

Perry breaks out the talk box for "Sweet Emotion" and says through the device, "Do you feel alright?" a tip of the hat to Peter Frampton's new live album released in January. "Rats In The Cellar" has a false start, so Tyler scats in an intro and Kramer counts the tune in. The song really rolls when it gets going, the phasing in full effect on the tune. The effect had been used more and more on the 1976 tour.

Tyler starts to enter a verse too soon during "Walk This Way," but he recovers. He and Perry join to sing the opening verses to "Sick As A Dog," although as the song continues, the backing vocals wobble and are out of tune.

Before "Train Kept A-Rollin'" Tyler asks if the crowd can sing "All night long." There is only a cheer. Tyler asks again, and again a cheer, but no line. And a third time, but no luck. But on the fourth attempt the crowd gets it and yells back "All night long!" A touching moment as artist and audience connect transcending the language barrier.

Perry starts the tune channeling Hendrix as he gets feedback roaring before striking the first notes. Tyler and Perry do a little harmonica/guitar interplay as the song progresses. The crowd goes wild as it tries to coax the band back onstage for the "Toys In The Attic" encore, which comes.

While Japanese fans were said to be staid and quiet, this was not the case on this night. The recording was made by the famous Japanese taper "Mr. Peach," who did a wonderful job capturing the evening as he would on other nights.

Budokan Hall, Tokyo, Japan. Monday, January 31, 1977. Audience recording. Sound quality: B-

Mama Kin, Write Me, S.O.S. (Too Bad), Lick And A Promise, Big Ten Inch Record, Sweet Emotion, Rats In The Cellar, Dream On, Lord Of The Thighs, Last Child, Walk This Way, Sick As A Dog, Same Old Song And Dance, Train Kept A-Rollin'/Get The Lead Out, Toys In The Attic.

Perry delivers a great sonic intro to the set, repeating a chord then launching into "Mama Kin." Less screamers in more sophisticated Tokyo than the previous gig.

"Come on Tokyo!" Tyler says during the intro into "S.O.S. (Too Bad)," one of the finest versions ever recorded. Bursting with energy – Kramer does a great drum fill at the beginning – and crisp vocals, the band really outdoes itself on this one.

The audience is very receptive, clapping along to "Lick And A Promise," which Tyler calls a band favorite from "Rocks." Kramer's heavy intro certainly knocked a few boulders loose from Mount Fuji!

"If you're going to throw those eggs boy, scramble them up first," Tyler says suddenly. Are eggs being tossed onto the stage? Perry plays unique notes to punctuate Tyler's lyrics during "Sweet Emotion," with the guitarist adding a wild lick toward the end of the song.

During "Rats In The Cellar," Tyler sings seemingly unintelligible new lyrics, as if he knows the crowd won't fully understand anyway. He also gives the harmonica a workout during the tune.

"Dream On" gets another rousing cheer as its first notes are played, while Tyler gets behind in the verse as the song closes. "Walk This Way's" backing vocals sound flat, almost as though a roadie is singing along, maybe the relaxed Japanese tour allows for some playful moments.

Tyler calls Hamilton "the big ten inch" after the bass man concludes "Same Old Song And Dance" in the spotlight. Kramer gets his solo back in Tokyo, the first time since before the European tour, and the crowd gives it the biggest applause of the evening. Almost out of nowhere during Kramer's banging,

Perry chimes in with the ending of "Combination," before the solo continues. Perry pulls out the stops as he solos during "Train Kept A-Rollin'," creating wild sounds, sliding his pick up and down his guitar before jumping into the now familiar "Peter Gunn" theme.

The first few guitar notes are missing on "Toys In The Attic," so it becomes a drum intro reminiscent of Led Zeppelin's live version of "Train Kept A-Rollin'." Our friend Mr. Peach and his recorder attended again on this night to capture the show, and the recording is very good indeed.

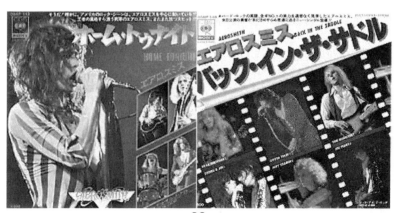

Nagoya-Shi Kokaido, Nagoya, Japan. Tuesday, February 1, 1977.
Audience recording. Sound quality: D+

Mama Kin, Write Me, S.O.S. (Too Bad), Lick And A Promise, Big Ten Inch Record, Sweet Emotion, Rats In The Cellar, Dream On, Lord Of The Thighs, Last Child (fragment), Walk This Way, Sick As A Dog, Same Old Song And Dance, Train Kept A-Rollin'/Get The Lead Out, Toys In The Attic.

Mr. Peach was not at this show, and the recording is not as strong as the previous two. Yet, there are some interesting moments caught by the taper.

Tyler misses the first verse of "S.O.S. (Too Bad)." The guitar solos on "Big Ten Inch Record" are super tight on this night, Perry not venturing out as he was want to do. A roadie seems to yell something into the mic in the middle of "Rats In The Cellar," another playful moment from the crew perhaps.

The first notes of "Dream On" are met with a wave of applause, but Perry then stops and re-starts the song. Tyler ad-libs the lyrics "sing for the ghetto, sing for the saints."

Interestingly, during the "Lord Of The Thighs" initial guitar solos, Perry and Whitford play more of a soundscape than individual notes, adding a new dimension to the song. The approach was heard in many of the 1977 shows.

We only get 15 or so seconds of "Last Child" before it fades as the tape must have run out. Tyler dubs Kramer "the greatest drummer in the world" as he takes his solo during "Train Kept A-Rollin.'" The crowd absolutely loves it. Who knew the Japanese loved drums solos so much? Or maybe it's the rock-solid Kramer that gets them going.

Perry again dips into the end of "Combination" in the middle of it all, starting by playing staccato notes. During his solo toward the end of the song, Perry hints at "Adam's Apple" before going into a subtle "Batman" theme.

The crowd begins a chant to get the band back on stage for the encore, with whistles being blown intermittently, the fans creating a song of their own. Good vibes in Nagoya!

Kyuden Kinen Gymnasium, Fukuoka, Japan. Friday, February 4, 1977. Audience recording. Sound quality: B-

Mama Kin, Write Me, S.O.S. (Too Bad), Lick And A Promise, Big Ten Inch Record, Sweet Emotion, Rats In The Cellar, Dream On, Lord Of The Thighs, Last Child, Walk This Way, Sick As A Dog, Same Old Song And Dance, Train Kept A-Rollin'/Get The Lead Out, Toys In The Attic.

The band faces the quietest crowd of the tour so far and the show seems to match that energy at some points as Aerosmith is a little more laid back on this night.

Perry sprinkles interesting licks throughout "Write Me." Kramer's intro to "Lick And A Promise" begins in a sound of fog and then gets louder, a cool effect, intended or not.

Tyler's harmonica intro into "Big Ten Inch Record" is soulful and extended, done at a leisurely pace. During "Sweet Emotion" the guitars suddenly jump to "11" in volume at one point in crunchy fashion – a real treat. Tyler scats during the song's break, slipping in "fuckin'" as the only intelligible word.

In his book, Perry recalls crowds applauding for 10 seconds and then stopping. Maybe it was this gig he remembered, as that's the exact response after "Sweet Emotion."

Kramer changes his drumming during parts of "Rats In The Cellar," rolling through his kit at points, eschewing the frantic beats he normally played. Right before the first solo, it sounds like a cow moos, and it's unclear if it's an instrument or a voice! Perhaps the road crew again? Perry plays some discordant notes as he solos along the way.

90

Tyler improvises lines toward the end of "Dream On" and gets a little tripped up, but it's interesting nonetheless. "Lord Of The Thighs" features some interesting jamming throughout, the rhythm section in a tight groove allowing the freedom for Perry and Whitford to wander off. Really one of the most unique versions of the song. Tyler breaks out a cowbell for the end of "Walk This Way."

He announces "Sick As A Dog" is "brought to you by Shakey's" referring to the pizza chain. Tyler also switches up the lyrics: "Please, I just got to sing to you..."

During "Same Old Song And Dance" Tyler says, "I feel like Alfalfa" (From the old TV show "The Little Rascals) and then proceeds to again improvise lyrics. Perry jams on "Combination" again during Kramer's solo in "Train Kept A-Rollin'." When the band jumps into "Get The Lead Out" Tyler sings "yes, yes" instead of "no, no" during parts and subs in "gotta take a piss" for a lyric. Perry plays the "Adam's Apple" intro as well.

As in Tokyo, the guitars go quiet during the beginning of "Toys In The Attic." The song is proceeded with the little blues jam, which Tyler sings over. Wonderful recording from this gig. Not only is the crowd quiet, but distant. Was this recorded from the stage? Or maybe just the fine work of Mr. Peach.

Kaikan Hall, Kyoto, Japan. Sunday, February 6, 1977. Audience recording. Sound quality: B-

Mama Kin, Write Me, S.O.S. (Too Bad), Lick And A Promise, Big Ten Inch Record, Sweet Emotion, Rats In The Cellar, Dream On, Lord Of The Thighs, Last Child, Walk This Way, Sick As A Dog, Same Old Song And Dance, Train Kept A-Rollin'/Get The Lead Out/Movin' Out, Toys In The Attic.

Road manager Kelly repeats the intro he gave back in Peoria during the summer of 1976: "Say, what are you fellows doing here, and a queer, no shit." It was probably lost on the Kyoto crowd as it is on us!

Perry begins the "Mama Kin" intro in the wrong key, but quickly rights the ship. Tyler switches up the "Write Me" lyrics, subbing in "entice me" and "excite me" for the "write me" line. Roadies again seem to pipe up in the middle of "Rats In The Cellar," an ongoing joke for this song in Japan.

91

Perry hits the wrong notes to start "Dream On," but the band carries on nevertheless. At the end of the song, the guitarists hold long notes as Kramer starts "Lord Of The Thighs." Whitford has trouble finding the notes to start "Last Child," a rare foul up for him.

"Walk This Way" starts with a fast shuffle by Kramer, who then slows it down to start the song proper. Perry strums some cool notes into "Same Old Song And Dance" on this night. Perry also gives a great intro into "Train Kept A-Rollin'," playing a bit of the "Stars Spangled Banner."

During his solo, he gets the band into "Get The Lead Out" then a brief "Adam's Apple" where Tyler joins him with a maraca. The real treat comes when Perry shifts the band to "Moving Out," which they jam on for a couple of minutes. The loud crowd claps to get the band back on stage for the encore. During the blues jam into "Toys In The Attic," Tyler takes on the role of auctioneer! Fabulous show in Kyoto recorded by Mr. Peach.

Festival Hall, Osaka, Japan. Monday, February 7, 1977. Audience recording. Sound quality: C+

Mama Kin, S.O.S. (Too Bad), Lick And A Promise, Big Ten Inch Record, Sweet Emotion, Rats In The Cellar, Dream On, Lord Of The Thighs, Last Child, Walk This Way, Same Old Song And Dance, Train Kept A-Rollin', Toys In The Attic.

Kelly introduces the band as the "Swine Flu Alumni Association," maybe a passing reference to some in the band being ill, as two tunes are removed from the setlist on this evening. The gig checks in at less than 75 minutes. The next gig would also see a shorter setlist.

"Write Me" is excised from the set. Kramer does an extended intro that turns into a mini drum solo into "Lick And A Promise," maybe to cover for a technical issue with one of the guitars.

Kramer steps on the intro into "Dream On," which gets its normal audience screams as the song begins. As in Kyoto, the opening notes to "Last Child" are flubbed by Whitford, but the rest of the song comes off fine. Perry extends the end of "Walk This Way" to connect to "Same Old Song And Dance." "Sick As A Dog," normally played, was left off the setlist.

Perry produces an electrifying intro into "Train Kept A-Rollin'," playing a bit of David Bowie's "Fame" with its descending riffs after the first verses. The mini "Get The Lead Out" is also missing on this night. After the encore, the fans go crazy and someone in the crowd blows a whistle in triplicate as the recording ends.

Budokan Hall, Tokyo, Japan. Wednesday, February 9, 1977. Audience recording. Sound quality: B-

Mama Kin, S.O.S. (Too Bad), Lick And A Promise, Big Ten Inch Record, Sweet Emotion, Rats In The Cellar, Dream On, Lord Of The Thighs, Last Child, Walk This Way, Same Old Song And Dance, Train Kept A-Rollin'/Get The Lead Out, Toys In The Attic.

After the opener "Mama Kin," Write Me" is played very briefly, but then the band goes right into "S.O.S. (Too Bad)," where Tyler starts the song with the second verse, "Salt Lake City..." then repeats it again.

"Bull Moose Jackson put that together after a nocturnal emission," Tyler slyly says after "Big Ten Inch Record." Perry again invokes Frampton's "Do You Feel Alright" as he starts "Sweet Emotion."

"Lord Of The Thighs" hits the nine-minute mark at the gig, with some great interludes along the way. It's a real musical treat, laid back, but full of intensity at the same time.

Tyler sounds like a mad dog during "Last Child" as he snaps, snarls and growls the lyrics throughout. During "Train Kept A-Rollin'" Tyler riffs the lyrics, "she was merry, like Joe Perry." Perry plays a feedback-drenched ending to the song.

Perry plays a little of "First Call" – the tune used before horse races – before "Toys In The Attic." Seems like the band is getting assistance during "Toys In The Attic's" backing vocals, maybe more roadie help during this wild version of the song that ends the tour.

"Will you hold still there please, what's this trouble down front?" someone on the crew says as the crowd is in hysterics. Much of this show is found on the vinyl bootleg "Spirit of Boston."

AEROSMITH — SPIRIT OF BOSTON — JAPAN TOUR 1977

SIDE A

INTRODUCTION
MAMA KIN (S.Tyler)
S.O.S. (TOO BAD) (S.Tyler)
LICK AND A PROMISE (S.Tyler/J.Perry)
BIG TEN INCH RECORD (F.Weismantel)
DREAM ON (S.Tyler)*
LORD OF THE THIGHS (S.Tyler)*

SIDE B

LAST CHILD (S.Tyler/B.Whitford)
WALK THIS WAY (S.Tyler/J.Perry)
SAME OLD SONG AND DANCE (S.Tyler/J.Perry)
TRAIN KEPT A ROLLIN' (Bradshaw/L.Mann/H.Kay)
GET THE LEAD OUT (S.Tyler/J.Perry)
BAT MAN THEME (N.Hefti)
TOYS IN THE ATTIC (S.Tyler/J.Perry)

Recorded live at Budo Kan, Tokyo on 31.1* and 9.2.1977 by somebody
Produced by nobody for the Vinyl Man Records

AEROSMITH & CBS/SONY CO-PILOT
SENSATIONAL FLIGHT OVER JAPAN

The early '77 high-altitude Aerosmith tour of Japan continues to establish records.
Aerosmith records selling in the stores, and Aerosmith records playing on the stations.
CBS/Sony is proud to be part of the team work it takes to bring home the really successful artist tours.

CBS/SONY INC.

Aerosmith: #1 album artist of the year.

NUMBER ONE, TIMES TWO.

Aerosmith: #1 album group of the year.

A fitting tribute from *Billboard* to America's premiere rock and roll band, Aerosmith. There's nothing like them anywhere in the whole wide world.
On Columbia Records and Tapes.

The "Draw The Line" album will not come out until December 1, 1977 (although one ad pegs it at December 8), but the band hits the road starting in the early summer of that year, playing dates in the United States. It also takes a second crack at the European market, playing several summer festivals. The album would be unjustifiably criticized; it's a great raw effort. Additionally, we see the band was on the road as they worked on the Lp, not an ideal circumstance.

During this tour the band is almost apologetic about not having the new record available. The 1970s were different days indeed, with artists expected to put an album out every year, not like today when years pass between offerings. That pressure the band faced probably helped with their undoing two years later. "Draw The Line" peaks at No. 11 on the Billboard charts on January 27, 1978.

The Summit, Houston, Texas. Friday, June 24, 1977. Soundboard recording from video. Sound quality: B+

Back In The Saddle, Mama Kin, S.O.S. (Too Bad), Big Ten Inch Record, Lord Of The Thighs, Dream On, Lick And A Promise, Adam's Apple, Sweet Emotion, Sick As A Dog, Draw The Line, Walk This Way, Rattlesnake Shake, Same Old Song And Dance, Toys In The Attic, Train Kept A-Rollin'/Helter Skelter.

The album "Draw The Line" has yet to be completed as the band jumps on the road, presumably to make some cash and keep their (or their managers') finances in order. While not a gig in support of a new album, we do get a song from the forthcoming Lp. But this was not dubbed the "Draw The Line" tour, but rather the "Aerosmith Express" tour.

The audio comes from a long circulating video recording apparently from the in-house system at The Summit. It's the first circulating video depicting an entire concert by the band.

Finally, after a year's wait, the band plays "Back In The Saddle" live. It's great on stage and a natural opener. It makes one wonder why it was not trotted out much sooner. The version here is sublime, with the band giving its all. Tyler, in particular, is focused on this song – as he was for this entire gig – singing a raspy, raunchy and blissfully ragged rendition of the song.

The show then follows the familiar pattern of 1976 shows. After another supreme workout of "Lord Of The Thighs," Perry trips over the intro into "Dream On" has he did on the following night. One wonders if this was a bit of passive/aggressiveness toward Tyler and the song, which Perry and now wife Elyssa openly mocked.

"Adam's Apple" makes a spectacular return to the setlist, the driving tune augmented by some on the fly Tyler lyrics: "something tried to crawl up her crack, all I wanted to do was get her in the shack."

Kramer does his talking on his kit, charging through each song with fire. Before "Sweet Emotion," Tyler comments on the array of clothing landing on the stage. "I'll tell ya something, I really get off on some the shit you people throw up here. You got the balls to walk in with it, I got the balls to wear it."

Tyler again improvises lyrics during the song, likely a flashback to the time cops roughed him up in Memphis in 1974: "You knocked me on my ass and hit me with a hose, and you tried to take the white stuff off my nose." Perry holds some long notes that evolve into feedback on the outro.

Kramer then yells out "Sick As a Dog!" and Tyler goes into a short ramble, "This is one here that sums up, it's off Rocks, you know the words to this one..." as Kramer starts the song before Tyler can finish. The backing vocals are shaky, which plague the song off and on.

The hyper Kramer starts to get into the "Walk This Way" intro, but then stops. Perry walks up to the mic and says, "I don't know if any of you are into buying our albums, but the next one coming out has a song that goes like this," and he strikes the intro chords into "Draw The Line," the first known live recording. A little ragged overall, but not a bad effort for one of the first times it was played, Perry's slide work and Tyler's vocal histrionics tying the tune together. One of the band's great live jams.

The band rediscovers "Rattlesnake Shake." Despite their fondness for the song, it had trouble catching fire on this night, with the off-key vocals sinking the effort. Tyler gets the crowd revved for "Train Kept A-Rollin'" by asking them to sing "all night long." But after some dead air, someone yells "Toys! Toys!" and Kramer starts in on "Toys In The Attic."

"Train Kept A-Rollin'" starts next with Kramer pounding out a faster than usual beat, and Tyler joins in with harmonica. Out of nowhere, the band jumps into The Beatles "Helter Skelter," which they had recorded in the studio. The familiar "Batman" theme, "Peter Gunn" theme and a snatch of "Combination" close the set out. A hot gig in Texas land.

The Summit, Houston, Texas. Saturday, June 25, 1977. Soundboard recording from video. Sound quality: B+

Back In The Saddle, Mama Kin, S.O.S. (Too Bad), Big Ten Inch Record, Lord Of The Thighs, Dream On, Lick And A Promise, Adam's Apple, Sweet Emotion, Sick As A Dog, Draw The Line, Walk This Way, Rattlesnake Shake, Same Old Song And Dance, Toys In The Attic, Train Kept A-Rollin'/Movin' Out.

The gig starts out as another sizzler, Tyler screaming the "Back In The Saddle" lyrics over the wall of noise the band creates. Is there a better show opener?

Kramer is again amped up, pounding out the "Lick And A Promise" intro after "Lord Of The Thighs." But it would have to wait for "Dream On," where the band carries on, despite a shaky opening to the tune.

Kramer barely lets the song come to a close before he starts "Lick And A Promise" again, playing like a demon. After "Adam's Apple," Tyler quips, "I had to sneak a little bible talk in here." Interestingly, The Summit later became home to preacher Joel Otseen and the Lakewood Church. Praise the Lord!

Tyler once again introduces "Sweet Emotion" as "Sweet Implosion." "Sweet Explosion" may have been more apropos for the song's fiery ending. Hamilton's bass lines to start the song sound sweeter than ever on this recording, a direct feed from the soundboard.

Tyler introduces "Sick As A Dog" as a song the band wrote "while working on the chain gang," a veiled reference to their never ending work during this period. Tyler vocalizes over the intro adding a little drama.

"In the last two months, we have been doing an album, we'd like to do a song off that album called 'Draw The Line,'" Tyler says, while rejecting an offer of a joint from a fan! Just say no! The song itself goes well enough until the end, when Perry seems to lose his place, and it wilts to a close.

"Rattlesnake Shake" gets another workout, with Perry and Tyler trading initial lines of the tune. Tonight's version is a little more fluid than the previous night's effort, but still lacks a groove Aerosmith's originals have.

"I know this guy, his name is Steve, and he don't care if he don't got no chick, he does the shake, the rattlesnake shake, he jerks away the blues," Perry humorously sings.

"Toys In The Attic" has an odd ending, the band failing to play the final section, and the song ends with a few guitar riffs. Iconic photos of Tyler and Perry sharing the mic through the years probably come from versions of "Toys In The Attic," where the pair sing the "toys" line together.

During "Train Kept A-Rollin'" after playing the "Batman" theme and the "Combination" licks, Perry moves the band into "Movin' Out." But the band members lose each other, and a longer version is aborted. The gig ends with a tape of Porky Pig saying, "That's all, y'all."

On the Fourth of July, the band would play Market Square Arena in Indianapolis. Parts of that show would end up on "Live! Bootleg" and "Pandora's Box." There was a fervor around the gig that included a ticket giveaway by the *Indianapolis News*. The band set attendance records at Market Square in the 1970s.

10 Residents Of City Win Aerosmith Tickets

Sorry, Linda, looks like you'll have to get another date to the Aerosmith concert.

Linda Harvey of Indianapolis was just one of 1,291 entrants in The News Aerosmith ticket drawing. In spite of her "desperate need" for tickets to the July 4th concert in Market Square Arena, she wasn't one of the 10 participants to win a pair of show tickets.

"The guy I've been dating said he would get the tickets as soon as they went on sale," Linda wrote on her entry blank. "He kept putting me off. He stood me up, and I haven't talked to him since. But now I'm stuck without a ticket and I've waited all year for this."

Linda wasn't as fortunate as these 10 entrants, all from Indianapolis, who each won a pair of tickets:

David Massing, 744 Fenster Court
Barry Bone, 2808 Saturn
Tony Gregory, 4950 W. Regent
Joyce Harts, 6705 Roundtree Court
Craig Storm, 6055 Ivanhoe
Angel LeVine, 8313 E. 35th Place.
Angela Olinski, 821 Windingbrook E. Drive
Donna Johnson, 202 S. Rural
Carole Hamilton, 6140 E. 10th
Peggy Green, 2954 S. Parker

Winners were contacted by phone.

Aerosmith played in the arena last spring to a capacity crowd of 19,000, and indications are that the place may be full for this one, too. Tickets for the 8 o'clock concert have been moving briskly, but there still are $7 general admission ducats available.

Civic Center, Baltimore, Maryland. Saturday, July 9, 1977. Audience recording. Sound quality: D

Back In The Saddle, Mama Kin, S.O.S. (Too Bad), Big Ten Inch Record, Lord Of The Thighs, Last Child, Lick And A Promise, Adam's Apple, Sweet Emotion, Sick As A Dog, Draw The Line, Walk This Way, Same Old Song And Dance, Toys In The Attic, Train Kept A-Rollin'.

"Good evening, Baltimore," Tyler says. The echo effect when Tyler sings "rat!" in S.O.S. (Too Bad) is in full force. Kramer and Tyler play a funky 90-second intro to "Big Ten Inch Record" on this night. The song leads right into "Lord Of The Thighs," in which Kramer plays a more deliberate drum intro than usual. The song has a deep jungle vibe in the middle, helped along with Kramer's drums.

Whitford also plays slow, deliberate notes to start "Last Child," a plodding version, though no less satisfying than how it's typically played. Kramer's intro into "Lick And A Promise" is thunderous on this recording. Perry goes wild during "Sweet Emotion" with feedback, as the machine that is Kramer pounds away.

Part of "Sick As A Dog" is played as an instrumental, as Tyler fails to sing some of the lines. After Perry introduces the new "Draw The Line," he tells the crowd: "If you don't like it, too bad," which gets a laugh from the audience.

"Instead of the usual guitar solo you hear every day and every night, I want to take this 1957 Stratocaster...and I want to show you how we did guitar solos in my day," Perry says during "Train Kept A-Rollin'" as he proceeds to smash up his instrument.

"The precious stringed relic of the pioneer days of rock 'n' roll flew 15 feet in to the air and crashed to the floor unattended," is how a report in *Creem* magazine explained the scene. Odd and wild ending to the show!

Aerosmith sound was faulty

By MINDY SCHERR and ERIC PRIPSTEIN

A faulty sound system disappointed the many fans who gathered at the Civic Center Saturday night to see and hear Aerosmith

Most disappointed, however, was Joe Perry guitarist for the heavy metal rocker band who expressed his frustration over the malfunctioning equipment through obscenities and mock violence.

Perry first voiced his opinions of the equipment to the stage crew, and later to the confused audience. When, during "Toys in the Attic," the public address system cut off, he kicked a monitor speaker into the orchestra pit.

Despite lead vocalist Steve Tyler's nightlong efforts to pacify Perry, the enraged guitarist punctuated the encore, "Train Kept A Rollin'," with a flying kick to the amplifier He ended the show by hurling his guitar into the air after yelling to the audience, "This is a '57 Stratocastor It's been in my family for a long time and this is how we do a guitar solo"

Compared to Perry, the other four members of the Boston-based band, were uncharacteristically passive.

The group began the show with "Back in the Saddle" from their latest album,

"Rocks." Next they performed "Mama Kin," their usual concert opener.

They played most of their biggest hits including "Walk This Way," "Sweet Emotion," and "Last Child," but omitted their biggest, "Dream On."

Aerosmith played for 75 minutes, offering 14 of their older songs and one from their soon-to-be-released album.

The show was enhanced by special lighting. Colored spots were reflected off a mirrored ceiling which produced a unique glowing effect supplementing the usual stage lighting.

Another unusual feature was the use of fans surrounding the stage, giving the players a windswept look.

The opening act, Nazareth, was less flashy, but still entertaining. Starting precisely at 8:03, the British band played 10 selections, including a two-song encore, and left the stage at 9:00.

Highlights of their performance included their biggest hit, "Love Hurts," an electric version "Peter and the Wolf" by guitarist Manny Charlton and the use of a talkbox disguised as a bagpipe on "Hair of the Dog."

The band makes its second foray into the European continent where summer rains have turned many of the concert sites to mud. Interestingly, the first and last shows of the two-week tour were documented, with none of the German shows in between surfacing to date.

Bilzen Jazz Festival, Bilzen, Belgium. Saturday, August 13, 1977. Audience recording. Sound quality: C/B
Big Ten Inch Record, Lick And A Promise, Adam's Apple, Dream On, Sweet Emotion, Sick As A Dog, Walk This Way, Same Old Song And Dance, Train Kept A-Rollin', Toys In The Attic (fades out.)

This Belgian jazz festival had morphed into a rock event by the year 1977. The Ian Gillan Band was on the roster the night Aerosmith played the outdoor venue. The band gets the prime spot for the three-day event, headlining Saturday's show.

Someone in the crowd made a strong, albeit short recording of the band, capturing about 20 minutes of the middle of the set. A second recording has now emerged and gives us more of the gig, but still not the full show.

Kramer's drum intro to "Lick And A Promise" hits a great groove. The polite Belgian audience gives the band applause throughout the gig.

Tyler ends up skipping a whole verse during "Dream On," forcing the band to concoct a new arrangement on the spot, resulting in one of the shortest versions of the song – about three minutes – ever caught on tape.

The band's rendition of "Sweet Emotion" stirs the crowd into rhythmic clapping by its end. Kramer dashes off a funky "Walk This Way" introduction. The version seems almost sped up, with Tyler going through vocal gymnastics during the tune.

"Toys In The Attic" starts with a blues jam and then later fades out as it seems the taper leaves the show!

Reading Festival, Reading, England. Saturday, August 27, 1977.
Audience recording. Sound quality: C

Mama Kin, S.O.S. (Too Bad), Big Ten Inch Record, Lord Of The Thighs, Lick And A Promise, Dream On, Walkin' The Dog, Sweet Emotion, Walk This Way, Draw The Line, Same Old Song And Dance, Train Kept A-Rollin', Toys In The Attic.

The mood is much different in England, where the crowd is loud and aggressive on this windy night. Aerosmith is not the headliner, but rather third on the bill behind Graham Parker and Thin Lizzy and trims their setlist accordingly.

"From The U.S. of A. would you please welcome, Aerosmith!" says the British MC. We hear the "Psycho" theme intro music for the first time here, although it was likely used at prior 1977 shows.

"Mama Kin" is first out of the blocks, as the band tightens its set to 60 minutes. Perry is playing loud tonight, as though he is turned up above the rest of the band – and it sounds good. The whole gig has an intensity, a controlled chaos, that was needed to win the British hard rock fans over.

Kramer's intro into "Lord Of The Thighs" is massive, as though he is playing a monster-sized drum kit. The band plays a hard-driven set that is cheered, a real victory for the band on foreign soil. "If you cheer a bit they might come back," says the festival's MC.

"You motherfuckers! You're ready to rock now?" Tyler says teasing the audience as the band comes back for an encore. "We are gonna do an old slow tune..." Tyler says as the band plays a mini blues jam before jumping into "Toys In The Attic" as a final assault on the Brits.

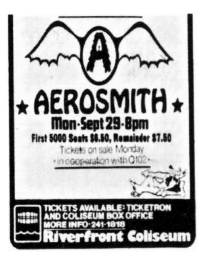

Riverfront Arena, Cincinnati, Ohio. Thursday, September 29, 1977. Audience recording. Sound quality: C-

Back In The Saddle, S.O.S. (Too Bad), Big Ten Inch Record, I Wanna Know Why, Lord Of The Thighs, Lick And A Promise, Walk This Way, Sweet Emotion, Dream On, Walkin' The Dog, Sick As A Dog, Draw The Line, Same Old Song And Dance.

Back in the States, the band hits its strongholds in the middle of the country, while continuing to finish up a new album. The recording here is distant, but "Back In The Saddle's" main guitar riff comes through.

105

"S.O.S. (Too Bad)" gets a drum intro by Kramer after a break, instead of segueing from a previous song as had been the case in more recent shows. Tyler's phrasing and emphasis changes on the line "my daddy was hard, face a little scarred," something the singer constantly did, bringing freshness to songs.

On "Big Ten Inch Record," Tyler does a scat and then blows the harmonica per usual to what normally is Kramer's launch of the song proper. But on this night, Kramer doesn't start the tune and Tyler scats again and blows the harp a bit longer before it does finally start. Whitford delivers a wild solo on the tune, instead of the precise hard hitting notes he is known for. Tyler changes the last line of the song, inserting "stink" and "pink" in the final verse.

"You might have been wondering what we have been doing with all this time off. We've been writing a new album. We're gonna do a song off it, it's called, "I Wanna Know Why," Tyler says, and we get the first known live version of the song and it comes off well.

"Lord Of The Thighs" continues to be a unique adventure every night, but always a great ride as the twin guitarists spin their magic. Perry creates undulating sound waves that whip across the arena in this version.

Kramer launches "Lick And A Promise" as the guitars are being tuned, but all is pulled together in time for the song to start without a hitch. Gunslingers!

The band knocks out its dog songs back to back: "Walkin' The Dog" and "Sick As A Dog." In the middle of the pair, Perry says "speaking of dogs" as he would in shows to come.

Perry then addresses the crowd: "This next song is the title cut off the album, it's called 'Draw The Line,'" as the band launches the tune. Some of Tyler's off-color comments toward the end of the song indicate some pushing in front of the stage, portending the tragedy at The Who show outside the same venue two years later. The recording cuts short on this night, it seems the taper only had a 60-minute tape on hand or maybe lost a second tape with the balance of the recording.

Cobo Arena, Detroit, Michigan. Sunday, October 2, 1977. Audience recording. Sound quality: C-

Back In The Saddle, S.O.S. (Too Bad), Big Ten Inch Record, I Wanna Know Why, Lord Of The Thighs, Lick And A Promise, Get It Up, Walk This Way, Sweet Emotion, Dream On, Walkin' The Dog, Sick As A Dog.

As with the previous recording, only the first part of the show has surfaced. As in Cincinnati, Tyler gives an extended harmonica workout as part of "Big Ten Inch Record." The show reveals the first live rendition of "Get It Up," which Tyler introduces as "Can't Get It Up." Not a blistering version, but satisfying nonetheless.

The last time the band was in Detroit, Tyler chastised the crowd for being quiet and he sounded a similar theme during Kramer's drum intro to "Walk This Way:" "Sitting your ass down...where you at? Detroit, what are you sitting for? Shit! Get up!"

Perry gets into a few discordant notes during the outro to "Sweet Emotion," an avant-garde approach. A unique reading for sure. "Sick As A Dog" is a perfect rendition of the loping song. Tyler then announces, "We're going to do the title track..." Presumably "Draw The Line" was next, but the recording ends.

Spectrum, Philadelphia, Pennsylvania. Sunday, October 9, 1977. Audience recording. Sound quality: C

Back In The Saddle, S.O.S. (Too Bad), Big Ten Inch Record, I Wanna Know Why, Lord Of The Thighs, Lick And A Promise, Get It Up, Walk This Way, Sweet Emotion, Dream On, Walkin' The Dog, Sick As A

The infamous gig where an M-80 — a powerful firework — was thrown at the band as they returned for an encore. The explosion cut Perry and burned Tyler's eye.

The "Jaws" theme is paired with the "Psycho" theme here to start things as the band breaks into "Back In The Saddle," with Perry augmenting his rhythm playing in a different way from his normal chords for the song.

Kramer's drum intro to "S.O.S. (Too Bad)" gets the primed crowd clapping along. Tyler says, "Let's see what kind of soul you have" during the beginning of "Big Ten Inch Record." He blows his harmonica then asks Kramer to stop drumming so the crowd can take over the beat with its clapping. A nice moment with the Philly fans.

"It's been so long since we have had a new album out, everyone has been asking this question," Perry said, as he introduces, "I Wanna Know Why." "Lord Of The Thighs" again gets some imaginative and inventive guitar work from Perry, who writes his own script for the song each show.

Tyler dedicates "Get It Up" to the guys in the crowd holding women up on their shoulders, a common sight during 1970s rock shows. Kramer's "Walk This Way" intro gets the crowd going. Perry uses his talk box mid song in unison with his guitar riffs and the vocals.

During "Sweet Emotion" Tyler utters "right back here!" after the "can't tell where I'll be in a year" line. It would be something he would use through the years. Perry goes completely off script during the song's outro, intent to not staying within the song's parameters. "Mr. Joe Perry!" Tyler says at the song's conclusion in recognition of the effort.

The crowd jumps out of its collective skin during the "Dream On" intro, where Perry plays the song's beginning. The crowd is hanging on every word of the tune. Despite the town's image as hard-scrabbled, they loved this rock ballad and what it meant. Tyler – for the first time caught on tape – utters, "everything you do, *motherfucker* will come back to you," another tweak that would appear for years to come.

"This is the title song off our new album, we have never played it in front of anybody, so we hope you like it, it's a totally different sound than what we have ever played before," Perry says, kicking off "Draw The Line."

Of course, the band has played the tune live before, but the slide work throughout was a departure for the band. Perry's backing vocals are loud and ragged in places, but adds to the cool, rough feel of the song. The slow section features harmonica by Tyler and Perry's slide guitar interlocking with Whitford's rhythm, all played in a groove of high style. "Draw The Line" is also marked by some staccato riffs that stand in contrast to all the slide work on the track.

"Get The Lead Out" is featured inside of "Train Kept A- Rollin'" and starts to wobble with missed cues and some rough backing vocals. Perry then plays the "Combination" lick then stops, then starts and stops again before he jumps in for good and jams with the rest of the band. Once they stop, so does the recording.

But from reports we know what followed. Perry and Tyler were rushed to St. Agnes Hospital and treated for their injuries. The following night's show at the Spectrum was cancelled and re-scheduled for December 19.

Aerosmith concert is rescheduled

The concert by the rock group Aerosmith, canceled Monday after two of the musicians were injured by a firecracker, has been rescheduled for Dec. 19 at the Spectrum.

A spokesman for the Boston-based rock group said that appearances in five other cities also would have to be rescheduled while lead singer Steven Tyler recuperates from a burned cornea, and guitarist Joe Perry from a cut left-hand.

They were injured at the Spectrum Sunday night when a firecracker was thrown at the group as it was returning to the stage for an encore. The spokesman said that the vision in Tyler's left eye is blurred and that Perry still can not play the guitar. However, he added, both men are expected to recover fully.

A spokesman for Electric Factory Concerts, promoter of the Aerosmith concert, said tickets for Monday's show would be honored at the Dec. 19 performance. Refunds may be obtained at the place of purchase until Dec. 17. Tickets for the Dec. 19 show are on sale now.

Philadelphia Inquirer

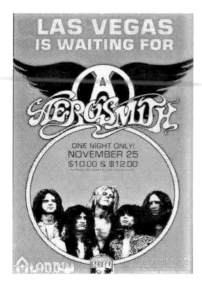

Aladdin Theater, Las Vegas, Nevada. Friday, November 25, 1977. Audience recording. Sound quality: C

Back In The Saddle, Big Ten Inch Record, I Wanna Know Why, Get It Up, Walk This Way, Sweet Emotion, Dream On, Walkin' The Dog, Draw The Line, Same Old Song And Dance, Train Kept A-Rollin'.

All that exists of this show are the tracks that appear on the vinyl bootleg album "Five The Hard Way."

"Back In The Saddle" is the opener and we hear for the first time Kramer's double beat on his drums after the line "calling all the shots tonight I'm like a loaded gun." A small nuance, but one that really stands out.

The stereo audience recording is edited after "I Want To Know Why" and before "Get It Up" as the bootleggers apparently cut tape to fit material onto one disc. A two-record set would have been welcomed!

"We got an album coming out next week," Tyler tells the Vegas crowd before "Get It Up."

Perry has the talk box in full effect for "Sweet Emotion," again mimicking Frampton. The song is greeted with big cheers as Hamilton lays down his famous bass line.

The first notes of "Dream On" seem to be lost on the crowd – maybe the volume was too low – and recognition of the song does not start until the second instrumental stanza. Tyler himself gives a quick double whistle with his fingers as part of the end of "Walkin' The Dog," which would be heard more in the future.

"Same Old Song And Dance" flows right into "Train Kept A-Rollin'" without Tyler's exalting for the crowd to sing along. Perry and Whitford double up nicely on the track's intro, with the slightest of delays between the two making the guitar lines really stand out. Perry launches the "Batman" theme and the "Combination" riff.

The latter must have been played in stereo at the gig because the guitar drops in and out as its played, as the tape recording was made from one side of the venue.

The name of the boot may have come from a comment Perry made to *Circus* that the next album would be called "Aerosmith Five." So, the bootleggers delivered this fifth album to fans.

Aerosmith, funny cover, sad recording

Appeared in the Regina Leader-Post.

111

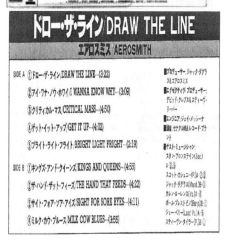

Print ads for "Draw The Line."
Japanese pressing material, below.

Done With Mirrors? Yugoslavian release reversed.

Maple Leaf Gardens, Toronto, Ontario, Canada. Saturday, December 10, 1977. Audience recording. Sound quality: D

Back In The Saddle, S.O.S. (Too Bad), Big Ten Inch Record, I Wanna Know Why, Lord Of The Thighs, Lick And A Promise, Walk This Way, Sweet Emotion, Walkin' The Dog, Mama Kin, Draw The Line, Same Old Song And Dance, Train Kept A-Rollin', Milk Cow Blues, Toys In The Attic.

This is the first known show that was recorded after the release of "Draw The Line" on December 1, 1977. The crowd is just not into the show enough as far as Tyler is concerned.

"Hey Toronto, you going to sit down all night or what? Get the fuck up! C'mon momma!" Tyler says during the beginning of "S.O.S. (Too Bad)."

"Lick And A Promise" seems to be a favorite among the friends who recorded this as they clap along, and one offers his own vocals at the beginning. Perry's guitar blasts into the foreground during the beginning of "Walk This Way."

There is some sort of technical delay in starting "Sweet Emotion," a rarity for the band whose crack crew kept the show always going. The song's intro gets another strong response as the tune becomes more popular, eventually becoming stitched into the fabric of 1970s hard rock, and remaining a radio staple today. Perry plays some wildly strange notes after the line "the rabbit gone and died" and during the ending there are more outer fringe notes from the guitarist, but he catches up to the rest of the band for the finale to the song.

Tyler again goes after the crowd during "Walkin' The Dog" screaming (almost salivating), "stop sitting on your ass and get the fuck up!" Rather than recoiling, the crowd screams in approval. "It's about time," he says as the band revives "Mama Kin" for the show.

During "Draw The Line" Perry does some quick finger picking in the slow middle section. Kramer ends the song with a drumbeat, and after a brief slide riff from Perry, the band jumps into "Same Old Song And Dance."

One of the shorter versions of "Train Kept A-Rollin'" is played allowing for a double combo encore of "Milk Cow Blues" and "Toys In The Attic." An oddity to the gig: "Dream On" was not played, or for any of the December shows caught on tape.

The Forum, Montreal, Quebec, Canada. Monday, December 12, 1977. Audience recording. Sound quality: D

Back In The Saddle, S.O.S. (Too Bad), Big Ten Inch Record, I Wanna Know Why, Lord Of The Thighs, Lick And A Promise, Get It Up, Walk This Way, Sweet Emotion, Walkin' The Dog, Mama Kin, Draw The Line, Same Old Song And Dance, Train Kept A-Rollin'/Get The Lead Out, Milk Cow Blues, Toys In The Attic.

The recording has a strange quality: it's flat, but when Tyler begins singing the volume comes up around his voice. Kramer plays a false start to "Big Ten Inch Record" on this night.

At the end of "I Want To Know Why" the drummer keeps riding the cymbals until he bangs the intro into "Lord Of The Thighs." Usually a highlight of the band's shows, this version comes off as listless and flat, with the guitars sounding more like worn out banjos.

"Do you have the new album?" Tyler quizzes the crowd before "Get It Up." Tyler again reverts to whistling with his fingers during "Walkin' The Dog."

Perry jams on "Combination" before launching the band into the mini cover of "Get The Lead Out" inside of "Train Kept A-Rollin'." The Montreal crowd does a lot of whistling at the show, but it's not as loud as Tyler wants.

After the crowd calls the band back for an encore after several minutes (it seems as though the band was debating whether to come back out) Tyler says, "All I can say is, it's about time! You want to kick ass now?"

"Milk Cow Blues" comes off well, the Aerosmith thunder is let loose on the blues tune. At the end of "Toys In The Attic" a few of the final notes are sampled and repeated over and over as the show comes to an end. The effect would occur in upcoming shows as well.

Aerosmith Willing To Forgive, Forget

PHILADELPHIA (AP) — Saying they hold no hard feelings, the rock group Aerosmith is returning Monday to Philadelphia, where a firecracker thrown onto a stage injured lead singer Steven Tyler and guitarist Joe Perry.

Both Tyler, who suffered an eye injury, and Perry, who was burned on the hand, have recovered, since the October incident at the Spectrum here, a spokesman for the group said.

Spectrum, Philadelphia, Pennsylvania. Monday, December 19, 1977. Audience recording. Sound quality: C

Back In The Saddle, S.O.S. (Too Bad), Big Ten Inch Record, I Wanna Know Why, Lord Of The Thighs, Lick And A Promise, Get It Up, Walk This Way, Sweet Emotion, Dream On, Walkin' The Dog, Mama Kin, Draw The Line, Same Old Song And Dance, Train Kept A-Rollin', Milk Cow Blues, Toys In The Attic.

Less than 10 weeks after getting bombed by someone in the Philly crowd, the band comes back for more. This show went off without a hitch, fortunately, but there would be more problems in the future in the city for the band.

Kramer crashes his cymbals during the "Back In The Saddle" drum intro. Perry's guitar is initially lost in the audio mire during the song, but suddenly emerges loudly, standing above the rest of the band. Kramer misses the beats to close the song, starting them too early, but then simply repeats them to close it out.

Perry's imprint is all over "S.O.S. (Too Bad)" filling in gaps with notes as he switches from rhythm to lead. Tyler yells to Perry, "Go cat!" before the latter takes his lead during "Big Ten Inch Record," an oft used introduction at that point in the song.

117

"Course ya'll got a new album called 'Draw The Line' don't ya?" Tyler says. "We're gonna do a song I wrote with Mr. Perry..." and he makes an odd noise before Kramer launches "I Want To Know Why."

As at other stops, the Philly crowd mistakes the "Lord Of The Thighs" intro as the beginning of "Walk This Way." The guitars are reserved and hold an elegance as they make their way through the middle sections of "Lord Of The Thighs," an interesting twist from the normal, exhilarating frenzy.

"Come here Joe!" Tyler says to Perry as he gets him to sing the "Bright Light Fright" line in "Get It Up." Tyler starts "Sweet Emotion" with a little scat before Kramer aids him with the lift off of the song. "All right, Philly!" Tyler says after, as the events of October seem long forgotten.

As the band segues from "Walkin' The Dog" into "Mama Kin," Perry begins the latter with a flurry of notes as he did when it was the opener during the Japanese shows at the beginning of the year.

"First time, the title cut off our new album," Tyler says as Perry plays some slick slide before kicking the song off. First time? We know better than that Steven!

"You knew we'd come back here," Tyler says, referencing the October incident. Then Perry smartly plays a little of the "Dragnet" theme, the American police television show from the 1960s.

"Toys In The Attic" is the finale, and Perry plays a few notes during the song that sound like they are from a different tune altogether. The show finishes with "Toys In The Attic," and as in Montreal, with a few of the last notes sampled and repeated electronically. When the house lights go up, "We Wish You A Merry Christmas" by a boys' choir is played to fans as they leave.

Aerosmith returns, without fireworks

By Jack Lloyd
Inquirer Entertainment Writer

The heavy-metal rock group from Boston called Aerosmith last night completed its two-night engagement at the Spectrum — which began last Sept. 10 and was forced into a "hold pattern" when a thrown firecracker injured the group's vocalist and lead guitarist.

This time, the capacity crowd restricted itself to loud shouting. There were no firecrackers.

larly the "heavy metal," hard-driv-

Philadelphia Inquirer

DEC. 21 & 22—8 P.M.
AEROSMITH
STYX
$7.75 Advance
$8.75 Day of Show

MON., JAN. 1—8 P.M.
THE MARSHALL TUCKER BAND
$7.50, $6.50

Tickets available at HECHTS, PENTAGON TICKET SERVICE and CAPITAL CENTRE BOX OFFICE, LANDOVER, MD. Add 45¢ service charge to all tickets except at Capital Centre. Capital Centre is located on Beltway Exit 32 E. No personal checks accepted. For info. Call 790-7490.

Capital Center, Landover, Maryland. Thursday, December 22, 1977. Soundboard recording from video. Sound quality: A-

Back In The Saddle, S.O.S. (Too Bad), Big Ten Inch Record, I Wanna Know Why, Lord Of The Thighs, Lick And A Promise, Get It Up, Walk This Way, Sweet Emotion, Dream On, Walkin' The Dog, Mama Kin, Draw The Line, Same Old Song And Dance, Train Kept A-Rollin', Milk Cow Blues, Toys In The Attic.

Whoops, this show starts with Tyler singing, "I'm back in the..." Instead of "I'm back." Despite the early flub, the song rocks and rolls and is caught beautifully in the recording. Toward the end of the song the singer makes noises of a whip cracking.

Kramer pounds out a sharp intro into "S.O.S. (Too Bad)." Tyler's harmonica is especially soulful on this night as he plays the "Big Ten Inch Record" intro as Perry strums along. Kramer, often the band's musical coordinator on stage, yells, "Let's go!" as the band launches "I Wanna Know Why." Tyler yells, "Keep your eye on the ball" as the drummer rides his cymbals into "Lord Of The Thighs."

119

Tyler switches up the lyrics during "Lick And A Promise" to the apropos: "He took their money, but forgot all their names and blew all his money on drugs."

"Get It Up" starts with some cool slide notes from Perry, and Tyler dedicates the song to a "couple of promoters that we went around with four years ago." Kramer plays an interesting "dry" drum line in the middle of the song, adding a new dimension. Perry plays a particularly fierce solo and uses the talk box to emphasize what he plays.

Perry then uses the talk box to say, "we have one more for you" before "Sweet Emotion," and Tyler calls him the "Italian Stallion" for one of the first times. Perry dabbles in a new rhythm pattern as "Walkin' The Dog" gets underway.

The clear recording reveals some of the problems with the backing vocals on "Draw The Line," although out in the crowd the fine details were likely lost in the din.

Hamilton is dialed way up at the end of "Same Old Song And Dance" and his intricate bass patterns stand out. Tyler gets tongue tied on the first verse of "Milk Cow Blues."

There are some weird backing vocals on "Toys In The Attic," as if the roadies have taken to the mic. Perry slips in a little of "Have Yourself A Merry Little Christmas" on the guitar during the song before it closes out with the repeating guitar notes and the "We Wish You A Merry Christmas" tape. A fine end to the year 1977!

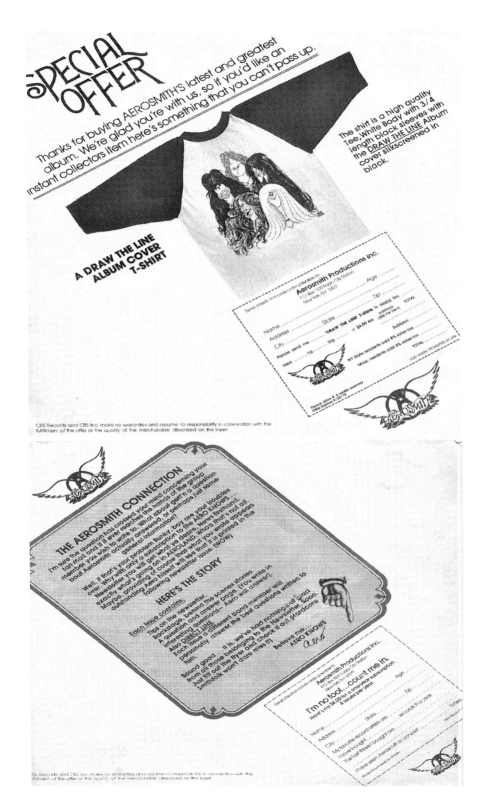

121

You could miss out on one of the great rock albums of '78 but it depends where you draw the line...

A succession of Great British rock acts have emerged ever since the mid '60s to achieve world wide success. More recently though, the influence of British hard rock has spawned several equally dynamic bands in America, who are challenging the big established tradition: British is best.

Among the most successful of these acts is Aerosmith, who have proved during the last few years that their appeal to American audiences is at least equal to that of their British counterparts. Aerosmith's new album, 'Draw The Line', produced by Jack Douglas, invites you to experience at first hand the music with which America has challenged British rock dominance.

You can draw the line at the established British names, but in doing so you'll be ignoring some of the best American hard rock you're ever likely to hear.

Draw the line around Aerosmith

New Album 'Draw The Line'

82147

Records & Tapes

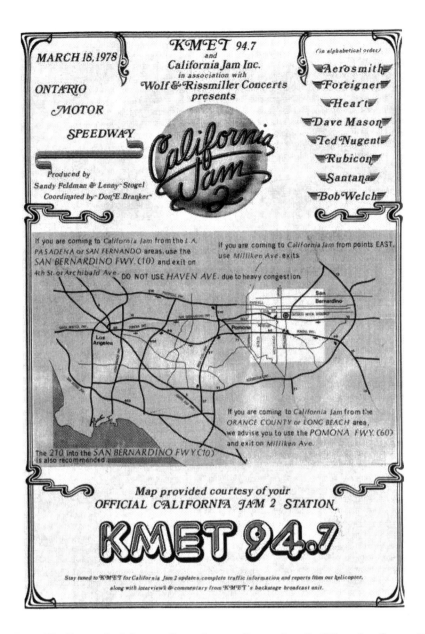

Map provided courtesy of your
OFFICIAL CALIFORNIA JAM 2 STATION

KMET 94.7

Cal Jam II, Ontario Motor Speedway, Ontario, California. Saturday, March 18, 1978. Soundboard recording from video/radio broadcast. Sound quality: A/A-

Rats In The Cellar, I Wanna Know Why, Big Ten Inch Record, Walk This Way, Seasons Of Wither, Sweet Emotion, Lord Of The Thighs, Dream On, Chip Away The Stone, Lick And A Promise, Get The Lead Out, Get It Up, Draw The Line, Same Old Song And Dance, Toys In The Attic, Milk Cow Blues, Train Kept A-Rollin'.

An exciting period for the band, which has now added Mark Radice on keyboards and backing vocals. They play a series of spring shows, many of which are being recorded for what would become the "Live! Bootleg" album. These Spring 1978 shows are among the bands most exciting and fertile, with wide-ranging setlists spanning the band's albums. It's really their zenith live in many ways.

The Cal Jam show is the largest gig the band would play, with some 350,000 packed into the speedway in Southern California. The band begins their set with an energetic "Rats In The Cellar," but Tyler's mic is not working for the first verses.

The band gets into a funky little jam to start "Big Ten Inch Record." Whitford and Perry play individual notes during "Walk This Way," giving the tune a more funky feel. The band has added the moving and powerful "Seasons Of Wither" to its setlist, a refreshing change. The song is a fan favorite and likely is played for the first time on stage since 1974. The band does the song justice in front of the massive crowd, boosted by the addition of Radice, who adds his touches on keyboard and backing vocals.

Perry gets some great feedback together before the close of "Sweet Emotion." Whitford and Perry again do a masterful job of trading licks throughout "Lord Of The Thighs."

During "Dream On," Tyler sings "Dream on, dream on, dream on until your dreams come *huge,*" as he looks out over the mighty gathering.

Perry gives Radice a formal introduction to the crowd before the new "Chip Away The Stone" written by Tyler pal Richard Supa. An offbeat song that was memorialized in Aerosmith lore on "Live! Bootleg" (see more on that below.) But the tune was not played much after this period.

Tyler starts with the wrong line on "Lick And A Promise" and mumbles nonsensical lyrics until he can right the ship. The band now does a stand-alone version of "Get The Lead Out," which was regulated to part of "Train Kept A-Rollin'" until now. Radice's background vocals are strongest during the song.

Perry does a fantastic slide solo during the start to "Draw The Line." The song is made more iconic by the film of the event and is arguably the definitive live version from this era.

Perry sings the first verses to "Milk Cow Blues" like the old days. "No More No More" is pleasantly revived for the gig. Perry sounds out a little of "Strangers In The Night" during the finale, "Train Kept A-Rollin'."

A strong set by the band, which showed a willingness to change, with a fresh setlist and the addition of a musician into the mix. The gig created momentum that would continue over the next several months as Aerosmith eased into the role of one of the biggest bands on the planet. Road manager Kelly left the band after this gig.

Of note: The "Cal Jam 2" album has three songs from Aerosmith, but they are not from the Cal Jam. "Same Old Song And Dance" is from Columbus, March 24, 1978, while "Draw The Line" is from Philadelphia, March 26, 1978 as heard on "Live! Bootleg." "Chip Away The Stone" is from "Live! Bootleg" as well, but not from Santa Monica as that album states. More on that later.

HEAR AEROSMITH LIVE ON WKQX 101. F.M. THURSDAY MARCH 23 AT 9:00 P.M.

Aragon Ballroom, Chicago, Illinois. Thursday, March 23, 1978. Radio broadcast. Sound quality: A-

Rats In The Cellar, I Wanna Know Why, Big Ten Inch Record, Walk This Way, Sight For Sore Eyes, Seasons Of Wither, Sweet Emotion, Lord Of The Thighs, Dream On, Chip Away The Stone, Get The Lead Out, Get It Up, Draw The Line, No More No More, Same Old Song And Dance, Toys In The Attic, Milk Cow Blues, Train Kept A-Rollin'.

"This one is for you, Hillary!" Tyler says before the band jumps into "Rats In The Cellar" with great energy at the intimate venue. From best what we can tell, Hillary is a sick fan, as Tyler references her later in the show telling her to get better.

A rollicking spring 1978 show that sees the recorded debut of "Sight For Sore Eyes." "Can you hear us all right?!" Tyler asks the crowd before launching into the song. "What about you mothers in radio land?!" The band is broadcasting the string of shows as its building material for their live album. Perry again introduces Radice before "Sweet Emotion."

The version of "Lord Of The Thighs" is the one that makes it onto "Live! Bootleg." And true to legend, it's just as raw here as it is on the album; just pure, kick-ass rock and roll, no overdubs were done.

Tyler says "for you Jack" before the guitar solo during "Dream On" as Jack Douglas was on the tour to record them. He introduces the song as "one for you old codgers."

"Chip Away The Stone" sees Radice use of a synthesizer for a rising then falling note, a distinct feature of the song. "That right there is a song off of California Jam that's going to be our new single," Tyler says.

The band plays energetic versions of "Get It Up" and "Draw The Line" that can barely be contained by magnetic recording tape! Just an all-out assault. Tyler inserts some additional lines into "No More No More" behind the backing chorus, adding a fresh element. Perry starts the lyrics to "Milk Cow Blues" reminiscent of older live versions.

One hell of a gig!

Veterans Auditorium, Columbus, Ohio. Friday, March 24, 1978. Radio broadcast. Sound quality: A-

Rats In The Cellar, I Wanna Know Why, Big Ten Inch Record, Walk This Way, Sight For Sore Eyes, Seasons Of Wither, Sweet Emotion, Lord Of The Thighs, Dream On, Chip Away The Stone, Get The Lead Out, Get It Up, Draw The Line, Same Old Song And Dance, Toys In The Attic, Milk Cow Blues, Train Kept A-Rollin'.

"Rats In The Cellar" flies out the door pounding the audience, starting another high energy show. Kramer's use of percussion during "I Wanna Know Why" creates a distinctive sound for the song. Perry plays rapid fire notes during "Big Ten Inch Record."

Tyler mucks around with the lyrics at the beginning of "Walk This Way," which now has a great, smooth flow as the band has mastered playing it on stage. "They lettin' you dance tonight?" Tyler asks during the familiar "Sight For Sore Eyes," which appears on the "Live! Bootleg" album.

We also hear the "Live! Bootleg" intro for "Sweet Emotion" but the actual song used for the album was culled from the previous night in Chicago. It's not clear where the album's firecracker burst comes from. Perry's controlled mayhem on "Sweet Emotion" plays out on stage in a wonderful way. "Do you people know you're being recorded on the radio tonight? Speak to yourselves!" Tyler says to the cheering crowd.

126

"Chip Away The Stone" is used on "Live! Bootleg," but in this case with some studio vocal alterations. Given the band's hopes for the song (see ad below), they likely wanted a pumped-up version on the live album. The doctored version also made its way onto the "Cal Jam 2" album.

"Sing that song, you bitch!" Tyler yells indiscriminately as the band returns to the stage for its encores. Then he says, "The Liberace of guitar players, the Italian Stallion...this song is inspired by Elvis Presley, 'Milk Cow Blues!'" Tyler plays some harmonica on the tune, getting off some initial high notes on his harp.

Another great spring show in Columbus and there are not enough superlatives to capture the energy and power coming from the stage. The band seems to top itself each night.

Interestingly, this would be the last show where "Dream On" would turn up until January 1980. (The date of the "Classics Live" version is questionable. More on that later.) As mentioned, it has been written that Perry and his wife – standing nearby – would mock the song when it was played, which bothered Tyler. This is the logical reason why one of rock's most stunning ballads was buried for some time.

The show would be pressed onto bootleg vinyl as "Get Your Lead Out Momma" in the 1980s.

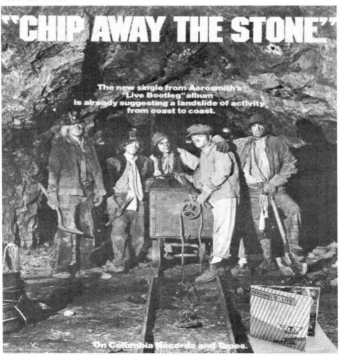

127

Tower Theater, Upper Darby, Pennsylvania. Sunday, March 26, 1978. Radio broadcast. Sound quality: A-

Rats In The Cellar, I Wanna Know Why, Big Ten Inch Record, Walk This Way, Sight For Sore Eyes, Seasons Of Wither, Sweet Emotion, Lord Of The Thighs, King And Queens, Chip Away The Stone, Get The Lead Out, Get It Up, Draw The Line, Same Old Song And Dance, Toys In The Attic, Milk Cow Blues, Train Kept A-Rollin'.

A little of the "Close Encounters Of The Third Kind" theme music slips into the intro tape along with "Psycho" as the band jumps into another wild ride of "Rats In The Cellar." During "Big Ten Inch Record" Whitford's nimble fingers pluck through a searing solo, followed by Perry who massages only a couple of chords, but quite effectively.

"It's good to be back," Tyler says to the Philly crowd, subtly acknowledging the band's troubles in the town as the band launches into "Sight For Sore Eyes." Tyler invents new, unintelligible lyrics for a verse of the song, but gets back to the standard words soon enough. Some might say this was a sign of drug use, but it sounds more like the work of a creative mind looking for a new way to present familiar music.

"Do you know you're being recorded live tonight?" Tyler asks. "Do you know you're going out live on the radio tonight? Express yourselves!" Interesting rhythms populate "Lord Of The Thighs" as the two guitarists banter on their strings between themselves.

The addition of Radice allows for the band's first known live attempt at "Kings And Queens," a fan favorite and it comes off quite nicely. Whitford's isolated solo has the same drama as the studio version, while there is some intricate interplay with Radice and Hamilton. "All right, that was a nice try for the first time," Tyler says afterward. This time he was telling the truth.

Whitford does some on-the-fly tuning during the "Get The Lead Out" intro chords as the band gets into a taut version of the song, though some of the backing vocals are rough even with Radice's help. "Draw The Line" is familiar as it's the version on "Live! Bootleg," but the tune and location is uncredited on that album, mimicking real bootlegs.

Perry's opening salvo on "Same Old Song And Dance" is strong and loud, a gripping reading. "You stiffs in the front, c'mon will ya!" Tyler says as he tries to get the crowd involved in the song. "What's your mother going to think when she hears you on the radio?!"

He comes back with more taunting after the crowd calls the band back for an encore: "You have the balls to stand up now? Now? You wanna rock now? After all that shit? It's about time! I want to thank the station for putting us on the air..."

Perry plays a clipped intro into "Milk Cow Blues," with the last note omitted as he shapes a new sound. As Perry hits his "Strangers In The Night" segment during "Train Kept A-Rollin'," someone grabs a station mic and yells, "All right, rock and roll!"

Another stellar night, one of the best ever for the band.

Soundcheck. Music Hall, Boston, Massachusetts. Monday, March 27, 1978. Soundboard. Sound quality: A

Krawhitham, Kings and Queens, I Wanna Know Why, Big Ten Inch Record, Seasons of Wither.

The band jams on the tune dubbed "Krawhitham," which would appear in a more complete version on the Pandora's Box collection.

Tyler sings select lyrics to "Kings And Queens" as he listens to the overall sound, as the band repeats the end section, trying to perfect it.

Hamilton plays a little of "Mama Kin" before the band jumps into "I Wanna Know Why."

Tyler requests "Big Ten Inch Record," and the band goes through a loose workout of the tune. The band also works on "Seasons of Wither" with Tyler telling Perry when to come in as the ending is worked out. An interesting session.

Music Hall, Boston, Massachusetts. Tuesday, March 28, 1978. Radio broadcast. Sound quality: A-

Rats In The Cellar, I Wanna Know Why, Big Ten Inch Record, Walk This Way, Sight For Sore Eyes, Seasons Of Wither, Sweet Emotion, Lord Of The Thighs, Kings And Queens, Chip Away The Stone, Get The Lead Out, Get It Up, Draw The Line, Same Old Song And Dance, Toys In The Attic, Milk Cow Blues, Train Kept A-Rollin'.

Another incredible show that starts with a rocket-fueled "Rats In The Cellar." The band seemingly wants to set a speed record for the song – and they succeed! Not a beat is missed as they fly through the opener.

"Boston, I want you all to know we are going out live on BCN tonight, did you know that? You didn't know that? Well goddammit, express yourselves! Say hello to your momma!" Tyler says. The band recorded several live versions of "Seasons Of Wither" during this spring run, but none made it onto "Live! Bootleg" unfortunately.

On the version this night, we can hear Kramer yell "yeah" just before Tyler begins his vocals, no doubt the drummer caught up in the song. The crowd is all over the floor of the hall and Tyler gives a half-hearted warning: "They told us to clear the aisles, or they are going to have to cut the show."

"Kings And Queens" is the familiar version that turned up on "Classics Live" almost a decade later. Karen Lawrence (reportedly wearing a see-through plastic top) reprises her role on the studio version of "Get It Up" here on stage. It's a great version of the inherently sloppy, rocking jam tune.

There is a little break between "Get It Up" and "Draw The Line" on this night; the pair are typically joined at the hip by Perry's slide guitar work.

Radice jumps in again with the "Close Encounters" theme as the band comes back on stage for the encore. Tyler goes on a ramble: "Before we do this next song, I want to say a couple of things. The reason the cops stopped this gig before, and *The Phoenix* (newspaper), and the press and the shit around town here…They go on about all the crap you kids do in these halls. They never bring up the fact that at the hockey games how many people died! They bring up how much you did to the halls, see? They don't like it. I don't fucking like it either, so express yourselves momma, just don't break the place down."

With that, Perry starts in on "Milk Cow Blues" where Tyler dedicates his harmonica solo "for you at BCN." Tyler and Perry sing the lyrics in an offset way at one point, bringing out the vocals in a nice way. Perry taps into "Strangers In The Night" one more time before ending "Train Kept A-Rollin'."

THE LINE IS BUSY.

Busy at places like:

WCAO	Baltimore	WBBF	Rochester(#28)	WOKY	Milwaukee
WRKO	Boston(#27)	WOLF	Syracuse	WZUU	Milwaukee
WVBF	Boston	WPJB	Providence(#23)	KSLQ	St. Louis
WYSL	Buffalo	WBBQ	Augusta	WOW	Omaha
13Q	Pittsburgh(#29)	WRFC	Athens(#30)	KTOQ	Rapid City(#22)
WIFI	Philadelphia(#29)	WFLB	Fayetteville	KIOO	Los Angeles
WPEZ	Pittsburgh(#34)	WKLO	Louisville	10Q	Los Angeles
WTRY	Troy	WFOM	Marietta	KCPX	Salt Lake City
WDRC	Hartford	WSGA	Savannah	KQEO	Albuquerque
WFEA	Manchester(#27)	WGCL	Cleveland	KAFY	Bakersfield
WAVZ	New Haven	WAYS	Charlotte	KCBN	Reno
WPRO-FM	Providence(#30)	WDRQ	Detroit (#29)	KNDE	Sacramento
		KWWL	Waterloo		

Busy at album radio, with an avalanche of across-the-board support.
And busy on the charts, where the number has been changed to
☆ *Billboard,* ⊙ *Cashbox* and ▣ *Record World.*

"DRAW THE LINE."
A PREDICTABLY ENORMOUS AEROSMITH SINGLE.
FROM THEIR FORTHCOMING ALBUM, "DRAW THE LINE."
ON COLUMBIA RECORDS.

JOE PERRY of Aerosmith and his
B.C. RICH Mockingbird
in concert..

Ace Music — 828-5688
1714 Wilshire Blvd.
Santa Monica, Ca.

International Warehouse Sound
338 Brunswick St. — 419-3397
Fitzroy Victoria, Australia

Long & McQuade — 964-8808
459 Bloor St.
Toronto Ont. Canada.

Music Crib — 636-5545
9753 Southwest Hwy.
Oak Lawn, Ill.

Pastore Music — 863-3424
507 - 32nd St.
Union City, N.J.

Hollywood Music — 653-9598
734 N. Fairfax Blvd.
Hollywood, Ca.

Stuyvesant Music — 221-5821
173 W. 48th St.
New York, N.Y.

Photo by Ron Pownall

TICKETS BY LOTTERY

Aerosmith Small Hall Tour Set

Aerosmith, which headlined before an estimated 300,000 persons last week at the California Jam 2 rock concert, returns April 7 and 8 for appearances in the 3,000-seat Santa Monica Civic Auditorium.

"The concerts are both part of Aerosmith's current 'small hall' tour and their way of thanking L.A. for the turnout at the Jam," said a spokesman for Wolf & Rissmiller Concerts.

Because of heavy ticket demand, a lottery will be conducted. Self-addressed envelopes should be mailed to KMET/Aerosmith, P.O. Box 38, Hollywood, Calif. 90028. Envelopes drawn will be mailed by Wolf & Rissmiller with a purchase voucher that allows the holder to buy two tickets at the Civic box office. No money should be sent in the lottery envelope, the spokesman said.

AEROSMITH'S RETURN: Aerosmith's April 7 and 8 concerts at the 3,000-seat Santa Monica Civic Auditorium will provide the first small-hall look here at a major rock band since Jethro Tull played the Pasadena Civic and Dorothy Chandler Pavilion early last year.

Larry Vallon, vice president of Wolf & Rissmiller Concerts, said Aerosmith added the Santa Monica shows to its national "small hall" tour as a thank you to local rock fans after the success of last week's California Jam 2 concert which drew 300,000 people to the Ontario Motor Speedway.

THE AEROSMITH LOTTERY: An estimated 100,000 letters were received for the lottery last week to determine who will be able to buy tickets for Aerosmith's concerts Friday and Saturday nights at the Santa Monica Civic. The 3,000 winning envelopes were drawn Friday and notifications—authorizing persons to buy tickets at the Civic box office—were mailed Monday.

Three clips from the Los Angeles Times on the Santa Monica gigs.

Civic Auditorium, Santa Monica, California. Friday, April 7, 1978. Audience recording. Sound quality: C-/D

Seasons Of Wither, Sweet Emotion, Lord Of The Thighs, Chip Away The Stone, Get The Lead Out, Get It Up, Draw The Line, Same Old Song And Dance, Toys In The Attic, Train Kept A-Rollin'.

A rough, incomplete recording of the second part of the gig. It's hard to hear all that's happening through the cacophony, still, there are some cool moments. Perry pulls off some great solos during "Lord Of The Thighs."

"We are going to do something off the Jam, something off the Jam album. It's going to be a single off the Jam album, entitled 'Chip Away The Stone,'" Tyler says, as there is still a lot of hype from the previous month's gig.

I bet a few people in Santa Monica watching Aerosmith on this night were at the Cal Jam gig. But instead of 350,000 people, the crowd is 3,500!

Tyler introduces Radice as Perry plays the intro to "Get The Lead Out." The riffs really stand out on the rough, unbalanced recording. Perry again does "Strangers In The Night" during "Train Kept A-Rollin'."

Civic Auditorium, Santa Monica, California. Saturday, April 8, 1978. Soundboard recording. Sound quality: A-

Rats In The Cellar, I Wanna Know Why, Big Ten Inch Record, Walk This Way, Seasons Of Wither, Sweet Emotion, Lord Of The Thighs, Chip Away The Stone, Get The Lead Out, Draw The Line.

An alternative universe from the previous night's recording. It's incomplete too, but in solid quality: This sounds like it's from a board tape versus an FM broadcast. The band was broadcasting many of its shows around this time, but it's doubtful if this went out over the radio. Perry's guitar is mixed down for most of what exists on tape here, giving the listener a better chance to focus on Whitford's unique rhythm and lead style.

Perry's first solo of the night during "Rats In The Cellar" is an odd one, he seems almost disinterested before turning it on. Radice's piano work is prominent during "I Wanna Know Why," in which Tyler sings improvised lyrics during parts including "ain't schoolin' me." Kramer plays an extended intro into "Walk This Way."

During "Seasons Of Wither" the sounds of wind conjured up from Radice's keyboards add more flavor to the beautiful song. It seems like someone is dialing up Hamilton's bass during the song as you might hear on a board tape.

More Tyler lyric changes during "Sweet Emotion:" "I ain't one to stop and grab..." Perry's and Whitford's twin guitars become one during "Sweet Emotion" as they get their feedback into perfect sync before a whistle signals the beginning of the end of the song, quite a moment! Cool stuff.

Tyler does a stream of consciousness mentioning a McDonald's restaurant Quarter Pounder and Fish Filet (!) as Kramer then bangs out the beginning of "Lord Of The Thighs." Whitford jams out on the song as Kramer taps out some interesting rhythms on another wholly unique version of the tune.

Fans might recognize this date from "Live! Bootleg." That album lists "Chip Away The Stone" as from this night, but it is not the case. A close listen to the 4/7/78 audience of "Chip Away The Stone" reveals it's not from that night either. Rather it's from Columbus the month before. "Remember the Cal Jam?" Tyler says before the song, then, "Are you alive out there tonight?"

**Texxas Jam, Cotton Bowl, Dallas, Texas. Saturday, July 1, 1978.
Soundboard recording. Sound quality: A**

*Rats In The Cellar, I Want To Know Why, Big Ten Inch Record, Walkin' The
Dog, Walk This Way, Seasons Of Wither, Sweet Emotion, Lick And A
Promise, Lord Of The Thighs, Get The Lead Out, Draw The Line, Same Old
Song And Dance, Toys In The Attic, Milk Cow Blues.*

After some May dates in the South and a couple of more in the Midwest in
late June, the band ends up playing the famous Texxas Jam. This is an
officially-released video recording, although the audio – save for a couple of
tracks on the "Pandora's Box" box set – was never officially released in a
separate manner.

It initially sounds as "Rats In The Cellar" is edited here as though a chunk
is missing. But concerts from this period show the song was cut down by the
band, maybe to add more punch.

Tyler repeats the same "Swing low, sweet cherry-o..." line during "I Wa
Know Why." While the set starts off well enough, one senses a certain
weariness on stage (the video only confirms this.) The heat may have been a
factor.

Kramer yells out loud as the band gets into "Seasons Of Wither." Perry's
guitar accentuates some of the lyrics of the song on this night.

As at the second night in Santa Monica, the guitar players try to match
harmonics on "Sweet Emotion" in a cool way, even if not as in-synch as that
gig.

Kramer's run up into "Lick And A Promise" is chopped out of the audio
mix, but the furious version gets things moving again onstage. "Lord Of The
Thighs" features some curious soloing by Perry, who plays what he feels
versus rote notes, yet they always fit the mood of the song.

"Toys In The Attic" does appear to be edited in the release. Ted Nugent
comes out to join the band for "Milk Cow Blues." Interestingly, the band
also had brought up Richie Supa on his song, "Chip Away The Stone." He
can be seen in the official video of the tune, but the audio remains stashed in
a vault.

The video was shot by NFL Films. "Big Ten Inch Record" and "Lord Of
The Thighs" were released on "Pandora's Box."

**Selland Arena, Fresno, California. Saturday, July 15, 1978. Audience
recording. Sound quality: B-**

*Rats In The Cellar, I Want To Know Why, Big Ten Inch Record, Sight For
Sore Eyes, Walk This Way, Walkin' The Dog, Chip Away The Stone, Seasons
of Wither, Sweet Emotion, Lord Of The Thighs, Get The Lead Out, Get It Up,
Draw The Line, Same Old Song And Dance (incomplete), Train Kept A-
Rollin'.*

The band lands in California's Central Valley in the summer of 1978. As
with Dallas, the show is at a slower pace and more methodical than the
shows from the jet-fueled pace of spring, but no less powerful. The band is
at its live peak in 1978!

Perry uses the talk box to sing along some of the "Walk This Way" lyrics
on this night. Radice adds some stout backing vocals on the track as well.

"Is there any room for you people in the balcony to move? Full house tonight!" Tyler says. "We're going to do a song for you older fuckers. It's off our first album, hey I see it, pass that joint up here," as he introduces "Walkin' The Dog." Usually joined in a segue, it sounds odd in isolation here. Tyler spreads the lyric "Mary, Mary, quite contrary, how does your garden grow?" over several beats.

Perry takes issue with the crowd's quietness: "I knew you guys were dead when you didn't dig AC/DC (the opener.) So, this is a song just for you," as he starts "Seasons of Wither."

Kramer seems to be ready to start "Walk This Way" before going into "Sweet Emotion." Perry again addresses the crowd: "We have a slight technical problem here, (the) guitar doesn't work. We will be back in about two minutes, so smoke a joint, beat up on your neighbor." Then Tyler chimes in, "Sabotage is what it is," seemingly blaming someone for the foul up.

But after Tyler gets the crowd clapping along, everything is soon fixed and the band launches "Get The Lead Out." The recording begins to undulate during "Draw The Line" as the batteries powering the recorder begin to run out of juice, but because Perry is playing slide on the tune, it's not too noticeable.

The opening chords to "Same Old Song And Dance" are loud and raw here. The recording ends as the batteries fail and the tape goes into hyper speed before cutting off. But an audience video of the show does present "Train Kept A-Rollin" almost in its entirety.

Author's 1970s-era belt buckle.

Comiskey Park, Chicago, Illinois. Saturday, August 5, 1978. Audience recording. Sound quality: B-

Rats In The Cellar, I Want To Know Why, Big Ten Inch Record, Sight For Sore Eyes, Walk This Way, Walkin' The Dog, Chip Away The Stone, All Your Love, Lick And A Promise, Sweet Emotion, Lord Of The Thighs (incomplete.)

Lively audience recording of the show that plays out in a large baseball stadium. The recording gives a much more intimate feel. It's too bad the tapers left after the first 45 minutes.

Really a superb show, Aerosmith's chaotic power on full display.

"Someone is taking a blow break up here," Tyler says, as the band jumps into a funky "Sight For Sore Eyes," not worried about the open consumption of drugs on stage.

"Chi-ca-go" Tyler says after "Walk This Way." "Last time we played here you burned the place down," he said, referring to the 1976 gig at the same venue when part of the stadium caught fire.

Perry seems ready to start "Same Old Song And Dance," but then goes into a version of "All Your Love" by Chicago native Otis Rush, a reverent touch and a fabulous live take.

"This is called, 'guess this tune.' If you don't get it in the first two seconds..." Tyler says before "Sweet Emotion." During the song, Tyler dedicates it to road manager Joe Baptista.

"Lord Of The Thighs" is the last song caught on tape, and even though incomplete, features great interplay between Perry and Radice, the latter sounding like Edgar Winter.

It's an interesting little jam for sure and illustrated Aerosmith was anything but stale, willing to re-work songs on the spot. "C'mon red eyes!" Tyler calls out to Perry before the jam begins.

two

140

**Giants Stadium, East Rutherford, New Jersey. Sunday, August 6, 1978.
Audience recording. Sound quality: D**

*Helter Skelter, Rats In The Cellar, I Want To Know Why, Big Ten Inch
Record, Sight For Sore Eyes, Walk This Way, Walkin' The Dog, Chip Away
The Stone, Seasons of Wither, Lick And A Promise, Sweet Emotion, Lord Of
The Thighs, Get The Lead Out, Get It Up, Draw The Line, Same Old Song
And Dance, Toys In The Attic, Milk Cow Blues, Train Kept A-Rollin'.*

A sweltering, rainy day at the gigantic football stadium, and the band
really delivers. This is it, the band at its biggest in front of a massive crowd.
Pictures from the show appear on the "Live! Bootleg" album.

To start, we get a surprise: The band kicks off the set with The Beatles
"Helter Skelter." The playing of the song calls into question the veracity of
the date of the studio version, listed as 1975 in the "Pandrora's Box"
collection. It would seem more likely pegged to 1977 or 1978 if the band is
playing it live at this juncture.

But we digress. The version is intense and dynamic as the band rises and
falls through The Beatles "heavy metal" tune. Great way to kick off the gig.

141

The band then falls into its more familiar "Rats In The Cellar." The crowd is into the set and cheers wildly at every turn.

Some radio interference comes across before "Chip Away The Stone" as fans call for "Back In The Saddle." Perry pauses briefly during the guitar intro and then creates a new song riff before Tyler starts singing. The vastness of the venue is captured on tape. While the quality is rough, the recording captures the ambiance of the event.

Kramer hints at "Lick And A Promise," but then Perry stops and starts the intro to "Seasons Of Wither" a few times before starting it up.

"Draw The Line" gets a large response from the mass, prompting Tyler to yell, "You have come alive!" Perry mentions the gig is the last of a six-week tour before the band jumps into "Milk Cow Blues." Perry plays a sinister sounding "Strangers In The Night" as he brings "Train Kept A-Rollin'" to its end.

A fantastic gig, a grand way to end the run of Aerosmith shows.

The Wherehouse, Waltham, Massachusetts. Thursday, August 10 and Sunday, August 20, 1978. Soundboard recording. Sound quality: A
All Your Love, Come Together (several takes), Downtown Charlie.

Wanting to add a live version of "Come Together" for the "Live! Bootleg" album, the band works on a version at their rehearsal space. The session starts off with "All Your Love'," a different take than would appear on "Pandora's Box," but in similar sound and style. The "Pandora's Box" version is credited to the "Draw The Line" sessions, but that may not be accurate. "Jack, you ready? Tyler asks producer Jack Douglas as the band readies to launch multiple takes of "Come Together." "We're rolling," Douglas informs the singer.

"Steven. Steven? Sounds pretty good, but we should do it again, though," Douglas says after the first take. "Let's work out that middle, after the instrumental," he adds as Hamilton plays the song's main riff.

"Hey Jack, is there anything I should change in the tone of the bass?" Hamilton asks. "It's getting better, let's go from the top again," Douglas says after another attempt by the band.

"Hey Joe, it would be better if you didn't sing and just concentrate on your guitar part and I can do the vocals over," Douglas says.

After one more attempt, the band jumps into "Downtown Charlie" another song that appears on "Pandora's Box," where its credited to the "Night In The Ruts" sessions.

During some of the later takes sans Douglas on the second date, Tyler begins to lose his patience: "Get me some fuckin' (sound spectrum) highs, there's nothing here!" And then: "We hear nothing...I'm no fool! I got a fuckin' stereo system at home!"

Various 45 sleeves for "Come Together."

143

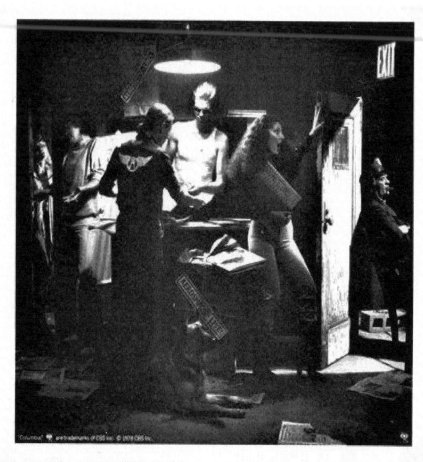

Tell your friends...and keep it quiet.

Aerosmith's "Live Bootleg." Sixteen classics recorded entirely in concert, including "Dream On," "Come Together," "Last Child," "Walk This Way," "Train Kept a Rollin'," "Sweet Emotion" and much more.

"Live Bootleg."

The new two-record set from Aerosmith. Under the counter, all over the world. On Columbia Records and Tapes.

Produced by Jack Douglas and Aerosmith for Contemporary Communications Corp. and Waterfront Productions Ltd. Direction: David Krebs-Steve Leber for Leber-Krebs, Inc.

Released in October of 1978, the live album was a way for Columbia to cash in on the band's popularity. It reached No. 13 on the Billboard chart on January 12, 1979 and successfully serves to give an honest representation of the band on stage. But it was not merely a one off, rather the band toured behind the album. As for the album, there are some dates and locations that are not correct. Some of the errors might be intentional or simple oversights. Here is a more accurate accounting:

LIVE! BOOTLEG

Back In The Saddle: Market Square Arena, Indianapolis 7/4/77
Sweet Emotion: Veterans Auditorium, Columbus 3/24/78
Lord Of The Thighs: Aragon Ballroom, Chicago 3/23/78
Toys In The Attic: Music Hall, Boston 3/29/78? (A recording of the 28th reveals the song is not from 3/28/78 as stated on the album; they did play the same venue on the 29th, so it could be from that show. Tape is sped up.)
Last Child: Paradise Club, Boston 8/9/78
Come Together: The Wherehouse, Waltham, Massachusetts 8/21/78
Walk This Way: Masonic Temple, Detroit 4/2/78
Sick As A Dog: Market Square Arena, Indianapolis 7/4/77
Dream On: Freedom Hall, Louisville 7/3/77
Chip Away The Stone: Veterans Hall, Columbus 3/24/78 (Vocal unknown, likely a studio overdub)
Sight For Sore Eyes: Veterans Auditorium, Columbus 3/24/78
Mama Kin: Market Square Arena, Indianapolis 7/4/77
S.O.S. (Too Bad): Market Square Arena, Indianapolis 7/4/77
I Ain't Got You: Paul's Mall, Boston 3/20/73
Mother Popcorn: Paul's Mall, Boston 3/20/73 (A little over a minute edited from the original broadcast.)
Draw The Line (unlisted on Lp): Tower Theater, Philadelphia 3/26/78
Train Kept A Rollin': Masonic Temple, Detroit 4/2/78
(Research: Darren North)

Friends in need

FORT WAYNE, Ind. (AP) — The rock group Aerosmith helped some of its fans get out of jail Wednesday.

After police arrested 62 people at an Aerosmith concert Tuesday night, the group posted bail for 13 of them.

Peter Minch, an accountant for the Boston-based group, said he paid out about $500 for bail and that he would appear in court to help pay the fines of those arrested.

Police arrested 34 adults and 28 juveniles at the concert on drug, alcohol and tobacco violations. During the performance, Aerosmith lead singer Steven Tyler stopped in the middle of a song to complain about the arrests and promised to post bail for anyone arrested.

Aerosmith bails out 13 of its busted fans

No one will ever accuse the rock group Aerosmith of being unappreciative of its fans, not after of its recent concerts. During an Aerosmith concert in Fort Wayne, Ind., police waded into the crowd and arrested 62 people on drug, alcohol and tobacco violations.

That night Aerosmith posted a total of $500 bail for 13 members of the audience. And Aerosmith accountant Peter Minch, promised to appear in court to help pay any fines levied by the judge.

Knight News Services

Incident at the Allen County War Memorial Coliseum, Fort Wayne, Indiana, October 3, 1978.

Capital Center, Landover, Maryland. Thursday, November 9, 1978. Soundboard recording. Sound quality: A

Chip Away The Stone, Dream On?

The first evidence of the "Live! Bootleg" tour comes via the Aerosmith "Scrapbook" video and "Classics Live."

The video shows the band on stage and intermingles footage from the Cal Jam Festival from earlier in the year for "Chip Away The Stone." The version is solid, but not spectacular.

"Dream On" on the "Classics Live" release is said to be from this date. The band, however, had not played the song on stage since March of 1978 and it's unlikely it was played here.

Before this gig, the band plays almost two-dozen shows in the Northeast, South and Midwest, but none have turned up to date.

Nassau Coliseum, Long Island, New York. Sunday, November 12, 1978. Audience recording. Sound quality: D

Toys In The Attic, S.O.S. (Too Bad), Mama Kin, I Wanna Know Why, Big Ten Inch Record, Sight For Sore Eyes, Lick And A Promise, Come Together, Back In The Saddle, Sweet Emotion, Lord Of The Thighs, Seasons Of Wither, Get The Lead Out, Chip Away The Stone, Walk This Way, Draw The Line, Same Old Song And Dance, Rats In The Cellar, Milk Cow Blues, Train Kept A-Rollin'/Happy Trails.

The first known complete show from this tour. Three months removed from its last dates, the band has refreshed its setlist, not satisfied to trot out the same set of songs. This show has a fast pace as the band goes from one song to the next, with few words from Tyler to the crowd during the first five songs. A trio of "oldies" starts the set.

147

"Come Together" has arrived in the setlist. What stands out is Kramer's rolling drum work throughout the tune. "Back In The Saddle" reappears, but the former show opener sounds out of place mid-set.

Mark Radice's piano work sticks out during "Lord Of The Thighs," but has a way of slowing the song's vibe and cutting into the Whitford/Perry guitar work that makes the track so fascinating live.

The band has a special guest for "Chip Away The Stone:" Richie Supa, who wrote the song with Tyler. He joins on vocals and guitar for a rollicking version, his singing adding to the unique rendition. Perry does a whipsaw opening to "Draw The Line," pushing wild notes through his guitar.

The guitars seem to be absent for the first vocal section of "Same Old Song And Dance" with Tyler and the rhythm section making due. Perry gets some feedback to signal the beginning of "Milk Cow Blues," which features a short drum interlude by Kramer.

"Happy Trails" appears suddenly during "Train Kept A-Rollin'" with Tyler putting on a country twang, a fun moment for sure.

Civic Center, Springfield, Massachusetts. Wednesday, November 15, 1978. Audience recording. Sound quality: C

Toys In The Attic, S.O.S. (Too Bad), Mama Kin, I Wanna Know Why, Big Ten Inch Record, Sight For Sore Eyes, Lick And A Promise, Come Together, Back In The Saddle, Sweet Emotion, Lord Of The Thighs, Seasons Of Wither, Get The Lead Out, Chip Away The Stone, Walk This Way, Draw The Line, Same Old Song And Dance, Rats In The Cellar, Bright Light Fright, Train Kept A-Rollin'/Happy Trails.

The band brings their A-game to Springfield, a great gig caught on an intense-sounding recording made from near the stage.

"How do you like our new duds tonight?" Tyler asks the crowd, as he was likely adorned in the finest rock and roll garb. Tyler plays great harmonica riffs into "Big Ten Inch Record." Whitford plays hypnotic rhythm during "Sight For Sore Eyes" as his partner in crime solos.

"Back In The Saddle's" guitar work seems particularly defined on this night as the guitars play the riffs in lockstep. Has there been a better rock and roll moment? I think not, and it's caught on tape!

"It's request time, what do you want to hear?" Tyler says afterward. "Bright Light Fright?" Perry asks. "Seasons of what?" Tyler asks, then, "Ain't Got who?" Tyler even tosses out "Major Barbara," which certainly was lost on most of the crowd as that track would not officially surface until eight years later.

The band settles on "Sweet Emotion," with Kramer's drums standing out as the song gets underway. Whitford and Perry again get their guitars revved up during the final section of the song, it's rock and roll bliss as their instruments pulsate.

Kramer adds a heavy backdrop to "Lord Of The Thighs" on this night, as Perry's guitar takes center stage. Perry plays a little country guitar on the intro to "Seasons Of Wither" adding a new flavor to the track.

"This next song is dedicated to 90 percent of the audiences we play to and I'm not talking about you," Perry says, as he launches "Get The Led Out" with an alternate riff to boot! He also alters the opening riff to "Chip Away The Stone," bending a note.

Perry plays a very energetic solo during "Walk This Way," dominating the track with wild playing. He also plays some soulful slide during "Same Old Song And Dance."

Finally, he does a stop/start on the opening "Rats In The Cellar" riff. Mr. Perry is on tonight, playing his instrument as though he is one with it.

"Who wants to hear, 'Bright Light Fright?'" Perry says. "Who wants to hear 'Milk Cow Blues,'" Tyler retorts, good naturedly. "Settled" Tyler says as the band jumps into the former, the first live version we know of.

Tyler really gets his cowboy on as he sings a little of "Happy Trails" Gene Autry style as "Train Kept A-Rollin'" ends the fabulous gig.

Madison Square Garden, New York City, New York. Friday, November 24, 1978. Audience recording. Sound quality: D

Toys In The Attic, S.O.S. (Too Bad), Mama Kin, I Wanna Know Why, Big Ten Inch Record, Sight For Sore Eyes, Lick And A Promise, Come Together, Back In The Saddle, Sweet Emotion, Lord Of The Thighs, Seasons Of Wither, Get The Lead Out, Chip Away The Stone, Mother Popcorn/Walk This Way,

Draw The Line, Same Old Song And Dance, Rats In The Cellar, Bright Light Fright, Milk Cow Blues, Train Kept A-Rollin'/Happy Trails.

Back in New York's big room, Kramer drums the hell out of "Mama Kin" tonight. "Now if we can get the monitors to work," Tyler says after the initial run of the first trio of songs before the band kicks into "I Wanna Know Why."

Radice's piano stands out on the tune. He also has a prominent roll and is introduced by Tyler on "Big Ten Inch Record." Perry gets in a trill during "Sight For Sore Eyes."

Kramer starts "Come Together" with a slow beat. While a hit for the band, live, it somehow slows the pace of the show on this night.

Kramer's slow, steady rhythm starts "Back In The Saddle" while Perry plays some notes before starting the riff proper. Two explosions go off in the Garden as the tune gets going.

Perry plays some wild high-pitched notes during "Sweet Emotion." Radice jumps into "Lord of The Thighs" again, this time with a more honky tonk flavor.

Perry's work on "Seasons Of Wither" sounds very majestic on this night. "Chip Away The Stone" again features an appearance by Richie Supa and the tune has the feel of a big party. Supa's vocals really stand out in a good way.

Kramer pounds out an intro to "Walk This Way," but sneaks into a bit of "Mother Popcorn," which the rest of the band picks up on before they stop and "Walk This Way" is started.

Perry does a lavish slide intro to "Draw The Line." Tyler jumps behind the drums and pounds the kit as the band returns to the stage for the encore.

"How would you like to hear 'Bright Light Fright?'" Perry asks the New Yorkers before the band plays the song. "Happy Trails" inside of "Train Kept A-Rollin'" closes things out.

Another apex gig for the band, playing the Garden as they had prestige and popularity. Just great rock and roll tunes one after another here.

The next night, things suddenly unravel and the band would lose some momentum.

Spectrum, Philadelphia, Pennsylvania. Saturday, November 25, 1978.
Audience recording. Sound quality: D

Toys In The Attic, S.O.S. (Too Bad), Mama Kin, I Wanna Know Why, Big
Ten Inch Record, Sight For Sore Eyes (partial).

A strange night at the Spectrum. "Ok, you foot fetish freaks. Quit throwing
your shoes up here," Tyler admonishes the crowd after "Mama Kin."

There is tension in the air. And Perry mentions something about "common
courtesy." But it would only get worse.

"If you wanna throw shit, throw bras, joints, c'mon, let's see it," Tyler says
during the "Big Ten Inch Record" intro as things continue to fly onto the
Spectrum stage.

Then the band starts "Sight For Sore Eyes." But within the first 30
seconds, a bottle from the crowd is thrown, hits a stage monitor, shatters and
spews shrapnel, hitting Tyler in the face.

The band stops and Kramer leaps out from behind his drum kit, rushing to
the mic.

"Now listen! We have been back here twice since the incident happened
with the fireworks. Steven just got hit in the face! The next person that
throws anything, we are going to leave the stage and we are not coming
back! And if you think I'm foolin', try me! We want to give you a good show
and we love you, but you can't throw things at us. Please," the drummer says
to a cheering crowd.

"Two times in three shows," someone says in the audience.

Then tour manager Joe Baptista addresses the crowd after a few minutes:
"Excuse me, this town has a real problem. A real problem. Every time we
come here – it's all because of one person, I know. I understand that. But
Steven got hit in the face, the doctor is looking at him now. It's going to be a
while. I don't know what's going to happen, we're just going to have to
wait."

Then we hear from the venue's manager: "Ladies and gentlemen, Steven
Tyler is hurt, the show will not continue. Please hold on to your ticket
stubs."

A woman in the audience loses it, shouting: "No! No!"

The Spectrum's manager continues, as he tries to quell the crowd: "Just a
minute, quiet please. Quiet please, let me finish. The band has left the

building, there is nothing to be done. They are gone, the show will not continue tonight. Hold onto your ticket stubs. We will announce what will happen. Thank you, good night."

For all the talk of bad performances of the band around this time (which are unfounded), it was really the crowds that could turn ugly at times. It was a bad end to a great run of shows.

For the band life was changing, and things wouldn't be the same in 1979.

Thrown Bottle Cuts Singer, Ends Concert

PHILADELPHIA (UPI) — The hard rock group Aerosmith has had its share of problems with unruly fans and a weekend concert at the Spectrum was no exception.

A spectator in the upper levels of the Spectrum Saturday night tossed an empty bottle at the stage, where it shattered, sending glass flying through the air, police said.

A piece of glass cut the face of singer Steve Tyler, forcing the band to cut short its performance. Tyler was treated in a dressing room by a Spectrum doctor.

Spectrum spokesman Mitchell Bass said that although the injury was not serious, it caused enough "emotional upset" to prevent Tyler from continuing the concert.

Bass said when officials cancelled the show 15 minutes later, the 19,500 fans reacted without anger.

"It was as if they understood," he said.

Bass said the Boston-based group had completed about 40 minutes of the show when the bottle broke on the stage about 10 p.m. Promoters were undecided over whether to give refunds.

Aerosmith was the chief attraction but had been preceded by another hard rock band, Golden Earring from Holland.

Aerosmith has been the object of spectator pranks in the past. Fans have thrown cherry bombs, bottles and firecrackers onto the stage.

In 1972, Tyler and guitarist Joe Perry were injured when a fan threw a firecracker as the group returned to the stage for an encore.

The cornea of Tyler's left eye was burned and Perry sustained a cut on his left hand. Neither injury caused permanent damage.

United Press International wire report.

Mediasound Studios, New York City, early 1979.

Chiquita, Three Mile Smile.

This recording is taken from a radio broadcast on KMET in Los Angeles as the band sits in with DJ Jim Ladd in April 1979. It's an almost complete version of "Chiquita" that is missing some of the guitar touches and horns heard on the final effort.

The vocals here are complete, meaning this was one of the first, if not the first song completed for the "Night In The Ruts" album. Tyler was notorious for being the last of the band members to add his part: lyrics, but he had them here. The song would be featured at gigs in 1979.

A working version of "Three Mile Smile" has appeared on YouTube.

Aero Knows (band newsletter), Spring 1979:

Aero update: Last Issue I told you about the album in pre-production in March. Since then, there have been some changes. First, we had problems with our recording truck that was at the Wherehouse. Rather than have to deal with all the hassles of the truck and the complex work of recording, we decided to can it for a while and take off for some gigs. To kick things off the boys decided to play a surprise show for their Boston fans.

Tuesday, March 27, 1979, Aerosmith played the Main Act in Lynn, Mass. They billed themselves as Dr. J Jones and the Interns, but it didn't really fool anyone. It was a great show and the band and crew were ready for two more relatively smaller appearances in Omaha, Nebraska and Wichita, Kansas before the big festivals.

> Another Boston rock unit, Aerosmith, played a none-too-secretive concert Tuesday night at the Main Act in Lynn.
>
> Again adopting the alias, Dr. J. Jones and the Interns, Stevie Tyler & Co. surprised nobody when they came on-stage at the new concert club, formerly the Harbour House.

Boston Globe mentions of the club show in Lynn above and the following page.

The upstairs also has a balcony that frames the stage below and tables (with leg room, no less) so that, sitting up here, you seem to be right on top of the performers. Meanwhile, down below, there's an open area in front of the stage (with no obstructing pillars), and the club is now experimenting with leaving that entire area open for dancing or for sitting on the floor a la the old Tea Party club in Boston. There have been tables in that area in the past, but not long ago, when Aerosmith made a sneak appearance (as Dr. J. Jones & the Interns), some of the crowd ended up jumping on them, breaking glasses and creating general havoc. On future nights, when hard rock is featured, the tables likely will be taken up beforehand.

The Main Act Concert Club at the Harbour House, Lynn, Massachusetts. Tuesday, March 27, 1979. Audience recording. Sound quality: D- to D+

(1st Set) Make It, Big Ten Inch Record, I Wanna Know Why, Walkin' The Dog, Seasons Of Wither, Bone To Bone (Coney Island White Fish Boy), Mama Kin, I Ain't Got You, Mother Popcorn.

(2nd set) S.O.S. (Too Bad), Somebody, Walk This Way, Get The Lead Out, Chiquita, Come Together, Lick And A Promise, Same Old Song And Dance, Toys In The Attic.

This is an interesting show in which we get a glimpse of the first songs from "Night In The Ruts," which the band is now working on. With bigger gigs upcoming, they take their show into a small club under the pseudonym Dr. J Jones and The Interns.

We must thank the taper who made his way in, even if the quality of the recording is dodgy at times. The taper has a stereo deck and is working to get into a good position to record from. But he is fighting the crowd in the cramped venue.

The band still uses the "Psycho" theme to open the show even though the gig is a more informal affair. The crowd is loud, funny at times, yelling at the band. "I can barely see them!" says someone in the crowd after the band breaks out "Make It" for the first time since 1975.

"Hey Joe! Hey Steven!" the crowd yells as their heroes are an arm's length away. The band is playing well and is very tight.

"It's great to play at clubs, you know what I mean," Hamilton says after "Walkin' The Dog," maybe the first time he has spoken to a crowd from the stage.

"We have been working on a new album," Hamilton says after "Seasons Of Wither." "We got this song we think you are really going to dig. If

155

anyone wants to dance, or has room to dance, they should do so on this song. You are going to hear this on the next album, but you're going to hear it a little different, but we are going to play it for you the way it is. It's called 'Bone To Bone'."

It's the first live version of the song, and musically sounds similar to the recorded version on "Night In The Ruts," although Tyler has yet to fully work out the lyrics.

The band trots out "I Ain't Got You" and "Mother Popcorn" for the intimate gig. The show is divided into two parts as they take a break after "Mother Popcorn."

The taper gets himself in a better position for the second part of the show. Perry plays well all night and is particularly fluid on "Walk This Way," his hands swooping up and down the guitar frets.

"We are going to give you a little bit of a taste," Tyler says as Perry strums the "Chiquita" riff, "of something we have been doing for our next album," as Perry hits another riff. "All you people with the tape recorders on, this is something off our new album." Tyler seems to call the song by another name, but it can't quite be heard. But it is what we know as "Chiquita," the first known live version. Sans horns here, the song's main riff really stands out.

Perry plays some sweet slide on "Same Old Song And Dance." Hamilton's bass threatens to collapse the club as it's turned up at the end of the song, per usual. A unique show that's challenging to listen to because of the poor sonics, but well worth it for the diehards.

Kansas Coliseum, Wichita, Kansas. Thursday, April 5, 1979. Stage recording. Sound quality: B
Bone To Bone (Coney Island White Fish Boy).

This is taken from a radio broadcast on KMET in Los Angeles as the band sits in with DJ Jim Ladd before the upcoming California World Music Festival show. Tyler and Perry played some of their favorite songs and unveiled this raw recording that the duo said was from a few days earlier in Wichita.

What we get is a formative version, lyrically at least, as in Lynn. Tyler almost sounds like he is ad-libbing the lyrics. Interesting recording and makes one wonder where the rest of the tape is!

California World Music Festival, Los Angeles Coliseum, Los Angeles, California. Saturday, April 7, 1979. Audience recording. Sound quality: C

Train Kept A-Rollin', S.O.S. (Too Bad), Mama Kin, I Wanna Know Why, Big Ten Inch Record, Bone To Bone (Coney Island White Fish Boy), Lick And A Promise, Come Together, Back In The Saddle, Lord Of The Thighs, Seasons Of Wither, Get The Lead Out, Chiquita, Walk This Way, Draw The Line, Same Old Song And Dance, Toys In The Attic, Milk Cow Blues, Bright Light Fright.

"Good morning LA!" Tyler yells – the band's late-night appearance apparently spilling over into the next day – after a fiery "Train Kept A-Rollin'" opens the show. Once the closer, the tune now moves to the front of the set.

"We are going to dedicate this here song to KMET for playing the shit out of the band and J.J. Jackson (later of MTV fame)..." as the band gets into "Big Ten Inch Record," which gets a 90-second introduction jam.

"We are going to do a little simple song off our new album, it's entitled 'Bone To Bone,'" Tyler says. The lyrics are still not the ones we would hear on the album.

Kramer's intro to "Lick And A Promise" is almost symphonic as his sticks bounce off the drums with impeccable rhythm. Tyler sings the wrong lyrics to start the song, which he has done a few times over the years, a bit of a mental block it appears. But the song hardly suffers for it.

Perry's one-man guitar army plays an improvised intro to "Back In The Saddle." Hamilton busks on the bass as Kramer pounds out the "Lord Of The Thighs" intro. Some of Perry's work on "Seasons Of Wither" has a sitar-ish quality, adding a new layer of sound to the song.

"The next song we are going to do now is right off the new album, it's called 'Chiquita,'" Perry says as he starts the stop-start riffs. The song comes off well and is without the horns. Perry swoops the frets as he brings "Walk This Way" to a close. Tyler brings out a maraca during "Draw The Line's" middle section as Perry adds his slide guitar.

"LA! We done it once before and we are going to do it again! Express yourselves!" Tyler says before "Milk Cow Blues," where Perry gets some

Link Wray-like sounds from his ax as he brings the tune to a close. Tyler and Perry share the mic during the "Bright Light Fright" jam to end the gig.

Florrida World Music Festival, Tangerine Bowl, Orlando, Florida. Saturday, April 14, 1979. Audience recording. Sound quality: C

Walk This Way, Draw The Line, Same Old Song And Dance, Toys In The Attic, Bright Light Fright, Milk Cow Blues and Johnny B. Goode with Ted Nugent.

Great energy by the band on this night. Only the last section remains. "Mr. Tom," Tyler calls out to Hamilton as the bass player begins his end bass run during "Same Old Song And Dance." Perry plays a flurry of notes before he kicks off "Bright Light Fright."

Ted Nugent was said to have joined the band at this gig for "Milk Cow Blues" and "Johnny B. Goode."

Canaddian World Music Festival, Exhibition Stadium, Toronto, Ontario, Canada. Monday, July 2, 1979. Audience recording. Sound quality: C

Train Kept A-Rollin', S.O.S. (Too Bad), Mama Kin, Big Ten Inch Record, Reefer Headed Woman, Lick And A Promise, Think About It, Seasons Of Wither, Bone To Bone (Coney Island White Fish Boy), Lord Of The Thighs, Sweet Emotion, Get The Lead Out, Walk This Way, Draw The Line, Same Old Song And Dance, Rats In The Cellar, Milk Cow Blues, Toys In The Attic.

The band headlines this large festival in Toronto on a hot summer day, and the band plays some new tunes on stage. The whole "Psycho" tape runs to its end and yet no band.

Finally, Kramer starts in on "Train Kept A-Rollin'" with some frantic notes by Perry getting the gig off to a start. Tyler purposely mumbles some of the lyrics to "Mama Kin" with a nice effect.

Tyler dedicates "Big Ten Inch" to Scott Cushnie, who played keyboards with the band in the mid-1970s. We can guess he was at this show. "Little breeze!" Tyler yells out during the tune as some wind cools the stage, at least for a few seconds.

Perry hints at "Heartbreak Hotel" before the band jumps into "Reefer Headed Woman" as Tyler says, "We are going to do something off our new album," as he introduces the song. The singer screams the title lyric at one point during the song, a great rock and roll moment. This is the first known version by the band since 1971.

"We are gonna do some of our new stuff," he says as Perry starts "Think About It," the first known live version since 1974. Tempers then flare between band members on stage after "Seasons Of Wither."

"How about a new song, Steve?" Perry says to Tyler, in a mocking voice. "How about up your ass, motherfucker!" Tyler shoots back.

The band then goes into "Bone To Bone (Coney Island White Fish Boy)." The tune is again more of a guitar jam as Tyler mumbles his way through lyrics that would never make the album.

The band gets into a fabulous jam on "Lord Of The Thighs." "What did you say, Brad?" Tyler says as the guitarist plays some sublime notes as Tyler shakes his maracas.

"Get The Lead Out" thunders over the massive sound system, giving a sense of how loud the sonics were at this gig. Tyler does some scatting during the song as well. Perry asks, "Is there a doctor in the house?" via his talk box before "Walk This Way."

Tyler does some more scatting during the slow section of "Draw The Line." During "Same Old Song And Dance" Tyler tries to get the crowd to clap along by saying "Let's see the (rhythm) in you." And later, "That's right, all you clapping sure can fuck good, can't you?"

Perry raises the devil, making his guitar scream during "Rats In The Cellar." The end of "Milk Cow Blues" has a Metallica-like ending as the twin guitars bang out notes in unison. "Toys In The Attic" now becomes the closer.

Day On The Green, Oakland Coliseum, Oakland, California. Saturday, July 21, 1979. Video recording. Sound quality: C

Back In The Saddle, Train Kept A-Rollin', Mama Kin, Big Ten Inch Record, Reefer Headed Woman, Lick And A Promise, Think About It, Seasons Of Wither, Bone To Bone (Coney Island White Fish Boy), Lord Of The Thighs, Sweet Emotion, Get The Lead Out, Walk This Way, Draw The Line, Same Old Song And Dance (partial), Come Together, Toys In The Attic.

The audio is from a Bill Graham Presents (the promoter) video. The audio is an amateur affair with sound pulled from ambient mics, not from the soundboard. Nevertheless, this is an interesting document, the last recording with Perry that circulates from his initial run with the band.

The recording starts with "Back In The Saddle," which has made its way to the front of the setlist again. It's followed by a solid version of "Train Kept A-Rollin'."

"Mama Kin" comes off with great power. Perry adds guitar histrionics to the end of the song in fine style.

The band is playing well here. It flies in the face of tales of the band being so out of it they could barely perform. It's simply untrue and borne out by the tapes. That's not to say drugs were not involved: "Goddamn, you got some fine Lebanese hash, don't ya?" Tyler says to the mass of Bay Area humanity.

Perry introduces "Think About It," which is played in a tight and taut manner. Perry plays a little run as "Seasons of Wither" lifts off. Because of the mix, Kramer's simple, but effective drum patterns stand out on the song.

The lyrics for "Bone To Bone (Coney Island White Fish Boy)" are still not developed here. "Mr. Joey Kramer!" Tyler says as the drummer beats out the intro to "Lord Of The Thighs." It's something to behold on film, Kramer's powerful and precise drumming on display.

"Reefer Headed Woman" gets a great bluesy reading from the band. "Lick And A Promise" has a long intro from Kramer, then things go a little askew as Tyler starts in on the wrong line on the song yet again. Then a high-pitched feedback kicks in. All well, who said rock and roll should be perfect?

A flash pod marks the beginning of "Toys In The Attic," and with the song's close it's the last we will hear of Perry with the band for the next five years.

It's a real shame, as the band was still playing very well and was developing new music. The rigors of the studio-album-to-tour-to-studio-album-to-tour the band dealt with for the last six years, along with an array of drugs, was too much to overcome.

The first era of Aerosmith was done after a gig in Cleveland the following weekend. Alas, some great photos of that gig have emerged, but no recording.

JOE PERRY

The L-500
(Pat. Pending)
Guitar Pickup

*

A sound
creation
of power
response
and sustain

*

Bill Lawrence Products

P.O. BOX 238   Madison,TN 37115   (615) 868-6976

GUITAR HEROES

pic by Ross Halfin

Aerosmith's Jimmy Crespo

WHEN DID YOU BEGIN PLAYING GUITAR? 1966. I was about 14 years old.

WHY DID YOU START? Mainly because of The Beatles, The Stones and The Yardbirds.

FIRST TYPE OF GUITAR: It was a Kent guitar, the most obnoxious thing I've seen in my life! All the strings were rusted up, it was a real piece of crap.

EARLY INFLUENCES: The Beatles and The Stones.

FIRST PUBLIC PERFORMANCE: Some school dance – my first indulgence in this silly profession!

FIRST APPEARANCE ON RECORD: Flame's 'Queen Of The Neighbourhood' album.

RECORDING BANDS: Flame and Aerosmith.

OTHER VINYL APPEARANCES: Studio work with Ian Lloyd and Robert Fleischman, who wrote some stuff for Journey, and one record with Helen Schneider. Also, a track for Stevie Nicks and a bunch of other people I can't remember.

EQUIPMENT LIVE: Musicman heads, re-done to make them more punchy in the mid-range, and basic Marshall bottoms with Celestions in them. As for guitars, at the moment I'm using a Les Paul that Gibson sent me – a re-issue of a '59 Flame Top that's really beautiful, and an old Fender six-string bass.

NUMBER OF GUITARS OWNED: I used to own 25-30 but now I've got about 10 – just the cream of the crop.

MOST MEMORABLE SOLO ON RECORD: It was on a song I did for the Ian Lloyd album. I played the solo with an Ebo; it was off-the-wall but somehow it fitted.

OTHER GUITARISTS YOU ADMIRE: a long list ... Clapton, Hendrix, Beck, Segovia, Bream, Big Bill Broonzy, Leadbelly, B.B. King, Freddie King and lots more.

165

Aerosmith. Right where it hurts.

"Night in the Ruts." Their new album.
On Columbia Records and Tapes.

"Night in the Ruts." Their new album.
On Columbia Records and Tapes.

The beginning of Aerosmith's three-month tour:

12/5	Binghamton, NY	12/18	Atlanta, GA
12/6	Portland, ME	12/19	Birmingham, AL
12/8	Hampton, VA	12/21	Cincinnati, OH
12/9	Pittsburgh, PA	12/22	Louisville, KY
12/12	Knoxville, TN	12/26	Chicago, IL
12/13	Augusta, GA	12/27	Indianapolis, IN
12/15	Greensboro, NC	12/28	Nashville, TN
12/16	Charlotte, NC	12/30	Memphis, TN
			More To Come

NIGHT IN THE RUTS TOUR

"Night In The Ruts" is released November 1, 1979 and peaks at No. 14 on the Billboard chart on January 18, 1980. Perry officially leaves the band on October 10, 1979, before the album was completed. Former Flame guitarist Jimmy Crespo gets the job after an audition. Much of Perry's work is on the Lp, with Crespo, Richie Supa and tech Neil Thompson filling out the guitar work on the album. The band launches an ill-fated tour. Tyler collapses on stage in Portland, Maine on December 6, the second date of the tour.

SUNDAY: David Bromberg at Alexander's in Browns Mills; Beaver Brown at the Fast Lane; Aerosmith at Nassau Coliseum in Uniondale, L.I.

Nassau Coliseum, Long Island, New York. Sunday, January 13, 1980. Audience recording. Sound quality: D+

Back In The Saddle, Mama Kin, I Wanna Know Why, Big Ten Inch Record, Three Mile Smile, Reefer Headed Woman, Bone To Bone (Coney Island White Fish Boy), Walk This Way, Dream On, Rats In The Cellar, No Surprize, Remember (Walking In The Sand), Lord Of The Thighs, Same Old Song And Dance, Milk Cow Blues, Toys In The Attic, Come Together, Train Kept A-Rollin'.

The first known live recording with Crespo on guitar. A new era for the band. Crespo is a fine player and adds his own signature to the band's classic canon. When he stretches out, he gives the band a new voice. Not better, nor worse, just different.

Some things have not changed: The "Psycho" theme is again used as the intro tape played to the crowd in the arena.

Tyler really screams his "baaaaaack" during "Back In The Saddle," at an almost frightening (but very cool) way. One fears his larynx will pop out of his throat and onto the stage! But alas, his voice bounces right back to sing the rest of the song. The crowd gives the band a loud response, a fervor that continues throughout the night.

"Three Mile Smile," "Reefer Headed Woman," and "Bone To Bone (Coney Island White Fish Boy)" are played back to back to back without a break. The gig is a real showcase for the new "Night In The Ruts" album.

This is the first known live recording of "Three Mile Smile." Tyler finally has the lyrics for "Bone To Bone (Coney Island White Fish Boy)," which had eluded him on stage for much of 1979.

With Perry gone, "Dream On" returns to the set. It's quite easy to hypothesize that Perry's mocking distaste for the song is why it had been dropped from the set after the March 1978 gigs. Now that he was gone, the tune is back and there is a frenzied reaction in the Nassau Coliseum. Through the din, Tyler plays an eloquent and exquisite intro into the song. Hard to believe the band dropped the classic for almost two years. Imagine Zeppelin not playing "Stairway To Heaven." "Thank you, momma!" an appreciative Tyler says to the crowd at its conclusion. No doubt it was satisfying moment for Tyler and the band.

"New York City!" Tyler says before the band launches into the first known live version of "No Surprize," which is played very similarly to the studio version. Richie Supa again gets a mention by Tyler.

"Remember (Walking In The Sand)," then gets its first recorded airing, full of moving soloing by Crespo. Hamilton gets to show off his bass work again at the end of "Same Old Song And Dance," it's loud, very loud! "Milk Cow Blues," which would become a concert staple of this era, gets a seven-minute workout.

"Come Together" turns up as an encore, with Supa providing some impassioned background vocals. "Train Kept A-Rollin'" lands in its more traditional spot as the show closer.

The tune is also a set up for Crespo's ending solo to prove he's a worthy successor to Perry, and he plays some fine guitar. All told, a great night on Long Island. Tyler talks about the show the next day on the Robert Klein Show and tells the host 20,000 crammed into the venue to watch the band.

Memorial Auditorium, Buffalo, New York. Thursday, January 17, 1980. Audience recording. Sound quality: D

Back In The Saddle, Mama Kin, I Wanna Know Why, Big Ten Inch Record, Three Mile Smile, Reefer Headed Woman, Walk This Way, Dream On, Rats In The Cellar, No Surprize, Remember (Walking In The Sand), Lord Of The Thighs, Same Old Song And Dance, Milk Cow Blues, Toys In The Attic.

"Buffalo, you motherfuckers!" Tyler yells out after "Back In The Saddle." Tyler is amped and this proves to be a high-energy gig, similar to the spring 1978 run of shows.

A tight and taut gig, the crowd is near delirium. It seems like a whole new set of fans have turned up, maybe those who were too young to see the band in the 1970s.

Supa is back on keyboards, adding funky piano to "I Wanna Know Why." Hamilton adds some bass to "Big Ten Inch Record" as Tyler blows his harp on and on.

"This is something off our latest album, it's called 'Fuck You *Rolling Stone*' or 'Three Mile Smile,'" says Tyler, referencing the less than flattering review the magazine gave the new album ("the finest moments on '*Night in the Ruts*' sound like inspired outtakes from '*Rocks*' and '*Toys in the Attic*'.")

But the band doesn't care as it blasts the tune into the arena to the screaming throngs, Crespo soloing like he is possessed as the Perry-less Aerosmith project is out to prove themselves.

169

"We got another ballad for you here, we are going to slow it down nice and pretty, just how you like it," Tyler says after "Dream On." But the band jumps into a blistering, frantic version of "Rats In The Cellar" that almost goes off the rails before the band guides it back home.

Tyler references the "new video" of "No Surprize." Crespo's solos his buttocks off during "Remember (Walking In The Sand)." Tyler does some bluesy harp work during "Milk Cow Blues" before "Toys In The Attic" fills out what was caught on tape.

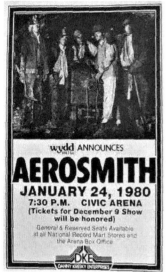

Civic Arena, Pittsburgh, Pennsylvania. Thursday, January 24, 1980. Audience recording. Sound quality: D

Back In The Saddle, Mama Kin, I Wanna Know Why, Big Ten Inch Record, Three Mile Smile, Reefer Headed Woman, Bone To Bone (Coney Island White Fish Boy), Walk This Way, Dream On, Rats In The Cellar, No Surprize, Remember (Walking In The Sand), Lord Of The Thighs, Same Old Song And Dance, Milk Cow Blues, Toys In The Attic, Come Together, Train Kept A-Rollin'.

The newly configured band gets another rousing response in Pittsburgh.

"You gotta push back a little," Tyler tells the crowd rushing the stage as the band gets into "Big Ten Inch Record." Kramer stops the beat for a second as he waits for Tyler, and the singer blows his harmonica long and loud.

The crowd is really responding, as if they can't believe the legendary band is right before them. It's likely a good portion of the crowd was a new generation of fans.

The audience quiets during the beginning of "Dream On," listening intently. "Shut your mouths!" Tyler yells during "Same Old Song And Dance" as he tries to get the throng to clap along to the tune. "Give me your hands, everybody...now dig yourselves, just your hands" as the band stops playing to take in the spectacle. "Yeah!" Tyler yells in approval. Another good night for the "new" band.

Capital Center, Landover, Maryland. Friday, January 25, 1980. Soundboard recording from video. Sound quality: A

Back In The Saddle, Mama Kin, I Wanna Know Why, Big Ten Inch Record, Three Mile Smile, Reefer Headed Woman, Bone To Bone (Coney Island White Fish Boy), Walk This Way, Dream On, Get The Lead Out, Remember (Walking In The Sand), Lord Of The Thighs, Same Old Song And Dance, Milk Cow Blues, Toys In The Attic, Come Together, Train Kept A-Rollin'.

Tyler again screams his "baaaaaack" during "Back In The Saddle," not holding anything back. Richie Supa adds some backing vocals during the tune that are isolated, really standing out. The clear recording reveals a band playing very well and excited to be on stage.

Tyler does a call and response with himself using his voice and harmonica during the "Big Ten Inch Record" intro, resulting in extreme bluesy funkiness.

"Oh, a little right in the nuts mama!" is Tyler's intro to "Three Mile Smile," which features a driving Crespo ending solo that leads into "Reefer Headed Woman."

A sizzling version of "Bone To Bone (Coney Island White Fish Boy)" follows, again driven by Crespo's guitar work. It may be sacrilegious, but this show makes one forget about Perry.

Kramer's beats into "Walk This Way" start fast, but then slow and the band gets into the groove properly. The "just give me a kiss" line becomes "just give me some head" as it would off and on in the future.

Lovely rendition of "Dream On" tonight, hitting all the marks. Interestingly, Tyler uses a different vocal emphasis on some of the lines during "Rats In The Cellar." The rhythm is really locked in during the song, which concludes with Tyler yelling, "Mr. Jimmy Crespo, magic man!" On this night it's really true.

Tyler punctuates the opening riffs of "Get The Lead Out" with a guttural grunt. The band is really cooking on the song. Crespo brings more intensity to "Lord Of The Thighs." Gone is the interplay between guitarists when Perry was in the band, replaced by Crespo wailing on his strat. But Whitford has a reply within the song and shakes up some notes of his own to great effect. Finally, the guitarists slow it down to end the long jam.

"Train Kept A-Rollin'" is the nightly showcase for Crespo, as he bends and pulls notes throughout his solo. A red-letter night in Landover!

24 arrested at Largo arena

Largo (Special) — Twenty-four persons at Friday night's Aerosmith concert at the Capital Centre were arrested in a police crackdown on drug trafficking at rock concerts in the arena.

Seventy-one officers from the Prince Georges county police force and the U.S. Park Police took part in the operation, in which undercover agents purchased drugs ranging from marijuana to LSD, PCP and amphetamines, a county police spokeswoman said.

Most of the 22 men arrested were charged with distribution of controlled substances. Some also were charged with drug possession.

Baltimore Sun

Kaleidoscope Presents . . .

AEROSMITH

with special guest,

"MOTHER'S FINEST"

Sun., Dec. 16 • 8:00 P.M.
Charlotte Coliseum

Limited Advance Tickets.......... $7
All Others $8

Ticket Locations both concerts: Coliseum Box Office • Ernie's Records (Cotswold, Park Rd.) • Records Plus (Sharon Amity Rd.) • Grapevine Records (Independence Blvd. • Ja Jo's (Gastonia) • Bobby's Music (Shelby) • Music City Records (Forest City) • Music Eye (Hickory and Whitnel) • WOOO Radio Station (Statesville) • Back Room (Albemarie) • Record Rack (Monroe) • Twilite Zone (Newton) • Square Record (Lancaster) • Record Cellar (Rock Hill) • Mercury Music (Spartanburg) • Tape Town (Morganton)
04-0-12-09

Charlotte Coliseum, Charlotte, North Carolina. Sunday, January 27, 1980. Audience recording. Sound quality: D

Back In The Saddle, Big Ten Inch Record (fragment), Three Mile Smile, Reefer Headed Woman (fragment), Bone To Bone (Coney Island White Fish Boy), Walk This Way, Rats In The Cellar, Lord Of The Thighs, Same Old Song And Dance (fragments), Milk Cow Blues, Toys In The Attic, Train Kept A-Rollin (fragment.)

Crespo adds background singing on "Back In The Saddle," and some interesting licks, including a brief ambulance sound passage. The crowd seems very receptive to the band on this night.

172

Aerosmith Cancels

The rock group Aerosmith has canceled scheduled concerts tonight in Greensboro and Sunday night in Charlotte.

Ticketholders for the concerts can use the tickets for rescheduled appearances by the group or receive a refund of the ticket price, according to a spokesman for Kaleidoscope productions, which scheduled the concerts.

The Charlotte concert has been rescheduled for Jan. 27; the Greensboro concert, Feb. 8.

The Kaleidoscope spokesman said Aerosmith lead singer Steve Tyler has been hospitalized for treatment of hypertension. Tickets to both concerts had been sold out.

For the Charlotte concert, refunds will be made 10 a.m.-6 p.m. Monday at the Coliseum Ticket Office, 2700 E. Independence Blvd., or they can be obtained by mail. For the Greensboro date, refunds can be obtained at that box office, 1921 W. Lee St., 10 a.m.-5 p.m. weekdays, or by mail.

For additional information, call the ticket offices: Charlotte, 372-3600, 10 a.m.-6 p.m. daily, or Greensboro, (919) 294-2870, 10 a.m.-5 p.m. weekdays.

Crespo goes off toward the end of "Three Mile Smile," playing some fantastic runs, tossing in Hendrix's "Spanish Castle Magic."

On "Bone To Bone (Coney Island White Fish Boy)," Crespo tosses in a stuttering guitar riff, a cool touch that made him just as unique as Perry.

Kramer sounds as funky as ever playing the "Walk This Way" intro, in which Crespo replicates Perry's effects. Crespo holds the last notes a bit longer, giving a new flavor to the song.

While Crespo may have not had the stage swagger of Perry, he certainly holds his own, playing an explosive solo during "Rats In The Cellar." That allows the band to explore free form playing within the tune's structure.

"Lord Of The Thighs" is another strong number, but there is not the strong rapport with Whitford. Richie Supa apparently made the trip to North Carolina to bang on the keyboards as Tyler announces him during "Same Old Song And Dance."

"Milk Cow Blues" is dedicated to Elvis as the band heads toward the finish line during the interesting show. The taper was on hand for the entire gig but recorded it in fits and starts.

Tyler's poor health forces the band to halt the "Night In The Ruts Tour" after a gig in Hollywood, Florida on February 2, 1980. As Tom Hamilton explained it during a 1980 radio interview, Tyler had burned out from being on the road and had health issues (likely related to drugs.) So, to keep their chops up and make a little money, it was into the clubs. After some strong performances earlier in the year, these club dates are less lucid affairs with the lead singer in the throes of drug use and abuse.

Speaks Club, Island Park, Long Island, New York. Sunday, April 20, 1980. Audience recording. Sound quality: C

(1st Set) Back In The Saddle, Mama Kin, I Wanna Know Why, Big Ten Inch Record, Dream On, Three Mile Smile, Reefer Headed Woman, Bone To Bone (Coney Island White Fish Boy.)

(2nd Set), Rats In The Cellar, Remember (Walking In the Sand), Walk This Way, Lord Of The Thighs, Same Old Song And Dance, Milk Cow Blues, Toys In The Attic, Train Kept A-Rollin'.

The first club date was in Long Island. Tyler sounds under the influence, but relatively coherent. The band, however, doesn't wait around for him to talk, instead launching into songs as he is mid-sentence.

Still, give Tyler credit, he sings the songs and doesn't miss much. He can barely be heard on "Back In The Saddle," but that is likely due to the club's sound system. The equipment sounds old and at one point a fan yells, "The PA sucks!" After "Mama Kin" a woman in the audience complains the sound is "too loud," meaning it was just right.

"We are starting to see the same faces," Tyler observes as the band kicks into "I Wanna Know Why." Tyler rambles "we are playing small places now, look at that motherfucker over there in the booth, he's snorting that shit off that lady's tit. Bring some of that over here." Not sure where the singer is going, Kramer starts in on a beat and counts in "Three Mile Smile."

A fan calls out for "Chiquita" before "Dream On." After "Bone To Bone (Coney Island White Fish Boy)" a female MC comes on stage and says the band will take a break.

The second part of the show is more lively and the PA has been replaced. Tyler mumbles something unintelligible before "Rats In The Cellar" giving pause as to how the tune might go. But as soon as it starts, the band is off and running with Tyler riding herd over the controlled chaos.

Crespo again plays beautifully on "Remember (Walking In the Sand)" always excelling on the song. The crowd gets into "Walk This Way" yelling out the lyrics.

Hamilton hints at "Sweet Emotion" and Tyler says the title. But it would be a surprise here, the band has surprisingly not played it live since the summer of 1979. And it was not to be as "Lord Of The Thighs" is the next tune, with some weird notes coming from Whitford at its outset, as if they are garbled. Crespo dominates its landscape as the tune progresses.

"You are louder than we are," Hamilton says. "We are going to do an oldie for you..." as he introduces "Same Old Song And Dance," the band changing some of the chord structure as they make their way through. A bottle rattling near the taper during "Milk Cow Blues" reminds the listener that the band is in a small club.

Crespo again gets the spotlight on "Train Kept A Rollin'," where he puts a bunch of notes into the guitar blender and hits frappé.

Club Detroit, Port Chester, New York. Tuesday, April 22, 1980. Audience recording. Sound quality: C

Soundcheck, Back In The Saddle, Mama Kin, I Wanna Know Why, Big Ten Inch Record, Dream On, Three Mile Smile, Reefer Headed Woman, Rats In The Cellar, Remember (Walking In The Sand), Lick And A Promise, Walk This Way, Lord Of The Thighs, Same Old Song And Dance, Milk Cow Blues, Toys In The Attic.

Tyler can be heard singing "Heartbreak Hotel" during the soundcheck before the show as the taper records even when repeatedly told by someone not to enter. Now that's the rock and roll spirit!

"Good evening hometown. Hello mommy and daddy," Tyler says sluggishly after the opening pair of songs. The recording apparently was made stage right, or Whitford's side, as Crespo is barely audible for most of the gig. The recording makes for an excellent study of Whitford's intricate and precise playing. More of the subtleties of the songs come out in the small club, but the tunes seem more plodding on this night. Someone in the crowd is obsessed with yelling, "You are number one!" at the band all night.

During "Lick And A Promise" Tyler's vocals become harder to hear and remain so for the balance of the show. Kramer's distinctive drum intros to "Lick And A Promise," "Walk This Way," and "Lord Of The Thighs" are played back to back to back here. The unbalanced recording provides a unique version of the latter.

Whitford's vibrato is super intense during "Milk Cow Blues." An interesting show. Tyler is definitely under the influence, but still hits all his cues, although sometimes in a sluggish manner.

Stage West, Hartford, Connecticut. Wednesday, June 11, 1980. Audience recording. Sound quality: B-
Back In The Saddle, Mama Kin, I Wanna Know Why, Big Ten Inch Record, Three Mile Smile, Reefer Headed Woman, Dream On, Lick And A Promise, Walk This Way, Rats In The Cellar, Milk Cow Blues, Come Together, Toys In The Attic, Train Kept A- Rollin'.

Tyler's voice warbles a little during "Back In The Saddle" tonight, but the band sounds good, the best so far of the club dates. Maybe a short period of rest since the last dates helped. Crespo plays some chaotic notes as the tune wraps up.

"You know we are recording tonight," Tyler says as the band launches into "I Wanna Know Why" after the guitarists do some quick tuning. The King Biscuit Flower Hour radio crew is on hand to record tonight's and tomorrow's gigs.

Tyler's voice echoes at times, even though the club is small, like a reverb effect. Hamilton does a walking bass line over the beginning of "Big Ten Inch Record."

"Dream On" appears mid set, without any piano introduction. Kramer's drumming is intense during "Rats In The Cellar," he's really on top of his game here, even if others weren't. He also plays an extended drum solo to "Walk This Way" with Crespo adding a talk box vocal.

While the band is in fine form, Tyler seems to lose steam in the middle of the show. Crespo sounds a little off at the beginning of "Come Together" as Kramer starts the tune with beats, but the guitarist plays an emotional solo to end "Train Kept A Rollin'"

Stage West, Hartford, Connecticut. Thursday, June 12, 1980. King Biscuit Flower Hour radio broadcast. Sound quality: A. Audience recording. Sound quality: B-

Back In The Saddle, Mama Kin, I Wanna Know Why, Big Ten Inch Record, Dream On, Three Mile Smile, Reefer Headed Woman, Rats In The Cellar, Remember (Walking In The Sand), Lick And A Promise, Walk This Way, Same Old Song And Dance, Milk Cow Blues, Toys In The Attic, Train Kept A- Rollin'.

The edited FM recording from the band's second night at this venue was broadcast and a complete audience recording also exists. The audience recording provides a more exciting presentation, with the radio broadcast edited in a way to render the show sterile.

An example: "Back In The Saddle" somehow fails to capture its normal excitement on the FM but sounds good from the crowd.

Crespo and Tyler double up on the vocals on "Mama Kin" to good effect. Whitford gets off a great solo on "I Wanna Know Why," as Kramer's drumming is spot on throughout the tune. Hamilton does some busking again during the "Big Ten Inch Record" intro. "Dream On" sounds passionate here and features a guitar intro.

"Something off our new album, titled tits in the crib and mom it ain't my fault there's feedback," Tyler says as "Three Mile Smile" gets going as feedback can be heard on the audience, but not the FM recording.

"Rats In The Cellar" sees jamming like the old days, although this version is truncated. Hamilton's bass really stands out here; he is locked in and propels the song along, his nimble fingers setting a driving pace.

Crespo reels off an emotive solo for "Remember (Walking in The Sand)," which segues into Kramer's frenetic "Lick And A Promise" drum intro.

"Same Old Song And Dance" shows off more of Kramer's rhythmic shuffle beats, mid tune. "Milk Cow Blues" sounds snappy and vibrant on this night and Crespo and Tyler share the mic on the final verses.

"The King Biscuit Flower Hour"

AEROSMITH

6/29/80

On _____, _____,
              day   date

at _____, _____-FM
              time   station

present THE KING BISCUIT FLOWER HOUR starring AEROSMITH
recorded live in concert. This show was recorded earlier this
month at a surprise club appearance in Connecticut. Included
in the program are live versions of songs from their lastest
release, "A Night In The Ruts". Be sure to be listening to
THE KING BISCUIT FLOWER HOUR starring AEROSMITH on _____
                                                          day

at _____ right here on _____-FM.
              time   station

****

The Tunes	The Players
"Back In The Saddle Again"	Steve Tyler - Vocals
"Big 10 Inch"	Tom Hamilton - Bass guitar
"3 Mile Smile"	Jimmy Crespo - Guitar
"Reefer Headed Woman"	Joey Kramer - Drums
"Dream On"	Brad Whitford - Guitar
"Lick"
"Walk This Way"
"Milk Cow"
"Toys In The Attic"
"Train Kept A-Rolling"

June 23, 1980

Dear Program Directors:

It has come to our attention that during the
KING BISCUIT FLOWER HOUR starring AEROSMITH
scheduled for June 29, 1980, at 2:08 on Side B,
during the song "Dream On", lead singer STEVE
TYLER uses language that may offend some of
your listeners.

We're sure that you're all familiar with this
in our everyday lives, but it is inappropriate
professionally. Although it's hardly audible,
we felt you should be informed so that you may
bleep this word. The rest of the show is great
and we regret this inconvenience.

Any questions or problems, please call us.

Sincerely,

Robert Kaminsky
Director of Production
THE KING BISCUIT FLOWER HOUR

Paul Zullo
Vice President   -and-
Station Operations

Bernadette Elliott
Associate Director
Station Relations

Private's, New York City. Monday , November 3, 1980. Radio broadcast. Sound quality: B+
Come Together

The band appears on a show intended to get people to vote during the presidential election the following day. The "Come Together" arrangement is augmented by Bobby Keys on saxophone, Rick Derringer, Richie Supa, Cyrinda Tyler, Mitch Weissman (of Beetlemania) and others. Pretty good version!

GREATEST HITS SHOW

As the summer of 1980 goes quiet for Aerosmith, Columbia releases "Greatest Hits" on November 11, 1980, and by the end of the year it climbs to No. 53 on the Billboard charts. Tyler suffers injuries in a motorcycle accident in August, but by some miracle, the band plays a show to celebrate its 10th anniversary at the venue that was once known as the Boston Tea Party. Odd in that Perry is not there for the big anniversary, and that the band was in some disarray. But Aerosmith carries on.

Club Boston Boston, Boston Massachusetts. Wednesday, December 3, 1980. Radio broadcast. Sound quality: A
Rats In The Cellar, Walkin' The Dog, Lord Of The Thighs, Three Mile Smile, Reefer Headed Woman, Mother Popcorn, Think About It, Seasons Of Wither, I Wanna Know Why, Big Ten Inch Record, Walk This Way, Lick And A Promise, Milk Cow Blues, Come Together, Train Kept A-Rollin'.

Tyler gives a short interview before the show and sounds tired. The band has not played in front of a crowd for almost half a year. But they play very

179

well, even if their front man drags at points. We do get a cross section of material from its career on the solid sounding recording.

The whip-cracking "Rats In The Cellar" kicks off the proceedings. "Good evening Beantown! And the rest of America," Tyler says

The show would be recorded and blasted on stations throughout the land. "Walkin' The Dog" is second out of the chute, a tune not played since the year prior.

After a good combination of "Three Mile Smile" and "Reefer Headed Woman," "Mother Popcorn" turns up again, with Tyler referencing "old Paul's Mall," in a tip of the hat to the venue immortalized on "Live! Bootleg."

"Think About It" re-appears and is perfectly executed by Crespo, who also provides some rough-hewn backing vocals and then just about a lead vocal at its end as Tyler wilts.

A fantastic version of "Seasons Of Wither" follows, it could not have been done better. "I Wanna Know Why" is less convincing, with Tyler mumbling his way through as if he has a set of alternative lyrics, but he does not.

Tyler sings a bit of gibberish during "Walk This Way" as well, not because he is stoned (although he most certainly is) but for the hell of it.

Crespo gets in on the vocals during "Milk Cow Blues" to nice effect, with Kramer providing some cool drum fills along the way.

"About 10 years ago, we were singing nothing but blues," Tyler tells the crowd. "But then the blues had a baby and we called it rock and roll," Tyler says, quoting the Muddy Waters song. The band then kicks into "Train Kept A-Rollin'."

A good gig overall given the circumstances. It would be Whitford's last gig with Aerosmith as a band member until 1984.

Boston Garden, Boston, Massachusetts. Saturday, February 28, 1981. Audience recording. Sound quality: D
Day Tripper, The Last Time.

Perry and Tyler make a surprise appearance on stage at the Garden with Cheap Trick for the band's encore. "We found him in the bar, we hope you don't mind, Joe Perry!" says Cheap Trick's vocalist Robin Zander.

Perry trades licks with the band's guitarist Rick Nielsen, but it's all a bit hard to hear because of the poor recording.

Next, Tyler comes out for The Rolling Stones "The Last Time" and trades verses with Zander, while Perry stays on stage for the tune.

"Mr. Joe Perry, Mr. Steven Tyler!" Zander says to the excited crowd.

While they were at odds, the divide was not so severe that the Toxic Twins could not share a stage.

> When ex-Aerosmith guitarist Joe Perry came out to do battle during an encore of the Beatles' "Day Tripper," Nielson matched him histrionic lead for histrionic lead. And when Aerosmith singer Steve Tyler popped up next for a red-hot cover of the Stones' "The Last Time," the mixture of intensity and spontaneity proved a steamy brew. And I've seen Cheap Trick in top form once again.

Boston Globe March 3, 1981

181

AEROSMITH

PURE GOLD
.999

Stereo Outtakes 1975
Criteria Studios
miami, fla.

side one
take it or leave it TAKE 13
bitches brew ALTERNATE TAKE
gut bucket blues
riff and roll
side two
the jig is up
jailbait ACOUSTICAL
when the lightning strikes ALTERNATE TAKE
cry me a river TAKE 4

Recorded in Full Stereo Sound

FIRST 50 PRESSINGS ON COLORED VINYL
WITH BOOKLET. YOUR COPY NO.

RECORDS

Recording Rock In A Hard Place 1981-1982

Growing tired of the band's inactivity, Whitford exits and Jack Douglas protege Rick Dufay enters. Drugs have taken Tyler to dark, shadowy places during this period, but he somehow manages to rally and record. Crespo proves to be up to the task of writing material with the singer, and the guitarist lights a musical fire under the band with Kramer and Hamilton responding with great performances.

Rock In A Hard Place Sessions. Criteria Studios, Miami, 1982. Soundboard recording. Sound Quality: A

Take It Or Leave It (Take 13), Bitches Brew (alternate take), Gut Bucket Blues, Riff And Roll, The Jig Is Up, Jailbait, Lightning Strikes (alternate take), Joanie's Butterfly (instrumental), Cry Me A River (Take 4.)

"Take It Or Leave It" is an early version of "Bolivian Ragamuffin," with Tyler scatting over the top of it, the lyrics not fully formed, though the final vocal run is. "Bitches Brew" is an instrumental showing off Crespo's strong and relentless guitar attack.

"Gut Bucket Blues" is an instrumental of "Bolivian Ragamuffin," close to what would be on the album. This take of "Riff and Roll" is different than what appears on "Pandora's Box." An interesting take, but one could see why it didn't make the final album.

"Jig Is Up" has different lyrics, that are punctuated by the vocal, "whip it out." "Jailbait" is the most fully conceived track of the bunch here. While the music is similar to the album version, the vocal isn't. Credit Tyler for going back and making changes to the lyrics.

"Lightning Strikes" lacks the swirling keyboard intro here. The music is close to what is a final take, minus the guitar lead and the first part of Tyler's vocal. The keyboards are more toward the end on this take.

The acoustic part of "Joanie's Butterfly" is an instrumental here, as Crespo had intended. Tyler had other ideas and added lyrics later. Percussion is also on the track. The "second" electric part of the tune is also without vocals here with a longer ending.

"Cry Me A River" has more guitar at the beginning and finger snapping as well. The vocals are here, but not the final take that Tyler would later perfect. Humorously, the end features Tyler intentionally mangling the vocal, then saying, "oh fuck!"

The sessions were pressed onto the bootleg: "Pure Gold .999." The back photo features Tyler with Perry. Oops.

ROCK IN A HARD PLACE TOUR

Released August 1, 1982, the new "Rock In A Hard Place" vinyl from the reconstituted Aerosmith reaches No. 32 on the Billboard charts on October 15, 1982. "Lightning Strikes" is the designated single and pushed by MTV's play of a video of the tune and would reach No. 21 on the Billboard Mainstream Rock Tracks charts.

The band launches the tour behind the album in Bethlehem, Pennsylvania in November, and the band keeps going until May of 1983. The summer of 1983 sees a star-crossed tour of the Southwest and West. Finally, a handful of dates are played in the East at the end of the year and into early 1984.

Opening for Aerosmith will be the Pat Travers Band. The concert is scheduled to begin at 7:30 p.m. Sunday in Stabler Arena. Tickets are available at the usual area outlets. Tickets have been selling very well, according to a spokesman for Makoul Productions. Because the concert may be sold out by show time, tickets are not expected to be available at the door.

Lehigh University, Stabler Arena, Bethlehem, Pennsylvania. Sunday, November 7, 1982. Audience recording. Sound quality: C

Back In The Saddle, Big Ten Inch Record, Three Mile Smile, Reefer Headed Woman, Lord Of The Thighs, Bolivian Ragamuffin, Lick And A Promise, Jig Is Up, Jailbait, Mama Kin, Sweet Emotion, Dream On,

Rock In A Hard Place (Cheshire Cat), Lightning Strikes, Walk This Way, Same Old Song And Dance, Milk Cow Blues, Toys In The Attic, Train Kept A-Rollin'.

It's a new era, but some things stay the same: The "Psycho" theme opens the gig as the band then blasts "Back In The Saddle" into the arena, the song's title having more meaning as the new band launches live.

"Big Ten Inch Record" has a shorter than usual Tyler harmonica intro, while Dufay lights a fire with a wickedly wild solo on the song. The song now features one guitar solo instead of two, a change. Bobby Mayo joins the tour and his keyboards stand out as well. Mayo would get a lot of air time during the tour and delivered every night.

"Lehigh! How high? Lehigh!" Tyler says, referring to the venue location. The Crespo/Dufay team bring some new energy to the old songs and jam nicely on "Lord Of The Thighs."

The first ever live "Bolivian Ragamuffin" comes off well and becomes the first tune off "Rock In A Hard Place" played on stage.

One of the most swagger-filled Aerosmith songs ever, "Jig Is Up," comes off strong as does "Jailbait," one of the hardest tunes ever penned by the band. These new songs are adding a new air to the stage show. It's too bad they were lopped off one by one as the tour continued.

Tyler misses the first line of "Jailbait," but soon joins in as the band verges on spinning out of control, fueled on drugs and opening night adrenaline. "Slow it down!" Tyler says mid song to try to halt the frantic pace, but it does little good! "Sweet Emotion" returns to the setlist, hard to believe it was ever dropped.

"Rock In A Hard Place (Cheshire Cat)" is played faithfully to the album version and comes off as a piece of cool on this hot night. Tyler provides a vocal lightning strike to kick off "Lightning Strikes," the Richie Supa song that was getting good airplay on MTV, despite revisionist history that asserts the video never got into rotation.

For all the stories about Dufay's erratic behavior on and offstage, he is quite a good player, getting off some agreeable opening notes to "Same Old Song And Dance." At the end of the tune, Hamilton and Mayo dominate the soundscape as though the guitarists are not on stage.

Crespo and Dufay trade solos in "Milk Cow Blues" matching intensities in different ways. "Toys In The Attic" ends the set, and the Stabler Arena crowd screams its collective lungs out to get the band back on stage for "Train Kept A-Rollin'." It has been a great first night of the tour.

The Centrum, Worcester, Massachusetts. Thursday, November 11, 1982. Audience recording. Sound quality: D
Back In The Saddle, Big Ten Inch Record, Three Mile Smile, Reefer Headed Woman, Lord Of The Thighs, Bolivian Ragamuffin, Lick And A Promise, Jig Is Up, Jailbait, Mama Kin, Sweet Emotion, Dream On, Rock In A Hard Place (Cheshire Cat), Lightning Strikes, Walk This Way, Same Old Song And Dance, Milk Cow Blues, Toys In The Attic, Train Kept A-Rollin'.

The band is home and the fans are accepting of the re-tooled band, cheering loudly throughout the night creating a din that permeates the recording.

Tyler's harmonica during "Big Ten Inch Record" gets a massive response, as the crowd responds to their hero, in the flesh.

"Reefer Headed Woman" features mournful harmonica playing by Tyler. The opening notes of "Dream On" (played by Mayo here) are again greeted with pure excitement from the throng.

"Rock In A Hard Place (Cheshire Cat)" is almost stopped by Tyler mid song as something seems to be thrown on stage. But Kramer keeps the beat going and Tyler re-starts his vocals.

"Drugs in the attic" is a verse inside "Toys In The Attic" and a truism for the band.

In his autobiography, Tyler calls going out on the "Rock In A Hard Place" tour a "disaster." But don't go back in time and tell that to the 12,000 rockers at The Centrum, who are having the time of their lives as the band puts on a great show.

The Boston Globe even gave a stellar review (see next page) of the gig and urged readers not to miss the show coming up five days later at the same venue.

That show would not go as well!

Aerosmith is back with a vengeance

REVIEW | MUSIC

AEROSMITH - In concert with Pat Travers and Rose Tattoo at the Centrum Thursday.

By Steve Morse
Globe Staff

WORCESTER – As brash as ever, Aerosmith has boasted of returning with a bang after a two-year absence from the big arenas. They've sounded almost too cocky – especially in view of their sludgy, scattershot days of old – but they backed up their boast with a convincing thunderclap of a show Thursday.

Rather than lapse into murky metallic sound, inaudible lyrics and clumsy musicianship, which were pitfalls in the past, they shed their old skin and played unexpectedly clear, barnburning rock 'n' roll.

There was plenty of grinding pelvic rock – an old Aerosmith trademark – but this time the rock was much sharper, more lively and more rhythmic. It was dance music, not Quaalude Muzak.

The reasons for the vast improvement were several – fresh personnel (new guitarists Jimmy Crespo and Rick Dufay are flashy but electrifying); time spent in rehearsal (two months rather than the few days of prior tours); and a solid recommitment from charter members Tom Hamilton on bass, Joey Kramer on drums and, most emphatically, Steven Tyler on lead vocals.

Looking his androgynous self in a purple Edwardian dandy suit with flowing tails, Tyler, fully recovered from a motorcycle accident, whipped the band into one peak after another. Thanks to a superb sound system that boomed

Steven Tyler at full tilt
PHOTO BY MICHELE McDONALD

the music but did not distort it, Tyler was audible on every song, whether belting his witchy tales of hedonism, scratching out a blues phrase or throwing in soulful hysteria on the back-to-back "Sweet Emotion" and "Dream On," two of the band's best-known hits which came midway through and prepped the capacity 13,500 crowd for a savage stretch drive.

But Tyler was hardly the night's only focus. Crespo's rapid-fire slide guitar riffs were galvanizing (he's a much cleaner player than former axeman Joe Perry), as was Dufay's crunching rhythm guitar and not infrequent lead licks of

his own. Dufay was also a great crowd-pleaser, stalking the stage with a wireless guitar, spinning around and often challenging the other musicians in face-to-face duals.

Songs were chosen from every phase of the band's 12-year career. Oldies were raved up considerably from the appropriate opener "Back in the Saddle" to an all-out "Walk This Way," while new ones leapt out of the speakers with more intensity than the new album "Rock in a Hard Place" would indicate.

Regardless of how skeptics view the band's machismo (there were no feminists in this crowd, that's for sure), Aerosmith put on the finest high-energy display since AC/DC. Hard rock lovers are urged to scoot out to Worcester for a repeat show Tuesday, or others in Providence Thursday and Portland Friday.

The Pat Travers Band was by far the best of the two warmup acts. Guitar hero Travers exhibited a night-to-day improvement from his desultory opening stint for Rainbow two years ago. No longer with a power trio, Travers had a new band (keyboards and harmonica were added for more of a J. Geils feel) and a new versatility.

Rose Tattoo, making their debut from Australia, were a sad letdown. Their three albums, especially the first two, reveal a fiery working-class band which sings graphically about survival on the streets. But they got off to a bad start Thursday as singer Angry Anderson (a Mickey Rooney with muscles) overreacted to debris thrown from the crowd and began insulting everyone.

Since the group, with two new members, also was not as good as the band on the old records, it made for a bleak scene.

Boston Globe review of the November 11, 1982 show.

The Centrum, Worcester, Massachusetts. Tuesday, November 16, 1982. Audience recording. Sound quality: C+

Back In The Saddle, Big Ten Inch Record, Mama Kin, Three Mile Smile, Reefer Headed Woman, Lord Of The Thighs, Rock In A Hard Place (Cheshire Cat), Bolivian Ragamuffin, Lick And A Promise, Jig Is Up,

Jailbait, Sweet Emotion, Dream On, Lightning Strikes, Walk This Way, Toys In The Attic.

Great atmospheric recording on what would prove to be an odd night for the band, and specifically Mr. Tyler. The band would not finish the gig as intended. Joe Perry turned up before this gig and snorted heroin with Tyler, according to lore.

There is a screw up during "Big Ten Inch Record" as the band gets lost midway through the song. And things would get worse.

"Three Mile Smile" has a tentative opening. There begins to be gaps between songs met with silence from the stage, though the band soldiers on as the setlist is changed somewhat from earlier gigs on the tour.

"Jailbait" ends with a superb jam, but by the time "Dream On" is played Tyler can barely be heard on stage. After stumbling his way through "Lightning Strikes," "Walk This Way" starts as an instrumental as Tyler can't seem to get to the mic.

Finally, Tyler appears, but sings sporadically. Sensing a problem with Tyler, Kramer starts the beat to "Toys In The Attic" as soon as "Walk This Way" ends. But Tyler says "Goodnight!" and then collapses. The band continues "Toys In The Attic" as a two-minute instrumental before ending the show. The crowd groans but doesn't quite know what to do and they shuffle out of the venue.

Tyler collapses on stage

WORCESTER – Aerosmith lead singer Steven Tyler collapsed on stage at the Centrum Tuesday night, 75 minutes into the band's concert.

Aerosmith completed playing the ballad "Dream On" and began to play the rocker "Toys in the Attic" when Tyler collapsed. He was carried off, the band left the stage, the lights went on, and no explanation was given.

Band spokeswoman Leah Grammatica said yesterday that Tyler had suffered food poisoning. She added that he is well now and Aerosmith will continue with their tour.

– JIM SULLIVAN

Boston Globe

189

Civic Center, Hartford, Connecticut. Thursday, November 18, 1982. Audience recording. Sound quality: C

Back In The Saddle, Big Ten Inch Record, Three Mile Smile, Reefer Headed Woman, Lord Of The Thighs, Bolivian Ragamuffin, Lick And A Promise, Jig Is Up, Jailbait, Mama Kin, Sweet Emotion, Dream On, Rock In A Hard Place (Cheshire Cat), Lightning Strikes, Walk This Way, Same Old Song And Dance, Milk Cow Blues, Toys In The Attic, Train Kept A-Rollin'.

Tyler's troubles two days earlier are erased and the band puts on a sparkling gig. Crespo muscles a strong solo during "Back In The Saddle," grinding out the notes from his guitar in a most exciting and physical way. The music is *heavy*. "Big Ten Inch Record" has no harmonica intro on this night, a real oddity.

The cool swagger of "Jig is Up" is followed by the frantic "Jailbait" played at an almost too fast pace again. Pure adrenaline!

These early "Rock In A Hard Place" gigs feature one song segueing into another, with Tyler having very little interaction with the audience.

Tyler makes up new lyrics to "Sweet Emotion" on the spot, his mind as sharp as ever.

"Radio has been playing a lot of Aerosmith lately, yeah? And do you like it? Do you really like it? All right," says Tyler as the keyboards sound for "Lightning Strikes."

"Milk Cow Blues" features scat vocals from Tyler as the climax of the song builds and comes to an end.

Cumberland Civic Center, Portland, Maine. Friday, November 19, 1982. Audience recording. Sound quality: C+

Back In The Saddle, Big Ten Inch Record, Three Mile Smile, Reefer Headed Woman, Lord Of The Thighs, Bolivian Ragamuffin, Lick And A Promise, Jig Is Up, Jailbait, Mama Kin, Sweet Emotion, Dream On, Rock In A Hard Place (Cheshire Cat), Lightning Strikes, Walk This Way, Same Old Song And Dance, Milk Cow Blues, Toys In The Attic, Train Kept A-Rollin'.

A very workman-like "Back In The Saddle" opens the show, which will be another strong showing for the band. "Shades of castration!" Tyler says after

"Big Ten Inch Record." Then, "Something old, something new, something old? Something old," as the band breaks into "Three Mile Smile."

Tyler gets a great "yelling cat" sound effect during "Rock In A Hard Place (Cheshire Cat)" followed by signature whistling by the singer.

Tyler announces, "Lightning Strikes," but then the band goes into the last known live version of "Bolivian Ragamuffin," which would be the first "Rock In A Hard Place" tune to get the ax from the setlist. The song is executed perfectly, Tyler rapping the vocals as smooth as could be. It has intricate outro drumming by Kramer, with Tyler scatting across the top.

It would be nice to hear one of these early "Rock In A Hard Place" shows in pristine quality, they are a hoot. Crespo burns up "Jailbait" yet again, riffing like mad. Even Tyler acknowledges the fretwork at the end: "For your entertainment: Mr. James Crespo!" Indeed!

Hamilton begins to ponder "Sweet Emotion" on his bass. Then Tyler says oddly: "Someone requested this song tonight. I don't know who it was, because we don't particularly like this song. But someone requested it."

"How come you are so good tonight!" Tyler says after "Sweet Emotion" in appreciation of the warm reception from the Portland crowd. Kramer plays an elongated drum intro to "Walk This Way," maybe as a cover until all of the band is ready to go.

Dufay plays some smooth descending riffs during the beginning of "Same Old Song And Dance." "Milk Cow Blues" features Tyler speaking some of the beginning lyrics, an interesting effect. The song is relaxed and jam like, with Tyler and Crespo doing a little call and response to each other mid song. Mayo gets some cool keyboards in along the way too, to which Tyler says: "Did you hear that shit!" Maybe Aerosmith at its most relaxed on stage.

During the finale, Crespo gets off on a long solo, firing notes all over the arena, really letting loose. A brilliant way to end the fabulous gig.

Rosemont Horizon, Chicago, Illinois. Wednesday, November 24, 1982. Audience recording. Sound quality: C+

Back In The Saddle, Big Ten Inch Record, Three Mile Smile, Reefer Headed Woman, Lord Of The Thighs, Lick And A Promise, Jig Is Up,

Jailbait, Mama Kin, Sweet Emotion, Dream On, Rock In A Hard Place (Cheshire Cat), Lightning Strikes, Walk This Way, Same Old Song And Dance, Milk Cow Blues, Toys In The Attic, Train Kept A Rollin'.

A strong audience recording, although the vocals are sometimes lost in the mix. The recording does highlight just how tight the band was at this point in the tour.

"You want it, so we are going to do it," Tyler says before "Dream On," apparently hearing calls for the tune from the front row. The band does have a little trouble getting back into the rhythm after the break in the middle of "Lightning Strikes."

Dufay has some strong vibrato at the beginning of "Same Old Song And Dance." He shows more of his flash playing as the song continues. He is really the fire to Crespo's cool, calculating ice. The contrasting formula made the band work during this period. They deserve a lot of credit for keeping the caliber of the Aerosmith guitars at an elevated level under less than ideal circumstances.

Mayo jams out again on "Milk Cow Blues" and gets a shout out from Tyler.

The Aerosmith concert, with Pat Travers and Rose Tattoo, begins at 8 tonight at Market Square Arena. General admission tickets are $9.50 and the doors will open at 6:30.

Market Square Arena, Indianapolis, Indiana. Saturday, December 4, 1982. Soundboard recording. Sound quality: B

Back In The Saddle, Big Ten Inch Record, Three Mile Smile, Reefer Headed Woman, Rock In A Hard Place (Cheshire Cat), Lord Of The Thighs, Lick And A Promise, Jig Is Up, Sweet Emotion, Dream On, Lightning Strikes, Walk This Way, Milk Cow Blues, Toys In The Attic, Train Kept A-Rollin'.

A show with a lot of personality, courtesy of Mr. Tyler. It's obvious he is high, but he's having a blast and it all leads to a rollicking great time. He is much more loquacious than at the start of the tour. It's all caught on a challenged, but not bad sounding soundboard recording. There was also a taper in the crowd, and that recording "breathes" a little more, but the soundboard is more complete and a more enjoyable listen.

192

"Back In The Saddle" starts off in a menacing way, the guitar players really bringing it. Old pal Richie Supa must be around as Tyler references him a few times, including before his harmonica into "Big Ten Inch Record." "Watch this Richie," Tyler says before blowing his harp. Dufay knocks off one of his wild solos during the song. He provided the most energetic guitar playing the band ever had.

"Right George? Uh huh, fuck you buddy," Tyler says in a joking way, talking to one of the roadies. Then: "We are going to do one of our first political songs. It's about breast cancer...no, it's about, uh...It's called 'Three Mile Smile.'" The intro is loud and crunchy! Tyler starts to talk the lyrics "OPEC boys you went too far, Lucy...Lucy..." That segues into "Reefer Headed Woman." After Tyler sings the first verses, he says, "Ain't that right, Bobby Joe Mayo..." as he addresses the band's keyboard player. For his part, Mayo adds some great piano, filling out the tune. He is a great addition to the touring band, really fitting the sound.

As Kramer starts out the beat to "Lord Of The Thighs," Tyler yells to the drummer, "Subtle! Subtle! Subtle!" Then as he gets his lyrics going, Tyler sings, "Oh Lord, my god, what the *fuck* do we have here." Dufay and Crespo get into a guitar battle during the song, Dufay playing some great ascending riffs. "I am the lord of your nose," Tyler sings. As Crespo massages a single note, Tyler joins him vocally, a nice moment.

Kramer starts in on "Lick And A Promise" and there are more humorous ramblings from Tyler: "Fuck you, what do you know?" He works in "James Crespo" into the lyrics as well. Oddly, Crespo plays a little of "First Call" – the little tune used before horse races – as Perry had done in Tokyo on January 31, 1977. A coincidence, unless Crespo has that tape too!

He then gets into a super funky "Jig Is Up," the last live airing caught on tape as the "Rock In A Hard Place" tunes continue to be shaved off one by one as the tour progresses. Kramer shows off his drumming after the guitar intro and Dufay faithfully holds down the song's rhythm guitar as Crespo solos away.

"Someone must have cut the toot tonight, eh?" Tyler says before "Sweet Emotion." Then: "Tom wants to tell you something and so does Terry (Hamilton's wife.)" Then, "Anybody seen my bottle on the stage?" is Tyler's not so eloquent intro to "Dream On."

Kramer pounds his bass drum more than 40 times as the band gets into the finale, "Train Kept A-Rollin'" in which Tyler wishes happy birthday to a "Mr. Rengo," whomever that may be, as Crespo solos into the night to bring the gig to a close.

Civic Center, Huntington, West Virginia. Sunday, December 12, 1982. "Classics Live" album.

Sweet Emotion.

The band rents the Huntington Civic Center for December 11 and 12. The main gig is on the 11th. The following day contest winners gathered at the Huntington Civic Center for filming of 3-D videos.

"Bolivian Ragamuffin," "Bitches Brew" and "Sweet Emotion" were filmed. The videos premiered May 3, 1983 at New York City's Studio 54 and then vanished. But the audio for "Sweet Emotion" was then used for "Classics Live" and is likely a mix of live and studio recordings.

Joe Freeman Coliseum, San Antonio, Texas. Thursday, December 30, 1982. Soundboard recording. Sound quality: A

Back In The Saddle, Mama Kin, Big Ten Inch Record, Three Mile Smile, Reefer Headed Woman, Rock In A Hard Place (Cheshire Cat), Lord Of The Thighs, Lick And A Promise, Sweet Emotion, Dream On, Lightning Strikes, Walk This Way, Milk Cow Blues, Toys In The Attic, Train Kept A-Rollin.

Great soundboard recording of this night. Cool to hear the band testing out their instruments as the "Psycho" theme tape plays to the crowd.

After "Back In The Saddle," Tyler teases Crespo, who apparently is having some trouble with his guitar. "Come on, Jimmy! Get that rig working! C'mon baby! C'mon baby, c'mon! C'mon!" Then you can hear Crespo say, "I'm getting there," then laughing. These strong recordings bring out the instruments more, including Hamilton's fine bass work that is sometimes lost in the low-fidelity audience recordings.

Tyler is in fine spirits on this night, really enjoying himself on stage. "All in a day's work!" Tyler says after "Big Ten Inch Record." "Just like your Alamo, we have some political shit going on here. Aerosmith's first and only political song we ever wrote. It's about looking your best." Tyler then announces the song's title (almost) in parts as the song begins: "Three," "Mile," "Stretch Those Lips!"

"Reefer Headed Woman" gets a really good treatment on this night, a super bluesy version in the South. Tyler yells some random things during the tune, including, "You wanna dance?" Crespo really bends some notes here, ala Jimmy Page on "You Shook Me," as he shows sometimes less is more. Tyler ends the song with some high-pitched vocals and Crespo shakes a note effectively.

On "Rock In A Hard Place (Cheshire Cat)," Tyler slips "Dufay" into the lyrics. Dufay gets into some harmonics and nice finger picking during "Lord Of The Thighs." "Overlay Dufay!" Tyler says afterword in admiration.

Kramer does an extended intro to "Lick And A Promise," really showing off his chops. Tyler sneaks a "Jimmy Crespo" reference into "Sweet Emotion." Tyler has a little fun with the "Dream On" lyric: "Dream on, dream, dream on until your jeans turn blue!"

"Spotlight on Mayo!" Tyler says as "Lightning Strikes" starts and the singer provides vocal lightning at the beginning and end of the song. A loose and free form "Milk Cow Blues' has Tyler laughing and scatting, the band again at its most relaxed. Kramer gets his stand-alone solo back here, his first recorded since the Japan 1977 tour.

Crespo bends some notes on the way out of The Alamo on "Train Kept A Rollin'," but comes to a halt at one point. Tyler would jump behind Kramer's kit and bang the drums on the tour, which he does here, before Crespo finishes with a flurry.

● Aerosmith, the group with six albums in platinum and seven in gold and hefty Mainland attendance records, performs at 8 p.m. at the Blaisdell Arena. Tickets are $12.50 and $11 and are on sale at the Blaisdell box office and all STAR ticket outlets.

Blaisdell Arena, Honolulu, Hawaii. Tuesday, January 4, 1983. Soundboard recording. Sound quality: A

Back In The Saddle, Mama Kin, Big Ten Inch Record, Three Mile Smile, Reefer Headed Woman, Rock In A Hard Place (Cheshire Cat), Lord Of The Thighs, Lick And A Promise, Sweet Emotion, Dream On, Lightning Strikes, Walk This Way, Milk Cow Blues, Toys In The Attic, Train Kept A Rollin'.

A great soundboard recording of this night. Aerosmith has really become the Steve Tyler Band to a large extent through the sheer force of his large personality. He is up to the task, more entertaining than ever.

He switches the lyrics on "Back In The Saddle" to the more inclusive "*We're* baaaack." Crespo helps provide some help with vocals on "Mama Kin."

"Hey, I don't know what's going on over there but you're missing something," Tyler says during the "Big Ten Inch Record" intro, likely referring to combatants in the crowd. Tyler inserts a bit of Fleetwood Mac's "Oh Well": "Don't ask me what I think of you, I might not give you the answer you want me to." Crespo gets a solo early in the tune, an addition to how it has been played on the tour. Mayo really gets into his boogie piano here, followed by Dufay's slick solo. Quite impressive.

Something gets unplugged on stage accidentally after the song. "Don't worry, that happens all the time," Tyler quips. "But does this happen all the time (Aerosmith playing Hawaii)? Bet your ass it don't. I wanna apologize, we wanna apologize for being away so long." As he waits for the on-stage repair, Tyler then addresses people sitting behind the stage.

"I want to know what's with the people back here. Can you hear us? I can't hear you. Ooohhh doggie! So, I'm not wasting my time when I sing to you," he says, as the band kicks into "Three Mile Smile." He then adjusts the song's lyrics for Hawaii. "Takin' a walk in the warm Kona sun." A nice touch. Crespo bends out a loud solo, cutting through the rhythm section.

Firecrackers get tossed on the stage in the middle of "Lord Of The Thighs" and Tyler is none to happy. "We're gonna bring it way down here, shit," he tells the band, but they continue on. "Hey, was that way down?" Tyler asks his mates. "I said we're gonna bring it way down here."

Then Tyler continues: "Hey you know what man? One of you motherfuckers is an asshole this big. I'll tell you one thing...The next motherfucker who throws a firecracker up here, we are not going to do anything to you, shit, we ain't violent," Tyler says, who then shushes Dufay who starts to play. "But the people around you motherfucker who throws it, is going to eat your face off," he says to the cheering crowd. "Then throw it up here and we'll trade it in for some cocaine or something. So it doesn't hurt him, we'll put the cocaine on his face. That's all, because we don't do that stuff. For medicinal purposes only." The rant was not unexpected given the band had been dodging missiles on stage for a decade.

Tyler wasn't finished as he quiets the band again. "There's something else that is real important and it's been bothering me all night. For some ungodly reason, see the bass player over here is Tom Hamilton, it's his birthday, so I'd like to change the key..." as Tyler leads the crowd through "Happy Birthday" with the band playing along. To the band's credit they segue right back into "Lord Of The Thighs" without missing a beat.

During the "Lightning Strikes" keyboard intro, Dufay plays some discordant scratch notes on his guitar. "Hey, are we running into all sorts of overtime Mr. Baptista?" Tyler asks his road manager during "Milk Cow Blues." "Oh, shit that will cost you another 2,500 dollars. How are we doing? Are we safe?" The band then proceeds to play a 20-minute version of the song, one of the longest recorded live pieces in the band's history. It's full of cool loose jams and some sweet country finger picking by Crespo in one passage. Mayo adds in his piano too, going back to "Happy Birthday" briefly. It's almost AeroJazz at some points.

"Toys In The Attic" gets more Crespo vocals. Kramer is ready to start "Train Kept A Rollin'," but no one else is. Finally, the band jumps in to end the interesting gig. During the tune, Tyler sticks his mic into the crowd for the fans to sing "all night long!"

seem so . . . There were a lot of sickos throwing firecrackers into the crowd at the Aerosmith concert at the Blaisdell arena Tues. night, says **Cammy Coble**.

Long Beach Arena, Long Beach, California. Thursday, January 6, 1983. Audience recording. Sound quality: D

Back In The Saddle, Mama Kin, Big Ten Inch Record, Three Mile Smile, Reefer Headed Woman, Rock In A Hard Place (Cheshire Cat), Lord Of The Thighs, Lick And A Promise, Sweet Emotion, Dream On, Lightning Strikes, Walk This Way, Milk Cow Blues, Toys In The Attic (fragment.)

197

The Long Beach Arena is in full uproar as the lights go out, "Tyler, yaaaa!" someone yells in the crowd as the "Psycho" theme plays out over the mass.

The band kicks into "Back In The Saddle" to a dark arena and finally the lights go on and there is Tyler, "I'm baaaaack." and the crowd is in complete delirium.

Aerosmith's Steve Tyler is still striking his rock-star poses.

"It's been a long time, ain't it motherfucker," Tyler says after "Big Ten Inch Record." "We apologize for that." The band jumps into "Three Mile Smile" before Tyler can properly give the song title, so he does it in staccato fashion over the intro: "Three. Mile. Smile." The singer gives another great cat call during "Rock In A Hard Place (Cheshire Cat)." Crespo gets ear-ringing feedback going during "Lord Of The Thighs."

The crowd recognizes the "Lightning Strikes" intro from the new album and MTV play, and begins calling out the song's name in celebration. Another free-form "Milk Cow Blues" gets going with Tyler calling out Mayo's name. The recording ends during "Toys In The Attic" with the taper asking "you wanna go backstage?" as he must have shut off his recorder as he and his pal made their move.

198

**Coliseum Arena, Oakland, California. Friday, January 7, 1983.
Audience recording. Sound quality: C**

*Back In The Saddle, Mama Kin, Big Ten Inch Record, Three Mile Smile,
Reefer Headed Woman, Rock In A Hard Place (Cheshire Cat), Lord Of The
Thighs, Lick And A Promise, Sweet Emotion, Dream On, Lightning Strikes,
Walk This Way, Milk Cow Blues, Toys In The Attic, Train Kept A-Rollin'.*

Great build up to this show as the "Psycho" theme plays with 14,000 souls
in attendance, then the lights go out, and Tyler appears in all his rock and
roll glory, a sight to behold! It seems en masse, the crowd joins Tyler with
the first line, "I'm Baaaack!" as "Back In The Saddle" starts the night and
the party begins.

"Oakland, momma! I didn't think you'd still be here!" Tyler exclaims after
"Big Ten Inch Record." "Did you miss us? How do you like the boys?"
Then it's onto "Three Mile Smile." "Mr. Jimmy!" Tyler says before Crespo
lays out his solo during "Reefer Headed Woman," which fills every inch of
the arena. Kramer's drumming behind him is just as intense.

Dufay again proves his mettle during "Lord Of The Thighs," driving the
fans into a frenzy. "Oh yeah?" Tyler says after the solo. "Mr. Rick Dufay,"
the singer says in acknowledgment, maybe surprised that "The Doof" could
really bring it onstage.

"The one, the only, Mr. Rimshot himself," Tyler says of Kramer as he
bangs out the intro into "Lick And A Promise." Tyler sings "Johnny come
lately on a Saturday night, his poor momma pacing the floor, he grabbed a
guitar and a couple of *queers*" at which point Tyler grabs Dufay around the
neck, as Dufay shakes his head in disagreement.

Tyler has a weird intro into "Sweet Emotion:" "We're going to do a
controversial song here. It seems as though, we have been told...correct me
if I'm wrong, it seems as though they...play a lot of (this) song, but they don't
play any of the other shit. Would you like to tell me why? Cause this one
ain't bad, you be the judge" as Hamilton plays the famous introduction.

"Dream On" is played superbly and fades out to the din of firecrackers in
the distance. "Lightning Strikes'" ominous keyboards then emerge in an all
too cool way. The guitars are locked in unison during the song, like an army
marching.

During "Milk Cow Blues" Tyler starts in on his harmonica. "Sounds kinda straight, don't it? Tyler says. "Let me sloppy this up a bit," as he plays more soulfully as he provides some vocalizations along the way. Mayo gets a Tyler intro again and Kramer sets a beat for the keyboard player who plays away into the darkened arena. After "Toys In The Attic," the crowd howls for an encore.

"Let me tell you something baby, you people, you've been the hottest crowd to fill this stadium in a long time...express yourselves!" Tyler says as the band launches into "Train Kept A-Rollin" in which Tyler gets behind the drum kit again for a spell. A wonderfully high-energy show in front of an Aero-ravenous Bay Area crowd.

```
OCB 5                BILL GRAHAM PRESENTS
5893      event      OAKLAND COLISEUM ARENA
  21
GA    ADULT              AEROSMITH
CAS   BUL51
GEN   11.50     FRI JAN 7 1983 8:00 PM
  1A                                ADULT
ADM  B10DEC  GA        GA-5158      11.50
```

McNichols Arena, Denver, Colorado. Tuesday, January 11, 1983. Audience recording. Sound quality: C

Back In The Saddle, Mama Kin, Big Ten Inch Record, Three Mile Smile, Reefer Headed Woman, Rock In A Hard Place (Cheshire Cat), Lord Of The Thighs, Lick And A Promise (partial), Dream On, Lightning Strikes, Walk This Way, Milk Cow Blues, Toys In The Attic, Train Kept A-Rollin'.

During the opener, "Back In The Saddle," Kramer does a trio of drum rolls during the song, drumming outside the box. "We are going to do a song we did way back when, a Yardbirds rendition...politically orientated..." Tyler says, introducing "Three Mile Smile."

During "Lightning Strikes" Tyler again provides the vocal lightning effect. The crowd is subdued compared to earlier gigs, and that's not lost on Tyler. "It took you this long to get up?" he says during "Milk Cow Blues."

Kramer pounds out a seeming motor-propelled drum frenzy at the end of the tune that's so intense, it distorts the recording. We now know why he tapes his hands! Tyler jumps behind the drums again during "Train Kept A-Rollin'" as the show concludes.

Tingley Coliseum, Albuquerque, New Mexico. Thursday, January 13, 1983. Audience recording. Sound quality: D

Back In The Saddle, Mama Kin, Big Ten Inch Record, Three Mile Smile, Reefer Headed Woman, Rock In A Hard Place (Cheshire Cat), Lord Of The Thighs, Lick And A Promise, Sweet Emotion, Dream On, Lightning Strikes, Walk This Way, Milk Cow Blues, Toys In The Attic, Train Kept A-Rollin'.

Tyler inserts a little of Fleetwood Mac's "Oh Well" into "Big Ten Inch Record" again as he did in Honolulu. The bit would find a new place by the next recorded show.

"Hey Albuquerque, how's your ass tonight? How's your heads tonight? I said, how's your heads tonight? Well, that's good," Tyler says to cheers. There is a little trouble at the start of "Three Mile Smile" as one of the guitars craps out, but the issue is resolved quickly as the song continues.

The "Lord Of The Thighs" jam is very cohesive on this night, with Crespo and Dufay feeling more comfortable with each other as they continue to play together. The version rivals the best night of the Perry/Whitford team.

"When's the last time a band like this has played for you!" Tyler, full of bravado, tells the crowd before "Sweet Emotion." Crespo fires off a great string of notes to play the song out.

"I'll tell you what, you're one of the best audiences we played to in the last week," Tyler says in appreciation. "The truth!" The crowd screams in approval during the "Albuquerque" reference during "Train Kept A-Rollin'."

Convention Center, Las Vegas, Nevada. Sunday, January 16, 1983. Audience recording. Sound quality: D

Back In The Saddle, Mama Kin, Big Ten Inch Record, Three Mile Smile, Reefer Headed Woman, Rock In A Hard Place (Cheshire Cat), Lord Of The Thighs, Lick And A Promise, Sweet Emotion, Dream On, Lightning Strikes, Walk This Way, Milk Cow Blues, Toys In The Attic, Train Kept A-Rollin'.

One of those tapes that went missing for decades but was unearthed by collector Rob Phaneuf. His impressions of the show and recording:

"I got the Vegas 83 show, finally! I'm listening for the first time right NOW! There's no speed flux, but the taper moves through the crowd A LOT, meaning the sound keeps changing. However, a GREAT version of 'Thighs,' and Tyler is in good form!! And they do ROCK IN A HARD PLACE (Cheshire Cat.) I'm liking it a lot, despite all the shortcomings!!

"Definitely an odd one, though! That taper doesn't stop moving. And on side 2, the recording sounds worse than side 1. 'Dream On' cuts over sides, and you can hear a big drop in quality. It slowly 'kind of' makes its way back over the next few songs. In 'Milk Cow Blues' the taper is literally running through the hallways of the auditorium, it sounds like!!! And then goes back into the crowd. Weird. But cool, I guess. It's a journey! Lol.

"During Joey's drum solo there's an EXTREMELY ANNOYING guy near the taper barking like a dog! I swear to F'n god! This guy does NOT stop. It gets to the point of 'how much of this can I take.' LOL! Thankfully he shuts up when the music starts again. but still barks between songs. Must've been some good LSD that kid was on...jeez."

Met Center, Minneapolis, Minnesota. Friday, January 28, 1983. Audience recording. Sound quality: D

Back In The Saddle, Mama Kin, Big Ten Inch Record, Three Mile Smile, Reefer Headed Woman, Rock In A Hard Place (Cheshire Cat), Lord Of The Thighs, Lick And A Promise, Sweet Emotion, Dream On, Lightning Strikes, Walk This Way, Milk Cow Blues, Toys In The Attic, Train Kept A-Rollin'.

The AM radio-like recording really brings out the guitars here. Those guitars on "Back In The Saddle" are really biting. The guitars are picked up so well during "Mama Kin," the sound of the chord changes can be heard as fingers move along the strings.

Crespo's guitar sounds like an angry bee during "Lord Of The Thighs." Dufay has some fun during "Lick And A Promise" plucking his guitar during the verse.

Tyler now inserts Fleetwood Mac's "Oh Well" into the beginning of "Sweet Emotion": "Can't help about the shape I'm in, singing blurry and my legs are thin. Don't ask me what I think of you, I might not give you the answer you want me to..." as he is joined by the band with some short riffs and drumming before Hamilton starts in on the opening notes. The high end recording also highlights the guitar players picking their way through "Walk This Way."

There is some great playing throughout "Milk Cow Blues." On the surface, this jam could be written off as a lazy way to kill off 10 minutes at the end of the gig. But each performance is unique. Dufay does some interesting Lynyrd Skynyrd-type noodling towards its end. An interesting show.

Doors tomorrow . . . Boston's Aerosmith, who are completing a national tour, have added a Feb. 11 Springfield Civic Center concert to their itinerary, but still no word on a rumored Boston date . . .

Civic Center, Springfield, Massachusetts. Friday, February 11, 1983. Audience recording. Sound quality: C

Back In The Saddle, Mama Kin, Big Ten Inch Record, Three Mile Smile, Reefer Headed Woman, Rock In A Hard Place (Cheshire Cat), Lord Of The Thighs, Lick And A Promise, Sweet Emotion, Dream On, Lightning Strikes, Walk This Way, Milk Cow Blues, Toys In The Attic, Train Kept A-Rollin'.

The band is late to the stage on this night. As "Back In The Saddle" ends, Kramer starts to play the first beats to "Big Ten Inch Record" but catches himself.

"Sorry for making you wait. We had a little drizzle in our gizzle," Tyler says way before Snoop Dog was known. "We'll make it up to you, we'll make it up to you," the singer says as the band starts "Mama Kin."

Hamilton does a little bass work on the "Big Ten Inch Record" intro before Tyler starts in with his harmonica as the guitar players add some isolated notes. Someone is lighting firecrackers intermittently during the gig.

"We're going to bring back some oldies but goodies for you," Tyler says as Kramer works his way into "Lick And A Promise."

203

"It's that time in the set when you gotta dig into the other pocket, right? The other pocket," as Tyler reaches for his stash before "Sweet Emotion" and recites the "Oh Well" lyrics. The band stumbles on the end of the song and Tyler covers it by announcing the song title as it comes to an end.

Tyler plays some emotive keyboard along with Dufay on guitar as "Dream On" begins, with the singer re-assuming the piano intro from Mayo.

"Milk Cow Blues" again is a long jam, with Tyler scatting and Mayo playing some honky tonk piano along the way. The Kramer solo is excised by the taper on this night.

We hear Tyler count in "Toys In The Attic" "1, 2, 3, 4. 1, 2, 3, 4." Dufay plays some descending notes in the song, giving it a new flavor. The crowd digs the show, chanting "Aerosmith! Aerosmith! Aerosmith!" as they wait for the finale.

WAPP

WELCOMES TO THE MEADOWLANDS

John Scher Presents
AEROSMITH
Special Guest Star
PAT TRAVERS
February 13
1983

Brendan Byrne Arena, Meadowlands, New Jersey. Sunday, February 13, 1983. Audience recording. Sound quality: C-

Back In The Saddle, Mama Kin, Big Ten Inch Record, Three Mile Smile, Reefer Headed Woman, Rock In A Hard Place (Cheshire Cat), Lord Of The Thighs, Lick And A Promise, Sweet Emotion, Dream On, Lightning Strikes, Walk This Way, Milk Cow Blues, Toys In The Attic, Train Kept A-Rollin'.

"New York, New Jersey!" Tyler exclaims after "Mama Kin," no doubt happy to be on a big stage in the New York area again.

Our taper gets so excited during "Reefer Headed Woman" he yells out before the harmonica solo, temporarily knocking out the sound!

"Lord Of The Thighs" reveals some fine playing by Dufay, wiggling notes out of his guitar. His playing is becoming more and more confident.

Kramer plays a few beats of "Write Me" before launching his barrage to start "Lick And A Promise." "You think you can get these things working sometime tonight?" an annoyed Tyler asks a roadie about stage monitors before "Sweet Emotion." Tyler changes up the lyrics again to the song.

More emotive, bluesy guitar before "Dream On" again on this night. "Second gear!" Tyler yells out as "Lightning Strikes" begins.

There is laid-back guitar jamming during another relaxed "Milk Cow Blues," really the loosest ever. But it works.

"Can you hear all right?" Tyler asks the crowd before "Train Kept A Rollin'" as the show comes to a close.

Spectrum, Philadelphia, Pennsylvania. Monday, February 14, 1983. Audience recording. Sound quality: D

Back In The Saddle, Mama Kin, Big Ten Inch Record, Three Mile Smile, Reefer Headed Woman, Rock In A

205

Hard Place (Cheshire Cat), Lord Of The Thighs, Lick And A Promise, Sweet Emotion, Dream On, Lightning Strikes, Walk This Way, Milk Cow Blues, Toys In The Attic, Train Kept A-Rollin'.

This tape starts with Tyler speaking on the radio show "Rockline" earlier in 1983 about the troubles in Philadelphia in 1977 and 1978: "I saw the billboard you people in Philadelphia put up, we appreciate it. I know it was only one or two people that did that. Don't worry about it. We're coming back."

And come back they did, playing two shows at the city's largest venue within a two-week period.

"Are we 'Back In The Saddle' or what? It's good to see you too, momma," Tyler says after "Mama Kin." This show features one of the most excited crowds of the tour, a din filling the arena.

Another ethereal guitar beginning to "Dream On." There's a great response to the start of "Lightning Strikes," the crowd giving its loud approval after the first line of the song.

Lots of love between the crowd and band as fences were mended between Aerosmith and Philadelphia on this night

The rock group Aerosmith will appear in concert Feb. 21 at the Glens Falls Civic Center.

Civic Center, Glens Falls, New York. Monday, February 21, 1983. Audience recording. Sound quality: C+

Back In The Saddle, Mama Kin, Big Ten Inch Record, Three Mile Smile, Reefer Headed Woman, Rock In A Hard Place (Cheshire Cat), Lord Of The Thighs, Lick And A Promise, Sweet Emotion, Dream On, Lightning Strikes, Walk This Way, Milk Cow Blues, Toys In The Attic.

The taper is a part of the entertainment on this night. "Wish you were here, Alan!" he says as house music plays before the gig. The taper mistakenly says the date of the gig is April 21.

Dufay plays Eric Clapton's "Cocaine" riff as the guitars are tested. Once the "Psycho" theme starts up, Dufay then plays a little of The Rolling Stones' "Beast of Burden."

"Holy Shit!" Tyler says after "Back In The Saddle." "Is it really you? It's good to be back home. Can you hear all right? You want it louder? Coming at you!"

Then after "Mama Kin:" "Is that the way you like it? Me too! Me too! Mr. Kramer is in rare form tonight, ain't he?" says Tyler as the drummer starts "Big Ten Inch Record."

A furious "Lord Of The Thighs" revs up the crowd even more. Dufay plays hard rhythm on "Lick And A Promise," really grinding the chords. "You know what time it is? Time for you to start passing up the joints," Tyler says before "Sweet Emotion." "He will put the microphone right up to the drums, watch," says our taper. And Tyler does just that during the song, as Kramer's drums get that extra volume pushing through the arena.

Tyler does some nice vocalizations before "Dream On," adding a layer to the moody intros to the song on this section of the tour. "You like that?" Tyler says after the song.

"Play a new song. 'Bitches Brew!'" our taper says. Well, he did get the new "Lightning Strikes" next. "Turn this place upside down," Tyler says during the nightly "Milk Cow Blues" jam. More of the descending riffs from Dufay help close out "Toys In The Attic," the last tune caught on tape this night.

Broome Show Listed Feb. 22 By Aerosmith

Aerosmith, one of the leading hard rock bands in the country, will make an appearance Feb. 22 at 7:30 p.m. at the Broome County Arena, Binghamton, sponsored by Freefall Presentation, Ltd.

Tickets at $10.50 each for general admission, are on sale at the Broome County Arena Box Office and at all Ticketron locations.

Consistent high scorers on the Billboard charts, Aerosmith has a reputation for toughness that attracts millions of fans to their live dates and millions more to buy their recordings.

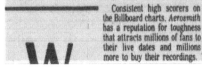

Broome County Veterans Memorial Arena, Binghamton, New York. Tuesday, February 22, 1983. Audience recording. Sound quality: C

Back In The Saddle, Mama Kin, Big Ten Inch Record, Three Mile Smile, Lord Of The Thighs, Lick And A Promise, Sweet Emotion, Dream On, Lightning Strikes, Walk This Way, Milk Cow Blues, Toys In The Attic, Train Kept A-Rollin'.

The band eliminates "Reefer Headed Woman" and "Rock In A Hard Place (Cheshire Cat)" from the set. As with many acts, as the tour progresses, tunes fall away. The band was late getting to the stage again, but at least Tyler is honest as to the reason why. "We're sorry we made you wait tonight," he says. "We were copping a buzz back there."

The crowd is amped to see the band and the recording captures that quite well. Tyler now plays a few floating notes on keyboards before starting "Dream On" properly. Tyler exclaims, "It's true!" after he sings, "everyone has their dues in life to pay."

"Lightning Strikes" has some offbeat guitar during the swirling keyboard by Mayo. Tyler gives a little yodel during "Toys In The Attic."

"The one and only, The Doof!" Tyler says of Dufay as the band returns for the encore. "But that's not all, let's kick ass. Shit, we will be having breakfast," Tyler says, as Kramer starts "Train Kept A-Rollin'." Crespo absolutely tortures his strat to end the song. Nice work, Mr. Crespo!

Tickets for Aerosmith
The rock band Aerosmith will be in concert at the Broome County Arena in Binghamton on Feb. 22 and at the Syracuse War Memorial on Feb. 24. Tickets for the Binghamton performance are now on sale at 723-7376.

Thursday
7:30 p.m. Syracuse War Memorial. The rock band Aerosmith in concert. Ticket information at (315) 425-2660.

Memorial Auditorium, Syracuse, New York. Thursday, February 24, 1983. Audience recording. Sound quality: C

Back In The Saddle, Mama Kin, Big Ten Inch Record, Three Mile Smile, Lord Of The Thighs, Lick And A Promise, Sweet Emotion, Dream On, Lightning Strikes, Walk This Way, Milk Cow Blues, Toys In The Attic, Train Kept A-Rollin'.

Kramer's drumming on "Back In The Saddle" gives the tune a plodding effect, but not in a bad way. "Yeah, you like that!?" Tyler says after. "You miss us? Good to see you all."

The band is really playing well here. A tight "Mama Kin" is followed by an equally taut "Big Ten Inch Record."

"We got some hardcore fans here tonight, don't we?" Tyler says before "Three Mile Smile" as he then vocalizes and grunts his way through the song's intro.

Crespo plays some great licks during "Lord Of The Thighs," his sweeping notes filling up fans' ears.

208

"You hear this song, you think of Aerosmith," Tyler says before launching "Sweet Emotion." "Thank you, Jimmy," he says as Crespo uses the talk box on the song.

Tyler gets his "lightning" effect going before "Lightning Strikes" begins, and then into the high, screaming registers as the song comes to a close. Amazing he has been able to keep in good voice over his career.

Tyler voices the "Leave It To Beaver" theme before "Milk Cow Blues," where Mayo and Dufay get into another good jam. Kramer's high-pitched exaltations can be heard during his solo.

"Did you get enough pictures?" Tyler says to the crowd during "Train Kept A-Rollin'" on which Richie Supa makes a guest appearance and adds a great guitar to the mix – one of the best versions of the song ever.

Forum, Montreal, Quebec, Canada. Friday, February 25, 1983. Audience recording. Sound quality: C

Back In The Saddle, Mama Kin, Big Ten Inch Record, Three Mile Smile, Lord Of The Thighs, Lick And A Promise, Sweet Emotion, Dream On, Lightning Strikes, Walk This Way, Milk Cow Blues, Toys In The Attic, Train Kept A-Rollin'.

A barrage of firecrackers is heard in the distance – Americans are not the only ones – as the set gets underway.

An amateur video of the shows what a whirling dervish Dufay is, running around the stage like a madman, a perfect foil for Crespo's stoic style. Tyler is also a ball of activity.

"Oh, Montreal. Did you miss us," Tyler asks the crowd after "Mama Kin." "Take a walk, in the warm Canadian sun..." Tyler sings during "Three Mile Smile."

"Do you get MTV up here?" Tyler asks, and from the tepid response it seems not. Tyler shrieks the words to "Walk This Way" with disregard for his tortured, straining vocal cords.

Tyler joins Kramer during the drummer's solo, banging away with him. The taper announces the date of the show during the encore break and we get a phalanx of female fans yelling, "Aer-o-smith!"

"Mr Jimmy!" Tyler says as Crespo hits the last notes of "Train Kept A-Rollin'."

Spectrum, Philadelphia, Pennsylvania. Monday, February 28, 1983. Audience recording. Sound quality: C+

Back In The Saddle, Mama Kin, Big Ten Inch Record, Three Mile Smile, Lord Of The Thighs, Lick And A Promise, Sweet Emotion, Dream On, Lightning Strikes, Walk This Way, Milk Cow Blues, Toys In The Attic, Train Kept A-Rollin'.

The second Philly show of the month. Crespo really manhandles the "Back In The Saddle" riffs, driving the song hard as the fans at the Spectrum lap it up.

His crunchy guitar playing continues into "Big Ten Inch Record." Crespo is really at the top of his game here. A great opening of the song too, with Tyler blowing his harmonica and vocalizing over Kramer's beat. Dufay also delivers a spicy solo.

Crespo plays bluesy notes and Tyler does an ascending vocal yell leading into the start of "Three Mile Smile." Tyler messes with the vocals, adding the line: "Please let your name be Dufay, Dufay...anyway."

"You remember an album called 'Rocks', 'Toys In The Attic,' we're gonna bring some of that oldies shit back, because that's what you want to hear, ain't it? That oldies shit? That kick ass, rock and roll, that you don't hear anymore? Mr. Kramer!" as the drummer pounds the intro into "Lick And A Promise." Tyler mucks up the "Oh Well" line intro into "Sweet Emotion."

The band is a little out of step at one point during "Dream On," but quickly finds its feet.

The band hears from a fan as he waits for them to return to the stage for an encore: "Come on, you motherfuckers!"

Philly love!

on the 26th...Aerosmith & Zebra will perform a the Nassau coliseum on March-1st.

Nassau Coliseum, Long Island, New York. Tuesday, March 1, 1983. Audience recording. Sound quality: C+

Back In The Saddle, Mama Kin, Big Ten Inch Record, Three Mile Smile, Lord Of The Thighs, Lick And A Promise, Sweet Emotion, Dream On, Lightning Strikes, Walk This Way, Milk Cow Blues, Toys In The Attic, Train Kept A-Rollin'.

The band now seems to start every show with an apology: "Sorry for being so late..." Tyler says as "Mama Kin" gets underway. Firecrackers greet the intro to "Big Ten Inch Record," which has another solid Mayo piano solo.

"Did you miss our asses? Give yourselves some credit too," Tyler says after the song. "This here is for all you people on the sides tonight who can't see, but who can hear," Tyler says, leading into "Three Mile Smile."

Calls of "Tyler!" go up from the crowd before "Sweet Emotion." "Second gear? Overdrive," he says after the song.

Kramer starts in on the "Walk This Way" intro, but the guitars lose power. It's a blessing as we get to hear Kramer's tubs in isolation playing the iconic beat until the power comes back.

As "Toys In The Attic" starts, popping can be heard. More firecrackers? No. Balloons? Yes. Hundreds drop from the rafters, smaller ones adorned with an "A" and the larger ones with "AEROSMITH" stamped on them. Some make their way to the stage where Dufay boots them back into the crowd. A fun moment.

211

Not so fun: the power goes off to the guitars again mid song, but Mayo and Kramer fill the void nicely until electricity to Crespo and Dufay is restored.

"We're sorry about that fuse. But that's when you start singing, like you automatically do," Tyler says.

Tyler assists Kramer again in the drum solo and stands to the side of his kit during "Train Kept A-Rollin."

Part of the gig can be found on an amateur video recording.

At the Augusta Civic Center on March 4, the eternal "raunch and roll" of Aerosmith will be featured and the band is expected to play many of their old classics, such as "Dream On," "Lord Of Your Thighs," and "Train Kept A-Rolling," "Sweet Emotion" and "Walk This Way."

Lead singer Steven Taylor will also perform many of the band's songs from the newest album, "Rock In A Hard Place."

Civic Center, Augusta, Maine, Friday, March 4, 1983. Soundboard recording, Sound quality: A.

Back In The Saddle, Lightning Strikes, Milk Cow Blues.

Three songs from this gig have turned up on YouTube. Because of the excellent quality, you can really hear all the details here. The band is really in fine form here after four months on the road.

Cape Cod Coliseum, South Yarmouth, Massachusetts. Saturday, March 5, 1983. Soundboard recording. Sound quality: A

Back In The Saddle, Mama Kin, Big Ten Inch Record, Three Mile Smile, Lord Of The Thighs, Lick And A Promise, Sweet Emotion, Dream On, Lightning Strikes, Walk This Way, Milk Cow Blues, Toys In The Attic, Train Kept A-Rollin'.

The last show of the band's first run of gigs. A soundboard tape has found its way to the light and someone recorded from the audience as well. The former is unbalanced at times, it's still a nice listen. There would be fan-incited drama on this night.

Tyler makes a gunshot noise after the "loaded gun" line during "Back In The Saddle." "Looks like you're having fun tonight, baby!" Tyler says before "Three Mile Smile."

As the band gets into "Lord Of The Thighs," a bottle flies out from the darkness and lands on stage. "Who threw that bottle?!" Tyler yells. "Bring him up here!" And the singer is serious. "Hey, anybody see who threw that bottle? Bring him up here. Bring that motherfucker up here. Point him out to me!"

The band keeps playing but tones it down. "Where is he? He did?" as the crowd points out the culprit. "You fucking asshole. C'mon up here and do some dancing with the big boys. C'mon baby," Tyler says.

The crowd may have taken some swings at the dude on the way up. "Wait a minute, don't hurt him. Just bring him up here, I want to see if he can sing. You can throw shit, let's see if you can sing."

As the fan gets onto the stage, Tyler tells him, "Let me hear you sing." He asks Tyler what to sing and Tyler advises, "Sing, 'I didn't do it.'" And the fan does just that: "Hey, I didn't do it!" in a not too bad rock voice!

Says Tyler, "How's that for a fucking solo? Meanwhile, back at the motherfuckin' ranch..." as one of the stranger moments ever caught on tape at an Aerosmith show comes to an end as the band carries on.

"Did you miss our asses? We missed you," Tyler says before "Sweet Emotion." "Rock and roll will never be the same," Tyler utters.

Dufay plays a few notes of "Sunshine Of Your Love" before "Dream On" after Tyler comments on "oldies but goodies." Crespo plays some lovely notes during the song.

"We have any MTV people in the house? Do you watch that station? That's good," says Tyler as the "Lightning Strikes" intro is played. The MTV influence in America is strong at this time and it helps the band.

"Do you know this is the last show of this tour? Now you're going to bitch at us because we didn't come here first," Tyler says as the band gets into "Milk Cow Blues." "You're sucking on that reefer and shit, pass it down here! Well, good things come to an end," Tyler says. As Mayo gets into his piano solo, Tyler puts on a Louis Armstrong-esque growl.

After the encore break, Dufay plays a few notes of Eric Clapton's "Cocaine" again, probably in reference to what was being ingested backstage. Dufay slips in Frampton's "Do You Feel Like We Do" as "Train Kept A-Rollin'" ends the show.

Aerosmith, 8 p.m. Friday, May 27, Cincinnati Gardens. Tickets: $8.50-$9.50.

Cincinnati Gardens, Cincinnati, Ohio. Friday, May 27, 1983. Audience recording. Sound quality: C

Back In The Saddle, Big Ten Inch Record, Mama Kin, Three Mile Smile, Reefer Headed Woman, Lord Of The Thighs, Lick And A Promise, Sweet Emotion, Dream On, Lightning Strikes, Walk This Way, Milk Cow Blues, Toys In The Attic, Train Kept A-Rollin'.

The band plays two festivals in Florida in April and then a trio of dates in the Midwest, beginning with this show in Cincinnati. The band changes its setlist's song order, flip-flopping "Big Ten Inch Record" and "Mama Kin." The guitarists add a little jam during the former's intro on this night. Crespo takes the mic during "Mama Kin," laughing slightly as he sings.

"Reefer Headed Woman" returns to the setlist, but in truncated form, checking in at about one minute. It serves as a bridge between "Three Mile Smile" and "Lord Of The Thighs." "Reefer Headed Woman" would be played in this manner for the rest of the Crespo/Dufay era and when the original members reunited during the "Back In The Saddle" tour.

The guitar solos in "Lord Of The Thighs" have changed throughout the tour and this night is no different. The band plays the main theme in unison before the way-out solos. "Mr. James Crespo!" Tyler says emphatically after the song.

Kramer pounds out another great opening to "Lick And A Promise." Tyler loses his place in the song for a verse. "Anyone got something to drink for me?" Tyler asks before "Sweet Emotion." He utters the wrong words during the "Oh Well" intro but finds his way out well enough. "What do you think about that!" Tyler says as the song ends to cheers.

"We'd like to close the show...no don't believe that shit. Do you watch MTV?" Tyler says as Mayo kicks off "Lightning Strikes."

"Excuse me a minute, I don't remember how to play this thing..." Tyler says of his harmonica as "Milk Cow Blues" gets underway. It's then a quick intro of Mayo, who bangs on his keyboards to get the nightly jam rolling. Crespo plays some long, extended notes on "Train Kept A-Rollin'" to end the show.

ALPINE VALLEY — Performers include: AEROSMITH, May 28; $11, reserved seats and $9 ...... Johnny Van Zant and Head East have been added to the bill for Aerosmith's May 28 concert at Alpine Valley, East Troy, Wis.

Alpine Valley Music Theater, East Troy, Wisconsin. Saturday, May 28, 1983. Audience recording. Sound quality: C

Back In The Saddle, Big Ten Inch Record, Mama Kin, Three Mile Smile, Reefer Headed Woman, Lord Of The Thighs, Lick And A Promise, Sweet Emotion, Dream On, Lightning Strikes, Walk This Way, Milk Cow Blues, Toys In The Attic, Train Kept A-Rollin'.

This is an odd one. Tyler again makes a gunshot noise after the "loaded gun" line during "Back In The Saddle" as the show gets underway. Tyler is definitely under the influence on this night, to a point where it is noticeable.

The "Big Ten Inch Record" intro goes on and on while Tyler does a bit of a ramble that is not intelligible. "Bobby! Bobby! Bobby!" Tyler says as he calls on Mayo for a solo during the song. Apparently, the venue was not filled. "I'll tell you what," Tyler says. "This place may not be sold out tonight, right? But you know what? It really doesn't matter. It really doesn't matter. Not when we have the likes of you here!"

"Lord Of The Thighs" gives us new solos, nothing rote in these waters from the band. "You going to sit down and ask me what?" Tyler asks before "Sweet Emotion," nonsensically.

215

Oddly, Mayo seems to disappear from the second half of the gig and "Dream On" begins with guitars and not keyboards. Tyler misses the entire second verse but picks the song up again.

Before "Milk Cow Blues" starts properly, there is four minutes of jamming, followed by more ramblings from Tyler. This is either interesting or embarrassing, depending on your view. Tyler tries to shush the band and crowd mid song.

"If I was trying to whisper which pocket my cocaine was in, wouldn't you be quiet!" as he then leads the crowd on a sing along of the song! Then he stops the proceedings again to get the crowd to sing loud so "that your mother back home hears it." Tyler then completes the verse in an almost unintelligible way and gives a loud scream. Crespo plays some tasteful guitar to try to bring the song to a close, but Tyler interrupts.

"Train Kept A-Rollin'" breaks down at one point as well before this strange gig ends.

 **Pine Knob Music Theater, Clarkston, Michigan. Monday, May 30, 1983. Audience recording. Sound quality: C-**

Back In The Saddle, Big Ten Inch Record, Mama Kin, Three Mile Smile, Reefer Headed Woman, Lord Of The Thighs, Lick And A Promise, Sweet Emotion, Dream On, Lightning Strikes, Walk This Way, Milk Cow Blues, Toys In The Attic, Train Kept A-Rollin'.

Tyler is in much better shape than the last gig. "Hey, can you play harmonica?" he says to someone in the crowd involved in a fight. "Then cut the shit" as he admirably tries to keep the peace during "Big Ten Inch Record."

"It was cold when we got out here. Did we warm you up a bit?" Tyler asks before "Three Mile Smile." "Take a walk, on old Pine Knob Hill," he sings during the tune. "One for the money, two for the show, three to get ready and four to go!" Tyler yells as Crespo fires off his lead in the song.

Dufay's guitar intro to "Lord Of The Thighs" is loud and choppy, played in a staccato style. He plays some wild lead in the song too, always ready to get the band energized. "Mr. Rick Dufay...Mr. Rick Dufay..." Tyler says mid song in appreciation. Crespo matches that energy and Tyler gives him a nod too after the tune is over.

Kramer bangs the hell out of his drums as he builds a furious intro into "Lick And A Promise." A marvel of rhythm! "Beethoven, I am not!" Tyler jokes as he hits some sour notes on the piano before starting "Dream On," which features some poignant guitar work overlayed by Crespo.

There is no keyboard intro into "Lightning Strikes," rather it's guitar driven. The tune has some rough backing vocals from unknown persons, maybe roadies!

Dufay again fires away on "Milk Cow Blues." Tyler tries to calm the crowd as people are being crushed up front. "Hold on! Hold it please, will you? Move back, please. Someone is going to get hurt. Let's have a good time, OK? Don't push!"

While he may have been on substances, he had the presence of mind to help protect the crowd. The jam-band style song resumes to its normal pace and no one is hurt.

"You people are beautiful," Tyler says after the encore break. "I want you to drive carefully on the way home please, because we are coming back, and I want you to be here," he adds, as Kramer starts "Train Kept A-Rollin'." Dufay and Crespo try to outdo each other to end the show, each throwing their best licks at each other.

AP Photo

Playing A Set: Tennis stars John McEnroe, left, and Vitas Gerulaitis, right, join Steve Tyler, lead singer for the the rock group Aerosmith, in a tune Saturday during a benefit concert, "Tennis/Rock '83," for the Special Olympics at Pier 84 in New York.

Special Olympics Benefit, Tennis Rock Expo, Pier 84, New York City, New York. Saturday, July 23, 1983. Soundboard recording. Sound quality: A-

Toys In The Attic, Train Kept A-Rollin', Milk Cow Blues, All Your Love, Blues Jam.

Tennis players John McEnroe and Vitas Gerulaitis staged this benefit for the Special Olympics. It was the first of a series of gigs that has Tyler in poor health, in the throes of his drug

217

addiction. While he was able to mask it before, and by and large the gigs came off well, his odd behavior was front and center in the summer of 1983, even if the band itself was playing quite well.

By JOAN HANAUER
United Press International

TENNIS, ANYONE?: The rock group Aerosmith was rehearsing in New York and its Tom Hamilton had a problem. "I decided to really get into tennis this year but I couldn't find anyone to play with in New York." Then he discovered two aspiring guitarists renting space in the same rehearsal studio – Vitas Gerulaitis and John McEnroe. Gerulaitis had lined up Clarence Clemmons, Stevie Ray Vaughn, Buddy Guy and Rush's Geddy Lee and Alex Lifeson to play with him and McEnroe at a benefit concert. "I told him Aerosmith would play, his concert if he'd play tennis with me." The next morning Hamilton and Gerulaitis paired off in a doubles match against McEnroe and rocker Billy Squire. Aerosmith played the benefit. "It just shows the lengths you have to go to find a good tennis partner," Hamilton said.

Aerosmith was the last of the acts to appear at the benefit.

"We'd like to end the show with some real rock and roll, I'd like to introduce Aerosmith! Steven Tyler and Aerosmith!" Gerulaitis announces.

"What? Shhh. Shhh. Hold on, what is that I heard?" Tyler says, egging on the crowd for more cheers. Kramer gives out a yell and hits the "Toys In The Attic" intro, the crunchy guitars giving it a real heavy metal feel. Crespo plays a little of "First Call" as Kramer starts "Train Kept A-Rollin'."

Tyler then goes on a rant: "It just so happens we are doing this for a benefit. Do you know that? We do not want, I repeat we do not want to go over time because these motherfuckers...OK, here we go, I'm gonna get accused of inciting a riot...They will not keep the lights on if we go over time. But if we do go over time, I was just told...this cat in the back said, 'shit, I'm in charge.' I said like fuckin' hell you are. Let me see your badge. I got the biggest motherfuckin' mouth of all of you. One hour is how much we'd like to go over the hour, not pay them, because we can't afford it. You don't believe that shit, but we and Vitas Gerulaitis and John McEnroe gotta pay for that net, you know, that fuckin' thing you try to hit. Why don't you let them know how much you think they should donate to this function. Let's hear it!"

Tyler continues: "Dig this shit, they are still gonna ask for the money. They are, they still are. But we don't give a shit, do we? We don't give a shit. So, we have gone and done, we got the motherfuckin' John McEnroe and that motherfucker Vitas Gerulaitis to play a song with Aerosmith. I thought that was pretty cool, so let's hear it..."

Crespo starts "Milk Cow Blues" and the ensemble follows. The tennis players can be heard a little, but hardly standout and Tyler jokes they are playing "air guitar." At one point Tyler asks the crowd, "Did you see Sgt. Pepper? Did you really? Well, I got nothing to say."

Buddy Guy joins the jam and then stays for a version of "All My Love." Stevie Ray Vaughan joins in along with Clarence Clemons during the smooth jam.

"We gotta curfew and we are going to get our asses cut in half because they are going to take all our money," Tyler says. "You all know it's a charity trip here, don't you?"

After some more rambling. Gerulaitis jumps in to wrap it up before the musicians launch into a blues shuffle. A good night of music for an important cause, but Tyler was out of it at times.

Aerosmith — And Dio, July 30, Compton Terrace.

Compton Terrace, Phoenix, Arizona. Saturday, July 30, 1983. Audience recording. Sound quality: C+

Back In The Saddle, Big Ten Inch Record, Mama Kin, Three Mile Smile, Reefer Headed Woman, Lord Of The Thighs, No More No More, Lick And A Promise, Sick As A Dog, Sweet Emotion, Same Old Song And Dance, Walk This Way, Milk Cow Blues, Toys In The Attic, Train Kept A-Rollin'.

On the day of the gig, the *Arizona Republic* runs a story about Tyler's arrest in June when the band made its way to Arizona's Lake Havasu City for a little rest and relaxation, renting a houseboat on Lake Havasu. While staying at the Nautical Inn, he was arrested by Kingman police June 23 and charged with two counts of possession of cocaine and for possession of Serex, a prescription drug. Charges were eventually reduced, and Tyler completed probation and paid a $5,000 fine.

"I assume there are a lot of people who look up to you, so maybe you should set an example rather than you be made an example of," Superior Court Judge Gary R. Pope told Tyler at his sentencing in January 1984.

219

Good recording of the show, but the recorder stops and starts throughout. Still, it's an enjoyable listen. As the "Psycho" theme starts up Tyler yells, "Hey, how ya doing!"

Tyler must have been aware of the newspaper article, singing the "Kingman cops said they got me..." during "Back In The Saddle." The band is energized, their first full gig in almost two months.

"Holy shit! It is some kind of hot tonight," Tyler said referencing the oppressive Arizona heat felt in full force at the outdoor venue. "Gentlemen of the jury, what song do you want to hear? 'No More No More,' just what I thought," Tyler says as the band launches into the old song, a new addition to the setlist. The last known airing was back in March of 1978 in Columbus, Ohio.

With "Lightning Strikes" now eliminated, there are no more songs from "Rock In A Hard Place" in the set, which is a good one. Tyler is high, sort of floating throughout the whole proceeding, but singing well and improvising lyrics all night.

"Sick As A Dog" is another new addition to the set, last heard in Philadelphia in October of 1977. Tyler puts together a humorous run of words during the break in "Sweet Emotion" referencing a "bitch with a mustache" before Kramer bangs away to start the ending segment of the song. No more Bobby Mayo on the tour, who has left to join Robert Plant's band.

"Same Old Song And Dance" also reappears. There is no Kramer solo as the band goes straight into "Toys In The Attic." Crespo plays a little of "Strangers In The Night" as "Train Kept A-Rollin'" gets underway to end the show.

Cal Expo Amphitheater, Sacramento, California. Tuesday, August 2, 1983. Audience recording. Sound quality: C+

Back In The Saddle, Big Ten Inch Record, Mama Kin, Three Mile Smile, Reefer Headed Woman, Lord Of The Thighs, No More No More, Lick And A Promise, Sick As A Dog, Sweet Emotion, Dream On, Same Old Song And Dance, Walk This Way, Milk Cow Blues, Toys In The Attic, Train Kept A-Rollin'.

The best show of the mini-tour, Tyler is at his most coherent. "What are you guys fighting about?" Tyler says after the opening tune, as he tries to stop fans going after each other. "Come on, come on."

The first verse of "Mama Kin" goes missing, but Tyler is back for the rest. He improvises "keep in touch with uncle Jim, tell him that you cannot swim!"

"How come you are so far away?" Tyler says, after noticing the crowd is kept back by barriers. Legendary rock promoter Bill Graham produced the show and was known for solid security. But Tyler continues, "I'd knock that down if I were you. Anyway, we're gonna do a lot of songs we haven't done in six, seven, eight years." Tyler calls Crespo over for the background vocals during "Three Mile Smile," "Come here, Jimmy!"

The warm summer night draws people from all over California's sprawling Central Valley. "How many people we got out here tonight?" Tyler says as he looks out over the ocean of fans in the open-air arena. "Thirty thousand? Forty?"

"No More No More" ends with a Kramer shuffle that starts "Lick And A Promise." "Kicking some ass tonight!" Tyler says as the band launches "Sick As A Dog," which comes to an end with Tyler saying, "The only acapella band in rock and roll history!"

Before "Sweet Emotion" Tyler addresses the crowd: "There ain't nothing like the real thing, is it? And I don't mean us, I mean you! I see faces I ain't seen in years. You fuckers, you come back! Ok, what do you want to hear?" Someone in the crowd asks for "Nobody's Fault," another yells "Come Together" and yet another, "Seasons of Wither." "Joe Perry: fuck him!" yells another fan.

"We'll show you how we write a song, OK?" Tyler says. "...Some person comes up with a lick at rehearsal, right? Just this one particular time this white-haired motherfucker over here started playing this little thing. And this big-lipped motherfucker grabbed one of these things and went like this," as Tyler shakes a maraca. "And all of a sudden it started to work. And I went, shit, that is sweet emotion," with Tyler then jumping into the "Oh Well" lyric.

Later, he says, "California motherfuckers used to throw joints up, what's going on? Do I have to be straight for the whole set? C'mon, throw me up a joint, will you? Something. A vial or something." Someone in the crowd then observes, "he's snorting something." Crespo then launches "Dream On."

During "Same Old Song And Dance" Tyler gets the crowd clapping and says, "Let's write a song, all right?" He then improvises some lyrics and Crespo joins in, but Tyler quickly realizes it's not going anywhere. "Oh, fuck that," he says to laughs from the crowd.

"We used to have someone who used to play piano, his name was Bobby Mayo. He's still here with us in spirit, but his name is Tyler Britt (a name Tyler used to use)," Tyler says as he jams out on the keyboard, playing some smooth, jazzy chords.

Before the "Train Kept A-Rollin'" finale, Tyler humors the crowd: "I just heard some horrible news. They couldn't hear us back there and so we are going to have to turn up, and we are going to have to start the show from the beginning. Anyway, I just got busted for smoking a joint, so are you going to chip in a buck so I can get out of jail tonight?"

BGP 75 Event
7046
26
CA ADULT
CAS BGL 51
GEN 13.15
1A
ADM B25JUL GA sec

CAL EXPO AMPH-SAC
PRICE INC.$1SURCHG
& APPLICABLE TAXES
TUE 8/2/83 8:00 PM
BILL GRAHAM PRES.
AEROSMITH

ADULT
GA-2315 nat 13.15

AEROSMITH

TUESDAY • AUGUST 2 • 8 P.M.
CAL EXPO AMPHITHEATRE
SACRAMENTO

MONDAY • AUGUST 8 • 7:30 P.M.
RENO-SPARKS CONVENTION CENTER

**Fairgrounds, Ventura, California. Wednesday, August 3, 1983.
Audience recording. Sound quality: C+**

*Back In The Saddle, Big Ten Inch Record, Mama Kin, Three Mile Smile,
Reefer Headed Woman, Lord of The Thighs, No More No More, Sweet
Emotion, Walk This Way, Toys In The Attic.*

Wow, a real disaster of a show at this outdoor venue that sits a few hundred
yards from the Pacific Ocean. Pacific means peaceful, but this gig is
anything but!

What to say about Ventura...pure bedlam. This show illuminates the shape
Tyler was in during the summer of 1983 thanks to a steady diet of
stimulants. To be fair, only Tyler goes off the rails here, and the band of
Hamilton, Kramer, Crespo and Dufay try to save him from himself by
playing on as he tries to stop the show with his ramblings.

As the "Psycho" theme starts, Tyler begins: "Let me say something, let me
say something, let me just say something! Hold on, hold on. Let me say
something before Joey starts playing on his drums. California, California
has been our new home ever since Boston, you all know that, don't ya? Well
don't ya! Well don't you!! Shit, talk to me. So when we play here they don't
know when we're playing here, back there, anyway...we thank ya'll kindly,
and if you ever think we are going to stop doing this, you're fuckin' crazy.
Let's do it to it!"

After he makes his way through "Back In The Saddle," Tyler is back at it.
"...You know this is an easy time tonight. There ain't no Bill Graham over
here doing this or David Krebs over here...this is rock and roll tonight...I
gotta act drunk, otherwise if I don't, I'll get blamed for being something I
wasn't. This song happens to be one of Bill Graham's motherfuckin' favorite
songs. I heard him tell me that last night when I whupped his ass at ping
pong!" Kramer then starts informally on "Big Ten Inch Record."

After that song there is more from the singer. "You know what? I'm fuckin'
pissed off. Do you hear me? I'm fuckin' pissed off. Don't even ask me why
I'm pissed off. You wanna know why? Do you really wanna know why?

Because..." Fearing what he might say next, Kramer smartly starts "Three Mile Smile" as Tyler protests the drummer pushing ahead, "Hey!" he yells.

After "Lord Of The Thighs" the band huddles without Tyler. "They seem to be having a meeting," Tyler says. "Soo, I ain't gonna fuck up on any words tonight. I'll tell you what, they are making a movie on this and if I do anything fucked up...imagine saying something fucked up after the lead like he took! Dancer, turn me up a bit more," he concludes as he talks to a roadie. Amazingly he sings the first lines of "No More No More" without an issue.

"(You all are saying) what the fuck is wrong with Tyler tonight? He's fuckin' so stoned, he can't do shit," Tyler says. "Well, what would you do...if you had six inches...My dick is bigger than six inches!" Hamilton then scolds Tyler off mic..."He got mad, so I gotta put it to rest," Tyler says. But then: "Fuck that shit. Did you hear me? I don't think you did. If you heard me, you'd repeat it. Fuck that shit! I still don't think you heard me, fuck that shit! Because dig this...We ain't like women, you know. Women can come anytime they want. Boys, you know, it's a two-bit shuffle, you know, doin' it?"

Again, somewhat miraculously, the band gets "Sweet Emotion" off the ground. But during the song's break, Tyler again stops. "Can I have the spotlight. Now what would you do, what would you do if you..." but before he can finish, Kramer jumps back in and drums his way, and the band, to the end of the song.

The band jumps into "Walk This Way," and then "Toys In The Attic," where Tyler blows into his harmonica at the end. Tyler tells the band to "hold on," but they all leave the stage after 50 torturous minutes.

The crowd reacts to Aerosmith's early departure with a hail of obscenities and jeers: "Come on you fucking assholes! I want my money back! Fuck you!" one yells.

Pacific Amphitheater, Costa Mesa, California. Friday, August 5, 1983. Audience recording. Sound quality: D-

Back In The Saddle, Big Ten Inch Record, Mama Kin, Three Mile Smile, Reefer Headed Woman, Lord Of The Thighs, No More No More, Lick And A Promise, Sick As A Dog, Sweet Emotion, Dream On, Same Old Song And Dance, Walk This Way, Milk Cow Blues, Toys In The Attic.

Another outdoor gig on this night and more weirdness. The venue had just opened and incurred the wrath of local residents, who complained of excessive volume. One claimed he made a "perfect" recording from his backyard of an earlier concert, it was that loud. Aerosmith's appearance could not have been welcomed. Costa Mesa Police would record 66 noise complaints.

Not that Tyler cared. "Shit, rock and roll don't die!" he exclaims after "Mama Kin," sounding in much better shape than in Ventura.

Tyler seems to sing a whole new set of lyrics for "No More No More," but the poor quality of the recording makes it hard to decipher. Kramer plays a great loping intro to "Sick As A Dog." Crespo also plays atmospheric guitar on the track. Band producer Jack Douglas is at the gig and sings some background on the song as well.

"Who's got that pot? Pass that joint up here, will ya?" Tyler says before "Sweet Emotion," as Dufay plays a bit of "The Munsters" TV show theme.

All is fine until: "We're all having a good time, ain't we? Move the chairs aside!" Tyler implores the audience, and the crowd starts to do just that. Crespo starts in on "Dream On," but Tyler gets him to stop, and then tells the crowd to calm. "Please, don't be moving shit or I'll be arrested for inciting a riot."

The crowd continues to push toward the stage during the song, and Tyler says after, "You're fucking up my monitors." The band gets into "Same Old Song And Dance," but there are more problems after. "Move back a bit.

225

Please move back, cut the shit!" Tyler says. A fan can be heard saying, "I wanna go backstage!"

Kramer gets his solo back and leads the band into "Toys In The Attic," the last song caught on tape. Given the unrest in the crowd, it's very possible no encore was played.

AEROSMITH STIRS UP AUDIENCE

Aerosmith's concert Friday at the Pacific Amphitheatre in Costa Mesa was nearly terminated several times in the final 30 minutes when hundreds of overzealous fans crushed toward the stage, despite numerous warnings to "back off" from singer Steven Tyler. Luckily, there were no injuries.

Los Angeles Times

Aerosmith will appear at 8 p.m. Saturday at the San Diego Sports Arena.

Sports Arena, San Diego, California. Saturday, August 6, 1983. Audience recording. Sound quality: C+

Back In The Saddle, Big Ten Inch Record (cut), Three Mile Smile, Reefer Headed Woman (cut), Lord Of The Thighs (fragment), No More No More, Lick And A Promise, Sick As A Dog, Sweet Emotion, Dream On, Same Old Song And Dance, Walk This Way, Milk Cow Blues, Toys In The Attic.

"Do I hear someone knocking at my door?" Tyler says while the "Psycho" theme gets rolling, as the band moves indoors. The quality of the recording is good here, but there are several cuts in the tape, leaving many partial tracks.

Kramer plays a jungle-like shuffle, before falling into the more typical drum intro to "Big Ten Inch Record." Crespo plays a clean, crisp solo during "No More No More," adding vibrancy to the track.

"You wise-ass motherfuckers. We take one year off to fuck our old ladies and you give us all this shit?" Tyler says, obviously very stoned.

226

"I'm sure you love rock and roll...." Tyler sings in a bluesy tone as Kramer kicks off "Sick As A Dog." Remarkably, he sings the song quite well. He does disappear for a verse of "Sweet Emotion," but the band fills in nicely. He also does some vocalizing during the song's break, but more in tune with the song, not in a disruptive way as in Ventura.

"Milk Cow Blues" clocks in at 20 minutes on this night as Tyler dedicates the song to manager David Krebs. Tyler brings out Jack Douglas for vocals, David Krebs and his wife. "Which one of you people think they can play harmonica real good?" Tyler asks the audience.

Amazingly, Tyler pulls someone out of the crowd to play harmonica and the fan does so quite well. "If you don't sing your asses off, I'm going to personally run backstage, go around to the front of the building and kick each one of your asses as you walk out the door," Tyler says.

What an odd summer tour!

WINTER 1983/1984 TOUR, END OF THE CRESPO/DUFAY ERA

The beginning of the end of the Crespo/Dufay era. Rumors swirl about a reunion of the original members around this time, and Whitford shows up to play the band's New Year's Eve show.

Dufay provides some of the impetus for the reunion, telling Tyler he should get back together with his old guitar player, Perry.

Perry later thanked Dufay for "committing career suicide" during the band's enshrinement in the Rock and Roll Hall of Fame.

The band books dates in December, but Kramer develops a case of pneumonia and some shows are postponed into January and February. Interestingly, the band books smaller clubs, but larger venues as well, showing the band still had drawing power.

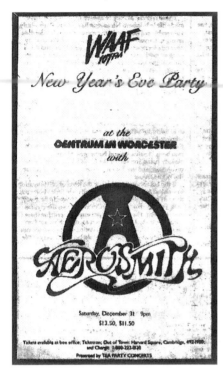

The Centrum, Worcester, Massachusetts. Saturday, December 31, 1983. Audience recording. Sound quality: C

Back In The Saddle, Big Ten Inch Record, Mama Kin, Three Mile Smile, Reefer Headed Woman, Lord Of The Thighs, Lick And A Promise, Sweet Emotion, Dream On, Lightning Strikes, Walk This Way, Auld Lang Syne, Come Together, Milk Cow Blues, Toys In The Attic, Train Kept A-Rollin'.

The band starts a winter tour and the first dates would be sans Kramer, but with a reappearance of Whitford on this night.

"Hey, this beats the hell out of watching Boy George on TV tonight, huh?" says a DJ from WAAF, the station sponsoring this New Year's Eve show.

"What a way to rock out the year," Tyler says, sounding better than he did over the summer. "As you can see Mr. Joey Kramer is not here tonight. My boy has pneumonia, true story, so we looked in our back pockets and we came up with someone who was playing with Rainbow at the time, Mr. Bobby Rondonelli," Tyler explains. Rondonelli does quite well in the fill-in role.

"Take a walk along Bleeker Street," Tyler sings during "Three Mile Smile." The concert demonstrates the Aerosmith brand is still strong, drawing some 13,000 to the venue. Tyler sings the "Oh Well" lines, but this time before "Lick And A Promise."

"As fucking usual, somebody fucked up," Tyler says as midnight has come and gone. But he resets time and does a countdown. The band then plays "Auld Lang Syne" with some scattered lyrics by Tyler.

Then, "We are going to ring in the new with a bit of the old, we have Mr. Brad Whitford over here on guitar," as the band launches "Come Together."

Whitford plays a cutting, standout solo. Rondonelli bangs out a seven-minute solo which leads into a 75-second "Toys In The Attic," no doubt the shortest version ever played! A fun, intense show.

Fountain Casino, Aberdeen Township, New Jersey. Friday, January 6, 1984. Audience recording. Sound quality: D

Back In The Saddle, Big Ten Inch Record, Mama Kin, Three Mile Smile, Reefer Headed Woman, Lord Of The Thighs, Lick And A Promise, Sweet Emotion, Dream On, Lightning Strikes, Walk This Way, Milk Cow Blues, Toys In The Attic, Train Kept A-Rollin'.

One of the postponed shows. Kramer is still out and Rondonelli is back behind the drums as the band plays some club dates.

"This is a rock and roll party, ain't it?" Tyler says to the receptive crowd. "Our drummer caught pneumonia, as you heard on the radio."

Someone in the crowd keeps calling for "Jailbait" not realizing the tune was retired soon after the band went on tour in November 1982.

"Sweet Emotion" begins with Hamilton's hypnotic bass, free of any of Tyler's pre-song stories or the "Oh Well" lyrics. This is a very good, workman like performance, the band sounding very professional.

The rattle of beer bottles on concrete can be heard throughout the show, again a reminder of the small venue. Someone in the crowd must have had a few concert recordings. As Tyler sings, "All the things you do," the fan yells "motherfucker" before Tyler continues "come back to you," Tyler didn't use the expletive in this version of "Dream On," but did at many shows. Rondonelli bangs on a gong to end his lengthy solo; Kramer rarely took so much time!

During Crespo's final solo, someone in the audience yells "you suck!" But there is no way Crespo heard him above the volume as the guitarist rises and falls with harmonics as he brings the show to a close.

CLUBS

Agora Ballroom, West Hartford, Connecticut. Wednesday, February 8, 1984. Audience recording. Sound quality: C

Back In The Saddle, Big Ten Inch Record, Mama Kin, Three Mile Smile, Reefer Headed Woman, Lord Of The Thighs, No More No More, Lick And A Promise, Sweet Emotion, Dream On, Train Kept A-Rollin'.

Kramer is now back and the recording captures the double thump of his bass drum during "Back In The Saddle" quite well.

Tyler is quiet during the set, but finally pipes up before "No More No More." "How's your heads tonight? Ya'll want to sing? Some vintage Aerosmith..."

The "Oh Well" lines appear in "Milk Cow Blues" on this night. "The boys!" Tyler yells as the set comes to an end.

Not a bad show, but the band cuts a couple of numbers and the whole affair has a subdued feel.

The Ritz, New York City, New York. Thursday, February 9, 1984. Audience recording. Sound quality: C

Lightning Strikes.

A show that had been scheduled for December 28, 1983, but postponed. Oddly, this is the only piece of this concert that seems to be circulating. But there is some significance: it's the last live outing of "Lightning Strikes" by the Crespo/Dufay lineup, which was its signature song. It was an important song for the band and helped them through some turbulent times. The song was so good in fact, that when Perry and Whitford returned, the song was revived in concert.

Calderone Concert Hall, Hempstead, Long Island, New York. Saturday, February 11, 1984. Audience recording. Sound quality: C+

Back In The Saddle, Big Ten Inch Record, Mama Kin, Three Mile Smile, Reefer Headed Woman, Lord Of The Thighs, No More No More, Lick And A Promise, Sweet Emotion, Dream On, Sick As A Dog, Walk This Way, Milk Cow Blues, Toys In The Attic, Train Kept A-Rollin'.

A lively night in Long Island, Tyler does some cool vocalizations during the "Three Mile Smile" intro. Tyler blows a whistle in the middle of "Lord Of The Thighs," a cool effect.

Tyler announces, "oldies but goodies" before "No More No More." It almost sounds like Richie Supa is singing on background here as he appeared at several New York area shows over the years.

Tyler ad-libs some lyrics during "Sweet Emotion." He again announces, "oldies but goodies" before "Dream On," this time saying, "since that is what you want to hear."

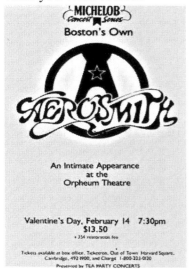

Orpheum Theater, Boston, Massachusetts. Tuesday, February 14, 1984. WBCN radio broadcast. Sound quality: A

Back In The Saddle, Big Ten Inch Record, Mama Kin, Three Mile Smile, Reefer Headed Woman, Lord Of The Thighs, No More No More, Lick And A Promise, Sweet Emotion, Dream On, Sick As A Dog, Walk This Way, Milk Cow Blues, Toys In The Attic, Train Kept A-Rollin'.

Six of the songs played tonight end up on the "Classics Live" album. A high energy show, with Tyler subbing in, "I'm back in Boston again" during "Back In The Saddle." "Mama Kin" becomes a great crowd sing along on this night. Crespo and Dufay provide cool layering of twin guitars on "Reefer Headed Woman."

Tyler's whistle again comes out as in Hempstead, this time on "No More No More." "The old Boston, kick ass BU (Boston University) song," Tyler says before "Lick And A Promise," which finishes with some great loud guitar work. After, Tyler asks the crowd to "wait a minute. It's time to change the tape."

"This here song is dedicated to the tightness of the underwear that's under the seats. It's a squeeze play!" Tyler says before "Sweet Emotion." He flubs the "Oh Well" lines, but oh well.

"They had us locked in the Hilton at the airport and someone said to us, 'son you're going to be a big star. Just write some songs,'" Tyler says before "Dream On." As Crespo starts the intro chords, Tyler continues, "Only if BCN plays us."

"The train that kept a rollin' all night long of rock and roll, which you cannot kill, it will live forever, is here again," Tyler says poetically before "Train Kept A-Rollin'" that ends the show, his words finding their way into print on the back of "Classics Live." This is a really great gig.

It's after this gig that the original band members talk about re-forming.

Mid-Hudson Civic Center, Poughkeepsie, New York. Thursday, February 16, 1984. Audience recording. Sound quality: C+

Back In The Saddle, Big Ten Inch Record, Mama Kin, Three Mile Smile, Reefer Headed Woman, Lord Of The Thighs, No More No More, Lick And A Promise, Sweet Emotion, Dream On, Sick As A Dog, Walk This Way, Milk Cow Blues, Toys In The Attic, Train Kept A-Rollin'.

The Poughkeepsie crowd seems particularly electrified this night and the band responds in kind with a great performance. Kramer's force and power are well documented in the recording, which captures the boom of his low-end attack.

"I like it, I like it!" Tyler says before "Three Mile Smile" noting the crowd's energy. During "Lord Of The Thighs" Dufay plays a prank as he signals the return to the song's main theme after his solo and Tyler starts to sing on cue, but he is forced to stop as Dufay then continues on with his solo!

"The one, the only, Joey Kramer!" Tyler says, thinking "Lick And A Promise" is up next. Kramer does a little cymbal work as an intro, but it's to "No More No More." After which, Tyler says "as I was saying, the one and only, Mr. Joey Kramer!" as the drummer does start up "Lick And A Promise."

Crespo adds some emotion-filled guitar work during the final verses of "Dream On," which segues nicely into an easy drum beat and "Sick As A Dog."

"You are all too kind," Tyler says after the encore break, acknowledging the loud crowd, "and we'll be back." As the band gets into "Train Kept A Rollin'," Tyler's vocals drop out, while the band keeps chugging along. This train stops for no one! Crespo comports himself very well on the final solo.

with Special Guest **JON BUTCHER AXIS**
FRIDAY, FEB. 17 8:00 P.M. Tickets $11.50 & $10.50

Civic Center, Providence, Rhode Island. Friday, February 17, 1984. Audience recording. Sound quality: C

Back In The Saddle, Big Ten Inch Record, Mama Kin, Three Mile Smile, Reefer Headed Woman, Lord Of The Thighs, No More No More, Lick And A Promise, Sweet Emotion, Dream On, Sick As A Dog (partial), Train Kept A-Rollin'.

Does Dufay know it's his last gig with the band? It almost seems so, as he plays some discordant notes as "Back In The Saddle" begins. "Good to see you again!" Tyler says to the familiar room after "Mama Kin." "Home sweet home!"

Dufay rides a long note during "Lord Of The Thighs" and plays a cool, wandering solo, Aerosmith's most flamboyant guitar player going out in a blaze of glory!

Crespo has a perfect response, playing his moody solo. In all candor, when Whitford and Perry returned, they were not as on point as Crespo and Dufay were here, at least initially. Dufay again is at it during "Sweet Emotion" playing some scratch rhythm during Hamilton's bass intro.

A rather sickly sounding "Sick As A Dog" is heard as the tape recorder apparently jams then shuts off, and a good chunk of the show goes missing. Thankfully, the recording resumes for "Train Kept A Rollin'," the last tune played by the Crespo/Dufay duo.

Aerosmith owes the pair a debt of gratitude, allowing the band to soldier on to what would be a world of riches that no one would have predicted in 1984.

Talks had been ongoing about a reunion of the original band members for much of late 1983 and early 1984...and then it happened. The band goes into rehearsals and emerges for public consumption almost off the grid in New Hampshire.

Steve Tyler, left, and Joe Perry at the Capitol Theater in Concord, NH.   PHOTO BY JIM COLE

Capitol Center, Concord, New Hampshire. Friday, June 22, 1984. Audience recording. Sound quality: C

Back In The Saddle, Mama Kin, Bone To Bone (Coney Island White Fish Boy), Big Ten Inch Record, Three Mile Smile, Reefer Headed Woman, Lord Of The Thighs, No More No More, Last Child, Get The Lead Out, Red House, Lightning Strikes, Same Old Song And Dance, Dream On, Sweet Emotion, Walk This Way, Milk Cow Blues, Toys In The Attic, Train Kept A-Rollin'.

AC/DC's "Rising Power" is heard pumping into the theater as fans brim with excitement waiting for the show to start. An MC appears: "Please welcome warmly, on their Back In The Saddle tour, the legendary, Aerosmith!"

A new intro tape now rolls, featuring booming drums with a Roman Empire feel and ominous keyboards and then..."We're baaaack! We're Back

In The Saddle again!" Tyler sings to the crowd as the original lineup takes the stage for the first time in almost five years.

The good airship Aerosmith is back flying the turbulent skies of rock and roll again. An unbelievable moment.

The band rocks and rolls, Perry getting feedback going across the track coming out of his solo. "Thank you!" Tyler says as the tune concludes. Wow, they are indeed back.

Tyler vamps some lyrics for "Bone To Bone (Coney Island White Fish Boy)" played for the first time since 1980.

As cries of "Aerosmith!" go up during the "Big Ten Inch Record" intro, Tyler responds "Yes, it is!" "Take a walk in the warm New Hampshire sun," Tyler croons during "Three Mile Smile."

As with the latter days of the Crespo/Dufay lineup, the band does a shortened "Reefer Headed Woman," which segues into "Lord Of The Thighs."

"Anything in particular you want to hear? C'mon, speak up!" Tyler says after. A lot of calls go out for "Dream On." "We'll get to that," Tyler says. "We're gonna do a song that lots of people asked for, but we ain't never played. Now we are gonna play it," and the band goes into "No More No More." Well, not exactly the truth. We know the tune has been played many times from New York to New Orleans, but few in the crowd probably knew!

Tyler comes back in too early during "Last Child," a sign of some rust that needed to be kicked off. It's is the tune's first outing since 1977.

Perry takes center stage as calls of "Perry!" reverberate in the hall. Without announcement, he launches into Hendrix's "Red House," a tune the Jam Band had done back in 1969. Perry sings and plays the song well, true to its original arrangement. It will be heavily featured over the next two years, allowing Perry to bask in the spotlight and allowing Tyler to take a break mid show. "Mr. Joe Perry!" Tyler says as the song concludes.

Maybe somewhat of a surprise, the band goes back to "Lightning Strikes." Sans the swirling, keyboard beginning of the Crespo/Dufay era, the band just jumps into the opening riffs here. "Dream On" is played for the first time with Perry since March 1978.

Tyler gets the crowd clapping along to "Same Old Song And Dance" and says, "Hey Joe, let's listen to them for a while." "Milk Cow Blues" is dedicated in part to sound man Nitebob. The song gets a more traditional reading as heard on "Draw The Line," versus the long 1983 jam versions, and becomes a showcase for Tyler's fine harmonica playing on this night. There is no Kramer solo tonight, but a straight lead into "Toys In The Attic."

There is an MC announcement after the song: "Thanks for coming to the Capitol Theater tonight. Be nice to your neighbor, we'll be back in a few." Tyler comes back on stage: "We were told we are running into overtime...we're going to play one more song and we ain't splitting up again, motherfucker!"

"Train Kept A-Rollin" ends the somewhat unbelievable night — the original members of Aerosmith have reunited. The overall performance is very good, if not a little stiff. The *Boston Globe* gave a good review.

Aerosmith red-hot in warmup

AEROSMITH – In concert at the Capitol Theater, Concord, NH, Friday night.

By Steve Morse
Globe Staff

CONCORD, NH. – There are plenty of nay-sayers who think the charter members of Aerosmith have reunited only as a means of paying mortgage bills. One wonders what those cynics would have said over the weekend if they'd caught the reformed Aerosmith in a savage, skull-cracking show that was not only up to past glories but added a few new ones as well.

In their first gig since lead guitarist Joe Perry and rhythm guitarist Brad Whitford returned after a five-year absence, Aerosmith shook the rafters of the intimate, 1300-seat Capitol Theater with a thunderous assault. Rather than having the stink of an over-the-hill gang slobbering through a mortgage concert, it had the sharp tang of a band going back to its steely, acid-blues roots with renewed commitment and drive.

Both returning guitarists, Perry and Whitford, showed dramatic improvement from the old '70s days when Aerosmith cut a loud, snotty swath through stadiums around the country. Perry has perfected his traditional R & B/blues-based style and become more of an architect of guitar feedback than a coarse trench-digger. Whitford, meanwhile, is more authoritative and has added some smart experimental touches to his rhythm work.

Aerosmith, who expect to play the Worcester Centrum in August, detonated one hard-rock blast after another Friday. The band played with less flamboyance than the last Aerosmith lineup featuring guitarists Jimmy Crespo and Rick Dufay, but had more power, confidence and chemistry on stage.

Singer Steve Tyler, wearing a cutaway body suit of stitched-together T-shirts bearing the Aerosmith logo (a welcome-back theme created by Boston costume designer Francine Larnis), was his cocky, strutting self, booming out a blade-edged cross-section of tunes from all the band's albums.

Old favorites such as "Back in the Saddle" and "Reefer-Headed Woman" were bolstered by resurrected versions of "Bone to Bone (Coney Island Whitefish Boy)," "No More No More" (with Whitford added a striking third vocal harmony), "Last Child," "Get the Lead Out" and a cosmic treatment of Jimi Hendrix' "Red House," in which Perry unleashed a torrent of brain-shredding bent notes and crashing transitions. The rhythm team of bassist Tom Hamilton and drummer Joey Kramer also played like men possessed, creating a throbbing wall of sound.

With an excellent sound mix provided by a character named Night Bob (who also is returning to the band since the early days), Aerosmith climaxed their triumphant return with over-the-top slices of "Lightning Strikes" (as the house lights were flipped on and off to simulate lightning), "Dream On," "Sweet Emotion" and a crunching encore of "Train Kept-a-Rollin'."

The band was clearly ready for the gig. For the past two months they've rehearsed at the Glen Ellen Country Club in Millis (using small amps), the Marquee Theater in Brockton (where their stage was erected), the Cape Cod Coliseum (where their massive lighting truss and PA went up) and finally to the Capitol Theater, which is where they rehearsed two years ago and is not far from Sunapee, where the band started in the early '70s and where several members now own homes. All of this grunt work paid off, because it added up to a unanimous get-lost gesture to the cynics who've said they're washed up.

238

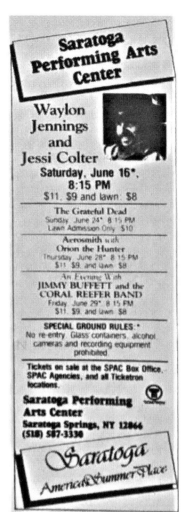

Performing Arts Center, Saratoga Springs, New York. Thursday, June 28, 1984. Audience recording. Sound quality: D

Back In The Saddle, Mama Kin, Bone To Bone (Coney Island White Fish Boy), Big Ten Inch Record, Three Mile Smile, Reefer Headed Woman, Lord Of The Thighs, No More No More, Last Child, Get The Lead Out, Red House, Lightning Strikes, Same Old Song And Dance, Dream On, Sweet Emotion, Walk This Way, Milk Cow Blues, Toys In The Attic, Train Kept A-Rollin'.

The same opening tape heard in New Hampshire runs here and would be used throughout this tour and again in 1986.

Things are coalescing more by this gig and the band rolls through its cannon almost non-stop. Perry introduces "Red House" as "from my heart to you." Tyler's vocalizations are eerie at the beginning of "Sweet Emotion" as the band takes a while to get the song going.

The reunion brings some giddiness on stage: "Mr. Fuckin' Joe Perry," Tyler says after the song, to which Perry responds: "Mr. Fuckin' Steve Tyler," to which Tyler says: "Mr. Fuckin' Joey Kramer" as the drummer starts "Walk This Way," in which Tyler mucks around with the lyrics.

There are some speed problems at the end of the recording, but overall a good document that captures the excitement of the show.

● Aerosmith, the popular hard rock band from the '70s, comes to the War Memorial with its original lineup of performers for a concert at 8 p.m. tomorrow. Tickets are

War Memorial, Rochester, New York. Saturday, June 30, 1984. Audience recording. Sound quality: C

Back In The Saddle, Mama Kin, Bone To Bone (Coney Island White Fish Boy), Big Ten Inch Record,

Three Mile Smile, Reefer Headed Woman, Lord Of The Thighs, No More No More, Last Child, Get The Lead Out, Red House, Lightning Strikes, Same Old Song And Dance, Dream On, Sweet Emotion, Walk This Way, Milk Cow Blues, Toys In The Attic, Train Kept A Rollin'.

"I don't know if it's us or you making the stage all wet tonight!" Tyler says before "Big Ten Inch Record," on a sweltering night. "Did you miss us?!" "Mr. Whitford!" Tyler yells out as the guitarist burns through a tight solo on the tune.

"Is it as hot out there as it is up here?" Tyler says before "Three Mile Smile." Tyler plays a cool harmonica riff during "Reefer Headed Woman," sounding as though it was transplanted via a time machine from the Mississippi Delta in the 1930s. "One of my favorite songs," the singer says as Perry starts "No More No More."

"You don't gotta push," Tyler says before "Last Child" as the fanatical crowd surges forward. "AM radio was on this song awhile back..." as Whitford plays the slow intro.

"Mr. Joe Perry is going to sing you a song," Tyler says. Perry takes the mic for "Red House." "It's great to be back in New York, it's great to be back in Rochester," he says, everything feeling renewed on stage.

"Blow that candle out," Tyler tells the spotlight operator before "Dream On," feeling it was ruining the effect he desired; he wanted to begin the piano intro in darkness. "Keep your eyes on the guitar players!" Tyler says before "Milk Cow Blues." Tyler adds some new lyrics to "Toys In The Attic."

"Now what do you want to hear? 'Train Kept A-Rollin'?" Tyler asks, as the band launches into the song to close the gig. Perry places his guitar on a mic stand at the end of the show and let's it swing, creating undulating feedback.

Merriweather Post Pavilion, Columbia, Maryland. Monday, July 2, 1984. Audience recording. Sound quality: C

Back In The Saddle, Mama Kin, Bone To Bone (Coney Island White Fish Boy), Big Ten Inch Record, Three Mile Smile,

Reefer Headed Woman, Lord Of The Thighs, No More No More, Last Child, Get The Lead Out, Red House, Lightning Strikes, Same Old Song And Dance, Dream On, Sweet Emotion, Walk This Way, Milk Cow Blues, Toys In The Attic, Train Kept A-Rollin'.

After the first two songs come off in fine fashion, a false start marks "Bone To Bone (Coney Island White Fish Boy)" and the band gets a little lost inside the song. Perry's slide work during "Lord Of The Thighs" is punctuated by Tyler's shaking maraca.

"Now a song we never played before..." says Tyler as he introduces "No More No More." Well, we still know that's not true, Steven! Perry plays a great "Red House," his solos floating effortlessly throughout the song. The tune is also a showcase for Whitford during the tour, as he adds his bluesy leads to the mix.

"Any of you watch MTV?" Tyler asks. Right away the crowd begins yelling for "Lightning Strikes" and Kramer's bass drum is captured nicely on the tune. Perry takes the mic to give the intro into "Same Old Song And Dance," which is given a bluesy vocal treatment by Tyler during the mid-tune breakdown.

Perry plays some ethereal notes during "Dream On," the song he once mocked has grown on him apparently. "C'mon up here and shake your ass!" Tyler tells the crowd before "Sweet Emotion." Kramer gets his solo back again on this night.

"Oh, that was loud as shit!" a fan says after "Toys In The Attic." A hot show.

Coming attractions at City Island, Harrisburg

JULY 3
Aerosmith, with Kix, $12.
Tickets available at Record City, South Gate Mall, and East Meets West, 7 E. King St., Shippensburg.

City Island, Harrisburg, Pennsylvania. Tuesday, July 3, 1984. **Audience recording. Sound quality: C+**

Back In The Saddle, Mama Kin, Bone To Bone (Coney Island White Fish Boy), Big Ten Inch Record, Three Mile Smile, Reefer Headed Woman, Lord Of The Thighs, No More No More, Last Child, Get The Lead Out, Red House,

Lightning Strikes, Same Old Song And Dance, Dream On, Sweet Emotion, Walk This Way, Milk Cow Blues, Toys In The Attic, Train Kept A-Rollin'.

The band plays an outdoor venue, and the lack of reverberation and good recording equipment yields a fabulous audience tape.

"Holy shit! Listen to yourselves, baby," Tyler says after "Back In The Saddle." As "Mama Kin" comes to a close, Tyler says, "And it ain't even dark yet. Did you miss us? Mr. Joe Perry and Brad Whitford? We back, momma, we back, with some ass kicking!"

"Front row motherfuckers, I know how long you've been here," Tyler says as he observes those up front as "Big Ten Inch Record" launches. He knows they got to the gig early to get that close. It may have been someone up front who recorded this, as it sounds as though Tyler's voice can be heard from the stage as well as the amplifiers, creating a slight echo.

Kramer sounds as though he is ready to launch the band into "Three Mile Smile," but Tyler stops him. He wants to talk about Three Mile Island, the nuclear plant near Harrisburg where a reactor meltdown occurred March 28, 1979, which inspired "Three Mile Smile." "Do you know you people are glowing? From here, with all the lights, I can still see you glowing. I can see you glowing from there to there. Must have something (to do) with Three Mile Island, huh? So, I wrote a song," as Kramer starts the tune. Tyler sings "Ahh, ah, blow it up!" then makes an explosion sound during the song.

A great version of "No More No More" ends with feedback. "Don't be throwing shit, we don't need that," Tyler says after the song. Tyler asks for a motorcycle jacket from the crowd, so he can wear it during "Lightning Strikes" and does indeed get one! After the song, he says, "whose jacket is this? C'mon up here...now go backstage and get drunk and stoned and we'll catch you later."

It's almost the Fourth of July and a loud firework goes off during "Same Old Song And Dance." "The instrument I'm supposed to be playing doesn't seem willing to work," Tyler says before "Dream On," but then his keyboard suddenly kicks in. "We are going to do some calypso…" Tyler says as "Walk This Way" starts.

"This one we used to do a long time ago, but we're going to do it now for you, it's called 'Milk Cow Blues'." "Toys In The Attic" brings another fireworks explosion from the crowd.

"We are going to end the show because the fire marshal is giving us some shit...we are going to end with some nice slow blues...ride 'em cowboy," as Tyler sings in a blues voice, but then Kramer starts "Train Kept A-Rollin'." Perry oddly hangs his guitar from a stage mic as if the tune is over, but it's not, and Kramer jumps in to end the song properly.

Orange County Fairgrounds, Middletown. New York. Thursday, July 5, 1984. Audience recording. Sound quality: C

Back In The Saddle, Mama Kin, Bone To Bone (Coney Island White Fish Boy), Big Ten Inch Record, Three Mile Smile, Reefer Headed Woman, Lord Of The Thighs, No More No More, Last Child, Get The Lead Out, Red House, Lightning Strikes, Same Old Song And Dance, Dream On, Sweet Emotion, Walk This Way, Milk Cow Blues, Toys In The Attic, Train Kept A-Rollin'.

A wet night at the open-air venue that eventually causes the taper to retreat and seek cover. But hey, he kept tape rolling.

Perry's fine fretwork can be heard very clearly on "Back In The Saddle." "Holy shit mamma, I'm home!" Tyler says after. "You all getting wet? Me too!" Tyler says, as he then blows his harp to start "Big Ten Inch Record."

"We played Harrisburg, a night and a half ago, by Three Mile Island. The first and only political song Aerosmith ever wrote, it's a song called 'Three Mile Smile' and it goes like this," says Tyler as Kramer starts the tune with two resounding drum strikes. Tyler changes up the lyrics to the tune.

Perry gets some off beat, high notes out of his guitar during "Lord Of The Thighs." "Mr. Joe Perry...Mr. Brad Whitford. Mr. Tom Hamilton. Mr. Joey Kramer!" Tyler says after, in acknowledgment of the workout of the song. Then Perry steps up to the mic: "And my favorite lead singer of all time, Steven Tyler."

"Someone asked for 'Last Child' down there, the rabbit lady? Wanna hear it? Remember it Brad?" Tyler says.

As the rain continues to fall, Perry says, "I'm sorry about the weather tonight. There's not much we can do about that. At least we got guitars and you guys came out. We are going to play a little blues for you right now and

243

see if we can dry up the sky," as he announces, "Red House." He sings the line "My baby don't want me no more," he then ads "Well, that's her loss and that's my gain, because I have better plans on the other side of town." It was a bit of reality there as Perry had split with Elyssa Jerret and had met Billie Montgomery. "Joe Perry!" Tyler says after. "Like he never left!"

"We're gonna do a song right now written by a friend of mine, a real good friend of mine, Richie Supa. Some of ya'll might have seen it on MTV. Big scar on my face, right, that wasn't real. Some of you young motherfuckers might of thought that was real shit..." as Tyler announces, "Lightning Strikes."

"I'm tired of singing, it's your turn to sing tonight," Tyler says as "Same Old Song And Dance" gets underway.

"This is dedicated to my daddy," Tyler says poignantly, as he introduces "Dream On." He would mention his dad in the nights to come as well. Tyler sings "drugs in the attic" during the penultimate "Toys In The Attic."

During "Walk This Way" the rain begins pouring and the taper is forced to leave his prime spot and the sound grows more distant. The show is lively, and Tyler is in the great form. Fireworks end the proceedings, even as the rain falls!

The Scope, Norfolk, Virginia. Friday, July 6, 1984. Audience recording. Sound quality: C

Back In The Saddle, Mama Kin, Bone To Bone (Coney Island White Fish Boy), Big Ten Inch Record, Three Mile Smile, Reefer Headed Woman, Lord Of The Thighs, No More No More, Last Child, Get The Lead Out, Red House, Lightning Strikes, Same Old Song And Dance, Dream On, Sweet Emotion, Walk This Way.

The entire opening tape runs to its conclusion before Kramer signals the beginning of "Back In The Saddle." Right away there is trouble. "You better quit throwing shit at us or we're gonna walk!" Tyler says. "And you're gonna get your ass kicked by everybody around you," as he slyly invites the crowd to police itself.

"You crazy motherfuckers," a somewhat stoned sounding Tyler says after "Mama Kin." "Are you glad we are back in the saddle?"

Firecrackers are thrown at the stage as Kramer pounds his drums to start "Big Ten Inch Record." The band stops momentarily, but rather than make an issue of it, Tyler blows into his harmonica after Perry re-counts the song in.

Tyler announces, "Three Mile Smile," but only gets as far as "Three" before Kramer starts in. Too much reverb is used during "Lord Of The Thighs" and Tyler's voice echoes over itself in one spot.

"A song that depicts our band and where it comes from," Tyler says as he announces, "No More No More."

"Mr. Brad Whitford, we wrote a song awhile back..." Tyler says as Whitford plays the opening notes and then Tyler sings, "I'm leaving tonight... "

Tyler notes all the male fans up front then says, "Let me tell you something, I need a woman up here to dance with," he says before "Lightning Strikes," but given the singer's condition, the band launches into the song not waiting to hear what he might say next.

"I'll dedicate this song to my daddy," Tyler says before "Dream On." Kramer adds some additional percussion over Tyler's "Oh Well" recital during the "Sweet Emotion" intro. Whitford and Perry really drive the song with their guitars. The last three songs were apparently not recorded.

Civic Center, Erie, Pennsylvania. Sunday, July 8, 1984. Audience recording. Sound quality: D

Back In The Saddle, Mama Kin, Bone To Bone (Coney Island White Fish Boy), Big Ten Inch Record, Three Mile Smile, Reefer Headed Woman, Lord Of The Thighs, Last Child, Get The Lead Out, Red House, Lightning Strikes, Same Old Song And Dance, Dream On, Sweet Emotion, Walk This Way, Milk Cow Blues, Toys In The Attic.

The first five tunes go down well, as the band is finding its groove as it continues to tour and get reacquainted on stage. Whitford and Perry show off their strong vibrato during "Reefer Headed Woman."

Perry plays some moving slide work during "Lord Of The Thighs," stamping his sound on the tune. Perry missteps on the intro to "Red House" and almost recovers, but not quite. It's unique nonetheless.

"I'm gonna put Coke-a-Cola in my hair and not up my nose," Tyler quips, as he talks about ways people used to slick their hair back in the old days as he introduces "Lightning Strikes." Perry purposely plays some discordant notes during the beginning.

The band has a false start on "Same Old Song And Dance," then pulls back. Perry plays some random notes before Whitford starts to play the rhythm to re-launch the song.

"Something my daddy inspired in me..." Tyler says before "Dream On" which is greeted by a flurry of firecrackers. A raucous "Sweet Emotion" features Tyler in the break saying, "Turn me up, turn me up!" as he puts his mic in front of Kramer's drum kit to capture the rat-a-tat to bring the song to a close.

"What time is it? It's time to kick some ass!" Tyler says before "Milk Cow Blues." And indeed, they do. "Train Kept A-Rollin'" was certainly played but was not recorded.

Kingwood Music Theater, Toronto, Ontario, Canada. Monday, July 9, 1984. Audience recording. Sound quality: C

Back In The Saddle, Mama Kin, Bone To Bone (Coney Island White Fish Boy), Big Ten Inch Record, Three Mile Smile, Reefer Headed Woman, Lord Of The Thighs, No More No More, Last Child, Get The Lead Out, Red House, Lightning Strikes, Same Old Song And Dance, Dream On, Sweet Emotion, Walk This Way, Milk Cow Blues, Toys In The Attic (halted), Train Kept A Rollin'.

This is a real "Joe Perry Experience" gig. Tyler yells to the crowd as the opening tape rolls and he gives a little yodel during "Back In The Saddle."

Perry is playing very energetically on this night, bending notes and taking license with the traditional solos. "What are you people on the lawn doing? Pass those joints up. We couldn't bring that shit over the border," Tyler says before "Last Child," which gets a warm reception from the Toronto crowd.

Perry fiddles with the end of "Get The Lead Out" as he continues to play loose and lucid on this night.

"It's good to be back in Toronto," says Perry, who has taken on demi-god status among those in the crowd based on the reaction he gets. His voice is put into some sort of echo as he tells the crowd he will find someone in "Toronto, Toronto, Toronto" to love him during "Red House."

Tyler mentions Richie Supa getting busted recently and makes the lightning strike by providing a vocal sound effect during "Lightning Strikes" that gets the crowd excited.

Tyler mentions Tchaikovsky and his father again, then plays a little riff on the piano he would expand on later in the tour before starting "Dream On." People standing during the tune gets some in the crowd agitated.

Perry plays sweet notes on "Sweet Emotion," really capturing the rhythm and feel of the song. He also plays a great, frenetic solo during "Milk Cow Blues."

Strangely, Tyler tells Kramer to stop "Toys In the Attic" after the first verse, just 30 seconds in, and directs the band to begin "Train Kept A Rollin'." It's unclear what caused Tyler to do this.

Hoffman Estates, Poplar Creek, Illinois. Thursday, July 12, 1984. Audience recording. Sound quality: C-

Back In The Saddle, Mama Kin, Bone To Bone (Coney Island White Fish Boy), Big Ten Inch Record, Three Mile Smile, Reefer Headed Woman, Lord Of The Thighs, Last Child, Get The Lead Out, Red House, Lightning Strikes, Same Old Song And Dance, Dream On, Sweet Emotion, Walk This Way, Milk Cow Blues, Toys In The Attic.

Perry gets some feedback together during "Back In The Saddle." Tyler lets the enthusiastic crowd take over during "Mama Kin," withholding the last word of each verse, a cool effect. Tyler chastises the security during "Big Ten Inch Record" for being too aggressive.

Tyler then criticizes local newspaper coverage of recent gigs as he sings "Three Mile Smile." "Don't believe it!" he says. Perry plays a country-ish solo during the tune.

"Mr. Brad Whitford!" Tyler says as the guitarist whips through a searing solo during "Lord Of The Thighs." Perry notes the band is in Chicago, northern home of the blues, as he launches "Red House." Tyler expands his piano riff before "Dream On" on this night.

247

The tape finishes with "Toys In The Attic," but "Train Kept A-Rollin'" was certainly played.

Two days later, a gig in Springfield, Illinois would see a meltdown.

Band's reunion marred by fight

SPRINGFIELD, Ill. (UPI)-- A reunion of the heavy metal rock group Aerosmith was marred by a fight that broke out among band members after the seemingly intoxicated lead singer Steven Tyler fell off the stage.

The band's scheduled 90-minute concert before an estimated 8,000 fans who paid $11 per ticket was cut short Saturday night by about an hour because of the scuffle at the Prairie Capital Convention Center.

Convention officials were undecided on whether to issue refunds.

Witnesses said Tyler, 36, appeared intoxicated before he stumbled off the stage. Tyler, who was not injured in the fall, then got involved in a scuffle with fellow band members when he returned to the stage, witnesses said.

Castle Farms Music Theater, Charlevoix, Michigan. Saturday, July 21, 1984. Audience recording. Sound quality: B-

Back In The Saddle, Mama Kin, Bone To Bone (Coney Island White Fish Boy), Big Ten Inch Record, Three Mile Smile, Reefer Headed Woman, Lord Of The Thighs, Get The Lead Out, Last Child, Lick And A Promise, Red House, Lightning Strikes, Same Old Song And Dance, Dream On, Sweet Emotion, Walk This Way, Milk Cow Blues, Toys In The Attic.

There is a lot of tuning up by Perry and Whitford as the opening tape rolls. A great recording from the audience on this night at the outdoor gig.

"Back In The Saddle" features an odd, premature ending, as the band gets off track.

Tyler invents new lyrics during "Mama Kin," and he again leaves off the last word of each verse to allow the crowd to sing. Kramer starts the beat to "Big Ten Inch Record," but it's "Bone To Bone (Coney Island White Fish

Boy)" that is next, with Tyler saying, "Mr. Perry, introduce this song, with your guitar, with your guitar, with your guitar, with your guitar."

"Hanging out in the parking lot for an hour and a half?" Tyler says as "Big Ten Inch Record" starts properly. "I was out there! I know what (you guys) are doing."

"Get The Lead Out" is played tightly and crisply, the nice recording bringing out all the details. A fine version of "Lick And A Promise" follows.

"We got a new member of the band tonight who is going to sing something for you," Tyler jokes before introducing Perry, who takes the mic before "Red House." Perry then comments on the venue: "I don't know where the hell we are playing, some enchanted castle or something like that. But we're gonna play some blues."

"You remember a group called Aerosmith who did a song called 'Lightning Strikes?'" Tyler says after, asking the crowd if they watched MTV. "We are all lucky it's not striking tonight." After the tune Tyler says, "There is a June bug in my Jack Daniels!"

"Same Old Song And Dance" has a rhythmic start, the band building the intro in a slow, bluesy way. Tyler again plays a piano intro to "Dream On."

Tyler does a little perverted poetry during the break in "Sweet Emotion": "I stuck my tongue in, and I licked and I licked," before Kramer comes in with his drums as the band finishes off a wild version of the tune.

"Sweet Jesus! We can't continue with the show right now, I ripped my pants!" Tyler exclaims before "Milk Cow Blues." It's too bad the recording ends midway through "Toys In The Attic," as Whitford's rhythm playing is sublime during the tune.

AEROSMITH. The hard-rocking Aerosmith band will perform at the Toledo Sports Arena Monday, July 23, at 8 p.m. Tickets are $11 in advance and $12 at the door. Orion the Hunter will appear with the group. Tickets are avvailable at Abbey Roads, the sports arena box office, 1 Main St., Boogie Records, Head Shed, Finders Records and Reflections in Fremont.

Sports Arena, Toledo, Ohio. Monday, July 23, 1984. Audience recording. Sound quality: C

Back In The Saddle, Mama Kin, Bone To Bone (Coney Island White Fish Boy), Big Ten Inch Record, Three Mile Smile, Reefer Headed Woman, Lord Of The Thighs, Last Child, Get The Lead Out, Lick And A Promise, Red House, Lightning Strikes, Same Old Song And Dance, Dream On, Sweet Emotion, Walk This Way, Milk Cow Blues, Toys In The Attic, Train Kept A-Rollin'.

Tyler switches up the lyrics to "Back In The Saddle" on this night. "Holy Fuckin' Toledo," Tyler says in a Spinal Tap moment.

Before "Momma Kin," Tyler thanks "Roz" for introducing the band. "Mama Kin" also sees some alternative lyrics, and a fan singing a line as Tyler dips his mic into the crowd.

"It's hot in here, ain't it?" Tyler says, then a large firecracker goes off to which he exclaims: "Shit!"

"Rumor has it that we ain't loud enough. Is that true? That we ain't loud enough?" Tyler says as "Big Ten Inch Record" gets underway. The guitars sound really sharp and crisp as they join the tune. Tyler tells the crowd to stop pushing. "You can see me just as well from over there, as well from here."

Perry plays a very melodic solo during "Lord Of The Thighs." "Do you know you're being taped tonight?" Tyler asks. "We might just use it for MTV or a live album." "Same Old Song And Dance" gets another nice jam to launch the tune.

"The infamous Mr. Joey Kramer" as Tyler calls him, starts "Walk This Way" with a little pause. "We're gonna do something Elvis Presley did, and he didn't even write it, and we picked up on that shit," Tyler says before blowing his harp to start "Milk Cow Blues."

Navy Island, Saint Paul, Minnesota. Friday, July 27, 1984. Audience recording. Sound quality: C-

Back In The Saddle, Mama Kin, Bone To Bone (Coney Island White Fish Boy), Big Ten Inch Record, Three Mile Smile, Reefer Headed Woman, Lord Of The Thighs, Get The Lead Out, Last Child, Red House, Lightning Strikes, Same Old Song And Dance, Dream On, Sweet Emotion, Walk This Way, Milk Cow Blues, Toys In The Attic, Train Kept A-Rollin'.

The exuberance of the crowd at the outdoor venue is caught well on tape this night; it's a non-stop party.

"Are you glad we're back?" Tyler asks the throng before "Three Mile Smile," hitting the song with great gusto. The mini "Reefer Headed Woman" is also played well.

The band tries to start "Same Old Song And Dance," but there is pushing in the front and Tyler warns the crowd to step back, and it takes a while before the band launches the song.

"I think they can hear us in that apartment building across the way," Tyler pointing toward the cluster of homes. He then leads the crowd to say, "Fuck You!" "You think they heard us?" Tyler asks.

Tyler again asks the crowd to stop pushing after "Sweet Emotion." Tyler gets agitated. "If you don't quit pushing we're gonna split!"

Finally, the band starts a bluesy "Milk Cow Blues." Tyler leads a version of "Happy Birthday" to an unknown person, then the band jumps into "Train Kept A-Rollin'" to end the show as Perry gets a "machine gun" tone from his guitar before it's all done.

While an ad for the show lists the 27th, and a write up in the Minneapolis Star Tribune on July 22 only discusses one show on the 27th, some tickets for the event list a 7/26/84 date.

Aerosmith — Batten down the hatches for Boston's hard-rocking Bad Boys, who blow into the Worcester Centrum tomorrow and Sunday, 7:30 p.m.

– STEVE MORSE

The Centrum, Worcester, Massachusetts. Saturday, August 4, 1984. Audience recording. Sound quality: D

Back In The Saddle, Mama Kin, Bone To Bone (Coney Island White Fish Boy), Big Ten Inch Record, Three Mile Smile, Reefer Headed Woman, Lord Of The Thighs, Last Child, Get The Lead Out, Red House, Lightning Strikes, Same Old Song And Dance, Dream On, Sweet Emotion, Walk This Way, Milk Cow Blues, Toys In The Attic, Train Kept A-Rollin'.

"We're baaaack," Tyler sings to the hometown crowd during a high-energy "Back In The Saddle." The crowd is massive and gives the band a warm welcome.

"A song we've never done before," Tyler says with a straight face as "Bone To Bone (Coney Island Whitefish Boy)" starts. Kramer's drumming to "Big Ten Inch Record" gets the crowd clapping along as Tyler dedicates the tune to band supporter WBCN.

"Oh yeah? Tyler says at the end of "Get The Lead Out," which is greeted by a loud cheer. Despite the rough recording, Hamilton's bluesy bass lines stand out during "Red House."

Tyler introduces the band and then the road crew: "There's going to be a big party with these (guys) at The Metro tonight! The boys!"

"Something Beethoven taught me," Tyler says as he launches into a brief piano reading of "One Way Street" before "Dream On."

"Every time Aerosmith plays here we break the house record! Every time! That's because of you!" Tyler says to the masses after "Dream On." Before "Sweet Emotion" Tyler quips: "Tom Hamilton and I wrote this song long ago and radio won't stop playing it! We are tired of them playing it!"

After the band leaves the stage before the encore, a WBCN DJ addresses the crowd: "I want to tell you how proud all of us over at BCN are of one of America's greatest rock and roll bands, Aerosmith! Let's hear it for Aerosmith and bring them on for one more song. Let them hear it. From the Rock of Massachusetts to you! Bring back Aerosmith!"

"Who is this kumquat (the DJ), who is this man?" Tyler jokes. "I hear a train a comin'."

✔ **Aerosmith**
A potent acid-blues mix is the dynamic trademark of Boston's long-lived, once-troubled but newly reunited band of rockers called Aerosmith.
Tonight 7:30 p.m.
Centrum, 50 Foster st., Worcester. Telephone 798-8888.
Tickets $11.50-$12.50.

The Centrum, Worcester, Massachusetts. Sunday, August 5, 1984. Audience recording. Sound quality: C
Back In The Saddle, Mama Kin, Bone To Bone (Coney Island White Fish Boy), Big Ten Inch Record, Three Mile Smile, Reefer Headed Woman, Lord Of The Thighs, Last Child, Get The Lead Out, Red House, Lightning Strikes, Same

Old Song And Dance, Dream On, Sweet Emotion, Walk This Way, Milk Cow Blues, Toys In The Attic, Train Kept A-Rollin'.

"You know you're being taped tonight," Tyler says (though only this audience recording has ever surfaced) before "Three Mile Smile," where Tyler takes a walk in the "warm Boston sun."

Interesting guitar playing from Perry and Whitford highlights "Lord Of The Thighs," as the duo revive some of their epic jams from the 1970s.

"We have done two nights in a row here, didn't we? Well, last night I read in the paper 'Steve' Perry, shit, so fuck them, OK," Tyler says before "Last Child," alluding to an error in the paper. He then says "Brad and I wrote this a long time ago when our dicks were real small and had no wrinkles at all, and it goes like this..."

"One Way Street" gets another short work through on piano by Tyler before "Dream On." "Shit, this is home for us!" Tyler says after "Sweet Emotion." "Walk This Way" features some non-band vocals on the "walk this way" line, maybe from a fan as Tyler puts his mic to those in the front row.

"Were some of you here last night?" Tyler asks before "Milk Cow Blues." "You have never seen rock and roll like this!" And he is right. "This show was a lot better than last night" a fan in the crowd can be heard saying before "Train Kept A-Rollin'," which ends the gig.

Spectrum, Philadelphia, Pennsylvania. Wednesday, August 8, 1984. Audience recording. Sound quality: C+

Back In The Saddle, Mama Kin, Bone To Bone (Coney Island White Fish Boy), Big Ten Inch Record, Three Mile Smile, Reefer Headed Woman, Lord Of The Thighs, Last Child, Get The Lead Out, Red House, Lightning Strikes, Same Old Song And Dance, Dream On, Sweet Emotion, Walk This Way, Milk Cow Blues, Toys In The Attic, Train Kept A-Rollin'.

AC/DC's "Girls Got The Rhythm" is the house music as the Philly crowd settles in for a night of Aerosmith. "We are taping your asses tonight!" Tyler announces after "Bone To Bone (Coney Island White Fish Boy). But as with other shows on this segment of the tour, the tapes have not seen the light of day. "Let the women up front!" Tyler says, as he notices a swarm of dudes at the barrier.

"Stop throwing shit," Tyler says before "Last Child." Fortunately, it's a small mention and there wouldn't be another Philly issue on this night.

"Red House" features cool descending riffs by Perry. "This chick has done me wrong, so I'm looking for a little love!" Perry says, strumming his guitar, adding, "this is how we do it in Boston," then brings the song to a close.

Tyler gets into a bit of "One Way Street" before "Dream On." As "Sweet Emotion" starts on its frenzied close, Tyler yells, "Say something, bitch!"

Tyler gets in some cool grunts during "Milk Cow Blues," as the band plays. Tyler gets out a guttural scream at its end. "This is one of our other road crew inmates. I want you to sing, 'Happy Birthday,'" Tyler tells the audience as he brings the roadie on stage.

BEST BETS

Tomorrow night, Aerosmith, back together for a little rough-house and spending money, trip all over themselves to get to the Forum. If Steve Tyler's in top form (keep the Jack Daniels flowing), it ought to be quite a spectacle.

The Forum, Montreal, Quebec, Canada. Saturday, August 11, 1984. Audience recording. Sound quality: D

Back In The Saddle, Mama Kin, Bone To Bone (Coney Island White Fish Boy), Big Ten Inch Record, Three Mile Smile, Reefer Headed Woman, Lord Of The Thighs, Last Child, Get The Lead Out, Red House, Lightning Strikes, Same Old Song And Dance, Dream On, Sweet Emotion, Walk This Way, Milk Cow Blues, Toys In The Attic, Train Kept A-Rollin'.

The band is greeted with a loud fireworks explosion from the crowd during the intro tape, making one wonder if Quebec separatists were planning an attack! During "Mama Kin" there is a slight pause after the opening notes, an oddity.

"Are you going to stop me from drinking beer at the party," Tyler quips as Kramer starts into "Big Ten Inch Record." At the end he says, "an old negro wrote that song," but it's said with full admiration for Bull "Moose" Jackson, who first recorded the tune in the 1950s.

"I got a reefer headed guitar player," Tyler sings during "Reefer Headed Woman."

Whitford and Perry are in fine form as they trade licks in "Lord Of The Thighs." God has never created such a fine pairing of players or a more perfect vehicle! Moody and full of emotion, the players create a textured feel. It's a shame such moments were not professionally recorded for dissemination but hats off to our taper.

"Lightning Strikes" again strikes without the more familiar keyboard opening and feels rather stark, although the song is played quite well. "Same Old Song And Dance" has the bluesy intro again and gets a nice cheer from the crowd as the song kicks in proper.

"This song is dedicated to anyone who is taking acid in this audience tonight," Tyler says strangely before "Dream On." During "Walk This Way," Tyler yells, "Get rid of the cops!"

"Train Kept A-Rollin'" is edited post show on the recording, likely to fit the gig on a C-90 cassette tape, the medium of the day. Remember those, kids?

Veterans Memorial Coliseum, Phoenix, Arizona. Monday, August 20, 1984. Audience recording. Sound quality: C

Back In The Saddle, Mama Kin, Bone To Bone (Coney Island White Fish Boy), Big Ten Inch Record, Three Mile Smile, Reefer Headed Woman, Lord Of The Thighs, Last Child, Get The Lead Out, Red House, Lightning Strikes, Same Old Song And Dance, Dream On, Sweet Emotion, Walk This Way, Milk Cow Blues, Toys In The Attic, Train Kept A-Rollin'.

M O N D A Y

Aerosmith

This reformed, hard-rock band will appear at an 8 p.m. concert in Veteran's Memorial Coliseum, 1826 W. McDowell Road. Opening the show will be Black and Blue. Tickets are $12.50 and available at the coliseum box office; Bill's Sight & Sound; Charts and Zia records; and the Paraphernalia Boutique.

"We're baaaack!" Tyler exclaims as the "Back In The Saddle" tour visits the Southwest. "My kind of crowd! Ya'll glad to see us back together?" as the crowd screams its approval before "Three Mile Smile." Perry strums a few chords of "Come Together" before the track.

"Lord Of The Thighs" features great slide work by Perry. Whitford employs a bit of tremolo on the last part of "Last Child."

Perry takes the mic during "Red House" and says of his former lady friend: "That bitch has been fucking with my head!" Tyler again bangs out a little "One Way Street" and seems to hit every key on the piano before settling into "Dream On." Tyler tells the crowd the band is recording the gig. "Drugs in the attic" again becomes the vocal refrain during "Toys In The Attic."

Perry dedicates a song to his mom who he says is in the crowd. "I'm going to play it for you just right," he says before the band launches "Train Kept A-Rollin'."

AEROSMITH, ROUGH CUTT (Golden Hall, 202 C St., San Diego, (619) 236-6510) Steven Tyler and company are back to rock your socks off. 8 p.m.

Golden Hall, San Diego, California. Wednesday, August 22, 1984. Audience recording. Sound quality: C

Back In The Saddle, Mama Kin, Bone To Bone (Coney Island White Fish Boy), Big Ten Inch Record, Three Mile Smile, Reefer Headed Woman, Lord Of The Thighs, Last Child, Get The Lead Out, Red House, Lightning Strikes, Same Old Song And Dance, Dream On, Sweet Emotion, Walk This Way, Milk Cow Blues, Toys In The Attic, Train Kept A-Rollin'.

Perry and Whitford decide to tune up their axes as the intro tape rolls. Kramer also bangs away on his kit. Well, better late than never.

"C'mon Trigger!" Tyler exclaims as he sings his way out of "Back In The Saddle" as Perry's feedback rings through the hall. "I'm going to dedicate this one to all the (people) who were here last time," Tyler says, maybe making a reference to the show in the city the year prior.

Whitford lays down a particularly smoking solo during "Big Ten Inch Record." "Rumor has it that politics and rock and roll don't mix. The first and only song Aerosmith ever wrote about politics or politicians...was involved in this song here, which we call "Three Mile Smile."

Tyler again mentions the gig is being recorded. Video recordings from later in the tour did in fact turn up, but it's not known if the singer was talking about audio or video here.

256

Whitford pours in another white-hot solo during "Last Child." His playing is truly sublime on this night. Kramer bangs out a machine-gun like flurry as "Sweet Emotion" winds down, always a highlight of the live show.

Tyler tells the crowd Kramer will introduce a brand-new song, but it's a Tyler joke, it's "Walk This Way." "I want you all to know I'm a liar."

Tyler says "Milk Cow Blues" is a tune Elvis Presley wrote, and has a prolonged opening featuring Tyler's harmonica work. "Hey Joe, come here a second!" as Tyler beckons Perry to close out the tune.

Kramer bangs on his kit before Tyler says: "If you listen real close, you'll hear something. Do you hear a train?" as the band jumps into the song to end the show, per usual.

Los Angeles Times

'Friday, August 24, 1984

AEROSMITH STANDS THE TEST OF TIME

By MATT DAMSKER,
Times Staff Writer

SAN DIEGO—A regrouped, presumably reformed Aerosmith is back, visiting its stormy '70s rock upon old loyalists and younger headbangers. Touring without benefit of a new album or, worse, without an MTV video, the band does have its original lineup intact for the first time since 1979, when it all but self-destructed in a willing the usual unstable mixture of ego, excess and ennui. By then, Aerosmith had laid down some classic hard rock, cannily bridging the gap between the swing of the Rolling Stones' R&B and the stalk of Led Zeppelin's heavy metal. Theatrically, the band has never seemed much more than a poor man's Stones, but by now Aerosmith performs with the polish and passion of men who've learned their lessons well. Lead singer Steven Tyler commands as the prancing, Jaggering jester—scarves streaming, his voice shrill yet rebel-soulful—while guitarist Joe Perry is the lucid, fast-fingered flash point, sparring with guitarist Brad Whitford as bassist Tom Hamilton and drummer Joey Kramer thunder skillfully.

None of this was lost on the more than 3,000 who packed Golden Hall here Wednesday night. They stood on chairs, rapt and responsive, from start to finish, as Aerosmith delivered its fierce, sardonic anthems. There was the dark bravado of "Back in the Saddle," the risque R&B shuffle of "Big Ten Inch Record," the erotic, infectious, chew-'em-up riffs of "Lord of the Thighs," "Walk This Way," "Sweet Emotion" and the baroque fervor of "Dream On." Aerosmith may have trouble withstanding its inner turbulence, but so far its best music is standing the test of time.

The group is slated to appear Saturday and Sunday nights at the Greek Theatre and Tuesday night at the Orange Amphitheatre in San Bernardino.

AEROSMITH with Black 'N' Blue. Greek Theater; Sat.-Sun., Aug. 25-26. Ticketron/Teletron 410-1062. Info 642-3888.

Greek Theater, Los Angeles, California. Sunday, August 25, 1984. Videotape soundboard recording.

Sound quality: B

Back In The Saddle, Mama Kin, Bone To Bone (Coney Island White Fish Boy), Big Ten Inch Record, Three Mile Smile, Reefer Headed Woman, Lord Of The Thighs, Last Child, Get The Lead Out, Red House, Lightning Strikes,

257

Same Old Song And Dance, Dream On, Sweet Emotion, Walk This Way, Milk Cow Blues, Toys In The Attic, Train Kept A-Rollin'.

Tyler is imbibed on this night, but the gig comes off without a hitch. "Big Ten Inch Record" is a "song about (roadie) Joe Baptista," Tyler says. During the intro to "Three Mile Smile," Tyler says politics and rock and roll pair like "escargot and ice cream."

Whitford lights up "Lord Of The Thighs" with some great jamming, though the band has a little trouble finding its way back to Tyler's vocal after. Some unique passages from the guitar players really stand out later.

"Big Bad Brad, also known as the main vein…," is Tyler's intro to "Last Child." Tyler creates a largely incoherent vocal intro to "Same Old Song And Dance," the tune highlighted by Hamilton's outro jam.

A sloppy, but fun "Sweet Emotion" this night as the band goofs at points, while Tyler squeezes his words out in a lethargic way. Whose says rock and roll must be perfect!

"Milk Cow Blues" has trouble getting off the ground. Tyler asks Perry to introduce the tune. "You talking to me? Perry says, mimicking the line from "Taxi Driver." Perry goes on to say the band has jammed on the tune on stage for years, but never put it on a record, forgetting it was on "Draw The Line." Whoops. The band then does an around the horn introduction of themselves, with Tyler calling himself "lips among lips!" The band then starts in with an old blues pattern before Tyler begins the theme properly with his harmonica.

Tyler's vocalizations can be heard on the soundboard recording during "Toys In The Attic," likely inaudible out in the crowd.

This is one of the shows were a pro-shot videotape has appeared.

Greek Theater, Los Angeles, California. Sunday, August 26, 1984. Audience recording. Sound quality: C
Back In The Saddle, Mama Kin, Bone To Bone (Coney Island White Fish Boy), Big Ten Inch Record, Three Mile Smile, Reefer Headed Woman, Lord Of The Thighs, Last Child, Get The Lead Out, Red House, Lightning Strikes, Same Old Song And Dance, Dream On, Sweet Emotion, Walk This Way, Milk Cow Blues (cut), Train Kept A-Rollin'.

"Welcome back Joe Perry and Brad Whitford! Ladies and gentlemen, Aerosmith!" yells the taper. A bunch of buddies decided to bring a recorder to this show. It's a funny group having a good time. They are all over this recording, but rather than detracting it adds to the ambiance. It seems like one of the gang must have said before the show that Black and Blue (the opener) would be better than Aerosmith, and his pals mock him. They also keep saying how this night was better than the previous night, when the band also played the Greek.

"There is magic in the air tonight!" Tyler gushes after "Mama Kin." Perry plays a particularly funky solo during "Three Mile Smile."

"Last Child" features a cool, sly solo by Whitford. "It's time for second gear, maybe overdrive," Tyler says as he introduces Perry before "Red House."

"Rick Dufay is in the audience somewhere," Tyler says before "Lightning Strikes." "He used to be with us, bless his soul."

"You recorded history!" one of the gang says to the taper after "Dream On." "Third gear baby, third gear," Tyler says before "Walk This Way," then makes a fuzzy Burt Reynolds reference. "Milk Cow Blues" is cut midway through and suddenly "Train Kept A-Rollin'" is there to end the recording.

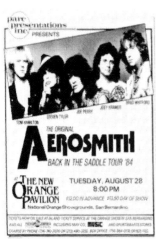

New Orange Pavilion, San Bernardino, California. Tuesday, August 28, 1984. Audience recording. Sound quality: C

Back In The Saddle, Mama Kin, Bone To Bone (Coney Island White Fish Boy), Big Ten Inch Record, Three Mile Smile (cut), Reefer Headed Woman, Lord Of The Thighs, Last Child, Get The Lead Out, Red House, Lightning Strikes (beginning cut), Same Old Song And Dance, Dream On, Sweet Emotion, Walk This Way, Milk Cow Blues, Toys In The Attic, Train Kept A-Rollin'.

"*We're* back, *We're* back in the saddle again!" Tyler sings inclusively as the gig gets underway in San Berdu.

Perry gets off a wicked solo during "Bone To Bone (Coney Island White Fish Boy)." The recording goes awry as Tyler introduces "Three Mile Smile," where (this time) he mentions that politics and music go together like "escargot and apple pie, it doesn't mix." The tape suddenly cuts out but comes back for "Reefer Headed Woman." There are sporadic speed issues with the recording, and some bleed through from Aerosmith studio albums is audible in the background.

Whitford displays powerful, energetic playing during a crisp "Lord Of The Thighs," which he continues on "Last Child." A great night for him. Not to be outdone, Perry shows off some nimble fretwork at the start of "Red House."

Whitford's solo during "Milk Cow Blues" cuts through the arena like a laser, sharp and focused. Tyler lets out one of his guttural grunts as Kramer concludes his solo.

"Toys In The Attic" gets a little too much echo at its beginning, as though Tyler is singing from The Alps.

The guitar players have a nice duel on "Train Kept A Rollin'" to close things out.

Oakland Coliseum Arena, Oakland, California. Friday, August 31, 1984. Audience recording. Sound quality: C. Videotape soundboard recording. Sound quality: B+

Back In The Saddle, Mama Kin, Bone To Bone (Coney Island White Fish Boy), Big Ten Inch Record, Three Mile Smile, Reefer Headed Woman, Lord Of The Thighs, Last Child, Get The Lead Out, Red House, Lightning Strikes, Same Old Song And Dance, Dream On, Sweet Emotion, Walk This Way, Milk Cow Blues, Toys In The Attic, Train Kept A-Rollin'.

The band books the 14,000-seat arena, but only 3,000 show up. Nevertheless, the band puts on a good show, even if Tyler is not at his healthiest.

Perry provides some backup vocals during "Back In The Saddle." "A song that we rarely play," Tyler says as he introduces "Bone To Bone (Coney Island White Fish Boy)."

Perry plays staccato guitar during "Big Ten Inch Record" as Tyler references KMET and Dr. Demento, where he first heard the tune he was inspired to record with the band.

"We'd like to play the first and only song we've ever done that was..." Tyler says as Kramer starts "Three Mile Smile." As the song begins, Tyler completes his sentence during the tune's breaks: "Political!" "Even if they don't," "Go together."

"The main vein!" is how Tyler introduces Whitford as "Lord Of The Thighs" launches. The description fits the rock solid Whitford; his contributions to the band can't be overlooked.

"Sorry, I took a whiz! Joe Perry!" Tyler says after "Red House." "Who's throwing their shoe up at me? Are you trying to give me some soul? I don't need your soul. I'm not an evangelist. I'm a rock and roll player, baby. You understand that shit? I'm here to get you off, and myself."

Kramer's drums are isolated in a unique way during a few beats of

"Lightning Strikes." Whitford solos wonderfully into the night on "Same Old Song And Dance" as the tune gets underway. Tyler gives a shaky vocal on "Dream On," yet sees it through.

Perry's guitar sounds like a motorcycle engine during the lead up to the close out of "Sweet Emotion." The guitarist then smashes his guitar and does so with efficiency! He is handed another to finish out the tune.

Perry and Tyler do a vocal pairing during "Walk This Way," heard well on the soundboard recording taken from a pro-shot video.

Toward the end of "Milk Cow Blues," Tyler places his harmonica on his shoulder and appears ready to flick it off with his finger, but then Perry — who is playing right behind the sitting singer on the drum riser — bonks Tyler on the head as he jumps out from behind him and across the stage, finishing the song as he knocks over a mic stand as he makes his way back across the stage!

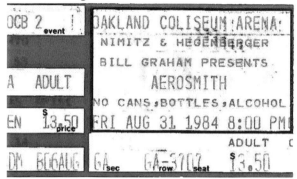

A circular lighting truss lowers over Kramer during his drum solo, appearing as though he is under a giant chandelier! The drummer breaks up his solo into bits, driving the crowd into a frenzy as he asks them if they want to hear more after each segment. They do.

"I hear a train a comin'! Something tells me a train is a comin'. A big fat, gray-haired old train!" says Tyler, who manages a backflip before the tune! This is the last gig of the summer run of shows.

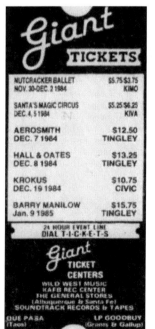

Tingley Coliseum, Albuquerque, New Mexico. Friday, December 7, 1984. Audience recording. Sound quality: D+

Back In The Saddle, Bone To Bone (Coney Island White Fish Boy), S.O.S. (Too Bad), Lord Of The Thighs, Three Mile Smile, Reefer Headed Woman, Movin' Out, Adam's Apple, Last Child, Walkin' The Dog, Let The Music Do The Talking, Red House, Seasons Of Wither, Dream On, Sweet Emotion, Walk This Way, Same Old Song And Dance, Toys In The Attic, Rats In The Cellar.

The band takes the rest of the summer off (some reports have Tyler going into rehab) and emerges on tour at the end of the year with an interesting new setlist, packed with goodies from the past.

First, the band pulls out "S.O.S. (Too Bad)" for the first time since 1979. "Movin' Out" appears for the first time since 1974. "Adam's Apple" gets its first live airing since 1977 and "Walkin' The Dog" for the first time since 1980. The band is looking to get in touch with its roots.

The band also works up a live version of Perry's "Let The Music Do The Talking" with original lyrics, later re-written for the "Done With Mirrors" album. This take sounds a little tepid in comparison to the later version, but a nice addition to the changing setlist.

The band also conjures up the first "Seasons of Wither" since 1980. There is an odd "Star Wars" -like theremin effect during "Sweet Emotion."

"Rats or Train? Rats or Train?" Tyler asks the crowd to pick a song for the encore. The band starts in on a bit of both before launching into "Rats In The Cellar," surely an oddity as "Train Kept A-Rollin'" has always been the de rigueur closer for this time period. Hot show with a fresh, wide-ranging setlist.

Memorial Coliseum, Corpus Christi, Texas. Monday, December 10, 1984. Audience recording. Sound quality: D

Back In The Saddle, Bone To Bone (Coney Island White Fish Boy), S.O.S. (Too Bad), Big Ten Inch Record, Three Mile Smile, Reefer Headed Woman, Lord Of The Thighs, Movin' Out, Adam's Apple, Last Child, Let The Music Do The Talking, Dream On, Lightning Strikes, Same Old Song And Dance, Sweet Emotion, Walk This Way, Rats In The Cellar, Toys In The Attic, Train' Kept A Rollin'.

"The one and only song we do off of 'Night In The Ruts,' called 'Three Mile Smile,'" says Tyler either forgetting or not knowing "Bone To Bone (Coney Island White Fish Boy)" is off the same album! I guess we can forgive him.

"Jumpin' Joe Perry!" Tyler calls out before "Movin' Out." "The skinniest, ugliest motherfucker up here, Mr. Brad Whitford would like to talk to you in his own special way," Tyler says. There must be a compliment in there somewhere. "Last Child" is the next tune.

"A song you never heard before, it's going to be on the next album," is the way Tyler introduces "Let The Music Do The Talking." I guess no one bought Joe Perry's debut album? "Muchas gracias" Tyler says at the end of "Dream On."

"Same Old Song And Dance" starts in a slow way until the band picks up steam. "Mr. Tom Hamilton, in the realm," Tyler chimes in before "Sweet Emotion," which includes the "Oh Well" lyric once again.

"Rats In The Cellar" is an all-out jam in Corpus Christi! It segues into "Toys In The Attic" without skipping a beat. "Train Kept A-Rollin'" features Perry's "Strangers In The Night" reference as the song comes to an end.

. · ·:. .... Headed for Reunion are
Aerosmith Dec. 13 · · : ·· ·:. . . ε.·. . .

AEROSMITH — In concert at Reunion Dec. 13. Tickets at Rainbow.

Reunion Arena, Dallas, Texas. Thursday, December 13, 1984. Audience recording. Sound quality: D

Rats In The Cellar, Bone To Bone (Coney Island White Fish Boy), S.O.S. (Too Bad), Big Ten Inch Record, Three Mile Smile, Reefer Headed Woman, Lord Of The Thighs, Seasons of Wither, Movin' Out, Adam's Apple, Last Child, Let The Music Do The Talking, Red House, Sweet Emotion, Same Old Song And Dance, Walk This Way, Milk Cow Blues, Toys In The Attic.

A pleasant surprise on this night: "Rats In The Cellar" is installed as the show opener. The high-energy tune is perfect for the slot. Good choice.

"Oh my God, 'Adam's Apple'," says an excited fan as the band plays the fan favorite.

Perry and Whitford really outdo themselves on "Red House," playing a high energy version. Highly inspired!

Perry lets the feedback fly during the "Sweet Emotion" break, sending the crowd into a frenzy: sonic sublimity!

The whole recording is hard to hear, and "Train Kept A-Rollin'" is missing, but what is caught on tape is fantastic.

The Summit, Houston, Texas. Friday, December 14, 1984. Videotape soundboard recording. Sound quality: B

Rats In The Cellar, Bone To Bone (Coney Island White Fish Boy), S.O.S. (Too Bad), Three Mile Smile, Reefer Headed Woman, Lord Of The Thighs, Movin' Out, Movin' Out, Adam's Apple, Last Child, Let The Music Do The Talking, Dream On, Lightning Strikes, Sweet Emotion, Same Old Song And Dance, Walk This Way, Milk Cow Blues, Toys In The Attic, Train' Kept A Rollin'.

Rats, Bone To Bone, SOS, Big Ten Inch, Three Mile, Reefer, Thighs, Movin' Out, Adam's Apple, Last Child, Let The Music, Red House, Dream On, Lightning Strikes, Oh Well/SE, SOSAD, WTW, Milk Cow Blues/Drum Solo, Toys, Train

Some great interplay between Perry and Whitford on "Rats In The Cellar" on this night.

"A song about a Texas whorehouse," Tyler announces as the band launches "S.O.S. (Too Bad)."

"C'mon baby, catch your breath," Tyler teases Kramer after the tune. "C'mon, c'mon." The drummer then starts a beat that leads into "Three Mile Smile," a unique opening indeed.

Tyler raps about a "backstage pass and free blow job" as he introduces Whitford as the band gets into a feedback-drenched "Lord Of The Thighs."

"A song I don't think you've heard Aerosmith play, someone else did it who is very close to us," Tyler says as he introduces "Let The Music Do The Talking." "That's going to be on the new album I think...if everyone votes for it," Perry says after.

"Lightning Strikes" returns to the set and starts with a guttural Tyler vocalization and Perry yanking his guitar strings.

Perry strums the opening notes to "Chip Away The Stone" before "Sweet Emotion," and then does it again before "Milk Cow Blues," but no one in the band joins in as Tyler blows some riffs on his harmonica. Tyler improvises "Hit The Road Jack" during the tune.

The ending to "Combination" is played before Kramer launches into his solo. Some light radio interference permeates the end of the show.

"We are going to do a very slow and funky song about the Middle East crisis," Tyler jokes as "Train Kept A-Rollin'" ends the show.

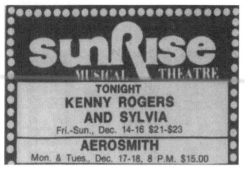

Sunrise Musical Theater, Fort Lauderdale, Florida. Tuesday, December 18, 1984. Audience recording. Sound quality: C+

Rats In The Cellar, Back In The Saddle, Bone To Bone (Coney Island White Fish Boy), Three Mile Smile, Reefer Headed Woman, Lord Of The Thighs, Movin' Out, Last Child, Let The Music Do The Talking, Red House, Dream On, Lightning Strikes, Sweet Emotion, Same Old Song And Dance, Walk This Way, Milk Cow Blues, Toys In The Attic, Train' Kept A Rollin'.

"I've been fortunate enough to be given a cowboy hat tonight by someone, and to honor you for that move..." Tyler says as the band adds "Back In The Saddle" back to the setlist, this time in the number two slot.

Whitford lets loose with a volley of notes during "Lord Of The Thighs," countered by Perry's slower, delicate notes. There is a great atmosphere this night as the band plays this smaller theater.

The crowd claps rhythmically along during "Moving Out," really feeling the song. The whole band is inspired during "Last Child." Tyler does some piano playing before settling into "Dream On."

"Sing that song, you bitch!" is Tyler familiar refrain after "Same Old Song And Dance." "Milk Cow Blues" has Perry leading the band into the frantic part of "Combination" before closing out the tune.

Aerosmith, with Black 'n' Blue: 8 p.m. Dec. 20; Orange County Convention/Civic Center, 9800 International Drive, Orlando; $12.50 (OCC, SAS).

Orange County Civic Center, Orlando, Florida. Thursday, December 20, 1984. Audience recording. Sound quality: C

Rats In The Cellar, Bone To Bone (Coney Island White Fish Boy), Three Mile Smile, Reefer Headed Woman, Lord Of The Thighs, Movin' Out, Last Child, Let The Music Do The Talking, Red House, Dream On, Lightning Strikes, Sweet Emotion, Same Old Song And Dance.

Perry plays over the opening tape before launching the band into "Rats In The Cellar." "Yeah, we back, baby!" Tyler yells, as the crowd cheers its approval.

"Bone To Bone (Coney Island Whitefish Boy)" starts with a few off notes, but the band recovers just fine. Perry plays some wild lead during the song, almost heavy metal in nature.

"The first song I wrote with Joe Perry, it dates back a millennium..." But Tyler is mistaken as the band goes into "Three Mile Smile," not "Moving Out." Perry almost sounds like he is playing part of Zeppelin's "Heartbreaker" as he solos away on the tune.

"As I was saying before, the first song Joe and I wrote together..." as the band does get into "Moving Out" this time. Perry does a great call and response with his vocals and guitar during "Red House."

"We only got one video on MTV, we are going to have more," Tyler says prophetically before "Lightning Strikes." As the song concludes Kramer repeats the roundhouse drum pattern of the song. "My momma told me there would be days like this!" Tyler exclaims after.

The recording ends after "Same Old Song And Dance" and with the familiar Tyler exhortation: "Mr. Tom Hamilton!"

Bayfront Center Arena, St. Petersburg, Florida. Friday, December 21, 1984. Audience recording. Sound quality: C

Rats In The Cellar, Back In The Saddle, Bone To Bone (Coney Island White Fish Boy), Three Mile Smile, Reefer Headed Woman, Lord Of The Thighs, Movin' Out, Last Child, Let The Music Do The Talking, Red House, Dream On, Lightning Strikes, Sweet Emotion, Same Old Song And Dance, Walk This Way, Milk Cow Blues, Toys In The Attic, Train' Kept A Rollin'.

Rats, Saddle, Bone To Bone, Big Ten Inch, Three Mile, Reefer, Thighs, Movin' Out, Last Child, Let The Music, Red House, Dream On, Lightning Strikes, Oh Well/SE, SOSAD, WTW, Milk Cow Blues/Drum Solo, Toys, Train

"We are back in the saddle again!" Tyler sings to the blissful crowd. "Take a walk in the warm Florida sun," Tyler sings during "Three Mile Smile."

Kramer pounds out the intro during "Lord Of The Thighs," but there is nary a word from Tyler who usually has something to scat about, an oddity for him not to.

"We are going to do a song off a Joe Perry Project album," Tyler says before "Let The Music Do The Talking."

Perry takes the mic to introduce "Red House." "I bet you thought I couldn't talk, huh?" he says.

Tyler is joined by the band tonight on a short jam that hints at "Darkness" before "Dream On."

"You are ugly motherfuckers in the front!" Tyler says before "Lightning Strikes," which features the singer giving out a little yodel as the tune starts, with Perry bending some notes.

Perry teases the crowd with false starts to "Same Old Song And Dance." "Do we have liftoff?" Tyler asks as the band finally jumps into the song.

Perry plays some chunky riffs to open "Walk This Way." "Milk Cow Blues" starts in a cool way, with the main theme played in a mellow way by Perry. Tyler calls it a "tune by Eddie Cochran."

"Someone here said the most requested song on FM radio is 'Train Kept A Rollin',' is that true? Is that true?" Tyler asks as Perry sounds some feedback as the band jumps into the finale.

Great run of Florida shows even if "S.O.S." and "Adam's Apple" were dropped. The band is energized and playing better than ever.

Civic Center, Providence, Rhode Island. Thursday, December 27, 1984. Audience recording. Sound quality: C

Rats In The Cellar, Back In The Saddle, Bone To Bone (Coney Island White Fish Boy), Big Ten Inch Record, Three Mile Smile, Reefer Headed Woman, Lord Of The Thighs, Movin' Out, Last Child, Let The Music Do The Talking, Red House, Dream On, Lightning Strikes, Sweet Emotion, Same Old Song And Dance, Walk This Way, Milk Cow Blues, Toys In The Attic.

"Rats In The Cellar" opens the show in front of an ecstatic crowd as Perry plays some cool stop and start riffs on the way out of the tune. "Merry

Christmas!" Tyler says to the throng. Two days late, but show tickets were no doubt Christmas gifts for many under a snowy Providence Christmas trees.

"Yeah, we back!" he continues. "Take a walk in the warm New Hampshire sun..." Tyler sings during "Three Mile Smile," maybe the singer feeling close to the area even though not in it proper.

"We are going to do a song Aerosmith never did before, it's off a Joe Perry album..." Tyler says as "Let The Music Do The Talking" gets underway.

"I bet you thought I couldn't talk," Perry again says before "Red House."

"We want you to all close your eyes, close your eyes...and dream on," Tyler tells the audience as he settles into the song. Perry plays a long loud note as "Lightning Strikes" gets underway.

> "It was complete chaos out there," city police Capt. Patrick J. McConaghy said today of the Thursday night crash. He said as many as 50 motorists, mostly young people who attended a concert by the band Aerosmith at Providence's Civic Center, were stranded and slept at the police station overnight.

Perry again teases the opening to "Same Old Song And Dance." The band fires into a bit of "Combination" again at the end of "Milk Cow Blues," but not before Tyler introduces Kramer. The tape ends with "Toys In The Attic."

Getting home from the gig proved to be difficult as a harsh winter storm set in during the show. The story was national news.

> Aerosmith, which recently welcomed back Joe Perry, plays two sellout concerts Sunday and Monday evening at the Orpheum ...
>
> **At Orpheum Theater** — Hamilton place, Boston. Telephone 482-0650.
> Aerosmith. Dec. 30, 7:30 p.m.; Dec. 31, 9 p.m. SOLD OUT.

Orpheum Theater, Boston, Massachusetts. Sunday, December 30, 1984. Audience recording. Sound quality: C

Rats In The Cellar, Back In The Saddle, Bone To Bone (Coney Island White Fish Boy), Big Ten Inch Record, Three Mile Smile, Reefer Headed Woman, Lord Of The Thighs, Movin' Out, Last Child, Let The Music Do The Talking, Red House, Dream On, Lightning Strikes, Sweet Emotion, Same Old Song And Dance, Walk This Way, Milk Cow Blues, Toys In The Attic, Train Kept A-Rollin'.

A WBCN DJ does the honors on this night in bringing the band on stage. "Merry Christmas!" Tyler says as "Back In The Saddle" begins. "We are Back In The Saddle!" Tyler sings, no doubt pleased to see his old band mates surrounding him as Aerosmith plays its hometown.

"No more politics in rock and roll," Tyler says oddly as the band plays its political song, "Three Mile Smile." "Take a walk in the warm Boston sun," Tyler croons. He sings "OPEC girls" on this night, not "boys."

"This is the perfect place to introduce this song," Tyler says. "It wasn't 5 miles from here that Joe Perry and I wrote our first song together, it goes like this..." as the band plays "Movin' Out."

"You some ugly motherfuckers..." Tyler teases the boys up front again before "Let The Music Do The Talking." Perry has some reverb on his guitar as he plays "Dream On."

"You watch MTV? The only song Aerosmith ever had on MTV goes like this..." as the band launches "Lightning Strikes."

Some fine guitar and harmonica interplay start "Milk Cow Blues." Perry plays a little of the fast riff to Bill Haley's "Rock Around The Clock" during the jam before a bit of "Combination" finishes it out.

Tyler claims a WBCN DJ has told him that "Train Kept A-Rollin'" is the most requested song on the radio, surely a tall tale that the singer repeated in other tour stops around this time. But it made for a good launching point for the song that ended the gigs. Perry's guitar goes into helicopter mode during his mid-tune solo, an effect usually saved for the end.

Orpheum Theater, Boston, Massachusetts. Monday, December 31, 1984. FM recording, first 30 minutes: Sound quality: A-. Incomplete videotape soundboard recording: Sound Quality B. Audience recording: Sound quality C

Rats In The Cellar, Back In The Saddle, Bone To Bone (Coney Island White Fish Boy), Big Ten Inch Record, Three Mile Smile, Reefer Headed Woman, Lord Of The Thighs, Movin' Out, Last Child, Let The Music Do The Talking, Red House, Dream On, Lightning Strikes, Sweet Emotion, Same Old Song And Dance, Walk This Way, Milk Cow Blues, Toys In The Attic, Train Kept A-Rollin'.

The WBCN DJ is back for the second night to introduce the band: "Please welcome warmly, the legendary Aerosmith!" as the band launches "Rats In The Cellar." Parts of the show would form the basis for the "Classics Live 2" album. Interestingly, the artwork for the remastered version of the cd release shows many of the recordings noted in these pages.

"Good evening Boston! Merry Christmas and Happy New Year, you crazy fucks!" Tyler says, welcoming the crowd in his own inimitable way. Perry does some intricate finger picking toward the end of "Back In The Saddle."

"We got TV here tonight, we got radio, we got BCN doing us, what do you say about that!?" Tyler says. "We're gonna do a little game here since we are on TV, we're gonna do 'Name That Tune,' you guess," Tyler says as Kramer pounds out the intro to "Big Ten Inch Record." "What's the tune?" Tyler asks.

"Lord Of The Thighs" features an epic "battle" between Whitford and Perry. "Nobody knows but Joe Perry" Tyler sings on "Movin' Out."

"Agent Orange," Tyler says before "Last Child," referencing Whitford, who is wearing an orange jumpsuit he donned during this period.

"I paid for that house too!" Perry sings during "Red House" as he laments his luck with women. Perry does some scat vocalization and displays a surprisingly strong falsetto to close out the song.

On the audience recording of this show, some poor fan cries out for "Walkin' The Dog" for the entire show, but alas, it was not to be played.

It's Hamilton's birthday and to mark the occasion, there is an impromptu sing-along of "Happy Birthday" and a not so spontaneous appearance of a stripper during "Walk This Way" in front of the bass player, much to his embarrassment. "You thought that would never end, didn't you?" Tyler says to Hamilton after.

Parts of show comprised the majority of "Classics Live II" released in June 1987.

Mexican and Yugoslavian cassette releases of Classics Live II.

Broome County Veterans Memorial Arena, Binghamton, New York. Wednesday, January 2, 1985. Audience recording. Sound quality: D

Rats In The Cellar, Bone To Bone (Coney Island White Fish Boy), Big Ten Inch Record, Three Mile Smile, Reefer Headed Woman, Lord Of The Thighs, Movin' Out, Last Child, Let The Music Do The Talking, Red House, Dream On, Lightning Strikes, Sweet Emotion, Same Old Song And Dance, Walk This Way, Milk Cow Blues, Toys In The Attic, Train Kept A-Rollin'.

Because the recording quality is poor, it's best to enjoy this show in its totality versus picking out individual merits that are hard to discern.

"Back In The Saddle" is excised from the show. Perry plays some long notes during "Lord Of The Thighs." Tyler gives a nice yell out during "Movin' Out."

There are lots of cuts between songs on the recording as though the taper was conserving his tape.

Perry twists some notes at the beginning of "Red House" and gets his guitar crying on "Sweet Emotion." Perry's notes are almost chime-like during the vocal breakdown of "Same Old Song And Dance."

Tyler ends the show with a hearty: "Good night and God bless!"

AEROSMITH
Legendary Rock Band
IN CONCERT
SPECIAL GUEST
DAVID JOHANSEN
THURS., JAN. 3, 1985
8:00 P.M.
ALL SEATS RESERVED
$12.50
●HERSHEYPARK ARENA

Hersheypark Arena, Hershey, Pennsylvania. Thursday, January 3, 1985. Audience recording. Sound quality: C-

Rats In The Cellar, Bone To Bone (Coney Island White Fish Boy), Big Ten Inch Record, Three Mile Smile, Reefer Headed Woman, Lord Of The Thighs, Movin' Out, Last Child, Let The Music Do The Talking, Red House, Dream On, Lightning Strikes, Sweet Emotion, Same Old Song And Dance, Walk This Way, Milk Cow Blues, Toys In The Attic, Train Kept A-Rollin'.

"Hey Hershey, Happy New Year!" Tyler exclaims after "Rats In The Cellar." "Oooooh" Tyler yells after his funky harmonica solo into "Big Ten Inch Record."

"Take a walk in the hot Hershey sun," was the lyric during "Three Mile Smile." Tyler sings "I got a ree-fer headed woman," a small gap in the words of the title of the tune. Tyler sings part of "Lord Of The Thighs" with a different inflection. The guitars go off on a chunk-a-chunk rhythm with Kramer and Tyler going over the top of it all during the tune, an interesting version.

Kramer drums over the intro of "Movin' Out." The slow part of the song features a cool Tyler yell and a real 1970s-type guitar breakdown.

After "Last Child" Tyler says: "One of my favorite songs! Why do I smell chocolate in the air?" Tyler introduces "Let The Music Do The Talking." "Ain't that right," he asks the crowd, referencing the song's title.

"Sing for Joe Perry's left ear" becomes part of the "Dream On" lyric on this night. "Lightning Strikes" starts with Kramer pounding the drums, but no one else is ready. "Fire two!" Tyler says as they have a second go at it. "And the hits keep rollin' on baby!" Tyler says after.

He then starts the "Oh Well" lyric to "Sweet Emotion," but stops, then starts again. "I can't tell where I'll be next year, probably Hershey," Tyler sings.

"A song by Eddie Cochran," Tyler says in a British accent, "and Elvis Presley" he says without the effect as "Milk Cow Blues" is introduced. Tyler does some stream of consciousness vocals over the beginning of the tune, adding to the bluesy feel.

Civic Center, Baltimore, Maryland. Monday, January 7, 1985. Audience recording. Sound quality: D-

Rats In The Cellar, Back In The Saddle, Bone To Bone (Coney Island White Fish Boy), Big Ten Inch Record, Three Mile Smile, Reefer Headed Woman, Lord Of The Thighs, Movin' Out, Last Child, Let The Music Do The Talking, Red House, Dream On, Lightning Strikes, Sweet Emotion, Same Old Song And Dance, Walk This Way, Milk Cow Blues, Toys In The Attic, Train Kept A-Rollin'.

Perry plays some melodic notes over the opening tape. "Baltimore you haven't changed!" Tyler says after "Rats In The Cellar." Perry plays strong guitar in the outro of "Back In The Saddle," capturing the spirit of the album version.

Great show in front of an enthusiastic crowd on this night. "How's your ass, momma?! Tyler asks as Kramer starts "Three Mile Smile" with a plodding drum intro.

"In person. Joe Perry!" Tyler announces before "Red House." The band sounds out "On The Road Again" before getting into "Milk Cow Blues" and jumps into the end of "Combination" to set up Kramer's drum solo.

The sound quality for "Train Kept A-Rollin'" is an improvement from the rest of the show as our taper may have moved closer for the encore. A great show, even with the dodgy sound here!

Holiday Star Theater, Merrillville, Indiana. Friday, January 11, 1985. Audience recording. Sound quality: B-

Rats In The Cellar, Bone To Bone (Coney Island White Fish Boy), Big Ten Inch Record, Three Mile Smile, Reefer Headed Woman, Lord Of The Thighs, Movin' Out, Adam's Apple, Last Child, Let The Music Do The Talking, Red House, Dream On, Lightning Strikes, Sweet Emotion, Same Old Song And Dance, Walk This Way, Milk Cow Blues, Toys In The Attic, Train Kept A-Rollin'.

Those who record this show can be heard offering instructions on mic position as the opening rolls, and this group produced a splendid sounding document.

"Hey Joe Perry!" Tyler exclaims after "Lord Of The Thighs." Perry begins playing "Adam's Apple" and then the whole band jumps in, a bit of spontaneity on this night. Tyler punctuates the tune with some nice vocalizations to boot. Perry supplies some locked in rhythm to Whitford's lead on "Last Child."

Some great acapella between Tyler and Perry on "Let The Music Do The Talking."

"When I first came to Merrillville I thought I was going to have the blues, but so far I have had the best three days I've had in a long time," Perry says before "Red House." "Even if I really don't mean it, I'll give it my best (to sing the blues)."

"Everyone close their eyes. You got it. 'Dream On,'" Tyler says. "The lid's going to blow up in Hell's Kitchen" gets the acapella treatment from Tyler on "Lightning Strikes." The "Oh Well" intro to "Sweet Emotion" gets a different vocal treatment. "The right stuff baby, the right stuff," he says after.

The band does what sounds like a version of "On The Road Again" as Tyler vamps some vocals and sings "hit the road jack" and blows on his harmonica as "Milk Cow Blues" starts.

"I hear a train a comin' do you? Tyler asks, as the band launches into a chug-a-lug train-type intro to "Train Kept A-Rollin'," which concludes with some interesting, isolated Perry riffs.

Joe Louis Arena, Detroit, Michigan. Saturday, January 12, 1985. Audience recording. Sound quality: C

Rats In The Cellar, Back In The Saddle, Big Ten Inch Record, Bone To Bone (Coney Island White Fish Boy), Three Mile Smile, Reefer Headed Woman, Lord Of The Thighs, Movin' Out, Last Child, Let The Music Do The Talking, Red House, Dream On, Lightning Strikes, Sweet Emotion, Same Old Song And Dance, Walk This Way, Milk Cow Blues, Toys In The Attic, Train Kept A-Rollin'.

"Back In The Saddle" seems to come and go in the setlist and is played. The band also flips "Big Ten Inch Record" and "Bone To Bone (Coney Island White Fish Boy)" on this night.

275

"You some crazy motherfuckers in front tonight. Lots of boys, too. You some ugly motherfuckers, yeah you are an ugly motherfucker!" Tyler says.

"Mr. Brad Whitford" Tyler says during "Lord Of The Thighs" after a involved solo before Perry starts in with his slide work.

Perry tries to relax the crowd before "Movin' Out" after a fight breaks out below. The tune finishes with a repeat of the final notes by Perry on guitar.

"Sing that song, you bitch," Tyler says before "Last Child," that familiar refrain it seems Tyler used when Whitford took center stage to introduce the song on guitar.

"We are going to do a tune from Joe Perry's first album, when he took off from Aerosmith..." Tyler says bluntly as he introduces "Let The Music Do The Talking."

"It's good to be back here in Detroit, our home away from home..." Perry says before "Red House."

The band gets into another loose "Hit The Road Jack" jam before "Milk Cow Blues." Tyler does some acapella and again vamps vocals during the song as Perry hits the "Rock Around The Clock" riffs. The band again jams on the end "Combination" before Kramer starts his solo.

■ The original Aerosmith is coming to Muskegon's L.C. Walker Arena Monday. Their show features vocalist Steven Tyler and guitarist Joe Perry who founded the Boston band in 1970. For ticket information (and credit card charges) call (616)

L.C. Walker Arena, Muskegon, Michigan. Monday, January 14, 1985. Audience recording. Sound quality: C and D

Rats In The Cellar, Bone To Bone (Coney Island White Fish Boy), Big Ten Inch Record, Three Mile Smile, Reefer Headed Woman, Lord Of The Thighs, Movin' Out, Last Child, Back In The Saddle, Lightning Strikes, Sweet Emotion, Same Old Song And Dance, Milk Cow Blues.

Tyler dedicates "Big Ten Inch Record" to "Tank" and again references the fellow during the tune. "Brad, do you remember what album 'Three Mile' was on?" Tyler quizzes Whitford before "Three Mile Smile." Whitford replies, "Aerosmith." Tyler responds, "First one? My ass the first one...Listen back to the tape."

Speaking of tape, the tape recorder runs into power problems as the speed fluctuates starting in the middle of "Lord Of The Thighs." Tyler does a stream of consciousness vocal during the tune, mostly unintelligible on the recording, but interesting nonetheless.

"Back In The Saddle" appears out of its normal position, almost as it was played per request on this night. "You will tear the stage down or turn over the soundboard if we don't do it? Tyler asks, then deadpans: "We ain't gonna do it," before they do.

"Proof that there is life on other planets, Mr. Brad Whitford," Tyler says during "Milk Cow Blues." An interesting recording that circulates with a pre-show press conference from local radio.

Rupp Arena, Lexington, Kentucky. Tuesday, January 15, 1985. Audience recording. Sound quality: C

Rats In The Cellar, Bone To Bone (Coney Island White Fish Boy), Big Ten Inch Record, Three Mile Smile, Reefer Headed Woman, Lord Of The Thighs, Movin' Out, Last Child, Let The Music Do The Talking, Red House, Dream On, Lightning Strikes, Sweet Emotion, Same Old Song And Dance, Walk This Way, Milk Cow Blues, Toys In The Attic, Train Kept A-Rollin'.

The arena is empty on this night. "Well, there ain't many of you here, but the ones we got are motherfuckers!" Tyler says as a compliment before "Big Ten Inch Record."

"Lord Of The Thighs" features some interesting passages by Whitford, almost like Hendrix's "Third Stone From The Sun."

"We have a song here from Joe Perry's first album, when he went so-lo," Tyler says, in a teasing tone before "Let The Music Do The Talking." Tyler really shakes his maraca during the tune.

"We cooking now, motherfucker!" Tyler yells after "Dream On." "I love you Steve!" a woman's voice cries out, as she somehow got a hold of his mic.

Nice isolated drumming by Kramer during "Lightning Strikes." Tyler uses an odd inflection during one verse of "Sweet Emotion."

Kramer starts to play "Walk This Way," but Tyler stops him to recognize "Elwood and Toby" in the crowd.

Another impromptu blues jam starts "Milk Cow Blues" with Tyler saying "Joltin' Joe Perry" as the song progresses as the guitarist gets some feedback together. The "Combination" jam follows.

"Rumor has it!" becomes part of the "Toys In The Attic" lyrics. "Someone told me Train Kept A-Rollin' was the number one requested country and western song in town, is that right?" Ha, not likely, but a good way to end the show!

The "Back In The Saddle" tour was a success overall, getting the band out and about after some troubled years. Now they would get a record deal, put out a new album and hit the road again.

The Muskegon Chronicle
MUSKEGON, MICH.
D. 45,845 SUN. 46,441

JAN 2 1985

RENAISSANCE

Aerosmith is back without bad-boy image

Aerosmith members are, clockwise from top left, Steven Tyler, Brad Whitford, Joey Kramer, Tom Hamilton and Joe Perry.

"Every time that I look in the mirror
"All these lines in my face gettin' clearer
"The past is gone.
"And all the things you do, come back to you."
– "Dream On" by Steven Tyler and Aerosmith.

By JEFF WOOD
Chronicle staff writer

Aerosmith is back. Also known as the Bad Boys from Boston, the group's back on tour after "five years of drugs and acrimony," as Rolling Stone Magazine recently put it.

They're older and not so bad anymore, according to most reviews. They're just acting up a bit.

Should they have taken the hint when they split in 1979? Should they have stayed off the road and out of the studio and called it quits while they were behind? Will lead singer Steven Tyler whale on the band members anymore in concert?

According to second guitarist Brad Whitford, the answer to all of the above is "no, the band isn't just dreaming on." This time around, the group is getting along better, the road show is receiving great reviews, a new album on a new label looms for this summer and they've only pounded on each other once.

MUSKEGON FANS will get a chance to see the renaissance when Aerosmith plays the L.C. Walker Arena Jan. 14. The show begins at 7 p.m. with warm-up group Black and Blue. Tickets are still available for $12.50 and are on sale at the arena box office, all Believe in Music stores in Michigan, the Disc-N-Tapes store in Muskegon and Sound Waves in Grand Haven.

Since the band isn't fronting a new album yet, there won't be much new material in the concert, Whitford said in a telephone interview with The Chronicle.

"The only thing we're doing that might be on the new album is 'Let the Music Do the Talking,' you know, the one Joe (Perry, lead guitarist) did on The Joe Perry Project album," Whitford said. He was enjoying a rare day off as the band made a swing along the East Coast.

"We do 'Let the Music Do the Talking' in the road show," Whitford said. "We do it in three-part harmony – Steve, Joe and myself. It's the first time we've ever done anything like that. We may throw that one on the new record.

"Joe's also doing a version of Hendrix's Red House," Whitford said. "Gives Steven a chance to go backstage during the middle of the show to blow dry his hair, shine his shoes and such," Whitford laughed.

AEROSMITH FANS will find a virtual live discography of the band on this tour. The hour-and-45-minute show includes numbers from the "Dream On," "Toys in the Attic," "Get Your Wings," "Rocks," "Night in the Ruts" and "Rock in a Hard Place" albums.

The only album that's missing a number in the current tour is "Draw the Line," and probably with good reason. "Draw the Line," cut in 1979, is to date the group's worst effort. It served little purpose beyond warning fans a break-up was coming.

The album followed Aerosmith's 1978 tour and the band's only double album, "Live Bootleg." "Bootleg" was sound evidence the band was burning out. Tyler was occasionally off-key in the tracks. His voice cracked and disappeared altogether when he tried to hit some high notes.

EVEN SOME BAND members said they didn't care for "Draw the Line," Bad press indicated Tyler and Perry were fighting. The group was dissatisfied with its management and record label, Columbia. Fans smelled a break-up.

"That's just what was happening," Whitford said. "We were all burned out to some extent, some more than others," he said in a transparent reference to Tyler and Perry.

"The cookie was crumbling. Everybody in the band was a rock star. We had the attitude, the old 'I don't care about anything anymore.' You can't run your newspaper like that and you can't run a rock band like that, either. It's a business."

The bad management and dissatisfaction with group's label didn't help matters any.

"I have demos from the 'Draw the Line' session that I still listen to in my car. There are some incredible tracks that never got on the record. They may even end up on the new album.

"That was mostly bad management. We weren't getting the attention we needed. It was the way the deals were handled. We've gotten rid of all that now, the old habits. We're getting back to the hard-core reason we started. We didn't start with any money and that's right where we're at now," Whitford laughed.

IT WAS SHORTLY after "Draw the Line" that lead guitarist Perry drew the line with Tyler. He left the group, citing irreconcilable differences with the group's lead singer.

Perry formed his own group, The Joe Perry Project, and made three albums that received mild air play. Perry's heroin habit prevented him from doing much of anything with class.

Whitford also left Aerosmith because he was dissatisfied with the direction it was taking. He recorded an album with Derek St. Holmes on the Columbia label and then disbanded his project.

Meanwhile, Tyler, bassist Tom Hamilton and drummer Joey Kramer kept the band together and even made one album, "Rock in a Hard Place." Hard-core Aerosmith fans disregarded it. Hamilton and Kramer's rock-steady blues thumping beat was there. Tyler's shrieking voice was healed, but the lack of Perry and Whitford's razor-sharp guitar licks running all over the group's music came through loud and clear. Replacement guitarists Jimmy Crespo and Rick Dufay just didn't have it.

THE BAND ALSO entered the video market with the "Rock in a Hard Place" cut "Lightning Strikes."

"They made the video," Whitford emphasized. "I wasn't with the band for that album. I've seen the video. They throw it on MTV every once in a while late Sunday nights when they throw in all the other junk.

"Aerosmith is a pre-video band. We were there before video and our music isn't written for videos."

After the break-up in '79, things slowly healed. Perry kicked his drug habit. Tyler dried out and recovered from road burnout. Then, in 1983, he and Perry began talking again.

"First Steven called me. Then Joe called me. Then we got together at Tom Hamilton's house and that was it. We realized once again what we're supposed to be doing," Whitford said.

WHITFORD SAID the band is now working to find the chemistry it had when it cut its first album.

"Dream On." Rather than simply crashing guitars a la Quiet Riot, Aerosmith will use the same "payin' dues blues-rock" formula it has always used to create what Whitford calls "foot-stompin' music."

"Our music has always flowed from our instincts," Whitford explained. "We've always tried to play what we've felt. We do a rehearsal and whatever ends up on the album seems to be foot-stompin'."

The band's first album was a combination of down-hard blues rock that immediately appealed to a hardcore fan group. The "Dream On" album came across like the band was still playing for its supper in some Boston bar, yet its title track was a rare slow-dance hard rock number that received plenty of Top 40 overplay on both AM and FM stations. "Dream On" joined Led Zeppelin's "Stairway to Heaven" as history's most overused theme song for high school proms and Christmas dances.

AEROSMITH TOOK its place among the top hard rock groups of the early and mid-1970s. The band's forte was its road show. It cranked out four platinum albums from 1973 to 1978. Tyler, with his rubber lips, blow-dried jet-black locks and on-stage strut was called America's answer to the Rolling Stones' Mick Jagger.

Aerosmith fans long for just such another album, so smooth and naturally blue steel as "Dream On," "Toys in the Attic" or "Rocks." So does Whitford, who allows that "Dream On" was his personal favorite.

"Absolutely, that was our music," Whitford said. "The synergistic effect the band had with each other was on that album, in songs like 'One Way Street.' We walked into the studio and they said, 'Go ahead and play your music.' All we were looking for on that track was excitement and that's exactly what we got.

"IF YOU WERE to look at the equipment we recorded that album on today, you'd die laughing," Whitford chuckled. "I happened to look at the original board we used to record the album a while back ... what a piece of junk! It looked like something you'd use to tune a car.

"But you see, it's what you get down on tape that counts."

Whitford says the band is letting the music do the

talking on its latest tour entitled "what else" "Back in the Saddle Again," which was the group's big hit of the "Rocks" album.

With the exception of a celebrated date last summer in Springfield, Mass., the current tour is getting good reviews.

"We deserved a bad review for the Springfield show. We screwed up. I guess we had to keep our image up of being trouble-makers."

IN THE SPRINGFIELD concert, Tyler drank before the show and started trouble on stage with the band. It ended with the group storming off stage, too off at Tyler just like in the good old days.

"We talked about it afterwards. That kind of thing doesn't happen anymore," Whitford said. "We're getting business taken care of now. We're playing auditoriums that hold from 8,000 on up and we're packing them to the rafters. Everybody in the band's getting comfortable with each other again."

REVIEWERS ARE still seeking a way to capture Aerosmith's unique style. Some persist in comparing the group, especially Tyler, to the Stones and Jagger. Whitford would prefer they take Aerosmith for what the group is.

"They always ask, 'What's it like touring with Steven Tyler? He's just like Mick Jagger.'

"And I always say, 'Is that so? Then you know Mick Jagger?'

"Of course they say, 'No.'

"So I say, 'Well then, 'or 'he' respective deleted do you know Steven's like him?' " he laughed.

"I think most fans have started figuring out that Aerosmith is its own entity," Whitford said. "We were labeled for the first three or four years. But the music's taken off and we've survived that stage.

"I feel stronger than ever," Whitford concluded. "Quitting totally has never entered my mind. These people keep coming to watch. I've kind of accepted the fact that I'll be strumming along until I drop."

"Time's always changing now it never stands still
"If I stop a-changing I'll-a write you my will."
– Steven Tyler and Aerosmith, "No More, No More" off "Toys in the Attic

WELCOME TO
THE AEROSMITH FAN CLUB

Dedicated to the best fans in rock n' roll . . . ours!
We'll always be a people's band, and it's you
Who prove there ain't no substitute
For the real thing!

So welcome aboard Aero Force One!
Together, we'll be kickin ass and rockin upward
For a long time to come.
And the greatest secret in the world? . . . You know—
You be the ones who light the fuse!

Blastoff!!

DAY	DATE	CITY	VENUE	BILLING
Thursday	Aug 22	E. Troy, WI	Alpine Valley Music Theater	Rehearsal
Friday	Aug 23	E. Troy, WI	Alpine Valley Music Theater	Headline
Saturday	Aug 24	Troy, MI	Pine Knob	Headline
Sunday	Aug 25	Rochester, NY	Silver Stadium	Spec. Guest Star w/Foreigner
Tuesday	Aug 27	Saratoga Springs, NY	Saratoga Perf. Arts Center	Headline
Monday	Sep 2	Phoenix, AZ	Compton Terrace	Special Guest Star
Friday	Sep 6	Cayuga Falls	Blossom Music Festival	Headline
Saturday	Sep 7	Lynn, MA	Manning Bowl	Headline
Sunday	Sep 8	Lynn, MA	Manning Bowl	Raindate
Sunday	Sep 22	Honolulu, HI	Aloha Stadium	Co-headline w/REO

*Note: This schedule is subject to change. Please contact Steve Barrasso if there are any questions.

AUGUST							SEPTEMBER						
S	M	T	W	T	F	S	S	M	T	W	T	F	S
				1	2	3	1	2	3	4	5	6	7
	5	6	7	8	9	10	8	9	10	11	12	13	14
11	12	13	14	15	16	17	15	16	17	18	19	20	21
18	19	20	21	22	23	24	22	23	24	25	26	27	28
25	26	27	28	29	30	31	29	30					

Collins/Barrasso, Inc.

280 Lincoln Street
Allston/Boston, MA 02134
617 783 1100

Unknown studio locale, 1985.

Jam

Here we have a short jam on a tape that was labeled "Done With Mirrors" test pressing. The majority of the tape is the "Done With Mirrors" album out of sequence, but in finished form, sans for a few count-ins. But this curious guitar-based jam is first up, unfinished and doesn't sound like anything on the album. The riffs are subtle, cool, and stick in one's head.

DONE WITH MIRRORS PRE-TOUR

The Alpine Valley Music Theatre lineup includes:
DEEP PURPLE · Aug. 17
MOTLEY CRUE · Aug. 18
AEROSMITH· Aug. 23

Alpine Valley Music Theater, East Troy, Wisconsin. Friday, August 23, 1985. Audience recording. Sound quality: B-

Rats In The Cellar, Bone To Bone (Coney Island White Fish Boy), Big Ten Inch Record, Mama Kin, Last Child, My Fist Your Face, The Hop, Walkin' The Dog, Red House, Back In The Saddle, Sweet Emotion, Let The Music Do The Talking, Walk This Way, Same Old Song And Dance, Toys In The Attic, Dream On, Train Kept A-Rollin'.

The first gig of the "Done With Mirrors" era. Not the start of the official tour per se, but a chance for the band to get out and play some dates and new material. "Rats In The Cellar" is still in the kick off position, with Tyler improvising some words along the way.

"A few years ago, I thought this was going to be a single off our first album, but Joe wised me up to it," Tyler says, as "Mama Kin" is reintroduced to the setlist.

"And now, we got something off our new album, it's so new, you can smell it," Tyler says, as the band plays the first known live "My Fist Your Face," which has Perry soloing in old time rock and roll fashion.

"The Hop" also gets its debut, with Tyler employing the harmonica midway through. "Walkin' The Dog" is dedicated to a Mary Durango. As Tyler starts the lyrics, the band seems to be turned down to church mouse level. Tyler says, "nice one, Bob," soon after, indicating a roadie may have made a gaff, cutting power to Tyler's accompaniment. Perry continues on, playing a heavy metal solo to round out the tune.

Tyler calls Perry the "Prince of Darkness" before "Red House." "I don't have anything to be blue about..." Perry admits, before the tune. "Did you get your nut on that one, baby," Tyler asks Perry after a fine version of the song.

"Back In The Saddle," appears mid-set. "I feel like a Texan right now," Tyler says as the song ramps up. "Yee ha!" is heard mid song as it ends with some wild Perry licks.

"I got a prediction: three months from now, every station in the United States will be playing this song," Tyler says before "Let The Music Do The Talking." While that didn't turn out to be true, the now re-worked version shows more of a groove than the Joe Perry Project version.

"Toys In The Attic" starts without a break after "Same Old Song And Dance," adding to the frenetic pace of the show.

Pine Knob Music Theater, Clarkston, Michigan. Saturday, August 24, 1985. Audience recording. Sound quality: C-

Rats In The Cellar, Bone To Bone (Coney Island White Fish Boy), Big Ten Inch Record, Mama Kin, Last Child, My Fist Your Face, Lord Of The Thighs, The Hop, Walkin' The Dog, Red House, Back In The Saddle, Sweet Emotion, Let The Music Do The Talking, Walk This Way, Same Old Song And Dance, Toys In The Attic, Dream On, Train Kept A-Rollin'.

The whole opening tape plays before the band jumps into "Rats In The Cellar" on this night, which features some interesting soloing. "Fucking Detroit!" Tyler says after.

"We got a guest who will blow some horn with us on this song," Tyler says before "Mama Kin." Perry makes the same intro, but the player's name is hard to hear, as is his work on the song.

"We just finished up our new album, and this is a song off of it," Tyler says as the band plays "My Fist Your Face." "If you like that, it must be good!" Tyler says after. Then, "Something new, something old" as the band launches "Lord Of The Thighs."

During "Back In The Saddle," Tyler lays back and lets the audience sing a verse. Kramer starts off with a quiet drum riff, then bangs his kit loudly as an intro to "Walk This Way." Later, he bangs out four, furious, loud beats to start "Toys In The Attic." Perry plays a supremely energetic solo during the tune, adrenaline flowing.

The guitarist plays some off-key notes during "Dream On," repeating them to make them part of the tune, an example of Mr. Perry thinking on his feet! Perry plays a little of "Think About It" before "Train Kept A Rollin'," which has its end cut on the recording.

Saratoga Performing Arts Center, Saratoga Springs, New York. Tuesday, August 27, 1985. Audience recording. Sound quality: C

Rats In The Cellar, Bone To Bone (Coney Island White Fish Boy), Big Ten Inch Record, Mama Kin, Last Child, My Fist Your Face, Lord of The Thighs, The Hop, Red House, Back In The Saddle, Sweet Emotion, Let The Music Do The Talking, Walk This Way, Same Old Song And Dance, Toys In The Attic, Dream On, Train Kept A-Rollin'.

"Sara Toga! Toga! Toga! Toga!" Tyler playfully exclaims after "Big Ten Inch Record," referencing the movie "Animal House."

The summer 1985 shows have "Lord Of The Thighs" starting from a dead stop, rather than being segued into as the band had done so often.

"The Hop" gets off to an odd start, as Perry begins the lick before Kramer gives it his intro. Perry then stops to give it the proper start. Perry introduces "Let The Music Do The Talking" after Tyler defers to him.

Kramer's "Walk This Way" intro is quite powerful on this night. "Same Old Song And Dance" starts off with a bluesy intro. Perry plays some pretty notes during "Dream On" during its last verses. "Now that we are warmed up...." Tyler says, "I hear a train a comin'!"

Compton Terrace, Chandler, Arizona. Monday, September 2, 1985. Audience recording. Sound quality: D+

Rats In The Cellar, Mama Kin, Big Ten Inch Record, My Fist Your Face, Back In The Saddle, Let The Music Do The Talking, Sweet Emotion, Walk This Way, Same Old Song And Dance, Toys In The Attic, Dream On, Train Kept A Rollin'.

Aerosmith opening for the Scorpions here and cuts its set to about an hour.

A real supersonic version of "Rats In The Cellar" kicks things off. "Some new Aerosmith baby, this song is dedicated to the photographers and security in the front row, it's entitled 'My Fist Your Face,'" Tyler says.

Perry plays some smooth slide guitar throughout "Let The Music Do The Talking."

"Hey, you better calm down here or you'll push the stage over," Tyler tells the crowd that was quite out of control, according to several reports.

One man died of a drug overdose and there were several stabbings. An AC/DC show set for the venue Oct. 17 was moved, and Compton Terrace Chairman Jess Nicks — father of Stevie Nicks — said he had no plans for more concerts at the venue.

Manning Bowl, Lynn, Massachusetts. Saturday, September 14, 1985. Audience recording. Sound quality: C

Rats In The Cellar, Bone To Bone (Coney Island White Fish Boy), Big Ten Inch Record, Mama Kin, Last Child, My Fist Your

Aerosmith concert gets Lynn permit

LYNN – In spite of about a dozen arrests Sunday night during the Kinks concert at Manning Bowl, a permit has been granted for a concert there by Aerosmith this Saturday, a Lynn city official said yesterday. Eugene Dooley, superintendent of parks and playgrounds and a member of the Lynn Stadium Commission, said the commission had given the Aerosmith promoters a limit of 25,000 tickets for the concert and that about 20,000 have already been sold. "If we survived the Motley Crue, we can survive anything," Dooley said. Fifty persons fainted in the August heat and others were arrested for disorderly conduct, drunkenness and vandalism at the Motley Crue concert. Sunday's arrests includes two for assault and battery on a police officer, public drinking and disorderly conduct, police said. On the whole, it was not an unruly crowd, Dooley said.

Face, Lightning Strikes, The Hop, Walkin' The Dog, Red House, Back In The Saddle, Sweet Emotion, Let The Music Do The Talking, Walk This Way, The Movie, Same Old Song And Dance, All Your Love, Toys In The Attic, Dream On, Train Kept A-Rollin'.

A pair of atmospheric recordings of this outdoor daylight show on the band's home turf exist.

Tyler turns in a little rap during "Big Ten Inch Record." "We will have no fighting in the front row tonight!" Tyler declares before "Last Child," but it was quite a rough time in the crowd, reports say.

"Awhile back, Brad Whitford brought a little song to me, I said 'eh.' Then he changed it around a little and it sounds like this." Whitford fires off a great solo in the song, while Perry's rhythm is sublime.

"This is dedicated to the guys in the front row, 'My Fist Your Face,'" Tyler says. "Must be the governor's daughter up there. OK, I have to say this: Please get off the towers," referencing the announcement made at Woodstock.

"Lightning Strikes" works its way back into the setlist, with Tyler saying it's being played on local station V-66, which incidentally is broadcasting part of this show on cable TV. "The Hop" gets off to a cool start with Kramer setting a great pace with his intro.

"It might seem pretty early in the day to play the blues," Perry tells the sun-drenched crowd. "Since I've been up all night, it seems fine," he says before "Red House." The band has a little trouble bringing "Sweet Emotion" to a close here.

286

"The Movie," the instrumental that would appear on "Permanent Vacation," is played as a 90-second jam here before Perry stops the proceedings: "Thank you for the brief musical interlude. We will now go into something called the 'Same Old Song And Dance.'"

Perry, born September 12, gets a belated, off-key rendition of "Happy Birthday" from Tyler and the crowd.

"Since we are in an intimate environment, now we are going to do a song that we used to play in clubs a long time ago. We'll have Steven play harp and have everyone get down here," Perry says before "All Your Love."

The event saw a dozen arrests, some for robbery, and Lynn officials voted to ban concerts from the Manning Bowl after this show.

Aerosmith has the momentum

AEROSMITH – At the Manning Bowl in Lynn, with Farrenheit and the Knee Tremblers. Saturday afternoon.

By Brett Milano
Special to the Globe

MUSIC REVIEWS

Good news for Aerosmith fans: The group is still in the middle of a full-scale comeback. It began last year, when guitarists Joe Perry and Brad Whitford rejoined the group; and it continued with their fiery New Years shows at the Orpheum. On their current tour, Aerosmith are returning to the large arenas where they spent most of the '70s. If they can keep rocking as hard as they did this weekend, Aerosmith's lean years are over.

The Manning Bowl crowd was considerably larger (estimates ranged from 30,000-35,000) and less peaceful than the Kinks audience a week ago. The main problems happened up front, where it was getting cramped and nasty. Singer Steven Tyler had to stop the show a few times, to ask the front rows to stop fighting. Ironically, the fights broke out during a new tune called "My Fist, Your Face." The song was an amusing bit of comic-book violence, but nobody had to take it literally.

The group is working hard to win back its reputation, which was tarnished by some sloppy shows in recent years. They're still proud to be the "Bad Boys from Boston," but Aerosmith have grown up a bit. Perry and Tyler have taken a stand against drug use, and both looked in good health over the weekend (Tyler even did a back-flip during "Bone to Bone"). They still play hard and loud, but they seemed better-re-hearsed. Drummer Joey Kramer sounded especially tough, while rhythm guitarist Whitford

stepped up to share the leads with Perry.

Opening with the punky "Rats in the Cellar" (which has replaced "Back in the Saddle" as their regular opener), Aerosmith played everything from early LP tracks ("Mama Kin," "Walk the Dog") to obvious hits ("Walk This Way" featured some funny, unprintable Tyler ad-libs). Perry took the vocals for a reverent version of Jimi Hendrix' "Red House," and Tyler played a boogie-woogie piano intro on "Dream On." But the best-received song was a surprise: "Lightning Strikes," from their one album without Perry and Whitford. Thanks to recent airplay on rock video channel V-66, it's finally become a local hit.

The set was nearly the same as last winter's show, with the addition of three new songs. The most obvious hit was "The Hop," a rock anthem with a '50s feel and the quotable lyric "You'll all be kickin' (bleep) tonight, with the boys from Aerosmith". (The album, due next month, is called "Done With Mirrors" – a reference to magic tricks, not to cocaine. Other LP tracks include "She's on Fire" and "Gypsy Moods").

The band loosened up later in the set, with a blues jam and a surprising snatch of Fleetwood Mac's "Oh Well." But they still sound best on the straight-ahead rockers, like the double-shot finale of "Same Old Song & Dance" and "Toys in the Attic." This was Aerosmith at their friskiest, and no-frills hard rock doesn't get much better.

The opening sets were a hit and a miss: Local band Farrenheit were a likeable bunch of hard-working rockers, but the Knee Tremblers (including former members of Foghat) went through the motions with sedate rock tunes, bombastic blues and endless guitar solos.

Boston Globe review

287

DONE WITH MIRRORS

THE NEW ALBUM FROM

AEROSMITH

WILL TURN YOUR LIFE AROUND.

CAST OF CHARACTERS:
STEVEN TYLER ON LEAD VOCALS, PIANO AND HARMONICA.
JOE PERRY ON GUITARS AND BACKGROUND VOCALS.
BRAD WHITFORD ON GUITARS.
TOM HAMILTON ON BASS AND JOEY KRAMER ON DRUMS.

PRODUCED BY TED TEMPLEMAN

ON GEFFEN RECORDS, CASSETTES AND COMPACT DISCS © 1985 THE DAVID GEFFEN COMPANY

GEFFEN
RECORDS

288

AEROSMITH HISTORY

1970   In the summer of 1970, Jam Band members Tom Hamilton on bass and Joe Perry on guitar join forces with vocalist Steven Tyler in Sunapee, New Hampshire. Joey Kramer is recruited on drums and guitarist Brad Whitford rounds out the Aerosmith lineup. Later that year the band moves to the closest big city, Boston, Massachusetts.

1971   Aerosmith develops original material and a stage show, playing as many (mostly low paying) gigs as possible. As a means of survival, all five band members share a small Boston apartment, "eating a lot of brown rice and soup."

1972   The group starts to pick up a following in the Boston area, attracting the attention of local promoter Frank Connelly, who briefly manages the group. In the summer of 1972, Connelly introduces Aerosmith to Leber-Krebs, Inc., who sign the band to a new management contract. A few weeks later, Clive Davis signs Aerosmith to a recording contract with Columbia Records after seeing them perform at Max's Kansas City in New York. Aerosmith's self-titled album is recorded in Boston with producer Adrian Barber.

1973   Aerosmith tours New England constantly behind the release of their first album, steadily building their following through college, club, and concert dates. The regional success of the single "Dream On" helps the group land opening spots for acts as diverse as The Kinks and Mahavishnu Orchestra. In the fall Aerosmith tours concert halls and small theaters as the opening act for Mott the Hoople. By the close of 1973, the band enters the recording studio to begin work on *Get Your Wings*, the first of several albums produced by Jack Douglas.

1974   Aerosmith tours constantly following the release of their second album, opening for major headliners in arenas and headlining their own shows in small concert halls and theatres. By the end of 1974, *Get Your Wings* approaches 500,000 units sold and the non-stop touring appears to be paying off.

1975   Early in 1975 Aerosmith begins recording *Toys In The Attic*. This album proves to be Aerosmith's biggest album ever, eventually selling over four million copies in the United States. With "Sweet Emotion" and "Walk This Way," great summertime singles, the group becomes one of the nation's top concert attractions, consistently selling out large halls. By the end of 1975, all of Aerosmith's albums are back on Billboard's chart; *Toys in the Attic goes platinum*.

1976   "Dream On" is rereleased as Aerosmith enters the studio to begin work on their fourth album. A regional hit in 1973, "Dream On" becomes the group's first national Top Ten single, giving them a heavy dose of AM airplay and pushing both their debut album and *Get Your Wings* to platinum. Their fourth album, *Rocks*, is released and immediately goes platinum. Aerosmith's success is not due to critical praise, but even the critics agree that *Rocks* is Aerosmith's most sophisticated effort and a classic American rock and roll album. The accumulation of studio experience and road work has paid off for Aerosmith; they headline arenas and outdoor stadiums. As the year comes to a close, "Walk This Way," from the group's third album, is released as a single. Eighteen months after the album's released, "Walk This Way" becomes Aerosmith's second top ten single. "Dream On" also cracked the Top Ten in much the same fashion.

1977   Aerosmith continues their heavy touring schedule in 1977 before recording their fifth album, *Draw the Line*. The album is recorded in a most appropriate setting for Aerosmith, a converted convent dubbed "The Cenacle" in Armonk, NY. *Draw the Line* is released shortly before Christmas and goes platinum faster that any other Aerosmith album.

1978   More concert dates, including a headlining appearance at the California Jam II concert, dominates the Aerosmith calendar. The band also makes an appearance as "F.V.B.," the "Future Villain Band," in the *Sgt. Pepper's Lonely Hearts Club Band* movie. They turn in a riveting performance of Lennon & McCartney's "Come Together," which rides the charts for three months. Aerosmith releases their sixth platinum album, *Live! Bootleg*, in October of 1978. The double record set contains live versions of songs spanning Aerosmith's career, from the nightclub cover version of James Brown's "Mother Popcorn" to stadium renditions of new material.

1979   Aerosmith slows their touring pace, but still plays a number of concert dates. The band switches producers, working with Gary Lyons on their sixth studio LP, *Night in the Ruts*. Upon release of the album in December, guitarist Joe Perry leaves Aerosmith to pursue a solo career. After auditioning several well known guitarists, ex-Flame guitarist Jimmy Crespo joins the Aerosmith line-up.

1980   Aerosmith resumes touring in 1980 and release their *Greatest Hits* album in November of that year. Joe Perry releases *Let the Music Do the Talking* in March and tours nightclubs and small concert halls with his new band, The Joe Perry Project, in support of the record.

1981   Guitarist Brad Whitford leaves Aerosmith and teams up with ex-Ted Nugent guitarist and vocalist Derek St. Holmes to record *Whitford/St. Holmes* for Columbia Records. The duo takes their band on the road playing club dates and supporting headliners in concert halls. Joe Perry changes the lineup in his solo project, records *I've Got The Rock 'n' Roll Again*, and tours America's nightclubs and smaller concert halls. Aerosmith's *Greatest Hits* is certified gold in March of 1981. The band remains inactive during this period, as vocalist Steven Tyler recovers from a motorcycle accident.

1982   Guitarist Rick Dufay is named as the replacement for Brad Whitford. Aerosmith teams up again with producer Jack Douglas to record *Rock In A Hard Place*. The group returns to extensive touring after the album's release in August 1982. Although there are major changes in Aerosmith's personnel, the band continues as a strong concert attraction, selling out coliseums and arenas. Joe Perry continues touring clubs and small halls with the Joe Perry Project, again with a new line-up. Brad Whitford and Derek St. Holmes disband their group with Whitford teaming up with Joe Perry for several Joe Perry Project dates. Whitford also does session work during this time, including an album with singer Rex Smith.

1983   Aerosmith continues touring large halls and doing brisk business. The Joe Perry Project leaves Columbia and records *Once A Rocker, Always A Rocker* for MCA. His band goes on another club and small hall tour.

1984   On Valentine's Day, Joe Perry and Brad Whitford visit their old bandmates after an Aerosmith show at the Orpheum Theater in Boston. More meetings continue until the announcement in April that the original Aerosmith line-up would reunite for the "Back in the Saddle Tour." After extensive rehearsals at several New England locations, the band hits the road from June to August, playing several sold out shows all over the United States. After a short break, Aerosmith goes into more rehearsals before embarking on the second leg of the "Back in the Saddle Tour" in December. The tour is a success despite the fact that there was no new album or video.

1985   Aerosmith completes their tour in January and begins writing and rehearsing material for the first album by the original line-up in six years. A new record deal with Geffen Records is signed and producer Ted Templeman comes to Boston to work on pre-production with the band. Aerosmith and Templeman begin recording *Done With Mirrors* in July at Fantasy Studios in Berkeley, California. The album is completed in August at The Power Station in New York. Late August and September find Aerosmith playing eight outdoor festival dates dubbed the "Preview Tour," with the band performing material from their forthcoming record. Aerosmith gears up for the release of *Done With Mirrors* and the start of an extensive world tour set to begin in January. More to follow....

289

"DONE WITH MIRRORS" TOUR 1986—PART I

DAY	DATE	CITY	VENUE
MONDAY	January 13	Seattle, WA	Seattle Arena—Rehearsal
TUESDAY	January 14	Seattle, WA	Seattle Arena—Rehearsal
WEDNESDAY	January 15	Seattle, WA	Seattle Arena—Rehearsal
THURSDAY	January 16	Portland, OR	Memorial Coliseum
FRIDAY	January 17	Seattle, WA	Seattle Center Coliseum
SUNDAY	January 19	Spokane, WA	Coliseum
TUESDAY	January 21	Medford, OR	Jackson Expo Arena
THURSDAY	January 23	Reno, NV	Lawlor Events Center
FRIDAY	January 24	San Francisco, CA	Cow Palace
SATURDAY	January 25	San Francisco, CA	Option—Cow Palace
MONDAY	January 27	Fresno, CA	Selland Arena
TUESDAY	January 28	Bakersfield, CA	Civic Auditorium
THURSDAY	January 30	Las Vegas, NV	Thomas & Mack Center
FRIDAY	January 31	Los Angeles, CA	LA Sports Arena
SATURDAY	February 1	San Bernadino, CA	Orange Pavilion
MONDAY	February 3	Albuquerque, NM	Tingley Coliseum
WEDNESDAY	February 5	El Paso, TX	Civic Center
THURSDAY	February 6	Lubbock, TX	Coliseum
SATURDAY	February 8	Lafayette, LA	Cajun Dome
SUNDAY	February 9	Austin, TX	Frank Erwin Center
TUESDAY	February 11	Corpus Christi, TX	Memorial Coliseum
WEDNESDAY	February 12	San Antonio, TX	Hemisphere Arena
FRIDAY	February 14	Odessa, TX	Ector County Coliseum
SATURDAY	February 15	Oklahoma City, TX	Myriad Convention Center Arena
SUNDAY	February 16	Amarillo, TX	Coliseum Civic Center
TUESDAY	February 18	Beaumont, TX	Civic Center Assembly Center
THURSDAY	February 20	Dallas, TX	Reunion Arena
FRIDAY	February 21	Houston, TX	Summit Arena

From Aero Force One

290

DONE WITH MIRRORS TOUR

The long-awaited reunion album "Done With Mirrors" is released November 4, 1985, peaking at No. 36 on the Billboard charts on December 27, 1985. The album did solid business and the band now had a record label (Geffen) and an album to tour behind.

Orpheum Theater, Boston, Massachusetts. Thursday, November 7, 1985. **Audience recording. Sound quality: C**
The Hop, Walkin' The Dog, My Fist Your Face, Blues Jam, Mother Popcorn, Big Ten Inch Record.

Life imitating art. This recording was made at the video shoot for "Let The Music Do The Talking." The video storyline: a group of young Aerosmith fans are going to see the band and they want to document the performance by recording it.

The story is told fairly accurately from the bootlegger perspective, as the young crew sneak in equipment and nervously look around, worrying about security. They are eventually spotted, but make off with a recording. The final scene shows the band and its crew enjoying the video with the bootleggers.

Well, the night of the video shoot, there was a fan inside making an audio recording.

In between the band miming for the song, they play live to an audience. The crowd is none too thrilled when the video director comes out and stops the live music. "Kill that director!" says one fan.

Tyler fires off a few limericks in between songs, all hard to hear, but it's clear they are risqué. The band plays a loose "Mother Popcorn" that gets tighter as it moves on.

Tyler humorously starts a "fuck Joe Perry" chant. A fan in the crowd predicts "Big Ten Inch Record" when he sees Tyler's harmonica and he's right as the band plays a taut version before the affair ends.

Center Coliseum, Seattle Washington. Thursday, January 16, 1986. Soundboard recording. Sound quality: B

No Surprize, The Hand That Feeds Jam, Same Old Song And Dance, Back In The Saddle, Bone To Bone (Coney Island White Fish Boy), Big Ten Inch Record, Last Child, My Fist Your Face, She's On Fire, Shame On You, Mother Popcorn, Red House, Lightning Strikes.

The date of this recording is not clear. The 13th has been mentioned, but the Seattle Supersonics played a game that day at this arena, making it unlikely. A Portland concert date has been listed for the 16th, but that show seems to have been moved to the 18th or 20th. It's likely this recording is from the 16th, as the band readies itself for the next night's opening of the tour.

"You have never heard this played live. I really think you haven't," Tyler can be heard saying before "No Surprize" to an empty venue. But, indeed the band had played it during dates in January of 1980 as we know. Tyler mumbles his way through part of the lyrics. "Is that good enough to put into the show?" Tyler asks after.

The band jams on "The Hand That Feeds" briefly, then goes into a blues jam. Kramer plays Hendrix's "I Don't Live Today" and Perry jumps in, as Tyler counts the seconds away, "45 seconds Joe, 50 seconds Joe..."

The first non-studio version of "She's On Fire" is here, with Tyler commenting after, "that's a nice effect." "Shame On You" also gets its first non-studio airing. "Joe Perry, ooh Mr. Style, better get ready Nitebob, to make it buzz awhile," Tyler sings, with a nod to the band's sound man.

Tyler is the band leader here, instructing everyone along the way as the session continues.

"Lightning Strikes" features a discordant keyboard intro that would be heard on versions of the song during the first shows of the tour. Tyler finishes the set with a risqué story of an older woman's sexual desires.

Aerosmith — 8 p.m. Friday, Jan. 17, at Seattle Center Coliseum, with the Divinyls. Tickets $14.50. To charge by phone, call 628-0888 or 272-6817.

Center Coliseum, Seattle, Washington. Friday, January 17, 1986. Audience recording. Sound quality: C

Same Old Song And Dance, Back In The Saddle, Bone To Bone (Coney Island White Fish Boy), Big Ten Inch Record, No Surprize, Last Child, My Fist Your Face, Shame On You, Mother Popcorn, She's On Fire, Red House, Lightning Strikes, The Hop, Come Together, Shela, Walk This Way, Let The Music Do The Talking, Sweet Emotion, Toys In The Attic, Dream On, Train Kept A-Rollin'.

The opening night of the official "Done With Mirrors" tour.

"We are going to get us a Western flavor, you asked for it," Tyler says after a crisp version of "Same Old Song And Dance," which opens the show, before the band goes into "Back In The Saddle." The guitarists make their instruments "gallop" as the tune ends.

Lots of literal fireworks at this show, with explosions heard coming from out in the crowd. Maybe the stash was left over from New Year's Eve?

"You remember an album called 'Night In The Ruts?" Tyler asks. "Well, for those of you who don't, and it doesn't sound like many of you have, we are going to do a song we never played on tour before called 'No Surprize.' And it isn't."

After that song, Tyler announces, "Shame On You," but he has misread the setlist and asks Perry to make the correction, which he does: "Well, on the setlist it says, 'My Fist Your Face'," which is played and well received by the crowd.

"Are you ready for a groove tune? You got the new album?" Tyler says, then "Look out mamma!" as Perry starts the ultra-cool riffs for "Shame On You." Sadly, the song made limited appearances during the tour. It segues into "Mother Popcorn" with Tyler saying, "Aerosmith Bootleg album."

Our taper suddenly calls out for the stage manager, "Where's Jeffers!?" he asks. Then it's back to Tyler: "Yeah, baby, my face be changing colors now...I always had it in me, you got to be born that way don't you know...these lips didn't come from nowhere."

Perry ramps up "She's On Fire" with some long slide notes. "I'm going to sing a little bit if you don't mind, and if you mind, fuck ya," Perry says, recalling Hendrix's intro at 1970's Isle of Wight festival as heard on "Hendrix In The West." Perry does "Red House" in Hendrix's hometown. "This is for you, Jimi!" he says, soloing away.

Tyler has a stream of consciousness as he introduces "Lightning Strikes": "I was walking down the street...and someone comes up and says, 'I got a $20 bag,' only you got no money on you, lightning strikes in your head...you think someone is fucking with your mind...I need the boys behind me!" as the band intro builds, the song featuring a newly constructed musical opening.

Next up, "The Hop." "It's simple, straightforward, balls to the wall," is the way Tyler introduces the new tune. "You all seen the movie 'Sgt. Pepper...' You remember the (Future) Villain Band?" Tyler asks as the band starts on "Come Together" as an "El salute to John Lennon," the singer says.

"Shela you out there!" Tyler says as the first known live rendition of the well-executed song follows, segueing into "Walk This Way."

"You all watch MTV? Well, neither do we. But they made us put a song on it," Tyler says before "Let The Music Do The Talking."

"I don't know where I'll be next year and that's a fact baby!" Tyler sings during "Sweet Emotion." "Dream on until your balls turn blue!" Tyler sings comically during "Dream On." Tyler uses a joking falsetto at one point during the song. A lively, great show and opening night to the tour!

Coliseum, Spokane, Washington. Sunday, January 19, 1986. Audience recording. Sound quality: C

Same Old Song And Dance, Back In The Saddle, Bone To Bone (Coney Island White Fish Boy), Big Ten Inch Record, My Fist Your Face, No Surprize, Last Child, She's On Fire, The Hop, Walkin' The Dog, Red House (fragment), Lightning Strikes, Come Together, Shela, Walk This Way, Let The Music Do The Talking, Sweet Emotion, Toys In The Attic, Dream On, Train Kept A-Rollin'.

"We are gonna rock you until you're dead mamma!" Tyler exclaims after the opening tune to an enthusiastic crowd. Kramer plays a cool drum fill on the intro to "Bone To Bone (Coney Island White Fish Boy.)" "It never gets old, does it?" Tyler says after the tune.

He then does an impromptu rap during the "Big Ten Inch Record" intro. Tyler plugs the new album and says it will be "my fist your face if you don't buy it" as the band starts that song.

Tyler says "No Surprize" was inspired by Perry. Tyler gets a yowl out of Whitford during "Last Child" when he asks him to sing, one of the rare times the guitarist has been heard vocally on stage!

The mood then turns sour for a second: "Next motherfucker who throws something at me, I'm walking!" Tyler says before "The Hop." Then, all is forgotten. "Do you realize the last time we played here was with Three Dog Night?" Tyler asks. He then gives a ramble "...step by step..." as the band starts up "Lightning Strikes."

A young woman asks our taper to be lifted on his shoulders. "I'm recording," he says politely as "Come Together" starts, no doubt his priorities are in order!

"Does anyone watch MTV? It's OK, because we don't either," Perry says as he introduces "Let The Music Do The Talking." The band gets lost in the middle of "Sweet Emotion."

The power in the building blows right at the end of "Toys In The Attic." "You are the greatest and that ain't bullshit," Tyler tells the crowd, as the band comes back for the encore once the power is restored.

"The power just blew and we didn't think we'd come back here. But since we did, 'Dream On'!" Tyler says.

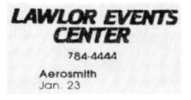

Lawlor Events Center, Reno, Nevada. Thursday, January 23, 1986. Audience recording. Sound quality: C+

No Surprize, Last Child, She's On Fire, The Hop, Red House, Lightning Strikes, Come Together, Shela, Walk This Way, Let The Music Do The Talking, Sweet Emotion, Toys In The Attic, Dream On, Train Kept A-Rollin'.

Our taper shows up late for the gig. "One of our favorite songs of all time..." Tyler says of "No Surprize." He adds the tune "has the feel of 'Rocks'" as the song starts. Tyler changes the lyrics up during the tune in a clever way.

"Once upon a time in a far-away enchanted land called Whitford Junction..." Tyler says as he introduces "Last Child."

Perry provides some sustained feedback on "Train Kept A-Rollin'" to end the show.

Cow Palace, San Francisco, Friday, January 24, 1986. Audience recording. Sound quality: C

Same Old Song And Dance, Back In The Saddle, Bone To Bone (Coney Island White Fish Boy), Big Ten Inch Record, My Fist Your Face, No Surprize, Last Child, She's On Fire, The Hop, Walkin' The Dog, Red House, Lightning Strikes, Come Together, Shela, Walk This Way, Let The Music Do The Talking, Sweet Emotion, Toys In The Attic, Dream On, Train Kept A-Rollin'.

The opening tape runs in its entirety before Perry sounds the beginning of "Same Old Song And Dance," on which Kramer's drums really standout during the tune's quiet parts.

"San Francisco! We're back and it's a full moon! Since we play the Cow Palace, it's with due respect that we add on this song," is Tyler's introduction to "Back In The Saddle," which has a little trouble getting off the ground.

"We did this album ('Done With Mirrors') over in Berkeley...hey, if you throw another beer can...this song is dedicated to you, 'My Fist Your Face,'" Tyler says.

"Let's see if I got my dedications right. We dedicated 'Big Ten Inch' to the O'Farrell Theater, Mitchell Brothers (the infamous San Francisco strip club), and we gonna dedicate this song to Joe Perry, which is 'No Surprize.'" After the line "where the fuck are my royalties" Tyler says, "that's right, Krebs!" Perry says, "where *are* my royalties?" at the song's conclusion."

Whitford tops himself on "Last Child" with an amazingly fluid solo. "The Hop" gets off to a jam start after Tyler introduces Perry as though he thinks "Red House" is the next tune. He also changes up the lyrics during "Walkin' The Dog" to "walking the hog."

Tyler introduces Perry as the "last living toxic twin" before "Red House." Whitford plays a brief snippet of "Foxy Lady." "Bless Richie Supa's ass," Tyler says before "Lightning Strikes," which features a lightning vocal effect by the singer and the discordant keyboard opening.

"The night is young! This is like a club, I love it!" Tyler says, before singing "When I'm calling you…" a line from "Indian Love Song." Before "Come Together," Tyler calls the tune John Lennon's "all-time favorite song."

"Joanie, Joanie" Tyler subs for "Shela" at one point during that song. "Someone out there kicking? No more shoes," Tyler said of a souled stage missile. Oddly, it was in nearby Oakland in 1984 when shoes flew on stage as well.

Kramer starts "Let The Music Do The Talking," with a beat. Tyler says of the drummer after his solo, "He walks, he talks, he crawls on his belly like a reptile!" before "Toys In The Attic," which almost breaks down mid song, but the band keeps it afloat.

More evocative guitar during "Dream On" from Perry. 'Cisco, I hear a train a comin'" as "Train Kept A-Rollin'" really does sound like a train coming down the tracks. The tune ends with sustained feedback.

COW PALACE — COB124
BILL GRAHAM AND — ADULT
MILLER HIGH LIFE PRE — N 13345
AEROSMITH — CA
NO CAMERA/BOTTLE/ALCOHOL — ORF 75
FRI JAN 24 1986 8:00 PM — GEN
GEN. ADM. ADULT — CA 6JAN
CA GEN ADM $14.50 — ADM
NO EXCHANGE / NO REFUND
0159769

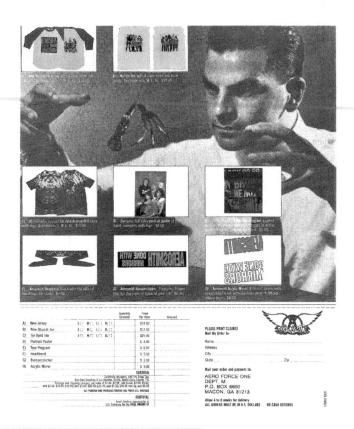

Selland Arena, Fresno California. Monday, January 27, 1986. Audience recording. Sound quality: C+

Same Old Song And Dance, Back In The Saddle, Bone To Bone (Coney Island White Fish Boy), Big Ten Inch Record, My Fist Your Face, Last Child, She's On Fire, The Hop, Come Together, Lightning Strikes, Shela, Walk This Way, Let The Music Do The Talking, Sweet Emotion,

Toys In The Attic, Dream On, Train Kept A-Rollin'.

The guitar players start off low in the mix, as Kramer's drums dominate the first seconds of "Same Old Song And Dance." Tyler works out some cool, affected vocals during the tune. "Young Frankenstein! Mr. Tom Hamilton," Tyler says as the bass man finishes off the song with his nimble finger work.

This gig is out in farm country, the middle of California's Central Valley and we get, "Since we are so far out in the sticks...is that true? Where are we here?" Tyler asks as he introduces "Back In The Saddle." It's a tune "my daddy taught me," Tyler says.

"Well the mouse that roared...you are about to get your socks rocked off by the best rock and roll band in history," Tyler says, full of bravado before "Bone To Bone (Coney Island White Fish Boy)." "Tighter than a crab's asshole in mating season," he says after.

During "Shela" Tyler sings "yeah, it's a city," repeatedly during the intro and it fits somehow. "Oh Brad, did you fart again, boy?" Tyler says after "Last Child."

Perry's slide work in "She's On Fire" is right on, really a wall of sound. "In honor of John Lennon..." says Tyler as Kramer pounds out the intro to "Come Together."

"What slinky thing took this off? I can't see you, momma, but I can smell you. Joe, add this to your collection," Tyler says. "Joe says 'shucks.'"

Perry uses the talk box for part of the lyrics during "Sweet Emotion." The good recording captures Kramer's drum solo quite perfectly here, including his reverberating bass drum. What power. "There's blood all over the drums Joey, that's a hell of a solo you took," Tyler says. The band gets a little lost inside of "Dream On" on this night.

Civic Auditorium, Bakersfield, California. Tuesday, January 28, 1986. Audience recording. Sound quality: C

Same Old Song And Dance (partial), Back In The Saddle, Bone To Bone (Coney Island White Fish Boy), Big Ten Inch Record, My Fist Your Face, Last Child, She's On Fire, The Hop, Come Together, Red House, Lightning Strikes, Shela, Walk This Way, Let The Music Do The Talking, Sweet Emotion, Toys In The Attic, Dream On.

"Don't look like too many people," Tyler says looking out over the audience. "We should take our clothes off and fuck it..." as the band starts "Back In The Saddle." "The Hop" leads right into "Come Together" on this night, the last known "Come Together" on this tour.

Perry repeats "one-half days" during "Red House," emphasizing the lyric. There are some technical difficulties before "Let The Music Do The Talking" and Tyler gets the crowd clapping as a way into the tune.

"What did they do, raise the drinking age here? Are the cops busting people for smoking pot?" Tyler says at one point, commenting on the perceived quietness of the gathering.

Perry plays a little of "Combination" as Kramer starts his solo. The beginning and ending of this show are missing.

Thomas and Mack Arena, Las Vegas, Nevada. Thursday, January 30, 1986. Audience recording. Sound quality: C

Same Old Song And Dance, Back In The Saddle, Bone To Bone (Coney Island White Fish Boy), Big Ten Inch Record, My Fist Your Face, Last Child, No Surprize, She's On Fire, The Hop, Red House, Lightning Strikes, Shela, Walk This Way, Let The Music Do The Talking, Sweet Emotion, Toys In The Attic, Dream On, Train Kept A-Rollin'.

"Since we started this tour in Seattle we have been moving south...this is a song called 'Back In The Saddle,' so it's appropriate," Tyler says at the top of the show.

"Just when we thought everything was going downhill, Joe Perry came up with a song called 'Bone To Bone,'" the singer tells the crowd.

"Aerosmith has never been a video band, but I'd love to do one for this," Tyler says as he ramps up "Big Ten Inch Record" with some mighty fine harmonica playing. "Some old Aerosmith, you get off on that shit, don't you? So do we. But there comes a time when you have to move on and do something new..." Tyler says introducing "My Fist Your Face."

"It's one of my favorite songs, so fuck you. I like it and my old lady likes it," Tyler says introducing "No Surprize." Tyler seems obsessed with the tour's lighting director Sparky Anderson, referencing "Sparky!" during these early shows.

Tyler says the crowd needs to call local radio stations and ask for more music from the band. "That's what the world needs, more Aerosmith!" Tyler says before "The Hop," which has a sudden, odd ending on this night. Perry tells the crowd "when I left the casino last night, I had the blues," before "Red House."

Tyler then references the bust in late June of 1983 at nearby Lake Havasu. "So, I was fucking around in Lake Havasu and I got caught with my pants down, so they arrested my ass. I got to write a letter every month...it seems every night the bags were getting better and better" the singer says.

"So MTV said, 'how would you like to be on TV,' I said, 'We did Cal Jam, so why not?'" Tyler says as "Lightning Strikes" gets going.

"My mama said there would be days like this...." Tyler sings before "Let The Music Do The Talking."

"I hear a train a comin', the train of good fortune..." But then Tyler gets quite angry..."who threw that fuckin' shit!?" before calming by the end for, "Good night, God bless."

Sports Arena, Los Angeles, California. Friday, January 31, 1986. Audience recording. Sound quality: D

Same Old Song And Dance, Back In The Saddle, Bone To Bone (Coney Island White Fish Boy), Big Ten Inch Record, My Fist Your Face, Last Child, No Surprize, She's On Fire, The Hop, Red House, Lightning Strikes, Shela, Walk This Way, Let The Music Do The Talking, Sweet Emotion, Toys In The Attic, Dream On, Train Kept A-Rollin'.

"Good evening LA!" Tyler yells after the opener, no doubt the singer feeling the rush of being on stage at a big venue in the massive market. "Dr. Demento! KMET!" Tyler says after "Big Ten Inch Record." citing his source for his discovery of the song.

"Enough with the silver bracelets, baby," as the band is once again under assault from objects tossed from the crowd. "My favorite song, this week, is a song titled, 'No Surprize.'"

"Hey Templeman, where's your ass, baby!" Tyler says before "She's On Fire," referring to "Done With Mirrors" producer Ted Templeman, who was at the venue this night.

"Everyone's a star here. There are more Limousines out front, we came in a Jeep," Tyler says before "The Hop." Tyler then references former management, who were working on "Classics Live" around this time.

"I was in Alphabet City in New York City trying to cop myself a bag of dope, the lady came up to me and said, 'don't you know that shit is poison.' I said I know. It's damn good,'" Tyler says.

Kramer plays an elongated drum intro into "Walk This Way" as the rest of the band is not quite ready to go. The talk box is employed by Perry during "Sweet Emotion." The beginning of Kramer's solo sounds more machine than human as the drummer plays maniacally, but he never loses his groove.

"You haven't had enough have you?" Tyler asks the crowd. "Say goodnight? Fuck that shit...the LA Times tomorrow will say dream on, baby," as he introduces the song. "I think I hear a train coming right through this building. It starts here, and ends right here, at Perry Place while going through the Aerozone!" is the way Tyler introduces the closer.

A new/old Aerosmith plays San Bernardino

Stories by MIKE STEPHENS
Special to The Sun

AEROSMITH with Divinyls. L.A. Sports Arena; Fri., Jan. 31, 8 p.m. Ticketmaster/ charge (213) 480-3232 or Ticketron/Teletron (213) 410-1062. Info (213) 748-6131. Aerosmith with Y & T at the New Orange Pavilion, National Orange Showgrounds, San Bernardino; Sat., Feb. 1, 7:30 p.m. Ticketmaster/charge (213) 480-3232. Info (714) 884-0178 or 825-1122.

"Back in the Saddle." It's a classic anthem of hard rock 'n' roll from one of the most talked-about power bands of the '70s: Aerosmith.

This time around, however, vocalist Steven Tyler shouldn't be screaming the line, "I'm back," but instead "we're back." The original Aerosmith has been reborn.

San Bernardino fans will be able to judge for themselves whether or not the "Bad Boys from Boston," as they used to be known, have returned in spirit as well as flesh when the group plays the Orange Pavilion at the National Orange Showgrounds Saturday. If the advance indicators are right, fans shouldn't be disappointed.

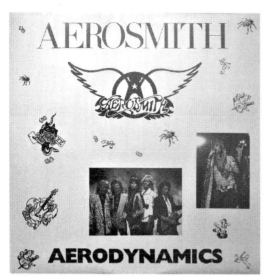

New Orange Pavilion, San Bernardino, California. Saturday, February 1, 1986. Audience recording. Sound quality: C- and C+

Same Old Song And Dance, Back In The Saddle, Bone To Bone (Coney Island White Fish Boy), Big Ten Inch Record, My Fist Your Face, Last Child, No Surprize, She's On Fire, The Hop, Red House, Lightning Strikes, Shela, Walk This Way, Let The Music Do The Talking, Sweet Emotion, Toys In The Attic, Dream on, Train Kept A-Rollin'.

Part of this show was released on the "Aerodynamics" bootleg Lp. It is a very clear audience tape. The balance of the show is from an average recording, but it helps flesh out the whole gig.

"So, we got a full house tonight?! We have some ripples on this stage. We got to loosen up the floorboards tonight. From Houston, Texas, on the six-string bass guitar, Mr. Joe Perry," says Tyler, as "Back In The Saddle" gets underway.

Then, the missiles, yet again, fly on stage. "The next person that throws something, a bottle or a shoe...you will get your ass passed up here and I'm gonna kick it," Tyler says before "My Fist Your Face." He adds "Done With Mirrors" went "gold last night."

"There is no denying I didn't write 'Big Ten Inch,' but when it came time for Joe Perry to put his hands on me, he entitled it 'No Surprize.'" The tune has a sloppy ending on this night.

Tyler has new lyrics for "She's On Fire" that work well, even if not fully intelligible. There is an all-out jam the band gets into during "The Hop."

Tyler starts in on his "bag of dope" stream of consciousness into "Lightning Strikes." "It's a fucking three-ring circus in here!" Tyler says later. "Oh Lucy, oh Lucy" Tyler says as "Shela" gets underway. Kramer is dubbed the "Darth Vader of drummers" by Tyler as the drum solo starts, the singer scatting over its beginning.

Coliseum, Albuquerque, New Mexico. Monday, February 3, 1986. Audience recording. Sound quality: D

Back In The Saddle (partial), Big Ten Inch Record, Bone To Bone (Coney Island White Fish Boy), My Fist Your Face, Last Child, No Surprize, She's On Fire, The Hop, Red House, Lightning Strikes, Shela, Walk This Way, Let The Music Do The Talking, Sweet Emotion, Toys In The Attic, Dream On, Train Kept A-Rollin'.

The band can't seem to decide whether to play "Big Ten Inch Record" or "Bone To Bone (Coney Island White Fish Boy)" and Kramer decides the matter with his drums, it's the former.

"Two of my favorite all time songs back to back," Tyler says of "Last Child" and "No Surprize," with Kramer ending the latter prematurely. Tyler plays some sprightly harmonica to introduce "The Hop."

Perry curves some notes during the "Red House" intro. "We are going to give you a little musical interlude while Steven goes back and perms his hair or whatever the fuck he does..." he says as he introduces the tune.

"So, MTV asked us to do a video. It was not the original band, but it worked..." Tyler says introducing "Lightning Strikes." Kramer's drum work shakes the building during the tune.

"I've been waiting all night to do this song. It gives me a chance to say, 'we made a stop in Albuquerque,'" Tyler tells the crowd, as "Train Kept A-Rollin'" finishes with odd feedback.

SOARING THRU THE SOUTHWEST!

* TOUR '86 *

IN CONCERT: Aerosmith, with special guest Y&T, 8 p.m. Saturday, Lloyd Noble Center. 325-5404 or 235-9040.

Lloyd Noble Center, Oklahoma City, Oklahoma. Saturday, February 15, 1986. Audience recording. Sound quality: D

Same Old Song And Dance, Back In The Saddle, Bone To Bone (Coney Island White Fish Boy), Big Ten Inch Record, My Fist Your Face, Last Child, No Surprize, She's On Fire, The Hop, Red House, Lightning Strikes, Shela, Let The Music Do The Talking, Sweet Emotion, Toys In The Attic, Walk This Way, Dream On, Train Kept A-Rollin'.

"On six-string bass, weighing in at 144 pounds," Tyler says of Perry as he starts "Back In The Saddle."

"Oklahoma, it's good to be back!" Tyler exclaims. "This is something we will dedicate to our old manager, it's called 'Bone To Bone'." Tyler says "Last Child" is a "song about Brad's brother."

Perry introduces "No Surprize" as a song that is seldom played, as the band gets into a perfect version of the song.

"The Hop" features a jam to close out the song. Perry plays a little of "Black Velvet Pants" before starting "Red House."

Whitford sounds out the intro to "Nobody's Fault" before "Shela." There is no evidence the band tried to tackle that song on stage during their early period. "Let The Music Do The Talking" has an extended intro as Tyler gets the crowd clapping.

The guitarists' torment their axes during the "Sweet Emotion" break, making them screech and howl. Tyler sings part of "Dream On" in a flat, but effective new way, then finishes the last verses with great emphasis adding, "won't you dream on…"

A sea of feedback from Perry ends the show on this night. Energetic show in Oklahoma City!

Aerosmith
DATE: Thursday, Feb. 20, 8 p.m.
PLACE: Reunion Arena, 777 Sports St., Dallas
DETAILS: Opening act: Y&T. Tickets $17.25 at Rainbow outlets (787-1500)

**Reunion Arena, Dallas, Texas.
Thursday, February 20, 1986.
Audience recording and soundboard.
Sound quality: D and A.**

Back In The Saddle, Same Old Song And Dance, Bone To Bone (Coney Island White Fish Boy), Big Ten Inch Record, My Fist Your Face, Last Child, No Surprize, She's On Fire, The Hop, Red House, Lightning Strikes, Shela, Walk This Way, Let The Music Do The Talking, Sweet Emotion, Toys In The Attic, Dream On, Train Kept A-Rollin'.

The band flips the first two tunes here and it works better in terms of flow. "Dallas does Dallas does Dallas," Tyler says before "Big Ten Inch Record." Whitford gets a rendition of "Happy Birthday" from the crowd.

Perry plays a little of "On The Road Again" during "The Hop" intro. Tyler gives another stream of consciousness intro to "Lightning Strikes." "Something Aerosmith will never need to teach Dallas how to do," says Tyler introducing "Walk This Way."

Perry dips into "Life Has Been Good to Me So Far," before "Sweet Emotion." "Sweet Jesus! Sweet Jesus! Sweet Jesus! Mr. Joey Kramer," Tyler says introducing his solo on this night.

A cascade of feedback on "Train Kept A Rollin'" ends the gig. About 30 minutes of the show can be found on a clear soundboard recording.

"DONE WITH MIRRORS" TOUR 1986—PART II

DAY	DATE	CITY	VENUE
FRIDAY	March 7	Largo, MD	Capitol Center
SATURDAY	March 8	Philadelphia, PA	Spectrum
TUESDAY	March 11	Worcester, MA	Centrum
WEDNESDAY	March 12	Worcester, MA	Centrum
SATURDAY	March 15	New Haven, CT	Coliseum
SUNDAY	March 16	Springfield, MA	Civic Center
TUESDAY	March 18	Providence, RI	Civic Center
WEDNESDAY	March 19	Syracuse, NY	Memorial Auditorium
THURSDAY	March 20	Pittsburgh, PA	Arena
SATURDAY	March 22	Norfolk, VA	Scope
SUNDAY	March 23	Richmond, VA	Coliseum
TUESDAY	March 25	Atlanta, GA	Omni
WEDNESDAY	March 26	Lakeland, FL	Civic Center
FRIDAY	March 28	Hollywood, FL	Sportatorium
SATURDAY	March 29	Ft. Meyers, FL	Lee Civic Center Arena
SUNDAY	March 30	Jacksonville, FL	Coliseum
TUESDAY	April 1	Augusta, GA	Civic Center Arena
WEDNESDAY	April 2	Knoxville, TN	Civic Center
FRIDAY	April 4	Charlotte, NC	Coliseum
SATURDAY	April 5	Johnson City, TN	Freedom Hall
SUNDAY	April 6	Asheville, NC	Civic Center
TUESDAY	April 8	New York NY	Madison Square Garden
THURSDAY	April 10	Hershey, PA	Hershey Park Arena
SATURDAY	April 12	Glen Falls, NY	Arena
SUNDAY	April 13	Allentown, PA	Stabler Arena

Some of these dates are tentative and subject to change!

Capital Centre, Landover, 792-7490 (Baltimore number). March 7: Aerosmith.

Capital Center, Landover, Maryland. Friday, March 7, 1986. Audience recording. Sound quality: D

Back In The Saddle, Same Old Song And Dance, Bone To Bone (Coney Island White Fish Boy), Big Ten Inch Record, My Fist Your Face, No Surprize, Last Child, She's On Fire, Walkin' The Dog, The Hop, Red House, Lightning Strikes, Shela, Walk This Way, Let The Music Do The Talking, Sweet Emotion, Toys In The Attic, Dream On, Train Kept A-Rollin'.

Another good, high-energy show. Maybe having Ted Nugent as the opener pushes the band. Hard to hear Tyler's comments on the cacophonous recording.

"The Hop" gets a great response from the loud rock and roll crowd, which is in the mood for a party. No wonder this was the site for "Heavy Metal Parking Lot," which was shot two months after this concert.

Perry sends the notes flying during his blues riffing on "Red House." Tyler does another "drug rap" into "Lightning Strikes."

Tyler mucks up the lyrics during "Walk This Way," but finds his way back quickly. Kramer plays the intro to "Lick And A Promise" during his drum solo.

... Macho men **Aerosmith** and **Ted Nugent** play to the boys at the Spectrum tomorrow.

The rejunventated Aerosmith crunches out their raw rock at the Spectrum in Philadelphia tonight. The group will also be at Madison Square Garden and the Brendan Byrne Arena in April.

•Aerosmith, hard rock concert, Ted Nugent opens show, Spectrum, Pattison Place and Broad Street, Phila., 8 p.m. Tickets $13.50 and $11.50 at box office and Ticketron. Call 344-1770.

Spectrum, Philadelphia, Pennsylvania. Saturday, March 8, 1986. Audience recording. Sound quality: C+

Back In The Saddle, Same Old Song And Dance, Bone To Bone (Coney Island White Fish Boy), Big Ten Inch Record, My Fist Your Face, Last Child, Shame On You, Mother Popcorn, No Surprize, She's On Fire, Walkin' The Dog, The Hop, Red House, Lightning Strikes, Shela, Walk This Way, Let The Music Do The Talking, Sweet Emotion, Toys In The Attic, Dream On, Train Kept A-Rollin'.

Aerosmith had quite a tour history in Philadelphia. An M-80 (1977) and a bottle (1978) were thrown at the band causing injuries at the Spectrum. Then billboards went up in the city, begging the band to play the town again, and they did with two sold out shows in February 1983 (oddly two weeks apart.) That Philly intensity can be heard on this tape.

"Philly baby, it's so good to be back!" Tyler says after the opening tune. "You keep a knockin', but you can't get in." Tyler says, recalling the lyrics to the song of the same name popularized by Little Richard. He continues: "19,000 of you tonight!" before "Big Ten Inch Record."

It's a great gig with some rarities including "Shame On You," which was played only two other times on this tour, or at least taped two other times (in Seattle and New Jersey). Perry tried to resurrect it during subsequent shows, playing the licks, but none of the band would jump in. The song sounds under rehearsed here, but still finds a good groove and it clocks in at just over two minutes before "Mother Popcorn" follows. Tyler improvises: "Don't give me no lip, I got enough for everybody..."

Of course, the band is being pelted with items tossed from the crowd, as he notes before the tune. Hey, it's Philly! It's Tyler's parents' anniversary and they are at the gig. "Ain't that cool? They are up in the press box," the singer says.

A taut version of "Walkin' The Dog" is played, after which Tyler says, "How was that Uncle Eddie? The boys be kicking some ass tonight!" After Red House, Tyler says of Perry: "The boy be singing the blues, my microphone is full of slobber, too!"

During the intro to "Lightning Strikes, Tyler references living in The Bronx in 1972 and his father's piano. "My momma came along and said, 'Steven, you got all this energy, what are you going to do with it?' I said, 'I don't know mommy...I think...I think... I think...'" as he then sings the first line of the tune, which features Tyler/Perry dual verses.

"This one is going to be our new single, as far as I'm concerned it is an all-time classic already," Tyler says before "Shela." One of the best live versions of the song, although it never met Tyler's expectations as a signature piece for the band. "See, nothing to it!" he says after.

"Walk This Way" gets off to an odd start with Tyler providing some vocalizations until Kramer starts the song. The guitars seem to go quiet mid song as Perry and Tyler sing the lyrics.

After this gig the band famously began working on "Walk This Way" with producer Rick Rubin and Run DMC, which would change the band's trajectory.

Perry uses a talk box for a fiery version of "Sweet Emotion," which gets an intense reaction from the crowd. Perry really burns up his strat during the tune's break, making it screech, preach and howl!

"Drugs in the attic," becomes part of "Toys In The Attic" lyrics, as it did on other stops of the tour. Tyler sings the "Banana Boat Song" as he introduces "Dream On." This is a great gig.

Aerosmith
Ted Nugent

March 11
7:30 pm
$14.50, 12.50
CENTRUM in
WORCESTER

The Centrum, Worcester, Massachusetts. Tuesday, March 11, 1986. Audience recording. Sound quality: C

Back In The Saddle, Same Old Song And Dance, Bone To Bone (Coney Island White Fish Boy), Big Ten Inch Record, My Fist Your Face, Last Child, No Surprize, She's On Fire, The Hop, Walkin' The Dog, Red House, Lightning Strikes, Shela, Shame On Your, Mother Popcorn, Walk This Way, Let The Music Do The Talking, Sweet Emotion, Toys In The Attic, Dream On, Train Kept A-Rollin'.

The first three songs on this night are played non-stop. "This is what it's all about!" Tyler exclaims after the run of tunes.

Perry wants to launch into "Shame On You" after "Last Child," but he has no takers within the band and it dies. Instead "No Surprize" gets the nod, and toward the end Perry sounds some notes reminiscent of "Kings And Queens."

The band flip flops "The Hop" and "Walkin' The Dog" on this night, a pattern that continues for the next several gigs, but then the original order returns later in the tour. "Shame On You" does get another rare outing and its followed by "Mother Popcorn." Very cool!

"Boston knows how to rock and roll!" Tyler says, warming up the crowd after "Walk This Way."

The crowd provides some Beatle-esque screams after the line "after a month on the road I'll be coming in your hand" during "Sweet Emotion."

Tyler tells the crowd to give each other a "big kiss" on the cheek before "Dream On." Kramer punctuates the first lines of the song with his bass drum.

A solid show on this night that would serve as a warm-up for the following night's gig that would gain prominence for various reasons.

An anniversary gift from WBCN

By Ernie Santosuosso
Globe Staff

It's hardly a well-kept secret that WBCN-FM (104) is celebrating its 18th anniversary by giving away 13,000 tickets to a free Aerosmith concert March 12 at the Centrum in Worcester.

Tickets are given to every 10th caller to the station or at giveaway locations announced over the air. Five hundred pairs of tickets have have been handed out to the first 500 persons at the Worcester Metro, and 1,000 went to listeners who went to Rich's Car Tunes in Danvers, Strawberries on Route 20 in Sudbury, and Manufacturers Marketplace with more locations to be announced. WBCN will produce and pay all expenses for the event.

Boston Globe coverage.

Radio wars: Boston's WBCN and Worcester's WAAF have been battling over this week's Aerosmith shows at the Centrum. WBCN angered WAAF by renting billboards near the Worcester station and proclaiming that WBCN was giving away all the tickets to the band's show last night. Then it gave away the first 500 tix at the Metro in Worcester. Incensed by the territorial encroachment, WAAF sent interns down to pick up some of the tickets, then announced it had free tickets, too. They also circulated an internal memo saying they would never be shut out of tickets in New England. WBCN somehow got hold of the memo and was none too pleased.

The Centrum, Worcester, Massachusetts. Wednesday, March 12, 1986. Radio broadcast and audience recordings. Sound quality: A and C+

Back In The Saddle, Same Old Song And Dance, Bone To Bone (Coney Island White Fish Boy), Big Ten Inch Record, My Fist Your Face, Last Child, No Surprize, She's On Fire, The Hop, Walkin' The Dog, Red House, Lightning Strikes, Shela, Walk This Way, Let The Music Do The Talking, Sweet Emotion, Toys In The Attic, Dream On, Train Kept A-Rollin'.

The free show! WBCN in Boston bought all the tickets for this gig and hands them out to listeners. Part of the show is later broadcast by Westwood One and issued on various EPs and other promotional vinyl.

"Boston! What a party tonight! Tyler exclaims and indeed it is as the band jumps into "Same Old Song And Dance."

"My Fist Your Face" is dedicated to boxer Marvin Hagler, who grew up in nearby Brockton, Massachusetts. Tyler says the band is recording for an album. "The boys be smokin' tonight," Tyler says after "She's On Fire." "I'll never get used to this," he adds.

"This is like one gigantic frat party," Perry observes before "Red House." Tyler says the tape is being "changed in the truck," after the tune. There is a short stall, but the band kicks up the "Lightning Strikes" intro without much delay. The band quiets during a section of the tune, making Tyler's vocals stand out. They had done the same at the Philly show.

A wobbly "Happy Birthday" is sung to WBCN, which is celebrating 18 years of its existence and was a huge supporter of the band in good times and bad. Kramer pounds out Zeppelin's "When The Levee Breaks" drum intro before "Let The Music Do The Talking."

"WBCN lets the music do the talking," Perry says. This version made its way onto the "Classics Live 2" album. Tyler does some vocalizations on "Dream On." "The Flintstones" theme plays out the crowd on this night.

Maxi-single of "Darkness" with "She's On Fire," "The Hop" and "My Fist Your Face" from Worcester 3/12/86.

312

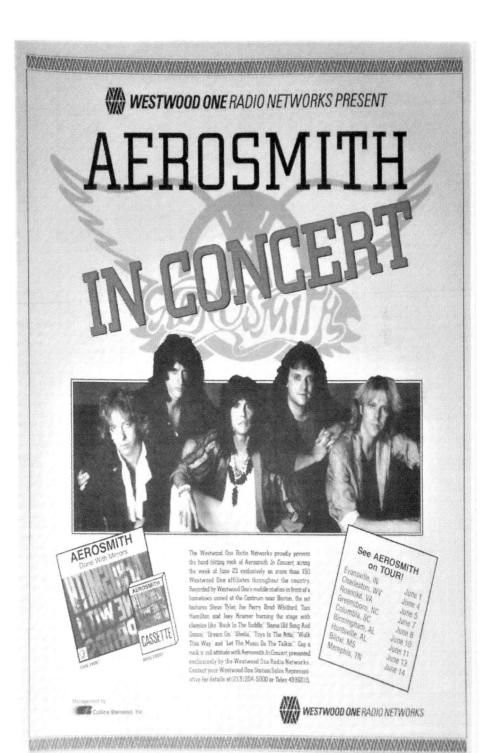

New Haven Coliseum, New Haven, Connecticut. Saturday, March 15, 1986. Audience recording. Sound quality: D

Back In The Saddle, Same Old Song And Dance, Bone To Bone (Coney Island White Fish Boy), Big Ten Inch Record, My Fist Your Face, Last Child, No Surprize, She's On Fire, The Hop, Walkin' The Dog, Red House, Lightning Strikes, Shela, Walk This Way, Let The Music Do The Talking, Sweet Emotion, Toys In The Attic, Dream On, Train Kept A-Rollin'.

The fuzzy recording makes it seem as though "Back In The Saddle" starts with Tyler's vocals as the band's opening is hard to hear. Kramer's beat for "Same Old Song And Dance" segues from the end of "Back In The Saddle" with Tyler yelling "New Haven, baby!"

"This place is tremendous!" the singer says before "My Fist Your Face" and then mentions something about all the women in the crowd "sliding down the aisles and into my mouth." The backing piano can be heard well on the song, despite the rough quality of the recording.

"Tell them a story, Brad," is Tyler's lead into "Last Child."

"Out of all of our favorite all-time Aerosmith songs, this is our favorite," Tyler says in introducing "No Surprize." Tyler switches up the lyrics for the song, not a bad trick for what at the time was a 7-year-old tune! Perry gets his slide groove going during "She's On Fire."

Whitford plays a unique solo during "The Hop," almost like it's not part of the tune, an example of how the band never played a song the same way. Perry plays a cool jangly, staccato ending to "Red House."

"Now we are going to shift into second gear," Tyler says later, and Perry again fires up the "Shame On You" riffs, but it doesn't go anywhere.

During "Let The Music Do The Talking," Perry takes his sweet time before playing the solo! Intentional feedback marks the beginning of "Sweet Emotion" before Hamilton begins the song. Perry's solo here lacks conventional structure, but in a good way. He definitely is playing outside the lines, very punk influenced, but then draws it back in as needed.

Kramer eggs the crowd on midway through his solo, cupping his hand to his ear, asking for more noise from the crowd, and they oblige. He then starts up again, playing slowly, seemingly banging his head against the drums, or was it his foot hitting the bass drum? Either way, his solos during this tour always got a great response before he led the band into "Toys In The Attic."

He then starts the end of the show by conjuring up images of a train coming down the track, bells and all, for "Train Kept A Rollin'."

Aerosmith, Ted Nugent — New Haven Coliseum, 275 S. Orange St., New Haven: Sat at 8. Tickets: $12.50-$14.50 (772-4330). Springfield Civic Center, 1277 Main St., Springfield: Sun at 7:30. Tickets: $14.50 (413-787-6600).

Civic Center, Springfield, Massachusetts. Sunday, March 16, 1986. Audience recording. Sound quality: C+

Back In The Saddle, Same Old Song And Dance, Bone To Bone (Coney Island White Fish Boy), My Fist Your Face, Last Child, No Surprise, She's On Fire, The Hop, Walkin' The Dog, Red House, Lightning Strikes, Shela, Walk This Way, Let The Music Do The Talking, Sweet Emotion, Toys In The Attic'.

The recording gives the feeling of an intimate gig, even though the venue is a good size. "Just like Haley's Comet, once a year..." Tyler says as the show gets underway.

"Brad Whitford best describes the situation like this..." Tyler says, as the guitar player starts "Last Child." Tyler adds some nice opening vocals, accentuating the "home" lyric.

"Full house tonight, if we all breathe in, the roof would cave in!" Tyler says before "No Surprise," the last time it was played on this tour. Perry does a nice long slide intro to "She's On Fire."

Kramer's middle break on "Lightning Strikes" is captured very well on the recording, really thunderous. "Hip, hip" Tyler says to the audience's "hooray" before "Shela."

"Without me on it, it was shit," Tyler jokes, introducing "Let The Music Do The Talking," as he gets the audience clapping along to the tune with "yeah, yeah, yeah, yeah!" Kramer's bass drum is loud during the tune; it knocks the recorder out for a few seconds!

"The greatest drummer since Darth Vader!" Tyler says again as a setup for Kramer's solo. Now there's an image!

315

Civic Center, Providence, Rhode Island. Tuesday, March 18, 1986. Audience recording. Sound quality: C

Back In The Saddle, Same Old Song And Dance, Bone To Bone (Coney Island White Fish Boy), Big Ten Inch Record, My Fist Your Face, Last Child, She's On Fire, The Hop, Walkin' The Dog, Red House, Lightning Strikes, Shela, Walk This Way, Let The Music Do The Talking, Sweet Emotion, Toys In The Attic, Dream On, Train Kept A-Rollin'.

"Oh baby, are we home, or what? You are higher than we are!" Tyler says after "Back In The Saddle" to a delirious crowd. The show has a homecoming feel as the band has spent much time in the town and performing in this venue over the years.

As "Last Child" begins, Hamilton continues to tune up! The Providence crowd knows "Done With Mirrors" well, cheering at the beginning of each new song. "Providence is our second home," Perry declares before "Red House."

Perry plays a little of "Get It Up" and then "Shame On You" before "Walk This Way." "Cream on!" Tyler sings during "Dream On."

A barrage of firecrackers goes off during "Train Kept A-Rollin'." Fireworks and rock concerts seemed to go hand in hand during this era. Perry plays some beefy riffs to end the song. "The Munsters" TV show theme plays as the gig ends.

TED NUGENT, AEROS-MITH, rock concert, Syracuse War Memorial, Syracuse. 7:30 p.m. Admission.

War Memorial, Syracuse, New York. Wednesday, March 19, 1986. Audience recording. Sound quality: C+

Back In The Saddle, Same Old Song And Dance, Big Ten Inch Record, My Fist Your Face, Last Child, She's On Fire, The Hop, Walkin' The Dog, Red House, Lightning Strikes, Shela, Walk This Way, Let The Music Do The Talking, Sweet Emotion, Toys In The Attic, Dream On, Train Kept A-Rollin'.

"Good evening baby," Tyler says after "Back In The Saddle." Welcome to Aerosmith's pleasure palace!" Whitford solos superbly throughout "Last Child," really leading the tune — his song.

"Watch this man over here!" Tyler says as Perry cranks up slide guitar for the moody "She's On Fire" intro.

316

Perry quips before "Red House": "We are going to give Steven a little break here, we're going to let him go back and dry his hair. He's been running around all over this place for you." He then adds, "I hear in Syracuse you don't have to take your aunt's abuse. It's an inside joke."

"A bunch of white boys from Boston is trying to tell you how to sing the blues? Tell it to me, daddy," Tyler says after "Lightning Strikes."

"God almighty, we have to clear the aisles, so you can do some tap dancing. I want to show you how to walk this way," Tyler says before Kramer bangs out a mini intro to "Walk This Way."

The drummer shuffles his playing in a cool way during part of "Let The Music Do The Talking." Then on "Sweet Emotion" he plays four staccato blasts on the way out of the song.

"Toys In The Attic" features some satisfying crunchy guitar. "Say good night Steven," Perry says to Tyler as "Toys In The Attic'" wraps up. Kramer pounds some interesting, but out of place notes during the beginning of "Dream On." A good recording of the show.

The Scope, Norfolk, Virginia. Saturday, March 22, 1986. Audience recording. Sound quality: C-

Rats In The Cellar, Mama Kin, Big Ten Inch Record, My Fist Your Face, Last Child, She's On Fire, The Hop, Lord Of The Thighs, Red House (cut), Lightning Strikes, Shela, Walk This Way, Let The Music Do The Talking, Sweet Emotion, Toys In The Attic, Dream On, Train Kept A-Rollin'.

This begins a great string of shows in the southern United States, where the fans really appreciate the band.

The band suddenly changes up its setlist. The new set brings a great energy to a downright fanatical crowd. This gig is one of the best of the tour.

An exciting beginning to the show. Perry solos away in the overdriven recording that captures the band in a loud, hard way. They jump into "Mama Kin" non-stop, the energy flowing.

"Brad was finger picking in the dressing room and I said, 'can you repeat that for the audience?'" Tyler says, as "Last Child" begins.

317

"Norfolk, crazy motherfuckers...you are like an army!" Tyler says before "The Hop." "Lord Of The Thighs" is suddenly back in the setlist. Some nice Tyler vocal gymnastics mid song drive the tune.

"Aerosmith is not a singles band, it's a rock and roll album band!" Tyler declares before "Shela."

Tyler says "Joe Perry!" as he hands the baton to the guitarist during "Toys In The Attic." A short, tight version of "Train Kept A-Rollin'" finishes the exciting show.

AEROSMITH AND TED NUGENT. More than 35 years of rock 'n' roll experience will be heard Tuesday, March 25, when Aerosmith and Ted Nugent (see today's More Music page) combine for a concert at The Omni, 100 Techwood Drive. Aerosmith, a five-man group, has been performing for 15 years, while Detroit rocker Nugent has been at it more than 20 years. Their current album is "Done With Mirrors"; his is "Little Miss Dangerous." Tickets, which are available at all SEATs outlets and The Omni box office, are $15. 577-9600 to charge by phone.

The Omni, Atlanta, Georgia. Tuesday, March 25, 1986. Videotape soundtrack. Sound quality: D

Rats In The Cellar, Mama Kin, Big Ten Inch Record, My Fist Your Face, Last Child, She's On Fire, The Hop, Lord Of The Thighs, Red House, Lightning Strikes, Shela, Walk This Way, Let The Music Do The Talking, Sweet Emotion, Toys In The Attic, Dream On, Train Kept A-Rollin'.

"Rats In the Cellar" is now firmly re-established as the opener, a fast-paced beginning that rocks the crowd.

"Mr. Brad Whitford!" Tyler exclaims, as the band jumps into the newly revived "Lord Of The Thighs" as the guitarist paints pictures with his notes. Perry does a falsetto at the end of "Red House."

Perry plays a wicked "skidding" solo during "Let The Music Do The Talking." "Cream on, scream on" are the ad-libs Tyler makes during "Dream On."

The train bells are sounded as Kramer cranks out the drum intro to "Train Kept A-Rollin'" as the show draws to a close with some great chunk-a-chunk guitar. The chaotic ending is drenched in feedback. The audio here is from a video shot from the audience.

Hard rocking is Aerosmith's cup of tea

Civic Center, Lakeland, Florida. Wednesday, March 26, 1986. Audience recording. Sound quality: C

Rats In The Cellar, Mama Kin, Big Ten Inch Record, My Fist Your Face, Last Child, She's On Fire, The Hop, Lord Of The Thighs, Red House, Happy Birthday, Lightning Strikes, Shela, Walk This Way, Let The Music Do The Talking, Sweet Emotion, Toys In The Attic, Dream On, Train Kept A-Rollin'.

Central Floridians can relive the hard-rocking '70s when Aerosmith and opening act Ted Nugent perform at 8 p.m. Wednesday at the Lakeland Civic Center arena, 700 W. Lemon St., Lakeland. Tickets, priced at $16, are available at the center box office and Select-A-Seat outlets.

Tyler subs in the more inclusive line "catch us if you can" for "catch me if you can" as "Rats In The Cellar" kicks off the stellar gig. Perry plays an ascending note right at the end of "Mama Kin" to punctuate the song.

"Brad, baby. This is Brad's chance to sing to you," Tyler says, marking the beginning of "Last Child." "Sing that song, you bitch!" Tyler says before "The Hop," a recurrent call from the singer that dots the band's touring history.

"The main man and 7th Wonder of the World, Mr. Brad Whitford!" Tyler says during the "Lord Of The Thighs" intro. Perry utters the "money for nothing and chicks for free" Dire Straits line as he brings "Red House" to a close.

It's Tyler's birthday and the crowd sings "Happy Birthday" at Perry's request as the guitarist sings the first few lines himself! A cool touch, and Tyler says, "Thank you. My cup runneth over."

The keyboard intro to "Lightning Strikes" is now gone as the band builds an intro which takes a while to find its groove. Tyler tells the crowd Whitford developed the riffs for "Shela" as the band moves into the song.

Yet another bottle flies onto the stage and Tyler chastises the thrower before "Let The Music Do The Talking." Tyler repeats the word "everyone" three times in the line "everyone's got their dues to pay" during "Dream On."

Lee County Civic Center, Fort Myers, Florida. Saturday, March 29, 1986. Audience recording. Sound quality: D

Rats In The Cellar, Mama Kin, Big Ten Inch Record, My Fist Your Face, Last Child, She's On Fire, The Hop, Red House, Lightning Strikes, Shela, Walk This Way, Let The Music Do The Talking, Sweet Emotion, Toys In The Attic, Dream On, Train Kept A-Rollin'.

"Rats In The Cellar" features Perry and Whitford lockstep as they bring the song to a close. "When you are louder than we are, we're talking some people," Tyler says before "My Fist Your Face."

"If someone were to give Brad singing lessons, it would sound something like this," says Tyler before "Last Child," with the singer sounding somewhat imbibed on this night. But his lyrics are unaffected.

"You like the new stuff, huh? So do I, so do we," Tyler says after "She's On Fire." "Lightning Strikes" has an almost avant-garde beginning until the band kicks into the song's traditional structure.

Tyler introduces "Walk This Way," but the next tune is actually "Shela" in which Perry plays some ascending riffs to end the song. "Keep your eye on the bouncing balls" says Tyler getting back to "Walk This Way," the intro marked by a long Perry note.

Perry plays a screaming guitar during the "Sweet Emotion" middle section. "The power of positive badness!" Tyler yells, introducing Kramer's solo.

Tyler chastises those who leave during the encore break before "Dream On." Perry plays wicked tones as "Train Kept A-Rollin'" ends the gig.

Memorial Coliseum, Jacksonville, Florida. Sunday, March 30, 1986. Audience recording. Sound quality: C-

Rats In The Cellar, Mama Kin, Big Ten Inch Record, My Fist Your Face, Last Child, She's On Fire, The Hop, Same Old Song And Dance, Red House, Lightning Strikes, Shela, Walk This Way, Let The Music Do The Talking, Sweet Emotion, Toys In The Attic, Dream On, Train Kept A Rollin'.

Whitford and Perry provide some fantastically frenetic guitar work on "Rats In The Cellar," as the inspired pair get more comfortable with the reintroduced tune.

Tyler plays super funky harmonica as part of the "Big Ten Inch Record" intro, cutting through the rock arena din. The singer does start in on the last verse too soon, but we shall forgive him. He was rarely off on stage, no matter what substance may have been coursing through his body. A true pro.

"You are making 4,000 sound like 10,000!" Tyler tells the crowd after the tune as he picks up on the surge of excitement. "Everyone has bathing suits here, all the time," the singer says before "Last Child" as he observes the Florida crowd.

"Same Old Song And Dance" rises out of nowhere after "The Hop," the band having fun, playing well and willing to switch up its set. Refreshing. "Take the delay off my voice," Tyler instructs the road crew before "Shela." "Oh Lucy, Oh Peter!" he adds, addressing a roadie in Ricky Ricardo's "I Love Lucy" voice.

"Another Joe Perry classic, dredged from the bowels of Aerosmith's back pocket," is Tyler's introduction to "Let The Music Do The Talking." Tyler's fertile mind changes the lyrics up on "Toys In The Attic."

"This is dedicated to those who left and who will miss the best part of the show!" Tyler says after the encore break as the band plays "Dream On." Perry and Tyler are quiet for the beginning of "Train Kept A-Rollin'" but suddenly both kick in as the song rolls along.

Civic Coliseum, Knoxville, Tennessee. Wednesday, April 2, 1986. Audience recording. Sound quality: C

Rats In The Cellar, Mama Kin, Big Ten Inch Record, My Fist Your Face, Last Child, She's On Fire, Lord Of The Thighs, The Hop, Lightning Strikes (cut), Shela, Walk This Way, Let The Music Do The Talking, Sweet Emotion, Toys In The Attic, Dream On, Train Kept A-Rollin'.

A radio ad for the gig starts the recording. That's followed by comments made by the house MC before the opening tape is played, adding to the ambiance of the night. We are transported (aurally at least) to Knoxville in 1986!

Kramer knocks out a steady beat to start "Rats In The Cellar." The guitar solo is crisp and exciting, Perry playing out of his mind, and then the band hits "Mama Kin" with great energy.

The piano can be heard in "My Fist Your Face." "Lord Of The Thighs" is played again on this night. Perry has trouble with the intro into "The Hop," but then rectifies it without stopping.

"Shela" begins without the verbal intro from Tyler, who proceeds to miss the first verse. Some of the guitar phrasing on the song varies from other live versions, making this a unique reading.

Tyler gets the crowd rhythmically clapping to start "Let The Music Do The Talking," but tells them to "slow down." To clear the musical pallet, Kramer bangs away on his drum and all gets quiet before the song starts. Tyler gets a sing along going for "Train Kept A-Rollin'."

Coliseum, Charlotte, North Carolina. Friday, April 4, 1986. Audience recording. Sound quality: C

Rats In The Cellar, Mama Kin, Big Ten Inch Record, My Fist Your Face, Last Child, She's On Fire, The Hop, Walkin' The Dog, Red House, Shela, Walk This Way, Let The Music Do The Talking, Sweet Emotion, Toys In The Attic, Dream On, Train Kept A-Rollin' (cut).

Tyler's voice really stands out on this recording. The band jams fabulously during "Rats In The Cellar," although Perry's guitar seems to crap out at one point. Another southern crowd is getting into the show and Tyler acknowledges the strong response. "This is what rock and roll is!"

"Brad is going to sing us this song his own way," Tyler says before "Last Child." "Got to get back to Charlotte's nitty gritty," Tyler improvises during the song.

"You like that? Well dig this..." Tyler says, as Kramer bangs the opening notes to "Walkin' The Dog." But the band does not follow. Instead, it's "The Hop."

"I'm so cold, ooooh, I'm so lonely," Tyler sings before "Sweet Emotion," a familiar refrain during this part of the tour. He then shakes the maracas to start the tune, joined by Hamilton's opening bass lines. Tyler's hands glide down the keys of the piano during the "Dream On" intro. "Holy shit, Charlotte!" Tyler says after. The end of "Train Kept A-Rollin'" is cut as the tape ends.

Freedom Hall Civic Center, Johnson City, Tennessee. Saturday, April 5, 1986. Audience recording. Sound quality: C

Rats In The Cellar, Mama Kin, Big Ten Inch Record, My Fist Your Face, Last Child, She's On Fire, The Hop, Walkin' The Dog, Red House, Lightning Strikes, Shela, Walk This Way, Let The Music Do The Talking, Sweet Emotion, Toys In The Attic, Dream On, Train Kept A-Rollin'.

The rhythm section chugs away during "Rats In The Cellar" in a most pleasing way on this night, the Aerosmith machine greased and gonzo. With no provocation other than the hypnotic music, the crowd begins to clap rhythmically to the tune.

"Good evening Johnson City! How's your Johnson tonight?" Tyler quips during the opening of "Big Ten Inch Record." "Walkin' The Dog" reappears again in the setlist after "The Hop."

"Mr. Sparky Anderson on the lights, let's give him a big hand!" Tyler says, acknowledging the lighting director mentioned throughout the tour. "And, of course, (sound man) Nitebob!" the singer says before "Lightning Strikes."

The guitar players come to a complete stop during "Sweet Emotion" before Kramer starts drumming to finish off the song.

"Roll over Beethoven, tell Tyschosky the news...and then we want you to 'Dream On.'" Tyler says. Tyler gets another sing along going for "Train Kept A-Rollin'."

Madison Square Garden, New York City. Tuesday, April 8, 1986. Audience recording. Sound quality: C+
Rats In The Cellar, Mama Kin, Big Ten Inch Record, My Fist Your Face, Last

323

Child, She's On Fire, The Hop, Walkin' The Dog, Red House, Lightning Strikes, Shela, Walk This Way, Let The Music Do The Talking, Sweet Emotion, Toys In The Attic, Dream On, Train Kept A-Rollin'.

A multi-layered "Rats In The Cellar" kicks off the gig. The recording is solid, with the crowd away from the taper's mic, giving the gig an almost club-like feel, even though the venue is cavernous.

"Hey Joe!" Tyler says as Perry joins him for some of "Mama Kin's" vocals. Boxer Marvin Hagler is again mentioned before "My Fist Your Face." Perry does some on the fly tuning during the intro to "Walkin' The Dog."

"No more throwing shit up here!" Tyler warns before "Red House." Tyler introduces Perry as the "Italian musical stallion" as he did many times during the tour.

It's New York, the Big Apple, the center of Western Civilization, but the too cool Perry is not impressed. "How are you doing tonight?" Perry asks the crowd, which gives a cheer. "I guess that means OK. Whatever..." the dismissive guitarist says before getting to the business of blasting the Garden with blues. "This is going to give a chance for Brad and me to beat on these motherfuckin' guitars," he says, before launching the song.

"Wowee! Talk about the boy from New York City," Tyler exclaims after the tune. "Lightning Strikes" features another guest appearance by Richie Supa, who wrote the tune. He adds some nice backing vocals. Tyler again warns the crowd about throwing things onstage before "Shela." Tyler says "Listen to Joe!" before the "Train Kept A-Rollin'" solo.

An amateur video recording also exists from this gig.

Hershseypark Arena, Hershey, Pennsylvania. Thursday, April 10, 1986. Audience recording. Sound quality: C+

Rats In The Cellar, Mama Kin, Big Ten Inch Record, My Fist Your Face, Last Child, She's On Fire, The Hop, Walkin' The Dog, Red House, Lightning Strikes, Shela, Walk This Way, Let The Music Do The Talking, Sweet Emotion, Toys In The Attic, Dream On, Train Kept A-Rollin'.

"Hey boys!" Tyler exclaims during the opener on this night in which he is full of "energy." Tyler purposely mixes up the lyrics during "Mama Kin."

"We are going to dedicate this next song to the banana I threw out front!" Tyler says before an impromptu rap leading into "Big Ten Inch Record," in which Whitford plays an ultra-tight solo.

"My Fist Your Face" is once again dedicated to boxer Marvin Hagler. The keyboards can be heard well here. On "Last Child" Perry plays some unique rhythm.

"So, you all bought our new album, right? Well, you better go out and buy it. We are going to play something off it, 'She's On Fire," Tyler says, right as a fan calls for that tune. "This guy knows his shit!" Tyler says of the fan.

"Excuse me!" Tyler exclaims before his harmonica solo during "The Hop."

Before "Red House" Perry says, "If it looks like I just woke up it's because I did, but I'm glad I did because I can play for you."

Tyler messes with the words to "Walk This Way"; he's not interested in a word for word recital on this night. Perry plays some warbly notes on the way out of the song.

Perry plays the "Smoke On The Water" riff at the beginning of "Let The Music Do The Talking."

"Oh, oh, she's so fine," is Tyler's intro to "Sweet Emotion" on this night as Perry is interested in making sounds and noises during, rather than the hard rock crunch during this version.

Before "Dream On" Tyler recites the lyrics to "No Surprize" in spoken form and then sings part of the song in his best Bob Dylan voice! "Daylight come and I think I hear a train," is Tyler's animated intro to "Train Kept A Rollin'," which ends the interesting and entertaining gig.

Meadowlands Arena, East Rutherford, New Jersey. Saturday, April 12, 1986. Audience recording. Sound quality: C

Rats In The Cellar, Mama Kin, Big Ten Inch Record, My Fist Your Face, Last Child, She's On Fire, The Hop, Walkin' The Dog, Shame On You, Red

House, Lightning Strikes, Shela, Walk This Way, Let The Music Do The Talking, Sweet Emotion, Toys In The Attic, Dream On, Train Kept A-Rollin'.

"I want to dedicate this song to our old managers," Tyler says before "My Fist Your Face." "How many of you were at Madison Square Garden?" Tyler asks, as cheers go up from the crowd before "She's On Fire."

Kramer starts in on "The Hop" as the last notes of "She's On Fire" drift through the arena, a very cool effect.

Perry jams out the opening to "Shame On You" again and this time the band is ready and joins in. Tyler starts his vocals too early, but overall, it's a solid version of the song that was rarely played on the tour. Perry gets some vibrato going to start his "killer bee" solo. "Is it loud enough for you? That's all I need to know!" Tyler says after.

As "Red House" closes, Perry says he will get a favor after the gig, not because of the way he dresses, but because of the way he plays. The twin guitarists exchange some cool notes to end the song.

"Richie Supa!" Tyler exclaims as "Lightning Strikes" begins, his longtime pal making another appearance with the band.

Civic Center, Glens Falls, New York. Tuesday, April 15, 1986.
Audience recording. Sound quality: C-
Rats In The Cellar, Mama Kin, Big Ten Inch Record, My Fist Your Face, Last Child, She's On Fire, The Hop, Walkin' The Dog, Red House, Lightning Strikes, Shela, Walk This Way, Smoke on the Water/Let The Music Do The Talking, Sweet Emotion, Toys In The Attic, Darkness, Dream On, Train Kept A-Rollin'.

An interesting gig, with many unique passages. "I love it when you sing!" Tyler says after "Big Ten Inch Record." "Kramer, Kramer, Kramer," Tyler says as "My Fist Your Face" starts.

"Play your guitar," Tyler says to Whitford in a heavy, Boston female accent before "Last Child." Kramer loses the beat in the middle of "She's On Fire," a rarity for the rock solid drummer.

A blues jam is played before Perry introduces what turns out to be a 10-minute version of "Red House," which features exquisite playing by the guitarists as they trade heavy blues and rock riffs in an amazing way. "That's how you do it!" Perry exclaims at the end of it all. Kramer pounds a groove on his drums before starting "Walk This Way."

Perry plays a fast-paced "Smoke On The Water" riff as "Let The Music Do The Talking" starts. Tyler sings some unique lyrics during the middle of the tune. "So what else can you do?" he asks Perry during his solo. "Oh yeah, oh!" Tyler responds to Perry's guitar answer.

Perry sounds out distant groans on his ax during the "Sweet Emotion" break, then plays a few notes of "Dream On" and then "Milk Cow Blues" before bringing the song to a close. Perry plays a wild ending to "Toys In The Attic," eschewing the tune's normal final structure.

"Darkness" gets its first known outing, another surprise. It comes to a sudden stop, but not after four minutes of the tune.

To top off the unique night, the band first does the slow, then fast version of "Train Kept A-Rollin'." Drug addled or not, the band is playing well and showed it could change things up. Fabulous gig!

Broome County Veterans Memorial Arena, Binghamton, New York. Thursday, May 1, 1986. Audience recording. Sound quality: C
Rats In The Cellar, Mama Kin, Big Ten Inch Record, My Fist Your Face, Last Child, She's On Fire, The Hop, Walkin' The Dog, Red House, Lightning Strikes, Shela, Walk This Way, Let The Music Do The Talking, Sweet Emotion, Toys In The Attic, Dream On, Train Kept A-Rollin'.

Perry mimics a British ambulance siren during the always fabulously frenzied "Rats In The Cellar." "The greatest rock and roll package out there, Nugent/Aerosmith," Tyler says before "My Fist Your Face."

"It's request time," Tyler says. Someone in the crowd yells "Somebody," not realizing they had not done the tune since 1979. "What do you want to hear? 'Last Child?' Brad, can you play 'Last Child?'" Tyler says as Whitford starts up the song. Not exactly spontaneous, but few knew that in Binghamton.

The guitarists play another blues jam into "Red House," this one leading right into the song. Perry's first lyric of the song gets a cheer from the crowd. The approach to the song on this night is more mellow and bluesy than on previous outings.

"Dig yourselves!" Tyler yells as he gets the crowd clapping along to "Let The Music Do The Talking." During "Sweet Emotion" Tyler sings, "can't say where I'll be in a year, Binghamton!" In this case, the words were true: The band would start their proper "Permanent Vacation" tour at this venue October 16, 1987.

Perry plays a flurry of notes at the end of "Train Kept A Rolin'" to end the show.

Civic Center, Erie, Pennsylvania. Friday, May 2, 1986. Audience recording. Sound quality: C+

Rats In The Cellar, Mama Kin, Big Ten Inch Record, My Fist Your Face, Last Child, She's On Fire, The Hop, Walkin' The Dog, Red House, Lightning Strikes, Back In The Saddle (partial), Shela, Walk This Way, Let The Music Do The Talking, Sweet Emotion, Toys In The Attic, Dream On, Train Kept A-Rollin'.

"Uh oh!" Tyler says as the band launches into "Rats In The Cellar." "Simon and Garfunkle outtakes" Tyler jokes, as "My Fist Your Face" starts.

Nice maraca work by Tyler during "Walkin' The Dog" on this night. "If you didn't bring any blues with you we have a little for you right now..." Perry says before "Red House," mirroring Hendrix's own words before the same song at the New York Pop Festival in 1970.

"Just give me some head!" Tyler sings during "Walk This Way," a sly variation he used often in lieu of "give me a kiss." "He walks and talks and crawls on his belly like a reptile! Amphibious!" Tyler says at the end of Kramer's solo on this night.

Perry plays a few notes of Hendrix's "Little Wing" before "Dream On." The tape runs out on "Train Kept A-Rollin'"

Aerosmith rocks in show tonight in War Memorial

By Andy Smith
Democrat and Chronicle pop music critic

Get set for a crunching evening of high-volume rock tonight as **Aerosmith** headlines a show in the War Memorial, with the Motor City Madman, **Ted Nugent**, as opening act.

Aerosmith is a no-frills rock band that last appeared in Rochester during the "Grand Slam" concert last summer at Silver Stadium, where the group exerted more energy than the headliner, **Foreigner**.

War Memorial Coliseum, Rochester, New York. Sunday, May 4, 1986. Videotape soundtrack. Sound quality: D+.

Rats In The Cellar, Same Old Song And Dance, Big Ten Inch Record, My Fist Your Face, Last Child, Lord Of The Thighs, She's On Fire, Walkin' The Dog, The Hop, Sweet Emotion, Red House, Back In The Saddle, Shela, Walk This Way, Let The Music Do The Talking, Milk Cow Blues, Toys In The Attic, Dream On, Train Kept A-Rollin'.

The band changes its setlist up yet again. "Same Old Song And Dance" suddenly takes the second slot in the setlist. Whitford delivers an on-point solo during "Last Child," his playing flowing and fluid. "Keep your eyes on Kramer," Tyler says as the drummer starts "Lord Of The Thighs" which reappears.

Tyler starts the lyric to "She's On Fire" too soon, but cleverly elongates it to make it fit. Kramer's end to "Sweet Emotion" sounds slightly off, but not in an unpleasant way. This is live rock and roll after all!

"Back In The Saddle" reappears as well: "That's right baby, we're back!" Tyler reminds the crowd. Tyler leads a "Happy Birthday" to local radio station WCNN, 17 years old at the time. "Milk Cow Blues" also comes into the setlist.

Sports Arena, Toledo, Ohio. Tuesday, May 6, 1986. Audience recording. Sound quality: C+

Rats In The Cellar, Same Old Song And Dance, Big Ten Inch Record, My Fist Your Face, Last Child, She's On Fire, Walkin' The Dog, The Hop, Sweet Emotion, Red House, Back In The Saddle, Shela, Walk This Way, Let The Music Do The Talking, Toys In The Attic, Dream On, Train Kept A Rollin'.

Perry plays some old-time rock and roll sounding guitar licks during "Rats In The Cellar." The guitar starts too early on "Big Ten Inch Record," then later Tyler comes in too early with a lyric! Oops!

"My Fist Your Face" again goes out to boxer Marvin Hagler after Tyler queries the crowd on their possession of the new album. Perry joins Tyler on some of the vocals during the tune.

Tyler's sexual references abound during "Last Child" from "hands on the titties" to "pulling your meat." Perry plays a bunch of cool, stuttering incomplete notes during the "Sweet Emotion" break.

Perry and Whitford play an elongated end to "Red House," the players trading licks. "Jumping Joe Perry!" Tyler says after.

Then, "We back, baby, and to prove we are back…" as the band begins "Back In The Saddle." Tyler introduces "Shela" with, "It ain't even a year old and it's a classic, that's what they say, so I'm going to take their word for it," sounding unsure of his own hubris over the song.He punctuates the tune with "that's right," to good effect.

"The power of positive badness, Mr. Joey Kramer!" is how Tyler introduces the drummer's solo, the low-end boom caught very well by the recorder. After a break, the band comes on for the encore, knocking out "Dream On" and "Train Kept A Rollin'." This show was also videotaped from the crowd.

Ticket information will be announced later this month. Aerosmith and Ted Nugent team up May 9 at Met Center. The Cult and Divinyls appear

Met Center, Bloomington, Minnesota. Friday, May 9, 1986. Audience recording. Sound quality: B-

Rats In The Cellar, Same Old Song And Dance, Big Ten Inch Record, My Fist Your Face, Last Child, She's On Fire, Walkin' The Dog, Sweet Emotion, Red House, Back In The Saddle, Shela, Walk This Way, Let The Music Do The Talking, Milk Cow Blues, Toys In The Attic, Dream On, Train Kept A Rollin'.

A wonderful atmospheric recording. "Get ready, Nitebob!" Tyler says to the sound man as the intro tape rolls. "Here we come!" Tyler yells as the band crashes into "Rats In The Cellar." Some interesting harmony at the beginning of the tune, and a discordant start to the song's solo by Perry.

"That's right!" Tyler repeats as "Same Old Song And Dance" gets underway, with Hamilton playing a funky bass line on the way out of the song. The solid audience recording renders his work quite audible.

"Big Ten Inch Record" features some fine caterwauling by Tyler. Tyler tries to calm the aggressive crowd after the tune. He over sings the beginning of "Last Child," and he raps about getting a seizure during the tune because of the light in his eyes.

"Speaking of getting laid, this song is from our first album, which we got royally fucked on," Tyler tells the crowd during the "Walkin' The Dog" intro.

"Hey Nigel, where's my maracas! I need maracas for this song, anyone got any maracas?" Tyler says as "Sweet Emotion" gets ready to roll. Perry creates quite a sonic assault during the end break of the song, filling fans' ears with pleasant noise. "Hit 'em hard, Brad!" Perry says to Whitford during "Red House."

Some interesting single notes from Perry during "Shela." Tyler blows some harp during the "Let The Music Do The Talking" intro. "Milk Cow Blues" turns up in the setlist with Tyler blowing his harmonica.

"Tyler mocks those who leave before the encore...'Let's beat the traffic, dear.'" "Looking so good Steven, I couldn't let it go," Perry sings slyly during "Train Kept A-Rollin'" a cool moment.

Aerosmith and Ted Nugent combine for a hard rock festival at the Ohio Center, Columbus, on Friday 8 p.m. Tickets are $14.50, and are available in Mansfield at Renee's in the Johnny Appleseed Shopping Center.

Ohio Center, Columbus, Ohio. Friday, May 16, 1986. Audience recording. Sound quality: C+

Rats In The Cellar, Same Old Song And Dance, Big Ten Inch Record, My Fist Your Face, Last Child, She's On Fire, Walkin' The Dog, Sweet Emotion, Red House, Back In The Saddle, Shela, Walk This Way, Let The Music Do The Talking, Toys In The Attic, Darkness, Dream On, Train Kept A Rollin'.

"Thank you, Tom, the amplifiers do work," Tyler says after Hamilton rumbles through the end of "Same Old Song And Dance" as the show gets off to its start.

Tyler raps some semi-nonsense into "Big Ten Inch Record" as Kramer pounds the beat. "The 'Honky Tonk Women' of guitar players" is how Tyler introduces Whitford before "Last Child."

Before "Sweet Emotion" Tyler notices someone in the crowd with a tattoo similar to his own. "Walk This Way" has a funky drum intro on this night, Kramer's soul influences on full display as Tyler encourages the crowd to sing.

"Did you say play 'Darkness'?" Tyler asks. The band then goes into the beginnings of the song, but then aborts it for "Dream On."

The Columbus crowd is a full-on participant in the "all night long" line of "Train Kept A-Rollin'."

INDY MUSIC: Headbangers Aerosmith and Ted Nugent will appear in concert in Market Square Arena Saturday, May 17. Tickets for the show are $15.85, and are available at Freddie's Records, 413 S. Tillotson.

Market Square Arena, Indianapolis, Indiana. Saturday, May 17, 1986. Audience recording. Sound quality: C

Rats In The Cellar, Same Old Song And Dance, Big Ten Inch Record, My Fist Your Face, Last Child, She's On Fire, Walkin' The Dog, Sweet Emotion, Red House, Back In The Saddle, Shela, Walk This Way, Let The Music Do The Talking, Toys In The Attic, Darkness, Dream On, Train Kept A Rollin'.

It seems those who recorded the previous night were back at it for this gig. We thank them! While an audience recording, it sounds almost bare bones at times, with the crowd distant.

"We're gonna bust out the first album blues. Hey, Joey!" Tyler says, prompting the drummer to start "Walkin' The Dog," an energetic workout of the song.

Perry and Whitford get into some layered interplay at the end of "Red House." Tyler declares "Darkness" should be the next single before "Shela." The former tune would begin to appear more often on this leg of the tour. Oddly, "Darkness" was left off the original album vinyl at a time when Lps were still a popular medium.

"Looking so good Steven, I couldn't let it go," Perry sings again in Indy during "Train Kept A-Rollin'" in which the guitarist — with a few precisely played chords — makes sounds reminiscent of Godzilla's footsteps.

Wings Stadium, Kalamazoo, Michigan. Monday, May 19, 1986. Soundboard recording from video soundtrack. Sound quality: B

Rats In The Cellar, Same Old Song And Dance, Big Ten Inch Record, My Fist Your Face, Last Child, She's On Fire, Walkin' The Dog, Sweet Emotion, Red House, Back In The Saddle, Shela, Walk This Way, Let The Music Do The Talking, Toys In The Attic, Dream On, Train Kept A Rollin'.

"The man who once got cranial vertigo, Mr. Tom Hamilton!" Tyler says as "Same Old Song And Dance" comes to a close. Tyler quotes "Hit The Road Jack" during the beginning of "Big Ten Inch Record."

Tyler has fun all night saying "Kalamazoo!" Perry's remarkable slide work is heard loud and clear on the soundboard audio from the soundtrack as he plays "She's On Fire."

Tyler reiterates "Darkness" will be a hit before "Shela." "Not bad for a white boy!" Tyler says after "Shela." During the tour, Tyler would often learn the call letters of the local rock station and say radio people at said outlet were saying "Shela" would be a hit.

Kramer starts in right away with a cool drum intro to "Walk This Way" as Tyler goes into a casual rap: "Second gear, right, second gear...which way to talk, which way to walk, which way to soothe, which way to groove..."

"Are they doing 'Darkness'?" a roadie can be heard saying after "Toys In The Attic," but it was not to be on this night.

Wendler Arena, Saginaw, Michigan. Tuesday, May 20, 1986. Audience recording. Sound quality: C

Rats In The Cellar, Mama Kin, Big Ten Inch Record, My Fist Your Face, Last Child, She's On Fire, Walkin' The Dog, Sweet Emotion, Red House, Shela, Walk This Way, Let The Music Do The Talking, Toys In The Attic, Darkness, Dream On, Train Kept A Rollin'.

Perry plays another frenetic solo during "Rats In The Cellar," with Tyler missing the cue to come back in after the guitarist finishes. Delicate rhythm sets up the quiet section of the song.

Tyler later admonishes the crowd for throwing things on stage. "Awww, Joey," Tyler exclaims as Kramer drum rolls into "Big Ten Inch Record."

Whitford delivers a spry, exciting solo during "Last Child." Tyler raps in blues fashion before "Sweet Emotion," which features a feedback-drenched Perry solo. The tune stretches out to nine minutes on this night. Tyler talks about "Back In The Saddle" and the band almost goes into it, but after some indecision it's "Shela" instead.

A shirt is thrown up on stage during Kramer's solo and the drummer proceeds to tie it around his head, then bangs his drums with his skull. "Toys In The Attic" features staccato rhythm guitar.

The band plays "Darkness" in its entirety, ending and all. Tyler's piano intro to "Dream On" really rings out. "Can I get an amen!" Tyler says as the band starts "Train Kept A-Rollin'" to end the gig. An animated show!

Joe Louis Arena, Detroit Michigan. Thursday, May 22, 1986. Audience recording. Sound quality: C-

Rats In The Cellar, Same Old Song And Dance, Big Ten Inch Record, My Fist Your Face, Last Child, She's On Fire, Walkin' The Dog, The Hop, Sweet Emotion, Red House, Back In The Saddle, Shela, Walk This Way, Let The Music Do The Talking, Toys In The Attic, Darkness, Dream On, Train Kept A Rollin'.

"Nitebob!" Tyler yells out again to the sound man as Kramer then starts "Rats In The Cellar." Tonight will be one of those free-wheeling, rock and roll extravaganzas. Anything goes, everyone is in a good mood, the elements that make Detroit "Rock City."

Perry plays his fast solo and then cools it down for a sweet jam with Whitford during "Rats In The Cellar." The band should always open with this tune!

During "Big Ten Inch Record" there is some discussion among the tapers, and the sound improves somewhat thereafter. "I'll tell you what baby, no one can fuck with Detroit. You got your R&B, your rock and roll, you got your

334

new shit, you got your old shit, I mean you own it, it's yours, you own it!" Tyler says before "Sweet Emotion," singing, "Oh, I love Detroit...." as he starts the intro vocals for the song. The break during the song provides Perry with a chance to punish his guitar, creating sweet, screeching noise.

"The one who created it all!" is how Tyler introduces Perry before "Red House." Tyler calls for a screwdriver before "Shela," saying it refers to a joke.

"I want everyone to take a step backwards" as "Let The Music Do The Talking" starts, the singer says, trying to create space for the crush of fans against the stage. The guitars cut out at the end of the tune, forcing an odd ending.

"The beauty of this is that you're still around and you know what good rock and roll is," Tyler says, as Kramer bangs out the beginning of his solo.

Tyler notes "Darkness" was not on the vinyl or cassette version of "Done With Mirrors," but that the tune has just been released as a single. Tyler's piano sounds slightly out of tune in parts during the song.

Tyler leads the crowd in the "Banana Boat Song" with him singing "daylight come, and I want to 'Dream On,'" and he then starts the piano intro. This call and response was oft repeated during this time frame.

Kramer starts "Train Kept A-Rollin'" but then stops to slow the beat. "We're gonna get funky now!" Tyler says, as the slow version of the song eventually flows into a faster pace. A great night.

Riverbend Music Center, Cincinnati, Ohio. Saturday, May 24, 1986. Audience recording. Sound quality: C-

Rats In The Cellar, Same Old Song And Dance, Big Ten Inch Record, My Fist Your Face, Last Child, She's On Fire, Walkin' The Dog, Sweet Emotion, Red House, Back In The Saddle, Shela, Walk This Way, Let The Music Do The Talking, Toys In The Attic, Dream On, Train Kept A Rollin'.

Just the second concert held at the new venue.

Some jostling of the recorder is heard early during "Same Old Song And Dance," but it clears by Perry's solo. But things get worse from there. The crowd is obnoxious, seemingly yelling into the recorder at times, making the concert hard to focus on.

Tyler's words between the songs can hardly be heard. From what we can tell, Tyler sort of bumbles the first line of "Big Ten Inch Record." Band manager Tim Collins seems to be at the gig this night, Tyler referencing him during "My Fist Your Face."

Cincinnati gets the award for wildest crowd of the year, or it seems that way with the loud folk surrounding the taper. A raucous, rhythmic version of "Last Child" is one of the night's highlights.

Someone throws a hat on stage before "She's On Fire." You got sunglasses to go with this hat?" Tyler asks. Firecrackers blast midway through the tune, adding to the craziness of the night. Some discordant chords during "Walk This Way" mark the song.

Aerosmith will jam Iowa Jam

Rock fans should get their fill in Des Moines Monday. The Iowa Jam, featuring a number of bands including Aerosmith, begins at noon in front of the grandstand at the Iowa State Fairgrounds. Information: (515) 262-3111.

Iowa State Fairgrounds, Des Moines, Iowa. Monday, May 26, 1986. Audience recording. Sound quality: B

Rats In The Cellar, Same Old Song And Dance, Big Ten Inch Record, My Fist Your Face, Last Child, She's On Fire, Walkin' The Dog, Sweet Emotion, Red House, Back In The Saddle, Shela, Walk This Way, Let The Music Do The Talking, Toys In The Attic, Dream On, Train Kept A Rollin'.

Great recording, one of the best of the tour, helped by the open-air venue. It was pressed up into the "Hard" bootleg Lp.

"I think we are ready if you are," Tyler says as the intro tape rolls. A unique solo from Perry during "Rats In The Cellar" kicks off the night's proceedings. The guitars come in late on "Walkin' The Dog" for some reason.

"You have to cool out in the front, lay back..." Tyler says, noticing trouble down below in the crowd. "You got to get it real sweet," Tyler says, and then

 directs the band into "Sweet Emotion." Perry and Kramer lose each other on the way back after the song's break.

Perry doodles on Hendrix's "Wait Until Tomorrow" with Kramer joining in for a couple of beats before launching into "Red House."

Whitford's rhythm work on "Shela" shines on the unique recording and drives the song along. "What a pussy! I still want to do 'Darkness'" Tyler says to Kramer, as the drummer forgoes his solo and starts "Toys In The Attic."

Kiel Auditorium, St. Louis, Missouri. Tuesday, May 27, 1986. Audience recording. Sound quality: D
Rats In The Cellar, Same Old Song And Dance, Big Ten Inch Record, My Fist Your Face, Last Child, She's On Fire, Walkin' The Dog, Sweet Emotion, Red House, Back In The Saddle, Shela, Walk This Way, Let The Music Do The Talking, Toys In The Attic, Darkness, Dream On, Train Kept A Rollin'.

Perry plays some interesting, stretched notes during "My Fist Your Face." Kramer plays over the intro to "Last Child."

"We are doing the dog trilogy for you here tonight," Tyler says, noting "Walkin' The Dog." But "Sick As A Dog," nor "The Reason The Dog," would not be played.

"Ooh, Tom forgot to play the note tonight, ooh, I don't care," is the odd intro by Tyler to "Sweet Emotion."

"What were you doing when you first played this song?" Tyler asks Perry before "Back In The Saddle." (Perry says in his book he was high and laying on his back!)

"Darkness" gets the most dramatic and passionate treatment of the tour. "The Flintstones" TV show theme song plays through the arena as the band leaves the stage.

Alpine Valley Music Theater, East Troy, Wisconsin. Friday, May 30, 1986. Audience recording. Sound quality: B

Rats In The Cellar, Same Old Song And Dance, Big Ten Inch Record, My Fist Your Face, Last Child, She's On Fire, Walkin' The Dog, Darkness, Sweet Emotion, Red House, Back In The Saddle, Shela, Walk This Way, Let The Music Do The Talking, Toys In The Attic, Dream On, All Your Love, Train Kept A-Rollin'.

A unique setlist caught by another really good recording. "Rats In The Cellar" shoots out of the gates on this night, with some intricate give and take, and some apparent electrical difficulties!

A big crowd of 18,000 greets the band. Keyboard work can be heard on "My First Your Face," something the clear recording reveals.

Perry plays a little of "Think About It" before "Darkness," the latter appearing earlier in the set than usual. Perry jumps into a little of "Shame On You" with the talk box before "Sweet Emotion," a riff that seemed to stick with him throughout the tour. Someone throws a flashlight on stage to Tyler's anger after the song.

The crowd takes over much of the "Banana Boat Song" on this night before "Dream On."

"It's $45 for every 15 minutes of overtime, so we can play all night, can't we?" Tyler says, as he stops Kramer from starting "Train Kept A-Rollin'." "Fuck the train, let's do something you never heard Aerosmith do before, something by John Mayall and the Bluesbreakers, baby. Yeah, yeah, yeah! Let's get some blues here, Joe!" Perry then begins in on "All Your Love," featuring harmonica playing by Tyler.

Extended feedback by Perry ends "Train Kept A-Rollin'" at the loose and funky gig. Excellent show.

```
┌─────────────────────────────────────────────────────────────────────┐
│  "DONE WITH MIRRORS"  TOUR 1986 — PART III                          │
│                                                                      │
│  DAY          DATE        VENUE                        CITY          │
│  Sunday       June  1     Roberts Arena                Evansville, IN │
│  Monday       June  2     TBA                                         │
│  Wednesday    June  4     Civic Auditorium             Charleston, WV │
│  Thursday     June  5     Civic Auditorium             Roanoke, VA    │
│  Saturday     June  7     Civic Center                 Greensboro, NC │
│  Sunday       June  8     Coliseum                     Columbia, SC   │
│  Tuesday      June 10     Birmingham-Jefferson Coliseum Birmingham, AL│
│  Wednesday    June 11     Von Braun Civic Center       Huntsville, AL │
│  Friday       June 13     Mississippi Coast Coliseum   Biloxi, MS     │
│  Saturday     June 14     "Cotton Carnival"            Memphis, TN    │
└─────────────────────────────────────────────────────────────────────┘
```

Civic Center, Roanoke, Virginia. Thursday, June 5, 1986. Audience recording. Sound quality: C-

Rats In The Cellar, Same Old Song And Dance, Big Ten Inch Record, My Fist Your Face, Last Child, She's On Fire, Sweet Emotion, Red House, Shela, Walk This Way, Let The Music Do The Talking, Toys In The Attic, Darkness/Dream On, Train Kept A-Rollin'.

Detailed soloing by Perry on "Rats In The Cellar" marks the beginning of the show. "Something new, something old, something black, something gold, 'My Fist Your Face'" is Tyler's intro to the song.

"We are going to get to know each other real good tonight. We already do, don't we," Tyler says before "Last Child." "Sing that song, you bitch!" he says after.

Tyler invents a new intro to "Sweet Emotion" "Oh-oh, you drive me crazy...." The second half of this gig seems supercharged, driven along by Kramer's intense pace.

"Kramer, you're like a machine tonight!" Tyler says, as he drums through "Walk This Way" and "Let The Music Do The Talking."

"Nitebob!" Tyler says as he plays the intro to "Darkness," but moves away from the theme and into "Dream On," in which he flubs a line. A fiery "Train Kept A Rollin'" ends the stellar gig.

New York State Fairgrounds, Syracuse, New York. Monday, August 25, 1986. Audience recording. Sound quality: C+

Back In The Saddle, Rats In The Cellar, Bone To Bone (Coney Island White Fish Boy), Big Ten Inch Record, My Fist Your Face, Last Child, Three Mile Smile, Reefer Headed Woman, Red House, Draw The Line, S.O.S. (Too Bad), Sweet Emotion, Walk This Way, Let The Music Do The Talking, Toys In The Attic, Honky Tonk Women, Dream On, All Your Love, Jeff's Boogie/Long Tall Sally, Train Kept A-Rollin', Walkin' The Dog.

Wow. The real Bad Boys from Boston playing a fantastic, loose, inspired, rocking show in Syracuse that is full of surprises. This was recorded with very good equipment and then pressed up into the "Stone Cold" vinyl bootleg that captures most, but not all of the fabulous gig. Oddly the date on the Lp is listed as San Francisco, January 24, 1986. Alas, the San Fran gig was at the beginning of the tour, and here the band is winding down their "Done With Mirrors" shows.

"It may be the end of the summer, but it's only the beginning tonight," Tyler says as the intro tape rolls. The opening tunes flip flop here, with "Back In The Saddle" taking the lead spot ahead of "Rats in The Cellar" which Kramer starts with a thumping bass drum.

"Three Mile Smile," suddenly re-emerges as does "Reefer Headed Woman," "S.O.S. (Too Bad)," and "Draw The Line," (the first since 1979) all smashing additions! Perry plays some wicked slide on "Let The Music Do The Talking."

The band pulls out some rarities and once in a lifetime gems, including a full version of the Stones' "Honky Tonk Women," which Joe Perry must of had on his mind as he played a few notes of the intro earlier in the show before "Sweet Emotion." Tyler makes a reference to bootlegging before the tune, too. "For the record, so we know who has been bootlegging us, we are going to do something by the Stones. Shit, why not..."

What follows is an Aerosmithed rocking version, kicking up the intensity of the tune to another level beyond the Stones more staid approach.

Tyler then tries to get to "Dream On." But no. Perry strums a bit of "One Way Street." "You don't want to stop do you? You want to dance?" Tyler asks. What follows is a soulful version of "All Your Love."

After, Tyler says, "What do you want to hear? This is your night!" Then Tyler signals for "Train Kept A-Rollin'" to start. "I think I hear a train a comin'..." But there is discussion on stage and then Tyler says, "maybe I don't."

Perry then jumps in: "This is the last time we will be able to play in front of a live audience before we go in to do our new album, so we are going to jam out for you, here it comes..." The band jumps into a rollicking version of The Yardbirds "Jeff's Boogie" to which Tyler grafts on "Long Tall Sally" lyrics.

Even the standard "Train Kept A-Rollin'" is played in a unique way this night. "We will give you two versions," Tyler says before they start. And the band wasn't done. "Walkin' The Dog" finally ends the two-hour, wild show, a real highlight in the band's live history. What a whopper!

songwriter of Aerosmith, the Boston-based hard rock band that headlines a triple bill at Sullivan Stadium in Foxborough tomorrow

Sullivan Stadium, Foxborough, Massachusetts. Sunday, August 31, 1986. Audience recording. Sound quality: C+

Back In The Saddle, Rats In The Cellar, Bone To Bone (Coney Island White Fish Boy), Big Ten Inch Record, Seasons of Wither, My Fist Your Face, Darkness, Three Mile Smile, Reefer Headed Woman, Red House, Draw the Line, Last Child, S.O.S. (Too Bad), Sweet Emotion, Walk This Way, Let The Music Do The Talking, Toys In The Attic, Dream On, Train Kept A-Rollin'.

Guitarist Joe Perry and singer Steven Tyler in action at Sullivan Stadium yesterday afternoon.

On a glorious sunny day, it's the end of an era for the band. It's the final gig of the "Done With Mirrors" tour and the last show of the straight out rockin' days of the band, as a new style would develop and take hold.

"You remember 'Toys In The Attic' don't you? We got 'Rats In The Cellar'" Tyler says as the band moves into its second tune. "Big Ten Inch Record" features a great "breathing" harmonica intro from Tyler and it has a slightly extended guitar ending. We get another complete "Darkness" during the show.

"Any requests? Seasons of..." Tyler says as "Seasons of Wither" is resurrected, always a treat, and played in all its wistful glory here.

Tyler comments on the approval from city officials for the stadium gig, allowing the band to get "out in the open and out of the darkness."

"Three Mile Smile" is back in the set along with its connected "Reefer Headed Woman," the latter in abridged form with more remarkable Tyler harmonica.

Perry mocks the concerns of locals over the loudness of the show during his spoken introduction to "Red House," which gets a long workout from the guitarist too. It ends abruptly with guitar fireworks. "All right, thank you," Perry says at its end.

"Draw The Line" sounds as good as ever here. Kramer pounds out the "S.O.S. (Too Bad)" intro with force.

Perry "scratches" his guitar on the intro to "Walk This Way." "Let The Music Do The Talking" features an extended long slide part by Perry broken up by Kramer's drums. The song almost comes to a stop before the band picks it up. "What do you have to say for yourself, Joe!" Tyler says before Perry's solo.

Kramer's drums punctuate the recording, his powerful style on full display, a real hallmark of the band's live shows.

Tyler dedicates "Dream On" to a friend and to Boston. Perry adds some beautiful notes to the tune, with Tyler singing the last verse in an odd, staccato-like way.

"I do believe I hear a train a comin', but it's not your average train," Tyler says, as Kramer starts the "slow" version of the song, then the band continues on with the "fast" version. Whitford's rhythm guitar sounds funky through the 10-minute train ride, with a crescendo of cascading screaming guitars ending the show. A fitting end to the end of an era.

Aerosmith plays for 30,000 fans

AEROSMITH – In concert with Yngwie Malmsteen and Keel, at Sullivan Stadium, yesterday.

By Jim Sullivan
Special to the Globe

FOXBOROUGH – Aerosmith singer Steven Tyler carried a balloon bouquet onto the Sullivan Stadium stage just after 4:30 p.m. yesterday, and guitarist Joe Perry pricked four or five of them right away. Quickly, Aerosmith – patched back together after personnel shake-ups and creative stagnation – took flight before 25,000 people in the first Sullivan Stadium rock concert since 1983.

The two-hour flight path was not without its bumpy passages: They soared into the clouds at times, particularly the start with "Back in the Saddle," "Rats in the Cellar," "Big 10 Inch Record" and the three-song finish, "Toys in the Attic," "Dream On" and "Train Kept A Rollin'." At their best, Aerosmith put across a snotty, fiery set of taut guitar-based rockers, rooted in primal blues and R&B. Other times, though, particularly during a draggy, sludge-blues midset and during excessive solos from drummer Joey Kramer and Perry, they headed into the nearest mountain range. Aerosmith's got the chops and renewed fire, but somebody should hire them a navigator, a guy who'd keep them pointed in the street-wise direction of the "Walk This Way" collaboration with Run-D.M.C. – No. 15 in the US, heading to No. 1 in the UK. As is, Aerosmith drifts between raw, whipsawed rock 'n' roll and thudding arena rock, or the hip and ham-fisted.

Promoter Frank Russo wants to put shows at Sullivan Stadium next summer, said Aerosmith co-manager Tim Collins, and thus, the stage was placed on the long east side and capacity limited to 30,000. Also, Aerosmith had the stadium refrain from selling beer. So how was the crowd?

"It's been brutal," said the Foxborough officer manning a police wagon, as an occupant whaled on the door. "This isn't as obnoxious as I thought it would be," said one state trooper, gazing down from a roof box. "I know a lot of people have been taken into custody," said Foxborough Sgt. Edward O'Malley. Sullivan Stadium security head John Barry put the arrest total at 40 by the concert's end. (State police estimated another 20-plus had been arrested outside, mostly for under-age drinking and disorderly conduct.)

Aerosmith's comeback has been semi-successful nationally, but immensely successful on the home-front. Within the past year, Aerosmith has played to more than 100,000 fans in the Boston region. New England rock fans are nothing if not parochial, and Aerosmith gave 'em a crowd-pleaser yesterday – a good sound and good energy. Judicious editing would have helped, and next time Aerosmith plays with a Diamond Vision cameraman on the stage, Tyler should figure out whether he wants him there or not. Berating him and then mugging for him looked a little daft.

Technical problems delayed the start of Yngwie Malmsteen's middle set. Creative problems stalled it once it got under way. Think of guitarist Malmsteen as an advanced noise-maker with a degree in cliched art/metal. Thus, lighter textures rub shoulders with metal crunch and none of it adds up to more than a bull charging his way around a china shop.

Keel, early favorites in the As Dumb As Spinal Tap contest, maintained their lead throughout the afternoon. They opened with a half-hour set of generic pop/metal, exclaiming at the close, "You've got a right – to rock." Let's hear it for shaggy-haired, head-bobbing constitutional protectionists.

Boston Globe report on the Foxborough show.

343

Of course, the Aerosmith story continues. While this book focuses on the early years of the band, let's take a peek at the first two shows of what would be a new era. These shows are hybrid gigs, capturing the band at a time of transition.

Alpine Valley Music Theater, East Troy, Wisconsin. Thursday, June 18, 1987. Audience recording. Sound quality: C+

Let The Music Do The Talking, Same Old Song And Dance, Big Ten Inch Record, My Fist Your Face, Magic Touch, Last Child, Lightning Strikes, Movin' Out, Walkin' The Dog, Back In The Saddle, Rats In The Cellar, Sweet Emotion, Walk This Way, Toys In The Attic, Ragtime Doll, Dream On, Train Kept A Rollin'.

An enthusiastic crowd greets the band. Aerosmith hits the stage embracing a renewal and sobriety. The band has been sequestered in the studio in recent months working on a new album. It would come out two months later.

Perry sounds out some slide notes as the show begins. There is no opening tape here.

"Guess what?" Tyler says and without further words, the band starts in on "Let The Music Do The Talking," the first time the tune opens a show. Perry has a little trouble launching his solo, but the rust of the last 10 months quickly falls away and the band gets into a pleasing short jam on the tune.

The song segues straight into "Same Old Song And Dance" with great flow. The song is as powerful as ever here.

"You're beautiful!" Tyler says later before "My Fist Your Face. "It's going to be hot and nasty tonight!"

"Don't you know Aerosmith, for the last three months, has been doing a new album," Tyler says after. "It's called 'Permanent Vacation.'" Tyler then introduces "Magic Touch," the first song ever played live from the album. It is played very close to what would appear on record. "You like that?!" Tyler says after to applause. "Alright!"

Whitford plays a gentle intro to "Last Child," with Tyler saying, "Tell them how it is, Brad." Played with great clarity, it sounds slightly faster than previous live versions.

"Lightning Strikes" follows in rapid fashion from a standstill. Tyler sings some of the verses in a flat way, but it works. The lightning effect gets a cheer mid song.

Kramer pounds the bass drum out of the previous tune and Tyler yells "Vintage!" It indeed is, as the band plays "Movin' Out" and then it's right into "Walkin' The Dog," the two songs played beautifully.

A mid set "Back In The Saddle" follows, with the crowd pitching in on the chorus quite nicely at one point. Without a break, the band snaps into "Rats In The Cellar," which features a lucid, detailed, funky workout in the middle that wins the audience's approval before the tension builds back up and the song is polished off.

Tyler again employs the "Oh Well" lyrics before "Sweet Emotion." When he sings, "I don't know where I'll be next year," he adds, "That's a lie!" He sings the song's words more emphatically than usual on this version.

"I'm going to get you to sing now," Tyler says, "Mr. Joey Kramer, the power of positive badness," as "Walk This Way" begins crisply and clearly. "Toys In The Attic" follows non-stop and then it's, "goodnight, Milwaukee!" from Tyler.

"We'd like to do something off our new album, the boys talked me into it," Tyler says, as the band makes its way back to the stage for an encore. Tyler introduces what he calls "Ragtime Doll." The song, of course, would eventually be known simply as "Rag Doll."

But we also know Tyler fought to keep "Ragtime" as part of the song, only to be dissuaded by those with a more commercial interest in the band and the song. At this point of the song's evolution, Tyler slips "Ragtime" into the lyrics to start some of the verses. It's a great version, one that mirrors what will appear on record, although the intro guitars are more staccato-like and the end has not quite been worked out yet. Perry plays an absolutely sparkling solo that is different than the studio version. The first live version.

"Dream On" is next, sounding as sublime as ever. An electronic blip from the stage is heard as it begins. Despite its age and numerous playings, the song has an ethereal, timeless quality that keeps it fresh to this day.

"Milwaukee! I do believe I hear a train a comin'," is Tyler's intro to "Train Kept A Rollin'." He changes up the first lyrics: "She was a sweetie, tight, see the light…"

A wonderful gig!

Texxas Jam, Cotton Bowl, Dallas, Texas. Saturday, June 20, 1987. **Audience recording. Sound quality: C+**

Let The Music Do The Talking, Big Ten Inch Record, Magic Touch, Mama Kin, Last Child, Lightning Strikes, Movin' Out, Walkin' The Dog, Back In The Saddle, Rats In The Cellar, Walk This Way, Toys In The Attic, Rag Doll, Dream On, Train Kept A Rollin'.

A sweltering day in Texas. Some clips of this show, sans audio, can be seen on the "Scrapbook" video. Water hoses were used to help cool the crowd.

Slide notes from Perry start "Let The Music Do The Talking," signaling the beginning of the show, which will be a trimmed set. Boston is the headliner today.

"We got some new Aerosmith for you, ya'll been wondering what we were doing the last four months, been in the studio," Tyler tells the crowd, introducing "Magic Touch."

"OK, Mr. Whitford is going to sing to you," Tyler says, but instead of "Last Child," the band plays "Mama Kin," some spontaneity perhaps! After, Tyler says, "Now it's your turn, Brad," as "Last Child" starts.

"Lightning Strikes," "Movin' Out," and "Walkin' The Dog," are played non-stop as the band pushes through their set briskly.

"Rats In The Cellar" goes at its rapid pace, then the band slows it way down for a delicate jam in a cool, cool way. Then it's "Walk This Way" and straight into "Toys In The Attic."

"It's hot! Someone blow that candle out!" Tyler says, referring to a spotlight as darkness begins to fall.

"I'm outvoted," he then says. "Some more new Aerosmith for your listening pleasure." "Rag Doll" follows, this time with fewer mentions of "ragtime" as he sings. It still does not have a proper ending.

The beginning of "Dream On" sounds epic here as 80,000 watch and give a rousing response at its conclusion.

"Dallas City" makes its way into the "Train Kept A Rollin'" lyrics at this gig. The tune ends the show.

Tyler then says to cheers, "Goodnight, God bless you, we'll be back…"

In Search Of...

Through the years, recordings have been documented, but for one reason or another, have not been widely circulated. They include:

Winterland, San Francisco 4/13/74 or 12/8/74 (video)
Boston Garden 11/13/76 or 11/15/76
Madison Square Garden, New York City 12/16/76 (Soundboard)
Memorial Auditorium, Buffalo, New York 7/6/77 (Soundcheck)
Hammerheads, West Islip, Long Island, New York 4/23/80
Fountain Casino, Aberdeen Township 4/27/80
Joe Louis Arena, Detroit 11/27/82
Tangerine Bowl, Orlando 4/23/83
Capital Center, Landover 5/25/83
Pine Knob Music Theater, Clarkston, Michigan 7/11/84

A great thanks to all those who took a recorder inside to these gigs (sometimes at their own peril) to document the band they love. Without you, history would have been lost. And my appreciation for all the generous traders and collectors out there who help build this important music history.

*Also, a special thanks to **Mark Blair**, **Brian Elder** and **Rob Phaneuf** for generously sharing their collections, expertise and wisdom. A special thanks to **Allen Bright Jr.** for verifying all the setlists!*

If anyone reading this has their own tapes in the cellar of a concert from long ago, or knows anyone who does, please reach out to help build the live musical legacy of Aerosmith!
TapesFromTheCellar@gmail.com

AEROSMITH:

4-23-73 Paul's Mall; Boston 50m EX fm
1974 Counterpoint Studios, N.Y.C. 55m EX- fm 'Rattlesnake Shake' Lp
1-7-74 Detroit, MI 50m VG+ aud
4-14-74 Michigan Palace, Detroit 80m EX fm
7-2-74 My Father's Place, N.Y.C. 45m EX fm
10-20-74 Providence, RI 60m VG- aud
10-26-74 Mckeesport, PA 60m VG aud
11-2-74 Academy Of Music, N.Y.C. 50m VG- aud
4-28-75 War Memorial, Rochester, NY 80m G+ ** aud
5-15-75 Boston Gardens 11m EX fm **
8-23-75 Aragon Ballroom, Cleveland 65m VG+aud
8-29-75 Shaeffer Music Festival, N.Y.C. 45m EX sb 'Rock This Way' Lp
7-8-76 Milwaukee, WI 65m G aud
7-15-76 Peoria, IL 45m VG aud 'Stamp' Lp
7-24-76 Toronto, Ontario 30m VG/EX aud
7-28-76 Cleveland, OH 85m VG aud
8-27-76 Cow Palace, San Francisco 60m VG++ aud ** a.k.a 8-28-76
9-12-76 Angel Stadium, Anaheim, CA 10m VG aud encore w/Jeff Beck
10-26-76 Amsterdam, Holland 65m VG aud
11-1-76 Paris, France 80m VG+ aud
11-26-76 Offenburg, W.Germany 70m VG aud
1-31-77+2-9-77 Tokyo, Japan 60m VG 'Spirit Of Boston' Lp aud
2-7-77 Osaka, Japan 70m VG+ aud
2-9-77 Budokan Hall, Tokyo 75m VG aud
6-24-77 Summit, Houston, TX 75m EX- sb
6-25-77 Summit, Houston, TX 40m EX- sb
8-13-77 Bizzen Jazz Festival, Brussels, Belgium 20m VG/EX aud
8-27-77 Reading Festival, UK 60m VG/VG+ aud
10-9-77 Spectrum, Philadelphia 75m VG aud
11-25-77 Aladin Theater, Las Vegas, NV 45m VG+ aud 'Five The Hard Way' Lp
12-10-77 Toronto, Ontario 85m VG aud
12-12-77 Montreal, Quebec 80m VG aud
12-19-77 Spectrum, Philadelphia 85m VG aud
3-18-78 Cal Jam II, Ontario Speedway, CA 30m EX+ fm *
3-23-78 Chicago, Il 85m EX fm
3-24-78 Veterans Auditorium, Columbus, OH 80m EX fm
3-26-78 Tower Theater, Philadelphia 90m EX fm
3-28-78 Music Hall, Boston 80m EX fm
4-7-78 Santa Monica, CA 45m VG- aud
8-6-78 Giants Stadium, E.Rutheford, NJ 85m VG/VG- aud *
11-12-78 Nassau Coliseum, LI,NY 65m VG aud *
11-24-78 Madison Square Garden, N.Y.C. 95m VG aud *
11-25-78 Spectrum, Philadelphia 25m VG aud Steve hit w/bottle
12- -78 Harbour House, Lynn, MA 75m G aud
12-3-78 Springfield, MA 85m VG+ aud
4-8-79 World Music Festival, LA 90m VG+ aud
4-14-79 Orlando, Fl 35m VG/VG+ aud w/Ted Nugent encore
7-2-79 Toronto, Ontario 90m VG/VG+ aud
12-16-79 40m VG- aud ** one of first w/Crespo,Charlottle, NC
1-13-80 Nassau Coliseum, LI,NY 85m VG/VG- aud *
1-17-80 Buffalo, NY 80m VG- aud
1-25-80 Landover,MD 95m VG & F 35m F cuz runs slow aud
3-8-80 'America Live' N.Y.C. Election 6m EX- fm
4-12-80 Club Detroit, Boston,MA 90m VG+ aud w/Tyler s'check
4-20-80 Speaks Club, LI,NY 85m VG/VG+ aud *
6-12-80 Stage West, Hartford, CN 50m EX fm
12-3-80 Boston, MA 90m EX fm 10th Aniversary show
9-82 'Rock In A Hard Place' Outtakes, Miami, FL 45m EX Sb
11-7-82 Allentown, PA 85m VG/VG+ aud. First show of tour.
11-9-82 New Haven, CN 90m VG aud
11-11-82 Centrum, Worcester, MA 90m VG/VG- aud *
11-16-82 Centrum, Worcester, MA 75m VG aud
11-19-82 Hartford, CN 90m VG aud
11-24-82 Rozemont Horizon, Chicago 90m VG++ aud
~~11-27-82 Detroit, MI~~
12-4-82 Market Square Arena, Indianapolis, IN 70m VG/VG+ aud
1-6-83 Long Beach, CA 70m VG aud *
1-7-83 Coliseum Arena, Oakland, CA 90m VG+ aud #
1-11-83 McNichols Arena, Denver, CO 70m VG+/++ aud **
1-13-83 Albuquerque, NM 80m VG aud
~~1-14-83 Las Vegas, NV~~
2-11-83 Springfield, MA 80m VG/VG+ aud *
2-13-83 Meadowlands Arena, NJ 85m VG aud *
2-14-83 Spectrum, Philadelphia 85m VG aud
2-21-83 Glen Falls, NY 78m VG/VG+ aud
2-22-83 Binghampton, NY 65m VG aud
2-24-83 War Memorial, Syracuse, NY 75m VG aud
2-25-83 Montreal Forum 75m VG/VG+ aud *
2-28-83 Spectrum, Philadelphia 75m VG/VG+ aud *
3-1-83 Nassau Coliseum, LI,NY 75m VG/VG+ aud *
3-5-83 Cape Cod Coliseum, S. Yarmouth, MA 85m VG+ aud *
5-27-83 Cincinnati Gardens 75m VG/VG+ aud *
5-28-83 Alpine Valley, East Troy, WI 80m VG/VG+ aud
5-30-83 Detroit, MI 70m VG Pine Knob aud
7-23-83 Pier 84, N.Y.C. 45m VG+/++ aud w/S.Guy Special Olmpics benefit
7-30-83 Compton Terrace, Phoenix,AZ 75m VG+/++ aud * cuts in tape
8-2-83 Cal Expo Amphitheater, Sacramento,CA 90m VG++ aud #
8-3-83 Ventura, CA 50m VG+ aud *, Tyler wasted, complete show
8-5-83 Pacific Amphitheter, Costa Mesa, CA 85m VG-
8-6-83 San Diego, CA 60m VG/VG+ aud
12-31-83 Centrum, Worcester, MA 85m VG aud * w/Whitford
1-6-84 Fountain Casino,NJ 75m VG- aud
2-9-84 Ritz, N.Y.C. 5m VG aud 'Lightning Strikes'
2-11-84 Calderone Concert Hall, Heampstead, LI,NY 80m VG++ *
2-14-84 Orpheum Theater, Boston, MA 80m EX fm *
2-16-84 Poughkepsee, NY 90m VG aud
6-17-84 Center, Providence, RI 50m VG/VG+ aud *
6-22-84 Capitol Theater, Concord, NH 90m VG+/++ aud * 1st w/Perry back.
6-28-84 Saratoga Springs, NY 85m VG- aud
6-30-84 Rochester, NY 90m VG+ aud
7-2-84 Columbia, MD 90m VG aud
7-3-84 Harrisburg, PA 90m VG++ aud
7-5-84 Middletown, NJ 90m VG/VG+ aud
7-6-84 Norfolk, VA 90m VG/VG+ aud — 7-8-84 Civic Center, Erie, PA 85m VG/VG+
7-9-84 Kingswood Theater, Toronto 85m VG aud *
7-12-84 Rozemont Horizon, Chicago 75m VG/VG+ aud
7-14-84 Castle Farms, MI 90m VG/EX aud
7-23-84 Sports Arena, Toledo, OH 90m VG+ aud *
8-4-84 Centrum, Worcester, MA 85m VG aud *
8-5-84 Centrum, Wocester, MA 90m VG/VG+ * aud
8-8-84 Spectrum, Philadelphia 90m aud
8-11-84 Montreal, Quebec 90m VG/VG+ aud
8-20-84 Veterans Coliseum, Phoenix, AZ 95m VG aud *
8-22-84 Sports Arena, San Diego,CA 90m VG+ aud *
8-26-84 Greek Theater, LA,CA 85m VG aud
8-28-84 San Bernardino, CA 90m VG+ aud
8-31-84 Coliseum Arena, Oakland, CA 95m VG aud #
12-13-84 Reunion Arena, Dallas, TX 85m VG- aud **
12-18-84 Sunrise Theater, Ft. Lauderdale, Fl 90m VG++ aud
12-20-84 Orlando, Fl 75m VG/VG+ aud
12-21-84 St. Petersburg, Fl 95m VG/VG+ aud
12-27-84 Civic Center, Providence, RI 90m VG aud *
12-30-84 Orpheum Theater, Boston 100m VG+ aud
12-31-84 Orpheum Theater, Boston 100m VG+ aud
12-31-84 Orpheum Theater, Boston 30m EX fm
1-2-85 Binghampton, NY 90m VG aud
1-3-85 Hershey, PA 75m VG aud
1-7-85 Capitol Center, Largo, MD 95m VG- aud
1-11-85 Merriville, NH 90m VG+ aud runs a little fast
1-12-85 Detroit, MI 90m VG/VG+ aud
1-15-85 Rupp Arena, Lexington, Ky 90m VG+ aud *
8-24-85 Detroit, MI 90m VG/VG- aud
8-27-85 Saratoga Springs, NY 85m VG- aud
9-2-85 Phoenix, AZ 55m G/VG aud
9-14-85 Manning Bowl, Lynn, MA 85m VG aud *
11-7-85 Orpheum Theater, Boston 45m VG aud Video shoot for 'Let The Music'
1-17-86 Center Coliseum, Seattle, WA 95m VG+ aud # First show of tour.
1-23-86 Reno, NV VG++ aud** 85m
1-24-86 Cow Palace, San Francisco 95m VG+/++ aud #
1-29-86 Bakersfield, CA 95m VG/VG+ aud
1-30-86 Las Vegas, NV 90m VG/VG+ aud
1-31-86 Sports Arena, LA, CA 90m VG/VG+ aud
2-1-86 San Bernardino, CA 90m VG/VG+ aud
2-3-86 Albuquerque, NM 75m VG+
2-15-86 Oklahoma City, OK 95m VG **
2-20-86 Reunion Arena, Dallas, TX 95m VG aud
3-7-86 Capitol Center, Largo, MD 95m VG aud
3-8-86 Spectrum, Philadelphia 100m VG+ **
3-11-86 Centrum, Worcester, MA 90m VG/VG+ aud *
3-12-86 Centrum, Worcester, MA 95m VG aud *
3-12-86 Centrum, Worcester, MA 45m EX fm *
3-15-86 New Haven, CN 95m VG- aud
3-16-86 Springfield, MA 90m VG/VG+ aud *
3-18-86 Civic Center, Providence, RI 90m VG/VG+ aud *
3-19-86 War Memorial, Syracuse, NY 100m VG+/++ aud
3-22-86 The Scope, Norfolk, VA 90m VG aud *
3-25-86 Atlanta, GA 90m VG
3-29-86 Lee County Civic, Ft. Myers, FL 89m VG- aud
3-30-86 Jacksonville, FL 90m VG/VG+ aud
4-3-86 Johnson City, TN 90m VG+ aud
4-4-86 Charlottle, NC 90m VG aud **
4-5-86 Glen Falls, NY 100m VG aud
4-8-86 Madison Square Garden, N.Y.C. 100m VG+ aud
4-12-86 Meadowlands Arena, NJ 100m VG+ aud
5-1-86 Broome County Arena, Binghampton, NY 95m VG aud
5-2-86 Civic Center, Erie, PA 90m VG/EX aud *
5-4-86 Rochester, NY 95m VG aud
5-6-86 Sports Arena, Toledo, OH 90m VG+/++ aud *
5-9-86 Minneapolis, MN 95m VG+/EX aud
5-16-86 Columbus, OH 95m VG+ aud **
5-17-86 Market Square Arena, Indianaplolis 95m VG+ aud *
5-18-86 Kalamazoo, MI 90m EX- sb (1st song G
5-20-86 Saginaw, MI 90m VG aud
5-22-86 Detroit, MI 95m VG aud
5-24-86 Cincinnati, OH 95m VG+ aud *
5-26-86 Iowa Jam, Des Moines 90m VG+/EX aud
5-30-86 Alpine Valley, East Troy, WI 95m VG+/EX aud
6-5-86 Roanoke, VA 75m VG- aud **
8-25-86 Syracuse, NY 110m G/VG aud w/Honky Tonk Woman
8-31-86 Sullivan Stadium, Foxboro, MA 90m VG+ aud *
6-20-87 Texas Jam, Dallas 75m VG- aud **
10-17-87 Memorial Auditorium, Buffalo, NY 80m VG/EX aud *
10-19-87 War Memorial, Syracuse, NY 80m VG aud
10-20-87 Maple Leaf Gardens, Toronto 94m VG aud *
10-25-87 Glen Falls, NY 95m G/VG aud
10-30-87 Civic Center, Providence, RI 90m VG/VG+ aud *
10-31-87 Civic Center, Providence, RI 90m VG/VG+ aud *
~~11-6-87 New Haven, CN~~
11-8-87 Nassau Coliseum, LI, NY 90m VG+/++ aud *
11-16-87 Civic Center, Hampton, VA 90m G/VG aud *
11-16-87 Civic Center, Hampton, VA 75m EX fm # w/o Bone,M.Touch,I'm Down
11-22-87 Raleigh, NC 90m G/VG aud *
11-25-87 Sports Arena, Toledo, OH 95m VG+ aud
11-29-87 Cleveland, OH 100m VG/VG+ aud *
12-5-87 Joe Louis Arena, Detroit, MI 100m VG+ **
12-6-87 Saginaw, MI 100m VG/VG+ *
12-12-87 Civic Center, St. Paul, MN 95m VG++ aud
12-28-87 Centrum, Worcester, MA 90m VG++ aud *
12-30-87 Centrum, Worcester, MA 110m VG+ aud
12-31-87 Centrum, Worcester, MA 110m VG+ aud
1-29-88 Cow Palace, San Francisco, CA 90m VG+ aud #
1-30-88 Coliseum Arena, Oakland, CA 90m VG+ aud #
2-1-88 Sports Arena, San Diego 95m VG+/++ aud *
2-13-88 Reunion Arena, Dallas, TX 100m VG++

Minneapolis 1-28-83 75m VG
Muskegon, MI 1-13-85 50m VG-(last 20m G-)
St. Louis 12-9-87 95m VG
Vancouver 1-20-88 100m VG/VG+
LA Forum 1-27-88 90m VG w/Bon Jovi encore
Long Beach 2-6-88 90m VG+
Austin, TX 2-12-88 95m VG/VG+
Wichita, KS 2-24-88 95m VG+
Oklahoma City 2-25-88 95m VG+
New Orleans 2-28-88 95m VG+
Greensboro 3-23-88 90m G/VG *
Charlotte 3-25-88 90m G/VG *
'Roc Talk' 4-88 30m VG+
Dayton 5-2-88 95m VG
Denver 5-20-88 95m VG+
Pueblo 5-21-88 95m VG+
Middletown,NY 8-7-88 95m VG++

An old trade list.